From Faith to Faith

WEAVING A TAPESTRY OF GOD'S GRACE

Elizabeth Grunick

CrossBooks™
1663 Liberty Drive
Bloomington, IN 47403
www.crossbooks.com
Phone: 1-866-879-0502

First published by CrossBooks 12/03/09

ISBN: 978-1-6150-7078-7 (sc)
ISBN: 978-1-6150-7080-0 (hc)

Library Congress of Control Number: 2009941735

Printed in the United States of America
Bloomington, Indiana

This book is printed on acid-free paper.

Dedicated to:

Gary,

My husband,

My soul mate,

My best friend

&

In Memory of:

Ann Marie,

Angel of God's Grace

Special Recognition to:

Susan Marie Werner for her journal entries

&

Julie Lee for her editing skills

Contents

Will The Circle Be Unbroken?

Truly, truly, I say to you,
unless a grain of wheat falls into the earth and dies,
it remains by itself alone;
but if it dies, it bears much fruit.
He who loves his life loses it,
and he who hates his life in the world
shall keep it to life eternal.

John 12:24-25 (NAS)

I was exactly on time to leave the house. As I grabbed my keys from my purse to head for the car, the phone rang. I glanced at the alarm clock on my nightstand it read 7:45 a.m.

I thought, "Who could be calling me so early in the morning?"

I picked up the phone, "Hello."

A familiar voice replied, "Mrs. Grunick, this is Mrs. Kyle from Luther Jackson Middle School. We had something happen here at school. I wanted to call and let you know. Yesterday, Mr. Muniz had a massive heart attack at school and died."

"Oh! Oh! I'm so sorry. So sorry to hear that," I replied slumping down on the bed beside the phone.

My mind started racing with memories of Coach Dave Muniz. Memories of his impact on our daughter's life, and Ann Marie's touch on his life. The thought came to me, "So now, we have come full circle. The first fruits of one small grain of wheat falling to the ground are beginning to be harvested."

"Mrs. Grunick, are you all right?"

"Yes, I'm all right. It is never easy." I replied choking back tears. "I think they are together in heaven now."

"Yes, Mr. Muniz was working out in the weight room when it happened. We have a team of crisis counselors at the school today to help the staff and students work through this," Mrs. Kyle said.

"You know, when we were there last year, Coach Muniz took us to the weight room and told us he would go there to workout and think about Ann Marie. Thank you for calling, Mrs. Kyle. Would you please let us know the funeral arrangements when you have them?"

"Yes, I will have someone call you, Mrs. Grunick. Goodbye."

~~

This is a true story about changed lives. It is a story of God's hand weaving threads in a tapestry of grace for His purpose and glory. It is a testimony of people in defining moments becoming conformed to His image and changed for eternity. It is an account of healing broken hearts, of saving faith giving hope, and earthly death leading to eternal life. It is the faithful story of a Sovereign God, who causes all things to work together for good to those who love Him, to those who are called according to His purpose.

There will come a day in heaven when we will rejoice together
for our work on this side of eternity.

Peter Vidu
Senior Pastor
Emmanuel Baptist Church
Oradea, Romania

CHAPTER ONE

The Lost Generation

How then shall they call upon Him
in whom they have not believed?
And how shall they believe in Him
whom they have not heard?
And how shall they hear
without a preacher?
Romans 10:14 (NAS)

It was the summer of 1978, my husband Gary and I had just come home to the United States from our three-year Air Force assignment in Germany. It felt good to be where life was so much easier and safer. We could actually understand the language when people spoke in the stores and on TV. The threat of terrorism and the Cold War were an ocean away. We were going through reverse culture shock with fast food and unlimited supermarket choices. After experiencing no speed limits on German autobahns, the 55 mph speed limit was another adjustment.

On a hot July afternoon in St. Louis the humidity was stifling. The temperature heading toward the 100°F mark would continue to rise. I was stretched out on a blanket determined to suntan my white skin. My mother had given me a book, *The Hiding Place,* by Corrie ten Boom, and I had taken the book to the backyard of my parents' home to read. Mom thought I would be interested in reading a true story about life in a German concentration camp during WW II. As I laid there reading and sunbathing, the words seemed to jump off the page at me. Images of my tour of the Dachau Concentration Camp outside of Munich, Germany, played in my mind. The pain and suffering millions of Jews and Christians had endured for their faith reminded me of the reason we had spent the last three years in Germany. This book, *The Hiding Place*, was plowing through my heart. It was churning up things that I had not known, and did not want to know. Like a tiller cutting through hard compact soil baked in the sun, the lessons dug into my soul. Something was happening as I read about the Christian witness of being thankful in all circumstances and how God can use weakness. Things like forgiveness, facing death and dealing with difficult people were hard to understand. Here on the pages of this book, God was beginning a work in my life. He was plowing and planting a seed that would change me forever.

It was not that I thought my life needed changing. Like many people, I had managed to remain in control of the first twenty-nine years of my life and thought I had done a rather good job. Gary and I had set goals for our future and worked hard to advance our education and professional opportunities. We had traveled all over Europe with the US Air Force. When our follow-on assignment to Scott AFB, Illinois came, we were ready to settle down in St. Louis and start a family. It never occurred to us that a Sovereign God had other plans for our future and our family.

Everything about my life appeared beautiful on the outside, but I was walking in darkness inside my soul. God was beginning to call me out from the darkness into the light. His plan from the foundation of the world was to put me in the right place at the right time. He had been preparing the various colored threads of my life to weave a tapestry of His grace in an amazing story of His love. Just as I had come home physically to St. Louis, it was time to bring my lost soul home to my Heavenly Father.

I stopped reading *The Hiding Place* and looked around at the backyard full of memories where I had grown up. For the last twenty years this had been my home. My family moved to this house when I was nine years old and just starting fourth grade. The sapling trees we used for bases playing whiffle ball had grown thick and tall through the years. The concrete patio where we staged backyard talent shows with the neighborhood kids had cracked and been re-poured.

Innocent times of childhood had grown into challenging teenage years. In ninth grade I made the freshman cheerleading squad and began to suffer growing pains. My parents decided not to move from St. Louis when a job offer at Cape Canaveral, Florida, had come for my dad with the space program. They knew how important it was for me to finish that year cheerleading. The decision not to move was a determining factor in meeting my future husband. High school brought peer pressure and romance to the center of my life. It was on the front porch of this home Gary first kissed me at age fifteen. We dated through all of high school.

The rest of the world and life passed us by as we only had time and life for each other. When Gary went off to college my senior year, every day I would walk to the corner mailbox and send him a letter. Every day the mailman would deliver a letter to the porch mailbox from Gary. From this home I went off to college and then married my high school sweetheart.

> My faith and confidence had been in my religious heritage and upbringing.

Who were these two people beginning life together? What did they bring to their marriage that would help them survive the tests that come to all marriages and families? What character traits and gifts passed down through generations did we inherit to help us deal with adversity and happiness? What had we learned from our own parents about being husband and wife or raising children? Did family tradition and moral standards, God or the Church have relevance to the postmodern culture in which we found ourselves rushing forward in time?

My faith and confidence had been in my religious heritage and upbringing, but I had no idea where I was heading in the postmodern culture. I trusted in a rich family legacy steeped in scarlet threads of religious persecution and the Reformation. A grand heritage of pastors looked on as a great cloud of witnesses. Their faith had passed to me a covenant of grace and many prayers for my regeneration. All of these scarlet threads in my bloodline had been woven in a tapestry to change my life. However, religious privileges will not save a soul. The grace I needed was the Holy Spirit. These religious privileges were valuable, but they could not replace the scarlet blood of Jesus Christ.

My mother's family heritage is a resounding roll call of Scotch-Irish Presbyterians. The *Irvine (Irwin/Erwin)* clan first appeared on the borders of Scotland during the reign of Malcolm II (1003-1034 AD). Living for hundreds of years in Annandale, Dumfriesshire, Scotland, they became a powerful clan. In Scotland few surnames are more ancient than that of *Logan*, which appears in the Royal Charter as early as 1278. Great-great-aunt Sarah Margaret Logan Morris compiled a book on our family genealogy entitled, *Irvins, Doaks, Logans & McCampbells of Virginia and Kentucky.*[1] In this treasure of research Aunt Maggie wrote about the history and the times in which my ancestors came to America, leaving their native land of Scotland and Ireland. In the years between 1729 and 1735, in the ship Queen Ann, they came to escape religious persecutions and found a home in the territory of Pennsylvania. Shortly after arriving in Montgomery County, Pennsylvania, they helped build a church and named it "Providence." The girls of the families carried the sand fifteen miles to make the mortar to build the church. Restrictive measures adopted against Scotch-Irish immigrants in Pennsylvania forced them to move to the Blue Ridge Mountains of Virginia in 1737. They soon built a new house of worship named "New Providence Church" in Augusta County, Virginia.[2]

Great-aunt Maggie wrote of their religious zeal:

> *In the following pages I have sought to rescue from oblivion and hand down to posterity at least the names of our ancestors, who not great in the ordinary sense, lived well in their day, and are worthy of this honor because of their religious zeal and the privations they suffered to maintain it. They were all Presbyterians of no uncertain type, and I am glad to say I have remained in their faith.*
>
> *The Bible was indispensable and transported at any cost. They were profoundly religious; before lying down to rest at night they did not omit to worship the God of their fathers and invoke His guidance and protection. Family worship was universal, and this institution was handed down in our family to the present day. During the early years of the 18th century the Scotch-Irish Presbyterians*

began to locate and patent tracts of land within the Shenandoah Valley, including Rockingham, Augusta and Rockbridge Counties, Va. Their innate desire to posses a home of their own, coupled with a love of freedom and religious liberty led them to plunge into the almost impenetrable wilderness, surmounting all obstacles, enduring privations, hunger and want, coupled with a fixed and steadfast belief in the guiding hand of the Great Dispenser of all things.

For about twenty years the immigrants were unmolested by the Indians, and many who had known wars in Ireland, lived and died in that peace in the wilderness, for which their hearts yearned in their native land. [3]

After the Revolutionary War, several of the Irvin and Logan clan moved to Kentucky and Indiana. Most were Presbyterian ministers following Benjamine Irvin, a Presbyterian minister who graduated from Princeton in 1776. Many became teachers and a few founded Christian colleges. Others were military men, lawyer/judges, plantation owners and farmers. On February 16, 1847, Elizabeth Eleanor Irvin married Robert Reynolds Logan from Shelby County, Kentucky. One year later in March 1848, they settled in Lincoln County, Missouri, where they spent the rest of their lives.

The family history records detailed information about my great-great-grandparents, Elizabeth Eleanor Irvin and Robert Reynolds Logan. Elizabeth was the second wife of Robert Reynolds Logan. He was the father to twelve children; ten of these children were from his second marriage to Elizabeth. Of these ten children, three became teachers and two Presbyterian ministers.

Aunt Maggie's genealogy of the Irvin clan gives a glimpse of Elizabeth's life. She was an excellent wife and mother, whose life must have been patterned after the Proverbs 31:10-31 woman.

She possessed the reputed characteristics of the Irvine's, light hair, florid complexion, energetic, resourceful, industrious, she kept things stirring from sun up to sundown, even into the late hours of the night. She could bring the largest results, from the least capital of any person I ever knew. Her children went respectably clad from the toil of her own hands. It was she who spun and wove the cloth for our clothes, spun and wove out of flax the table linen spread upon our table (and it was fine); she spun and knit our socks and stockings. It was she who taught us our individual self reliance, who gave us our lessons of rectitude and modesty, and taught us to reverence our father as a dignitary of the household; and never under any circumstances, before one of her children, took issue with him about parental government. Her cares and sorrows were many, but, like her husband, she trusted the guiding hand of an overruling dispenser of all things, which gave her strength to bear life's burdens.

I visited my mother's home, and the home of my childhood in August and September, 1895. She was not well at the time, but concealed her sufferings. On Nov. 8, same year, I received word to come to her at once, and on the 9th I reached her bedside, and found her suffering from an advanced stage of cardiac dropsy. I never witnessed such suffering, but notwithstanding her bodily pain and anguish, her mind was clear. She never let the hour for morning worship pass unnoticed even to the last morning, when we thought she would not notice, and had decided to leave it off; but at the hour, reminded us that it was time to assemble for worship, when we all assembled, for our last all together. She passed away at the dawn of day, November 20, 1895. [4]

Of my great-great-grandfather, Robert Reynolds Logan, Aunt Maggie wrote:

He possessed the traditional Irish wit, and was good in repartee. He bore locally the title of Colonel. In the times called "Muster days," when all able-bodied men over twenty and under fifty, met for military drill, he won the honor of Colonel. I remember his military outfit, his cocked hat and plume, his coat with silver fringed epaulets. He held the office of Squire from 1862 to 1870. Greatest of all was his innate and unfaltering Christian character. He had early been imbued with the principles and practice of sound moral, and religious training, received from good and pious parentage, and clung with unfaltering faith to the religion of his ancestors, who had suffered so much privation and peril to maintain. He embraced religion at the early age of sixteen and made a public profession with the united churches of Shiloh and Olivet in Shelby County, Ky. He was ruling elder of the Auburn Presbyterian Church in Lincoln County, Mo., for thirty six years, and lived to see all of his eleven children that came to maturity gathered under the sheltering wing of the Savior. My mind recalls the time when a large circle gathered at evening time around the big open fireplace in the old homestead, and my father always lead in family worship, reading a scripture lesson, and singing a hymn, when every member of the family joined in the singing. But the voices of that hearth are still and the circle that gathered there is broken only in memory.

On October 22, 1884, after life's battles had been fought, death came like the benediction that follows after prayer. The union of Robert Reynolds Logan and Elizabeth Eleanor Irvin proved to be a most happy one. I never heard an angry word, or saw an angry look pass between them. They were blessed with ten children all of whom lived to maturity save one. [5]

My mother's parents came from this Scotch-Irish stock. Settling in Lincoln County, they were country folks who spent their lives farming the rich Missouri soil. Grandpa Frazier was a hard worker who had left school after fourth grade to help support his eight younger brothers and sisters. He was a thin spry man. He knew more about farming and life than most with higher education. He would be up milking the cows by 4:30 a.m. every morning before breakfast. Grandpa kept his fields growing wheat, hay, or corn, and raised pigs and cattle.

He had hunting dogs and loved to hunt squirrel, quail, and coons. After Grandma's death, he remarried at age eighty-two and outlived his second wife, Kate. He drank strong black coffee, loved longhorn cheese and chewed tobacco the whole one-hundred years of his life.

Grandma worked from before dawn until sunset gardening, feeding the chickens, helping slaughter the cows or pigs, cooking on a wood-burning stove and pumping water from the well. She always served homemade biscuits and fried chicken when we came to visit. I remember watching her ring the neck of a chicken and it running around without a head. I was not too fond of fried chicken after that. Grandma was a women's Bible teacher in the Mt. Zion Presbyterian Church (ARP); the first Associate Reformed Presbyterian Church west of the Missouri River. Grandma died suddenly from a heart attack in her sleep on the day I graduated from high school. We had just been to visit the farm a few days before. She seemed so healthy and strong that the news of her death stunned me. It was the first time for me to have a close family member die.

My father's ancestors were Pennsylvania Dutchmen of German extraction in the Lutheran faith. They had moved into North Carolina in the late 1700s. On January 1, 1800, in a covered wagon, they crossed the frozen Mississippi River at St. Genevieve and entered Missouri territory. The Statlers were among twenty families lead by Col. George Frederick Bollinger as they proceeded to the White River and settled in the area later known as Cape Girardeau County, Missouri.[6]

We called my dad's father, Pop. He was a Methodist minister who began preaching in 1920, and retired forty-three years later from full time ministry after twenty-three moves in the Missouri Eastern Conference. He was a man of God who delivered a convicting sermon and loved the churches he served. I remember Pop as a tall, dark haired, extremely handsome man. His square jaw was clean-shaven and he wore "Old Spice" after-shave lotion. He wrote poems for all sorts of occasions and grew beautiful roses in his gardens. He could hug so tight the air squeezed out of your lungs. His marriage to Mimmy lasted for sixty-five years until his death at age ninety-three.

My grandmother, Mimmy, was a very attractive woman with steel blue eyes and silver white hair. She oversaw her family and church with matriarchal domineering conviction. She enjoyed the attention of being the pastor's wife. She had her favorite grandchildren and then there were the other grandchildren. Her acceptance of others was based on their performance and behavior. If you got on her list, you could never get off. I was fortunate to be on her good list. She kept her house immaculate. I learned early in life how to admire her violets without touching them. Pop loved her and never raised his voice to her. He wrote poems to his precious Mimmy.

From these roots came my parents. It was in church, during one of Pop's sermons, that my father spotted my mother in the congregation as he sat in the choir loft. He immediately was attracted to her and began to ask about her. My grandmother, Mimmy, informed him that my mom was too old for him. Actually, my mother was a year and a half older. Things progressed until my grandfather married them, while Mimmy sat on the front pew dressed in black and crying into her handkerchief.

My dad became an aeronautical engineer for McDonnell Douglas Aircraft Corp. in St. Louis, Missouri. In the mid 1950s, when the Russians sent the Sputnik space capsule into outer space, the US government formed the National Aeronautics and Space Administration (NASA). Dad was one of a dozen design engineers who answered NASA's question, *Can a man go into space?* He helped invent, design and draw the plans for the Project Mercury spacecraft, which McDonnell Aircraft Corp. manufactured. He was responsible for all of the equipment installation and structure of the left-hand console of the first Mercury spacecraft. In the mid 1960s, during the build-up of the Vietnam War, he was called off vacation one Friday afternoon. Working all weekend he helped design the 20mm M-61 Gatling gun installed in the F-4E fighter jet, replacing the photo recon camera with the gun. McDonnell Douglas employed him for thirty-six years, designing and drawing aircraft structure as a wing specialist for the DC-10, F-101, and F-15 fighter jets.

Dad was a very strict disciplinarian who set the standard high for his children. Once after I came home from college, he admitted to me that he thought he had been too strict as a father. I told him it may have seemed like it at the time, but I was grateful for the expectations he had set, which kept me from the rebellion of many in my generation.

A loving and forgiving woman, my mother was always there for us when we came home from school to share what happened that day. She cleaned the house, washed and ironed, and had a meal on the table every night when dad walked in the door. We always ate as a family at home. Mom loved us all equally and sacrificed to give us what we needed or wanted. My mother taught me to look for beauty inside of a person, not just the outward appearance. She challenged me to make friends with disadvantaged and lonely kids at school. To find the lovely in what might first appear unlovely.

My parents never let us miss church on Sunday. We sang in the children's choir and attended Vacation Bible School every summer. It was in the children's choir that my sister, Susan, was discovered. She had a very unusual beautiful voice, even as a child, and always got the solos. My brother Freddie and I sang the harmony. As we grew older, we attended youth fellowship. We went off to camp in Arcadia, Missouri, each summer, creating memories of climbing Pilot Knob Mountain and singing "Kumbya" around the campfires.

It was all part of growing up with a religious background in a Christian home. I was a good girl, and thought that surely I was going to heaven. Besides, my grandfather was a Methodist minister and that should count for something. I did not understand I could not get into heaven based on my parent's religion. Familiarity with sacred things had deceived my heart and soul.

Good things happen in church. My church had a yearly tradition of holding an October smorgasbord where the youth would wait tables. I was fifteen years old and waiting tables, when the church secretary and her family came and sat at my table. Her son was a handsome hunk in a football letter sweater, with a small band-aid over his left eyebrow. In the high school football game the night before, he was spiked in the eye and had fresh stitches. There he was sitting at my table! As I waited on him and his family, I found myself extremely attracted to him. It was not just the letter sweater and band-aid. The attraction was mutual. Within a few weeks, the church secretary's family switched from Baptist to our Methodist church. Her sixteen-year-old son's name was Gary.

Even though I was shy, I finally got the courage to ask Gary out for our first date. It was the Sadie Hawkins Dance where the girls ask the guys, and I almost fainted when he said, "Yes" to my invitation. I wore a tight pink knit dress, black fishnet stockings, and white patent leather heels and purse. My sister, Susan, thought I looked great. (I would not be caught dead in black fishnet stockings and white shoes now, and neither would Susan!) Gary wore a new brown suit, white shirt with a tie, and English Leather aftershave. That was the beginning of five more years of dating and courtship.

Gary's paternal grandparents were strong Russian Polish German heritage of the Catholic faith. Gary's dad was a blue-collar night shift worker. When Gary and his two sisters were home, their dad was sleeping, so everyone had to be quiet. His dad would get up for dinner and be off to work by 11 p.m. every night. He did not express love easily to his children, and often challenged them to try even harder by never complimenting them on a job well done.

Gary's mom, a gentle loving woman, placed her entire security and life in her husband. She was an orphan raised by her aunt who would not tell her about her parents. She learned a little about her parents through research done by her brother. Her mother had been a German and married an Italian man. Both parents died when she was quite young. Her childhood was very difficult and she married Gary's father at an early age. She worked as a church secretary for several years. Although his family was Catholic, when Gary was about eight years old they became Baptist. He walked the aisle at age nine; and was baptized. At sixteen, Gary's family switched to the Methodist church which had October smorgasbords.

I was only twenty years old, and Gary had just turned twenty-one when we married. Pop performed our marriage ceremony as the guest pastor. It was a large wedding party and reception in the Methodist church where we first met. Our wedding day was the last time Gary and I were in church for the next ten years. Our excuse was — there just did not seem to be time to go to church. It was too easy to sleep in on Sundays, especially since I began working full time and Gary was finishing his bachelor's degree.

In reality, we had a religion that left us unprepared for marriage and adulthood. There was very little substance to what happened in church except social relationships. The social gospel message was soothing and pleasantly preached from the pulpit. We felt un-convicted over possible sin or the existence of hell. We saw no need of a Divine Savior; only good humanistic works were required to be a Christian. The worship services were sleepy rituals of responsive readings and congregational prayers. The sermons addressed current political issues and not scriptural truth. People in church were either mad at each other or the pastor. It was easy to leave all of that behind. It was a lesson God would later use to remind us; when people leave church, their children leave church. When their children leave church, their grandchildren leave church. Soon a whole nation has left church. Once you have left, it is extremely hard to come back.

Gary and I had grown up in the "lost generation" of the 1960s. In a generation that seemed to have lost its way during the sexual/drug revolution and anti-Vietnam war protests. A generation sliding down the slippery slope of immorality and lack of respect for anyone over thirty years old, caught somewhere between Elvis and The Beatles. The generation testing all authority while refusing to take responsibility. It was the generation that "liberated" women. The profession of Mommy was a conversation stopper to any intelligent discussion at a cocktail party. A generation that was screaming, *God Is Dead* and *You Don't Believe We're On the Eve of Destruction?*[7]

CHAPTER TWO

On a Wing and a Prayer

For it is He who delivers you
from the snare of the trapper,
and from the deadly pestilence.
He will cover you with His pinions,
and under His wings you may seek refuge;
His faithfulness is a shield and bulwark.
Psalms 91: 3-4 (NAS)

"...ask not what your country can do for you—
ask what you can do for your country."
President John F. Kennedy
Inaugural Address, January 20, 1961

The 1960s began with the election of President John F. Kennedy, our youngest and first Roman Catholic president. The new NASA space program accepted the challenge to put a man on the moon before the end of the decade. A nation prayed on May 5, 1961, when the first astronaut, Commander Alan Shepard, lifted into space inside the tiny Mercury space capsule for a fifteen-minute suborbital flight. Nine months later, we cheered as John Glenn became the first American to orbit earth on February 20, 1962.

Between these two NASA achievements, the Cold War got colder in August 1961. The East German Communist government built a twenty-nine-mile-long wall in Berlin to halt the exodus of refugees to the freedom of West Berlin. Anyone caught escaping was shot down. Many found ways to escape at the risk of their lives, but would never see the loved ones they left behind the Berlin Wall.

The summer of 1963 heated up when race riots in Birmingham, Alabama, led to the "March on Washington." Dr. Martin Luther King, Jr. stood at the Lincoln Memorial and raised the nation's conscience to dream of voting rights, equal opportunity, and the end of segregation for African Americans. A nation wept on November 22, 1963, when TV anchor Walter Cronkite announced the assassination of President John F. Kennedy.

The walk from Selma to Montgomery, Alabama, in March of 1965, heightened racial tensions over civil rights. On the evening of April 4, 1968, we staggered at the assassination of Dr. Martin Luther King, Jr. Two months later, June 5, 1968, we watched in horror on television as Robert F. Kennedy was shot and died the following day.

August 22, 1968, during a Democratic Party hearing on Vietnam, U.S. Representative Hale Boggs interrupted the hearings: "Radio Prague announced today that Soviet troops have crossed the Czechoslovak borders."

At that moment, Secretary of State Dean Rusk rose from his seat and stated, "I think I will go see what all of this is about."[1]

The decade ended with "one small step for man, one giant leap for mankind" as Neil Armstrong and Edwin "Buzz" Aldrin walked on the moon, July 20, 1969. We could send a man to the moon, but we could not deal with a nation in moral and spiritual upheaval. Half a world away, a turbulent war was dividing America.

Do you support our country's involvement in the Vietnam conflict? That was the question on university campuses as we transcended into the Age of Aquarius. The pressure was mounting with every eighteen-year-old male facing a seven-year period of uncertainty about the military draft, which could send him involuntarily to Vietnam and possible injury or early death. High school friends were listed as KIA, MIA, or POW.

At the turn of the decade from 1969 to 1970, the landscape of our country had become a political minefield. The night of December 1, 1969 opened with an invocation and closed with a benediction for the future of eight-hundred and fifty thousand young men. Those young men could plan their lives according to the lottery-by-birthday draft drawing for induction into the United States Army. The "winners" of the draft lottery were those men born on September 14. Those in the top third of the drawing received the first call up by the Selective

Service under the new lottery system starting January 1, 1970. Those in the middle third would face a year of uncertainty, but would know by the end of 1970 whether they would be inducted into military service. The lower third of the birthday selection list knew they would not be drafted and could plan their lives accordingly.[2]

The rate of call up for 1970 was approximately thirty lottery numbers a month, from January to May. A man with a number 131 was ordered to report for his physical exam on February 18, 1970, and would be classified 1-A if he passed the physical. He would then report for induction May 20, 1970, and would be in the Central Highlands of Vietnam by February 1971, after basic training and advanced individual training at Fort Dix, New Jersey. By May 1970, the quota allowance called men with numbers 121 through 150 to report for physicals at their Selective Service Boards.[3]

Gary's birthday, July 18, placed him in the middle of the draft lottery, at number 190. His student deferment would end at graduation in May 1970 with his B.S. degree in Business Administration from the University of Missouri-Columbia. He wanted to go to law school at Mizzou. In the new draft lottery, his chance of going to Vietnam after graduation was very possible. He was ordered by the Selective Service to report for a physical. He made the decision to enlist in the US Air Force and get an ROTC deferment until he completed the three years of law school; giving him a four-year commitment as an officer in the Air Force. It was a decision that changed the next twenty-five years of our lives. God was weaving a red, white, and blue thread into the tapestry of our lives.

The Vietnam War was raging, and so were the protesters on campus at the University of Missouri-Columbia. Gary would have to wear his Air Force ROTC uniform once a week on campus, and keep his hair short while other students were becoming longhaired hippies. Many times, he was spit at or cursed by fellow students who protested the Vietnam War. Once, he took off running for our car when rocks were thrown at him.

On May 4, 1970, four students were killed during a Vietnam War protest on the campus of Kent State University. Student rioting rocked the university campuses of our nation, and the ROTC building of Washington University in St. Louis was set on fire. During 1970, draft cards were burned, and young men fled to Canada to escape being sent to Vietnam. An estimated seventy thousand draft evaders and "dodgers" were living in Canada by 1972.

The summer of 1970, Gary went for six weeks of basic training at Tinker AFB, Oklahoma. We had been married less than a year. When he came home from basic training with a crew cut, he had lost about twenty pounds and had red Oklahoma dirt ground into all of his clothes. He determined that basic training was the worst thing he had experienced in his life.

Then there was law school. We decided to move from our one-bedroom apartment building in town, into a new single-story apartment in the country. Our living space increased by a second small bedroom and a larger kitchen with a dishwasher for just ten dollars more a month. We enjoyed a small yard and area for a garden. Gary and I were living on three-hundred and sixty-nine dollars per month in law school. Our car payment was twenty dollars per month and rent one-hundred and ten dollars per month. We survived by eating macaroni and cheese or hot dogs for dinner almost every night.

When the German shepherd dog that lived behind us had a litter of eight puppies, we had a free choice. We picked out the runt of the litter, a little silver colored puppy with white chest and paws. Deciding what to name her was the trick. Gary had been studying in law school about cross-examination of witnesses. One professor had talked about not opening "Pandora's box" on cross-examination, and we decided that the name Pandora fit our precious pup.

Law school was three years of exhausting study. While I supported us by working for a state mental health center, Gary wore his eyes out cracking the law books. After graduation from law school in May 1973, everything came down to the final test--passing the Missouri Bar Exam. I had not prayed for years, but the morning of the bar exam I knelt at the side of our bed and cried out for God to let Gary make it. He came home deciding the bar exam had been worse than the six weeks of air force basic training in Oklahoma. Fortunately, he passed the bar exam the first time. My prayer was answered.

Gary was commissioned a second lieutenant in the USAF and received his orders to report for duty November 15, 1973. He entered the US Air Force as a judge advocate with the rank of captain, and a four-year commitment to serve his country. The Vietnam War had officially ended on January 27, 1973, and the remaining troops withdrew from South Vietnam on March 29, 1973. Eleven years of involvement made it the longest war in our nation's history. An estimated fifty-eight thousand Americans lost their lives in service to their nation.[4] Thousands more returned home, not with honor, but scorned by a nation, leaving them wounded in body, soul, and mind. The war in Southeast Asia was replaced with nightly TV news about a June 17, 1972 break-in at Democratic headquarters, a scandal dubbed "Watergate."

Our first air force assignment to the 436th Air Base Wing at Dover AFB, Delaware, was a new adventure for us. We were handed the keys to a three-bedroom, two-story base house on the golf course. Gary's base pay was four times more than what we had been living on in law school. I remember the first thing we bought was an oriental rug for the living room floor, and the one-hundred and fifty dollar check for the rug was the biggest check I had written in my life! I could hardly believe I could go into the base commissary and buy anything I wanted to eat. First, I got a good cookbook from the Officers' Wives Club, so I could learn how to cook something besides hotdogs and macaroni.

Since our base house was on the golf course, we were in danger every time we walked outside. Golfers were always hitting balls into our backyard, and Pandora would come charging out of her doghouse when a golf ball would hit it. One evening, I had just placed dinner on the dining room table and walked back into the kitchen, when a golf ball came crashing through the dining room window and landed in the bowl of corn. I was fortunate to have walked into the kitchen, and not cut with flying glass or hit with the golf ball. The teenage golfer knocked on our door and asked for the golf ball from our dining room disaster. He did not get it back!

Gary's boss was Major Dick Kautt. His wife, Margaret, was like a mother to me; and wise in the ways of air force life. Her home was always open for me to stop by and visit. Dick immediately challenged Gary by assigning him the court-martials in the office. While Margaret was teaching me how to cook a turkey for Thanksgiving or German sauerbraten and attend official air force functions, Dick was preparing Gary for a career in the courtroom.

We soon found in military life you learn to make friends quickly. They are your support group away from your family. Our neighbors had all been in the military for several years and were eager to help us make the adjustment. Next door was Major David, and his wife, Mair, from the Isle of Wight in England. They were such a delight to know because of their British accents and habits. Every afternoon was teatime at their house. I do believe Mair kept the cleanest house I had ever seen. She taught me how to play mahjong at the Officers' Wives Club once a week. She also helped me with proper dress for official air force functions, which length of gloves to wear for what time of day or evening. Many women still wore hats to everything, although it was becoming less common. The old Air Force guard was fading away and yielding to a newly liberated lifestyle. Some officers' wives were actually starting their own business careers instead of staying at home in a supporting role of their husband's military career.

On the other side of our house lived a crusty Lt. Col. and his wife, who had been in the Air Force for over thirty years. Our first night in our home, they invited us over for drinks. We had not eaten dinner yet, and Gary and I had not had much experience drinking in college, especially hard liquor. We could not afford it! The Lt. Col. suggested a pina colada for me. It sounded innocent enough and even tasted innocent. He served it to me in a tall ice tea glass. Things were warming up nicely with our new neighbors until I stood up to go home and nearly fell in the floor. Gary held on to me as we walked across the side yard and I collapsed on the kitchen floor unable to get up and cook dinner. I realized that drinking pina coladas on an empty stomach out of an ice tea glass was not the same thing as drinking tea.

One other neighbor became good friends with us. Lynn and John lived just next to the Lt. Col. who served pina coladas. They did not have children, so we got along fine. They loved Pandora. Lynn had been a nurse in the Air Force when she met John, who had served in Vietnam.

Lynn took me to a first aid seminar where we learned CPR and how to do self-breast exams. Not long after that class, I found a breast lump. After seeing a flight surgeon at the base hospital, he recommended I go off the birth control pill and wait three months to see if the lump would go away. Since I was only twenty-five, the doctor did not think there was a high percentage of the lump being cancer. When I told Gary, he became very upset. He was not waiting three months to find out that a cancerous lump had spread. Lynn and Mair suggested a surgeon in Dover. I made an appointment immediately and this surgeon was concerned. He said he would take the lump out if I could not get a surgeon on Dover Air Base within the week. That news sent Gary straight to the hospital commander. Within forty-eight hours I saw a military surgeon, who scheduled a biopsy of the lump the next day.

For the first time in my life, I had to deal with my own mortality. I was relying on the belief, if I was good enough my good would outweigh the bad and I would go to heaven. Had I been good enough? I was afraid to die! I was too young to die! What kind of God would let something like that happen?

The day of the surgery Gary had to be in court. He took me to the hospital and checked me in. The doctor did the surgery with local anesthetic removing the lump. He sewed me up and put a huge bandage around my chest. Gary took me home and put me to bed, and went to do the court-martial.

The lump was not cancer, but a fibroid tumor. The biopsy report was fibro-cystic disease, and I could expect more lumps in the future. It would serve as a constant reminder of my mortality. My grandmother, Mimmy, had breast cancer in her mid-forties. She had survived a radical mastectomy, but it was a warning for me that I was in a higher risk category.

Dick and Margaret had been stationed in Germany before coming to Dover, and were excited for us when our orders came eighteen months later for Wiesbaden, Germany. They gave us all kinds of tips, information, and maps as we packed up our household goods for our second assignment in less than two years. Three different packers and shipments put our furniture and clothes in either permanent storage, or a household shipment, or whole baggage. For a few weeks we boarded our dog Pandora at a kennel in New Jersey, and shipped her after we found housing in Germany. Our little Chevy Vega went on a ship headed to Bremerhaven, Germany, and took three months to get there.

Clearing base housing was an ordeal, since before leaving the air base a housing inspector walked through the house looking for damage and made sure it was spotless. The white glove inspector would check for dirt above the doorframes. The exhaust fan over the stove had to be grease free, and the molding on the side of the refrigerator had to be clean. We hired a cleaning company to guarantee passing the inspection.

The day our shipment of household goods was packed, I heard an ambulance come up our street. It stopped in the driveway of Lynn and John's house. The medical team went in and I took off running up the street to see what was going on. John had suffered a heart attack and they were taking him to the base hospital. Gary followed me into their home. Another neighbor, who was a nurse, had come to help. She offered to drive Lynn to the hospital. We stayed at the house in case Lynn needed us to bring something to the hospital. There lying in the middle of the living room floor was the small black medical bag Lynn had used on John. Next to the bag were his sweater and a small spot of vomit. Gary decided Lynn did not need to come back and see the reminders on the floor. He picked up the medical bag and put it in the hall closet. I folded up the sweater and tried to clean up the vomit stain.

In about an hour Lynn drove up with the neighbor, and came rushing out of the car crying to us. She was saying, "John didn't make it! John didn't make it!"

I just could not believe it. He was only thirty-seven years old. As soon as she got into the house the first thing she did was open the hall closet to hang up her coat, and there sat the medical bag. We talked for a while and she went up to the bedroom. She emptied her pockets of John's things, which she had brought home from the hospital. As she laid his watch on the dresser, she realized it had stopped running at exactly the time of John's death. Something seemed significant about the watch stopping. Knowing he would not wear it again. Knowing he did not need the watch anymore, searching for answers about life and death. Questioning why this sudden death should have happened. Wondering how Lynn could handle her husband's death in the days and months ahead.

I grieved her sudden loss and abrupt change for her future. Lynn was a young widow with no children. She was all alone. Gary was designated her summary court officer and helped her with clearing military housing and receiving air force benefits. In a matter of weeks, Lynn moved back to her home state to live with her mother. About that same time we left for our overseas assignment to Wiesbaden, Germany and new threads of friendship.

CHAPTER THREE

Guten Tag! Sprechen Sie Deutsch?

Cease striving and know that I am God;
I will be exalted among the nations.
I will be exalted in the earth.
Psalms 46:10 (NAS)

On my first air flight, I had flown to St. Louis and back to Dover for my grandparent's fiftieth wedding anniversary, and learned that I get airsick. The air flight to Frankfurt, Germany, was only my second trip by airplane in my life. When we left McGuire Air Force Base on a MAC flight and diverted to Tulle, Greenland, because of a hurricane, I was not feeling too great even with Dramamine. By the time we flew over the Rhine River and Gary was excited seeing the castles, I had one eye open and was searching for the bag. How I made it through customs and to the front door of the American Arms Hotel in Wiesbaden I do not remember. I left the airsick bag on the plane, but I will never forget the tree in front of the hotel where I left my breakfast. I made a great first impression on sponsor, Charlie.

That evening we were initiated into the German culture. Charlie picked us up at the American Arms Hotel, and we went to our first German festival along the Rhine River castle region. Twinkling lights led to a carnival celebration with merchants' booths lining the streets of a little village called Eltville. The evening was charged with excitement in the beer tents with polka music, delicious food and new wine to sample from the 1975 selections. The wine was the best I had ever tasted, so sweet and smooth to swallow. Charlie taught us how to order bratwurst in German. To order one bratwurst hold up a thumb and say, *Ein bratwurst, bitte.* If you hold up your index finger, the merchant will count your thumb and your index finger and give you two bratwursts. Your thumb is always *one.* I found a popcorn stand, held up my thumb and said, "Ein popcorn, bitte." The reply was "Mit zucker order salz?" Charlie just stood there smiling. Not knowing what the merchant had asked me, I shrugged my shoulders and handed over one Deutsch Mark. The popcorn bag was exchanged and I opened it for a taste. Then I realized the question had been, "With sugar or salt?" The popcorn was covered in sugar. This was not going to be easy learning the culture and language.

It would be three months before our Chevy Vega arrived from the States, so we bought a second car in Germany. A new French Peugeot Diesel, that sounded like a washing machine but could cruise fast on the autobahn unless it was going uphill. It was midnight blue, a five-speed stick shift without power steering, tan leather seats and a sunroof. The lack of power steering kept my arm muscles built up. Diesel fuel was cheap and plentiful giving us good gas mileage. There was no need for air conditioning in Germany; the sunroof would keep us cool.

Wiesbaden was a rich, snobby, city. It had not been bombed during World War II like the neighboring city of Mainz. Many movie stars lived in Wiesbaden and gambled at the Kurhaus Casino. The Germans refused to help any American in the stores. They resented the occupation forces thirty years after World War II. We soon learned to dress like Germans and took a quick German language class so we could get around. I found a job working for a Texas college extension and then for the Air Force logistics commander. Six months later, orders came to close Wiesbaden Air Base and give it to the US Army. All Air Force personnel moved to Sembach Air Base, which was an hour and a half south of Wiesbaden. We packed our bags for our third military move in two years.

My logistics job moved to Sembach Air Base along with Gary's job. We had been living in a small base housing apartment in Wiesbaden. All base housing at Sembach was taken before we arrived in Germany, and the German housing surrounding Sembach Air Base was already rented. Farther away, we found a large apartment on the first floor of a German house in Ramstein, Germany. Landstuhl Army Hospital was just across the autobahn in the next village. The Landstuhl Castle ruins glowed with lights every evening in the distant hillside. All day long, US fighter pilots pierced the sky above with take-offs and landings on sortie assignments to military air bases all over Europe.

The apartment we rented belonged to Karl and Gerda Haida who lived across the street. When Nazi troops invaded the Czech Republic, Karl was eighteen and had to fight in the German Army. He guarded Hitler's bunker at Berchtesgaden but was wounded in France. Karl and Gerda moved to Ramstein as Czech refugees after World War II.

Karl made money selling sporting equipment and guns to the American Rod and Gun Clubs on US military installations in Europe. He sold beautiful pewter beer steins and platters, which he gave to us for birthdays and Christmas. His basement was full of pewter and porcelain treasures. As an avid German hunter, he owned an awesome gun collection locked in his gun cabinet.

Gerda understood more English than she would speak. I learned German from her, because she would only speak German to me. She taught me how to clean windows, curtains, and floors the German way. Every Saturday, Gerda would scrub her front doorsteps while Karl would sweep the driveway, sidewalk and curb of the street. After cleaning all Saturday morning, Karl would take Gary and Pandora to the *Hundeheim* (German shepherd dog home) where the village hunters would gather for a few beers. Sunday afternoon was time for coffee and *kuchen* (German cakes) followed by a *spatzerin* (to go for a walk) in the woods.

Much of German traditional culture is a mixture of Catholic faith and superstition. After the fall harvest, Germans spend the dark winter months warding off evil spirits in celebrating the *Fasching Season* (Mardi Gras). Fasching starts on the eleventh hour, of the eleventh day, of the eleventh month and ends with the *Rosen Montag* (Rose Monday) Parade, the Monday before Ash Wednesday.

Karl and Gerda were very generous with their friendship and we thought of them as our German parents. They introduced us to the German culture and their friends in Ramstein Village. We attended many Fasching parties and festivities with them, and received a special honor from the Mayor of Ramstein as the American friends of the *Schwartzen Katz* (Black Cat) Ramstein Fasching Club. Gary would dress as a pirate, and I would go as a gypsy for the costumed parties.

The New Year's Fasching Ball was a formal affair where I wore a long black gown and black satin shoes trimmed with rhinestones. After singing, dancing, drinking wine and champagne into the wee hours of the night, we would walk home. Gary and I thought we were more fluent in German than we really were after one of those nights.

Karl's fiftieth birthday was a celebration for the whole Ramstein village. A local gasthaus was rented for the big birthday dinner party. The women wore long formal dresses, and the men wore suits and ties. Every party guest brought Karl a bouquet of flowers. The Ramstein village hunters came dressed in their hunting finery and serenaded us with their hunting horns. The finest *kassler rippchen mit sauerkraut* (thick sliced smoked pork chops and sauerkraut) with *kartoffelpuree* (whipped potatoes) was served within easy reach of the mustard pot and a stein of beer.

Karl's son, Gernot, was our age and lived a few hours away. When he would come to visit his parents he would stop by our apartment for a "Mr. Chivas Regal drink." He liked to practice his English and discuss American politics. Gernot and Karl both spoke excellent English mixed with a few cuss words. They smoked like chimneys, loved Americans and their money. They both referred to our US president as "Mr. Jimmy Peanut."

Karl would say, "If it wasn't for the Americans, all of Europe would be speaking either German or Russian."

We could afford to have a cleaning lady, which the Germans called a *putz-frau*. Frieda would ride her bike from the next village to my house and clean while I was at work. She had escaped from East Germany in the early 1950s when she had a six-week visa to visit her sister in West Germany. She did not return to East Germany after her visa expired, and for the next twenty years, Frieda could not see her family. If she dared to go back, she would be arrested and never be free. Finally, when she reached fifty years old, the East Germans allowed her to make once a year trips by train into East Germany to visit her family. She would save up all her money from cleaning homes to pay for the train trip. I would give her some of my used clothing to take to her family.

After I quit working for the Air Force logistics commander and was at home, I still had Frieda come to clean just so we could visit. Frieda loved American peanut butter and jelly sandwiches and popcorn. She would always stay for lunch.

One day she asked Gary, "How do you say in English what you do? Is it 'Liar'?"

Gary replied, "No! Lawyer!"

At Sembach AB, Gary became one of the first area defense counsels (ADC) in the Air Force. The Air Force was beginning to see the advantage of having defense counsels on each air base, who were not directly under the chain of command. These ADCs were to report to a Chief Circuit Defense Counsel (CCDC). The defendant in a court-martial would have the ADC to represent them.

Sembach was a small base and did not have many court-martials. Gary traveled all over Europe to defend military members charged with an offense. This was great experience with travel opportunities; but sometimes Gary was gone so much, I would wonder if he was ever coming home. Once he left in the middle of October for what was to be a week in Madrid, Spain, at Torrejon AB doing a court-martial. Each week he would call me in Germany, and say that the case was still going on. This went on for about four or five weeks. Then he went straight to another court-martial in Athens, Greece, without coming home. The second case was continuing just before Thanksgiving. We had made reservations for Thanksgiving weekend to ski the Matterhorn in Zermatt, Switzerland. When I saw Gary's commander at the Officers' Club one night, I asked if he thought Gary might be able to come home in time for our ski trip. Gary had been gone for seven weeks and only packed for one week. His commander told me there was only one military transport plane leaving Greece on the Wednesday night before Thanksgiving, and if the case was not over, Gary could not make it home. The case ended just in time for Gary to make a mad dash for the last plane out of Athens, and arrive home late that night. We headed off for the ski slopes the next day.

Two sports—tennis in the summer and skiing in the winter, were passions in our lives. Our first ski experience was at Dover AFB when one of the prosecutors had invited us to ski Blue Knob in Pennsylvania. We had rented our skis and strapped them on without taking a lesson. Our friend, Mike, was going to show us the ropes and slopes. There I stood at the top of the hill heading down on a pair of skis.

As I began to pick up speed, I yelled, "How do you stop these things?"

Mike said, "You go like this."

He slid his skis into a perfect snowplow position. When I tried it, my skis crossed and I descended the rest of the hill on my bottom backwards with my skis over my head. It was amazing that we ever got on skis again after that day.

Once we got to Germany, we found the beautiful "Alpen Gasthof Zur Post" in Erpfendorf, Tyrol, Austria. Roswitha and Helmut Purstinger were the English speaking Austrian proprietors who took American checks. A private room with bath and balcony was $99 per person for an entire week, including three meals a day and ski lessons from Austrian instructors. A week at Zur Post also included popcorn by the fireplace with hot chocolate and the choice of dominos or bingo after dinner. One night during the week, Tyrolean dancers would perform at the Larchenhof Hotel in Erpfendorf. Dressed in traditional Tyrolean costumes, they would sing, dance and yodel accompanied by accordion, guitar, and violin. We would enjoy a romantic evening in a horse-drawn sleigh ride through the snow-covered countryside to the woodland "Teepee." In the wooden hut with a fireplace and bar, we could get a drink to warm up. After a half hour of giving the horses a rest, wrapping up in wool blankets the sleigh would take us back to Zur Post, where we would collapse into bed under the warm feather comforters.

It was so special celebrating the week of Christmas in Austria skiing. Roswitha and Helmut would put up a live Christmas tree with ornaments and angel hair decorations, and they would light real candles on the tree. If a candle caught the angel hair on fire, Roswitha would just clap her hands around it until the fire went out. Musicians with French horns and violins would come and play carols during a big buffet spread for the Christmas meal.

On Christmas Eve, the community of Erpfendorf would gather outside the small Tyrolean village church and sing carols while the snowflakes would gently fall and blow around in the lights shining on the tall white steeple. At the stroke of midnight, the steeple bell would ring to announce the birth of the Christ child. It was like standing in a glass snow globe next to a tiny church with twinkling pine trees, as God would shake snow glitter down on us.

The finest skiing in Europe is in the "Snow Corner of Tyrol" at the Kaiser Waidring Triangle of St. Johann, Steinplatte, and Kitzbuhl. After a few trips to Tyrol, we learned to ski with a fluid Austrian *hip-nick* swishing style. We bought our own ski equipment. I loved my white Rossignol skis with the red, white, and blue French rooster on the tips. My ski instructor nicknamed me "Frenchie." At 170 cm in length, my French Rossignol skis were fast with the right wax for the snow conditions. The end of every week, skiers raced on a slalom course set by the ski instructors. The third year of skiing, I won the Super Gold Medal in the women's slalom race, barely beating an army nurse who skied on American K-2 skis.

All the ski instructors lifted me up and put me on their shoulders the night of the awards ceremony. I almost decided to leave Gary that week and run off with my Austrian instructor, Seppi. I realized that was probably not a good idea, because Seppi could only speak a few words of English. "Follow me, Frenchie!" was the extent of his vocabulary.

The most beautiful place in all of Europe is the Bernese Oberland region of Switzerland. Every ski run, terrace, and hiking trail is an impressive panoramic view of the majestic Swiss Alps with a beautiful waterfall plunging into an edelweiss-adorned valley. In warm weather, winding curves in the road yield scenes of dairy cows grazing in green pastures, beside dark wooden chalets dripping red geraniums from window-boxed balconies. Alphorn blowing, yodeling, and Swiss flag throwing are the timeless traditions of the region. Relaxing on the sun terrace of an outdoor café, and dining on cheese fondue, while gazing at the mountain peaks is breath taking.

Skiing the "Top of Europe" with the Eiger Glacier's North Wall majestically looking down on us was as close to heaven as we could get. The Oberland Hotel, in Lauterbrunnen, offered us a private balcony room with a view of one of the seventy-two glorious waterfalls. Walking to the Lauterbrunnen train station, we would take the mountain train up the side of the Jungfrau to the top at Kleine Scheidegg. From there, we could choose to ski several miles of runs to either Wengen or Grindelwald. During the Lauberhorn World Cup Races at the end of January in Wengen, Switzerland, the racers would ride the train. The racecourse was so fast and dangerous, that a safety net hung over the train tracks to catch any racer who might go off course and over the side of the mountain.

Skiing one morning after a fresh snowfall on the Murren side of the Schilthorn-Piz Gloria, the scene of a *James Bond Movie,* we heard an avalanche! Gary and I took off skiing as fast as we could straight down the mountain. Gary was in front of me and suddenly disappeared almost at the bottom of the mountain ski run. About the time I lost him, I went sailing off a drift that was ten feet high. It was a snow-covered wall dropping into the backyard of a farmer's mountainside home. At least we were down, and I must have been pumping so much adrenaline from the avalanche race, that I stayed up on my skis without falling. It was not until we got to the parking lot that we collapsed.

When family members came to visit us in Europe, we would plan as many countries to visit as time permitted. Gary's sister Donna, a beautician in Hollywood, came from Los Angeles to visit us for a few weeks. She cut my hair in the latest "Hamill" cut, named after Olympic ice skater Dorothy Hamill. We went by train for a weekend in Paris, leaving Gary to work the courtroom. Donna thought I needed a little updating in my style of clothes to go with my new haircut. I was wearing a light brown polyester jumpsuit, which I had made on my Singer sewing machine. We had the most fun shopping on the Champs Elysees for the latest fashions. I came home with a tight pair of khaki jeans and a baggy pink flowered blouse that looked like it had wings for the sleeves. Backless high heel shoes completed the outfit. I was ten years ahead of fashion in the United States. Donna bought a flowered peasant skirt and blouse with an off-the-shoulder fringed shawl. We wore our new fashion statements to dinner at the Eiffel Tower. Frenchmen certainly appreciate looking at women. The stares we drew were flattering. We giggled through the whole trip and could not wait to get home and show Gary our new clothes.

Our most interesting adventure came when Gary had a court-martial in West Berlin. We booked a flight into the West Berlin Airport. A driver in a Mercedes met us. The driver took us to Templehof Airfield. Hitler had built Templehof in the shape of an eagle with five stories above ground and five below ground. The Nazis constructed warplanes underground during WW II and rolled them out on the runway for takeoff. After WW II, Templehof was in the US sector of Berlin, and used for US military offices and VIP guest rooms. Our VIP room was huge. The bathroom was larger than any room in our German apartment. The place seemed bugged with communist spies recording all our conversations as they echoed against the walls. West Berlin citizens treated the American military like royalty. One evening, dinner was at the French Officers' Club overlooking a blue lake with beautiful white swans. The meal was fabulous French cuisine; chateaubriand and flaming baked Alaska.

The next day, we decided to cross over The Wall to East Berlin. Gary went through Checkpoint Charlie wearing his military uniform without a nametag. I had to go through a civilian checkpoint about a block down the street. For security I was not to have anything on me that connected me to a US military member; no military ID, no checkbook with a rank on it, only my US passport. I gave Gary my purse. As he walked toward the checkpoint, the East German border guard took Gary's picture with a long telephoto lens camera of the US Air Force captain carrying a woman's purse. I walked across the border and met up with Gary on the other side.

We began to explore East Berlin. It was amazing to see the stark contrast between East and West Berlin. The Berlin Wall had served its purpose as a dividing wall. It had kept the Western culture out of sight and influence of the East Germans. On every corner, a military officer stood with a machine gun. No flowers were growing. No dogs were walking or children playing. Color was gone. The buildings were gray concrete without windows or advertisements to tell what was inside. The long lines of people winding out of the doorways told us there was some kind of food inside the stores. Very few cars were on the street. Cars that were running were small and sounded like they had a rubber band for an engine. We heard that it took five years to get a car once you ordered one. Clothes looked twenty years behind in style. People walked with their head looking down at the ground, no smiles, no eye contact. It was depressing to see their despondent faces. They did not trust each other or any foreigner. There was no hope or happiness for these people.

On the way back to West Berlin, Gary and I separated to go through our checkpoints. I carried only my US passport. I entered the passport control station and gave the official my passport. He took it and walked through a doorway into another room. I waited, and waited. Other people were coming and going, but he was not coming back with my passport. After twenty minutes, I remembered the only identification I had to permit me back on the free side of The Wall was in the hands of the customs official. I started to panic thinking I might never get out of East Berlin. Gary was wondering where I was as he waited on the other side of The Wall. Finally, the customs official came out and handed me my passport. I realized what it might feel like to not be free. I walk into open air in West Berlin where flowers bloomed, children played, and dogs barked.

Our three years in Europe were full of wonderful treasured experiences, as we learned much about life and history. The flavor of each international country wove another colored thread into the tapestry of our lives. In Madrid, Spain, we saw the red glistening blood of a bullfight in the hot sunny afternoon. That evening we dined on yellow paella and fruity wine-colored sangria while watching a heel-stomping black and pink flamenco dance to the rhythm of handclaps and a steel guitar. We climbed the 2,500-year-old dusty white ruins of the Acropolis in the heat of the day in Athens, Greece. From Athens, we sailed in the cool blue ocean breeze to the island of Rhodes, watching old men mold clay pottery and multi-colored enameled tiles. From the top of the black iron Eiffel Tower, we gazed out over gleaming Paris streets. Climbing the steep steps in the cream-colored flying buttresses of Notre Dame into the ancient bell tower, we envisioned the hunchback ringing the bells. We enjoyed all the gaiety of life in Paris, from sweet café-au-lait in a quiet sidewalk café, to a night of wild can-can at the Moulin Rouge. In the Netherlands, we visited the stately government of The Hague, and the hidden cramped living quarters of Anne Frank's House. In Florence, Italy, I shopped for brown leather in the dirty market streets, and toured the golden Renaissance art museums of Michelangelo's David. We spent several days in jolly old London, sipping high tea outside of royal Windsor Castle, and taking a train to see our former neighbors, who had retired to the sparkling white ocean waters of the Isle of Wight.

We traveled all over the new green vineyard covered hillsides of Germany. Exploring Heidelberg Castle and the majestic fortresses lighted by spectacular evening fireworks along the "Rhine-a-Flame" river cruise. In the Black Forest, dark green pines hid the wooden farmhouses and tiny villages, where we stopped for hand-carved cuckoo clocks. I purchased a dazzling silver and hand-cut lead crystal chandelier for our dining room on a Czech border-shopping spree.

Traveling in Bavaria, we stayed in the high mountaintop Berghof Hotel built for Hitler in Berchtesgaden. We toured King Ludwig's fairytale Neuschwanstein and Linderhof Castles. The festivities of Munich's Oktoberfest at the Hof Brau Haus entertained us as buxom fraulines carried foaming mugs of beer, and Germans swayed to the frolicking music. Having learned to ski the black diamond slopes of Austria and Switzerland, we also became skillful at the game of tennis. Visiting the horror of the gas chambers and ovens of the Nazi Concentration Camp at Dachau gave us perspective on our assignment in Germany.

Behind the darkness of the "Iron Curtain," we dined at the top of the revolving TV tower overlooking a dreary East Berlin. The tower, known as "The Pope's Revenge," reflected a perfect silver cross when the sunlight would hit the globe-shaped top. The shimmering cross was a reminder of the gutted churches used to build a wall to separate a people and take away their hope. The cross shinning out of darkness on the highest building in East Berlin gave hope that one day that wall would come down.

God had given us a three-year history lesson. The scars remained in our hearts of a terrible World War crossing a continent leading to the Cold War. The effects of communism on the other side of a dividing wall would call us to champion our freedom at all costs. However, it was time to say *auf wiedersehen* to our special international friends and Germany. It was time for a change. Little did we know how dramatic and important the change would be for our lives. It was time to come home.

CHAPTER FOUR

Susan's Nose

For Thou didst form my inward parts;
Thou didst weave me in my mother's womb.
I will give thanks to Thee,
for I am fearfully and wonderfully made;
wonderful are Thy works,
and my soul knows it very well.
My frame was not hidden from Thee,
when I was made in secret,
and skillfully wrought in the depths of the earth.
Thine eyes have seen my unformed substance;
and in Thy book they were all written
the days that were ordained for me,
when as yet there was not one of them.
Psalms 139:13-16 (NAS)

Our original air force commitment was for four years. Four and a half years later, Gary and I were home from Germany. We were staying with my parents until we could find a home to buy in St. Louis. Closing the book *The Hiding Place,* I left the St. Louis heat in the backyard and walked into the air-conditioned house. It was good to be back with family and familiar surroundings. After traveling all over Europe, I still loved St. Louis with its famous Riverfront Arch and Busch Stadium. The Muny Opera, Forest Park and the Zoo held great summer fun. I was thankful we would settle in a city with so much art and entertainment. I was thankful to be back in the United States and home.

Our new air force assignment was Scott Air Force Base, Illinois, at the Military Airlift Command HQ/JAG Office. The assignment to Scott AFB got us back stateside at the government's expense. The plan was to get out of the military and find work at a St. Louis law firm. It was just the right assignment to ease into the civilian world.

The assignment to Scott AFB brought with it an extension of our air force commitment for one more year. By that time, we would be ready to start a family and get out of the military life. We had grown comfortable being just the two of us, and enjoyed spending time and money on traveling. However, we began to talk about having children, since we had been married for nine years.

After several weeks of looking for a home, we found one in south St. Louis off Grand Avenue. It was an older home, about sixty-five years old. The house was a real "fixer-upper." We were young and eager to remodel the kitchen, basement, garage, bedrooms, and bath. In September 1978, we started stripping and sanding off the paint from the detached garage that opened to an alley. We painted the garage white with green trim and put new German window boxes with red geraniums on the window ledges facing the house.

We had lived in our new home about two months when I suspected that I might be pregnant, and went to Scott AFB OB/GYN clinic for a pregnancy test. That night I had a dream. I was talking with my deceased grandmother in the backyard of her farmhouse. In a whipping wind, she was hanging clothes on the line by the old smokehouse.

I turned to her and said, "Grandma, am I pregnant?"

With a smiling look, she said, "Yes, my dear. You will be a wonderful mother."

I woke up from the dream in a sweat. My grandmother had been dead for eleven years. I was astonished that I could even remember what she looked like. The next day a phone call from the doctor's office confirmed that I was pregnant and due on June 17, 1979. We were surprised, but the timing seemed to fit right into our plans for staying in St. Louis. It also fit right into God's plan for us and our future.

Our family was excited about the news. Gary's parents lived within minutes of us, and were already grandparents to five-year-old Matthew. Gary's two sisters, Louise and Donna would now be aunts to our child. For my parents, this would be their first grandchild. My sister and brother would be Aunt Susan and Uncle Fred.

It had been nine years since we had any close relationship with our families. Old tensions in those relationships began to surface. Gary's parents began to warm up to the fact that we were married. They had visited us for a few days in Dover, Delaware, and that was about as long as we could stand each other. Now that we were going to have a grandchild, the thaw in our relationship began to take place.

My parents had come for a month visit to Germany. Although we had a great time traveling in Europe, Gary had little patience with them as his parents-in-law. Gary was somewhat jealous of the love my parents expressed to me. He had not received that kind of attention, especially from his father. When my dad tried to reach out to him, Gary would reject it. He just did not know how to accept a father's love.

These were complicated relationships that God knew needed work. My relationship with my sister, Susan, had issues that neither of us understood or acknowledged, until we tried to be part of each other's lives again. Susan had been a very insecure, highly emotional child growing up. I had been the stable, stoic, older sister. While I was off in Europe skiing, Susan had done some growing up and maturing that caught me off guard. She had married an attorney named Tom. She had received her Master's degree in voice. She also had become "born-again" in some religious experience with Campus Crusade for Christ in college.

She and Tom were involved as adult counselors in a youth ministry called Young Life. They were attending a highbrow rich Presbyterian church in Clayton, Missouri. She was running around the United States singing in churches on some kind of religious events called Lay Renewals. I was shocked to find out that she had actually become a "Jesus Freak!" The strange part was she had found something stable in her life. It was something that she wanted to share with Gary and me.

Susan and Tom began to share their faith and friends with us. They wanted us to meet John and Marcia Splinter. John was the St. Louis Area Director of Young Life. So one night we had Susan and Tom bring John and Marcia over for a special German meal in our newly wallpapered dining room. We had just found out I was pregnant. From that night on, John would always call me "Little Mama." God, The Father, was weaving a piece of the plan that would change our lives forever.

John and Marcia were great fun. When they discovered we knew how to ski, they asked us if we would like to be Young Life adult counselors at the weekly club meetings, and then go with the kids on the winter ski trip to Castaway Resort in Minnesota. We decided to try the weekly club meetings. Gary would go on the ski trip; I needed to stay home being about four months pregnant.

The Young Life Club meetings were amazing. First, we would meet as adults at the Splinter's home for a pre-meeting. John would brief us on how the meeting plan would go for the night, and we would pray. Then we headed out to a designated home. The Club meetings started with songs John would play on the guitar as the kids would sing, followed by outrageous skits. Finally, John would deliver the gospel in a simple message the teenagers could understand. Gary and I were there as basic crowd control adult chaperones. John needed all the adults he could get with 150-200 teens in the basement of a home.

Most of these kids had never been in church. Many were messing around with drugs and sex, and came from broken families. Young Life Club was the most fun they had all week. It was also the most love and acceptance that many had in their lives. They were the children of our "lost generation." What we had tolerated in our generation, this next generation was doing in excess.

At first, I was afraid of the kids, because I was an adult and almost 30 years old. I could not understand how they would relate to me. I became conscious of the fact that as I got farther in my pregnancy, I could not even dress like them. The tight jeans I bought in Paris would not zip any longer. I was really becoming "Little Mama"! Susan reminded me that I did not need to be like them. They did not expect me to be like them. They expected me to be the adult. They needed adults in their lives to model love and guide them.

Gary loved working with the teenagers. He went on the ski trip to Minnesota and came home pumped about Young Life. On the way home from skiing, the bus had slipped sideways on an icy farm road. It eased over on its side into a ditch, waking them all up. No one was injured, just scared to wake up sideways in the bus seat. A farmer had allowed them to sleep on the floor of his farmhouse, while he pulled the bus out of the ditch with his tractor. The bus accident made the trip more exciting.

John and Marcia Splinter knew when they asked us to help with Young Life that we were not "born-again Christians." What was happening to the kids at Club meetings was also happening to us. Young Life exposed us to talks that taught about the Bible and Jesus Christ. Many people were praying for us to know Jesus Christ in a personal saving relationship as our Savior and Lord. None of us had counted on what God was going to use to make that happen. Jesus Christ was weaving a piece of the tapestry into our lives.

Susan and I began to spend more time together, becoming not just sisters but best friends. One day after shopping at a mall, we had a very emotional and heated discussion over how our grandmother, Mimmy, treated each of us. Susan really struggled with Mimmy treating me as her favorite. Mimmy would openly praise me or give me gifts in front of Susan. Mimmy would rebuff Susan by ignoring her. If Mimmy felt like someone else was getting too much attention, she would develop a headache, needing to go home. We all knew what she was doing. Her playing favorites had destroyed many relationships in our family. It had driven a wedge between us as sisters, which we needed to acknowledge and heal.

I knew it hurt Susan for Mimmy to mistreat her, but it was not my fault. I tried to tell her I felt Dad over compensated for it by giving Susan more attention. He would always talk about her beautiful voice and go to all her recitals and performances. We cried and hugged. It was a family trait which we did not want to pass on to the next generation. We determined we had the power to stop it, and not ruin our relationship.

We were having so much fun getting to know each other again as sisters. Susan had one more friend for me to meet. I was not sure I wanted to meet this friend. His name was Bob Fenn. He was the founder of Lay Renewal Ministries. He was the man who kept taking my sister, my friend, away on trips to sing in churches. She would be gone for five to six days on these Lay Renewals and come home even more excited about Jesus. I did not appreciate my younger sister telling me something I needed to know about Jesus. In addition, I really did not appreciate some man named Bob Fenn taking her all over the country to sing about it.

In December of 1978, I was at Susan's house making Christmas cookies. She had a record by a Christian singer named Cynthia Clawson.

The song playing was *I Heard About a Man*. Susan was a district finalist for the New York Metropolitan Opera, and had always thought she would be a great opera singer. When she heard Cynthia Clawson sing, she decided to become a Christian singer. Susan was planning to cut her first Christian record sometime the next year. She told me Bob Fenn was stopping by that afternoon to leave some information with her about a Lay Renewal.

I was somewhat determined I was not going to like this Bob Fenn. When Bob showed up at Susan's door, he greeted me with such warmth and graciousness that I nearly melted in my shoes. He was about fifty-three years old. He was genuinely interested I was Susan's sister. His presence was over-powering in the room. The Holy Spirit was weaving this powerful piece of tapestry into my life.

During those nine months of pregnancy, the Lord was also weaving together a baby in my womb. I only weighed ninety-five pounds before I was pregnant. Each trip to Scott AFB hospital for my pregnancy appointments resulted in yet another physician's assistant giving me different advice from the last one. The first P.A. asked if I always carried my babies this small. I was disturbed the P.A. did not realize by reading the medical chart that this was my first baby. How was I to know if I was small or not? The P.A. told me to start gaining weight. The solution was simple in my mind. There are a few well-known unique places in St. Louis. One is Ted Drews Ice Cream. There just happened to be a "Ted Drews" on the corner of the next block from our house. Gary and I would walk up the street, down one block, cross over and have Ted Drews delicious vanilla custard several times a week. I was delighted when I started gaining weight.

The next pregnancy appointment, a different P.A. told me he was alarmed I had gained so much weight in one month. Test results showed I had developed gestational diabetes. I was put on a strict diet. I had to start counting my food exchanges. No more "Ted Drews." I could have plenty of fruit instead of dessert. The concern was that women with gestational diabetes could have problems with the delivery if the baby is too large. The OB/GYN clinic monitored my diet and weight. By June, I had eaten enough watermelon. If the baby had not started kicking me after eating White Castle Hamburgers one night, I would have thought there was a watermelon in my stomach and not a baby.

My due date, June 17, was based on being six weeks pregnant when my pregnancy test results were positive. On the night of June 16, I suddenly became hysterical with the thought things were never going to be the same again. It would not be just the two of us ever again. From now on our lives would change by including a child in the plans. I could do nothing. There was only one way out of this situation, and that was to have the baby!

When June 17 came and went with no sign of labor, the pregnancy clinic at Scott AFB decided to try to induce labor. I was hooked up to the drip and waited. Nothing happened. While I was waiting, a woman in the next bed who had come in for an amnio synthesis was moved into another room. During her procedure something went wrong. Gary was standing out in the hallway when several doctors rushed into her room. Her baby was delivered several months premature. Gary watched through the glass windows of the nursery as doctors worked on the baby to get it to breathe. The doctors looked up, saw him, and pulled the curtain. The reality that babies can die hit us both.

The next week I went back. The hospital staff was getting worried because our baby was now two weeks overdue. During the second try to induce labor, our baby's heartbeat slowed down so much the P.A. called a doctor. Our baby's heartbeat picked back up and I went home for one more week.

Finally, on July 7, I began to feel labor pains around 4:30 p.m. We got into the car with my suitcase, packed for three weeks, for the forty-five minute drive crossing the Poplar Street Bridge to Scott AFB Hospital in Illinois. At this point, three weeks overdue, I was hoping to wait a little while longer—just until midnight. July 8 was Susan's birthday. If this baby was going to wait three weeks, I was hoping that it would wait to be born on her birthday. That was not a problem. After a night of difficult labor, at 8:23 a.m. on July 8, 1979, we had a new baby.

Gary asked, "Is it a boy or a girl?"

I replied, "Oh, Gary! We have a little girl! Ann Marie is here! And she has Susan's nose!"

Ann Marie had waited to be born on that special birthday. She had this cute little distinct nose just like her Aunt Susan. She had needed those extra three weeks to grow, weighing only 4 pounds 6 ounces. The weaving of the tapestry was beginning to form a picture. A story of grace that would change everyone it touched. Our littlest angel had come with a message from God. She brought with her a delicate pink thread of Hope.

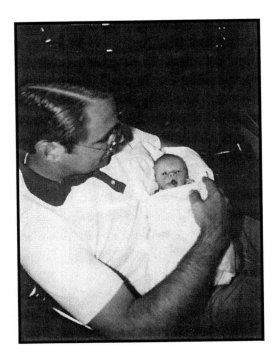

CHAPTER FIVE

A Church That Prays

He heals the broken hearted
and binds up their wounds.
Psalms 147:3 (NAS)

Several hours after Ann Marie's delivery, I woke up from a very deep sleep. The all night labor left me more exhausted than I had ever felt in my life. My eyeballs even hurt. Gary was there by my bed. He had been up all night with me in the labor and delivery room.

I said, "How is she? Is she O.K.?"

He was very quiet and took my hand.

He said, "Well, she is pretty little, Libby. She only weighs 4 pounds 6 ounces. They will have to keep her here until she gets to at least five pounds before they will let her go home."

Her weight shocked me. After all, she had been a ten-month baby! The medical staff had wanted to induce labor three weeks before because they were worried about her being too big. Now they were recounting months of pregnancy thinking she was pre-mature. There was no way that she was a preemie. It had been nine months since my pregnancy test was positive.

Later that afternoon I got up to walk. Everything in my body hurt. A hot shower loosened up my sore muscles. Ann Marie was not brought to me on the maternity ward like the other mothers. She needed to stay in the nursery because she was a little jaundiced. I walked down to see her. There she was under this bright light with nothing on but a diaper. She had an IV in her head and hooked up to a monitor. She was so tiny and thin; so delicate. I reached out to touch her and she made a little fist around my finger. She held on so tight. She was little, but she was strong. She was a fighter for life.

The nurse thought I should try to nurse her. Ann Marie cried because she was hungry. Nothing was happening. We were trying, but she kept going to sleep on me. The nurse told me to thump her feet and wake her up. She needed to eat. This went on for a day or two. Finally the decision was made she did not have the energy to nurse. I would pump my milk and put it into a preemie bottle with a very large hole in the nipple. That seemed to work, but she still barely sucked the milk until she would fall asleep again. We would measure how much she drank in centiliters. Most babies drink ounces of milk. Ann Marie was drinking centiliters of milk. If she drank one or two ounces we would cheer.

Gary was so excited about the birth of our new daughter, whenever he would jog during lunch his feet never touched the ground. He felt on top of the world as a new dad. During the first week of Ann's life, Gary was selected for promotion to the rank of Major one year "below the zone." This meant Gary was promoted one year ahead of schedule, and being groomed for command positions. It also meant he would have to extend two more years in the Air Force.

During that first week, the hospital moved me to a private room off the maternity ward. It was too hard to watch the other mothers with their babies in the room. After about a week of pumping and feeding with a tiny bottle, Ann Marie began to gain weight. She was hooked to an IV to supplement the fluids. A few times, she had been gavage fed with a tube. Once she had pulled the IV out of her head, so the nurse stuck it into her arm, then later into her leg. She was always being stuck with a needle somewhere. Her blood sugar was extremely low. I was excited at the ten-day point when she suddenly gained almost a half pound over night. I knew that meant we could go home. She was just over five pounds.

The doctor came in to check her out. He listened to her heart and lungs and looked at her chart. I was sitting in a rocking chair in the nursery waiting with Gary for the discharge paperwork to be completed. Suddenly several doctors were around Ann Marie. They were all listening to her heart and lungs. Finally Dr. Dichson, Chief of Pediatrics, came over to us. He was concerned about Ann Marie.

The doctors were hearing a heart murmur in her heart. He explained it was probably something very simple. Babies often have little heart murmurs that go away. Scott AFB Hospital was not equipped to handle infants needing the kind of test to find out what the problem was. They were sending Ann Marie by ambulance immediately to St. Louis Children's Hospital to the Cardiac Unit.

Gary and I packed my suitcase and drove home for me to change clothes and call our parents. Then we went to St. Louis Children's Hospital and were met by Dr. Arnold Strauss, Chief of Pediatric Cardiology. He explained Ann Marie had been given a diuretic because she was showing signs of heart failure. The sudden weight gain had been fluid her kidneys were not able to eliminate. Within a few hours, Ann Marie's weight had gone down to four pounds. He showed us x-rays. Her heart was enlarged, and he wanted us to sign papers allowing a cardiac catheterization. He explained how a small incision would be made in her groin and a tube inserted through a vein to her heart. Dye would be put into the tube, and from the flow of the dye, the doctors could tell what was causing her heart failure.

We were in shock. Things were happening so fast. We signed the papers and she went into surgery. We waited at St. Louis Children's Hospital for the results. Dr. Hartmann, who did the cardiac catheterization on Ann Marie, asked us to step into a small room with him for the results of the test.

"Ann Marie has two large holes in her heart," he began with this abrupt statement.

The room began to swim for me. I could hardly concentrate on what he was saying. Something about VSD and ASD as he began to draw a heart on a piece of paper and mark it with black circles where the holes were located. I was fading in and out of what he was telling us. This was our little girl. We had grown to love her in those first two weeks of life. How could this be happening?

He ended with the statement, "She is too little for us to even think of doing open-heart surgery to correct these two holes. She needs to weigh at least twenty-five pounds before we can work on her heart. Considering her condition and weight, I do not expect that she will live long enough to reach twenty-five pounds and have open-heart surgery. Do you have any questions?"

49

My mind was screaming, *What? What! He is saying she is going to die!*

Gary and I just held each other and cried. Sitting there in that cold little room together, we could not grasp what he had just told us. What questions could we think to ask? As we sat there with tears, the doctor got up and exited the room, leaving us alone.

After several minutes, we got up and left the room. We called our parents who were waiting to find out the news. It was devastating to them as well. Our world had suddenly come crashing down on us. We were no longer in control of life. We were facing death straight in the face. It was exactly where God wanted us to be. He wanted us to know weakness, so that He could be strong.

Little ones, to Him belong.
They are weak,
but He is strong.

Ann Marie was in heart failure and had to remain in the neonatal cardiology ward at St. Louis Children's Hospital. She started on a diuretic and heart medicine; and was put in an incubator. We hated to leave her there, but there were no arrangements for us to stay in the neonatal part of the hospital. Our home was only ten minutes away. When we got home, we collapsed on the couch in the front living room holding each other and crying. It was the first time I could remember us praying together. God was ready to move us from religious faith to a saving faith.

God was ready to move us from religious faith to saving faith.

Aunt Susan was devastated as if Ann Marie was her own child. The day after we received the cardiac catheterization report, Susan started a diary of letters to Ann Marie and prayers to God on her behalf. This diary of letters and prayers would be a source of strength for us in the years to come. It reaffirmed our testimony of God's grace and love. Reading how God had worked in our lives strengthened our faith that He is faithful. It is a book of raw and vulnerable treasured memories and emotions. Susan poured out her heart to God.

7/21/79

I want a miracle—more than I've ever wanted anything before—does that count?

I believe You have the power to do what I want—I don't know if You will, but I believe You can— Does that also count?

I'm sorry I'm so abrupt—but You know why better than anyone else right now. I am asking—I'm stomping my foot and screaming—and let me not pass up my opportunity to ask this question "WHY?"

Don't under estimate the asking, the questions—just because it's stuck between two lines doesn't mean it's small, insignificant—or even asked in humility— (Everything is crazy right now so why should I just happen to be humble?)

It's a fairly large and important "WHY?— "well not any bigger than the sun or the sky—but about that big.

Why did it have to happen in the first place? Now really—you could have taken care of it before anyone ever knew—couldn't you?

Or if it had to be, why couldn't it have been to someone who was trotting off to the abortion clinic—or going to give the baby away—

or to a squirrel or something for that matter— I'm sure a mother squirrel wouldn't shed a tear— she'd just look at it with slight curiosity and then run off.

God is the Mighty Creator of the Universe and yet one of the marvelous parts about our God is that He is able to enter into a personal relationship with anyone.

Rev. 3:20 "Behold, I stand at the door and knock, if anyone hears My voice and opens the door, I will come in to him, and will dine with him, and he with Me."

What did Joni (Erickson Tada) say last week—

I need to hear it now!

Lord, work something good out of this—Hearts are so important—don't let them all break—and please with all my heart I ask You to heal the tiny broken heart.

Do You love her?

Now I know You must—but I don't understand

I love her and if I could, I'd heal her immediately so why don't the two of you get together and work this out? She's so tiny and frail—

she's so pretty—

Lord—my attitude is awful—I'm upset and I can't think my true, healthy Christian thoughts.

Somewhere along the line I've let the anger, and outrage of this situation envelope me—

I get in a true crisis and my faith flies out the window— But it's hard when I see Libby and Gary and Ann Marie. Do something. Do a lot.

The day Ann Marie was born, Susan had sung for a vespers service and Joni Erickson Tada had been the guest speaker. Joni's message was ministering to Susan's heart and spirit. After beginning her prayer journal, Susan came to visit me. Her words left me confused and angry. They were words of confrontation I needed to hear. They were words of faith and truth.

She said, "Libby, I have been praying for Ann Marie. I have been searching the scriptures. I found a promise I am clinging to for the holes to heal in Ann Marie's heart."

She pulled out her Bible and opened it. She turned to the middle of the Bible and pointed to a red underlined passage.

"Psalm 147:3 says, 'He heals the broken hearted and binds up their wounds.'"

The Bible quote meant nothing to me. I was not interested in her trying to convince me there was something about this Jesus stuff. I was facing reality. She was not!

She continued, "My church is holding a twenty-four hour prayer vigil for Ann Marie right now. We are asking God for the holes to heal in her heart. We are claiming that scripture."

I said, "You can do what you want, but the doctors have said she is going to die."

Then Susan's words engraved in my heart forever. "Libby, the Jesus I know can heal today, the same as He did when He walked on the earth in the New Testament."

I did not know "THAT Jesus!" I thought the Bible was a good story if you might want to read it sometime. I did not know Jesus is God in the flesh. I thought he was a good man, if he had ever really lived. I did not know I was a sinner. I did not know I needed a Savior. I thought I was a good girl. I did not know a real Satan and Hell existed; and I certainly did not know I was headed straight to Hell. I had never heard Jesus is coming back. Somewhere I had missed this message. A gracious and merciful God was going to write this message on my heart for eternity. The tapestry of Grace was weaving through a child holding the pale pink thread of Hope for life.

Susan's church held a twenty-four hour prayer vigil for Ann Marie. The next day Susan wrote in her prayer diary.

7/25/79 2:30 am

Lord,

I have prayed so much for Ann Marie and Your divine will of healing for her. Now—we are all praying for these 24 hours and we pray with great expectancy because—You are a Great and powerful God, because You are a God who performs miracles.

I know I don't always say it correctly—my heart seems to be continually filled with sin—and yet I need to tell you that if I knew the right way—the best way to ask for her healing I would—

Well I don't know exactly how to say it the way I expect others have—but I do ask humbly and with all sincerity for You to heal Ann Marie— If You haven't already—

Take the wound in her heart and bind it up—so there is no trace—no wound left! I pray Jesus for Your healing power to intervene and perform this miracle of healing—in Your Precious Name—and for Your Glory and Honor—

Thank you Lord. Jesus, I am resting in the joy of what Thou art.

I am finding out the greatness of Thy loving heart.

Ann Marie

Ann Marie

Ann Marie

7/27/79

Thank you Lord for the way you fulfill Your promises to us. In everything you are so good —We can't always see what you have planned— yesterday was so discouraging for all of us— It seemed like things would never get better—but that is the crucial time when we really need to trust You— because You promise to take care of us—we can be hopeful and faithful as a result of believing in Your promises—

Ann Marie 4lb-8oz— 2 oz gain! She's alive and hungry!

My headache & oppression—gone! For as long as I want to give it up! I know You're in the process of teaching me to relinquish my beloved anxieties—Praise God from whom all blessings flow!

Ann Marie stayed at St. Louis Children's Hospital for about three weeks. We became quite familiar with the routine of the hospital and the nurses. Dr. Arnold Strauss and Dr. Cathy Henry were her pediatric cardiologists. The medications were stabilizing her and she was beginning to gain weight slowly but surely. A few days after the prayer vigil, our friend John Splinter came to the hospital for a visit. He had gotten into the neonatal ward by telling the nursing staff he was our pastor. He was the closest thing we had to a pastor at the time. It was a comfort for us to know he cared enough to come and visit. John and Marcia went to the same church Susan and Tom attended. He had been part of the twenty-four hour prayer vigil. He wanted to tell us something very special.

"Hey guys, I've been praying about this, and I have gotten a real peace about it. Ann Marie is going to be all right," he said.

I appreciated his visit, concern, and prayers, but I certainly did not have a peace about what was happening. How could I have a peace, I did not know Jesus who is the "Prince of Peace."

On August 6, 1979, Ann Marie came home for the first time. She weighed exactly five pounds. The next six months were continual doctor appointments between Scott AFB Hospital and the cardiologists at St. Louis Children's Hospital. Ann Marie would gain a little weight and then seem to stop. She began to exhibit her determined personality to demand her bottle and refuse to burp. This often led to her vomiting part of what we worked so hard to get down her.

I felt all the responsibility of taking care of her. Medications had to be exact and on time. Feedings measured and recorded. Charts made on when she eliminated and how much, to make sure her kidneys were functioning and she was not slipping back into heart failure. She had a repeated thrush infection in her mouth that soon became a yeast infection on her bottom. Every morning and sometimes in the middle of the night, I would wake up and go into her room. I would look into her bed expecting that she may have died during the night. I was preparing myself that she would not live long enough to have open-heart surgery.

Susan's prayer diary recorded the situation.

8/28/79

Need for prayers—we've been drifting along feeling like all is well—she looks so feisty—But she's not gaining weight—not like she should—she gains maybe an ounce a week—and should be gaining an ounce a day—

We have to figure something else out—

Lots more milk each feeding time to stretch her stomach— and a higher caloric content—

What a slow process!

At this rate she'll never grow—It can't stay this way— we've just got to make her eat more!

The solution was to stop feeding breast milk in a bottle. This was a relief for me. I was spending all my time either pumping or feeding Ann Marie every two or three hours. I needed some rest. The stress was overwhelming. Similac formula mixed with less water gave her greater calories for the small amount that she was taking. I asked the doctor about the nutritional value of switching to Similac. He answered that Ann Marie could live very well on Similac. In fact, she could take her case of Similac to college if necessary. It seemed to solve the problem in many ways.

Susan's diary expressed the personality of this little girl we had nicknamed

"Annie"

9/9/79

Annie —you and I sat together for the longest time tonight—

I gave you your bottle and you wanted to do some important things afterwards like look at your mobile, your hands, my face—

You actually talked to me—although I don't know what you said—

Your eyes are always searching my face to see if you can understand who or what I am—Sometimes you smile at me but most of the time its just wide eyed searching—

Thank you Lord because she's gaining weight now—7 lb. 1 oz!

She is so healthy looking—and so lively—and still very beautiful.

Ann was winning the hearts of all of those around her. Her will to live and her delicate beauty had drawn many to love and pray for her. Her extended family was so proud of her. She had a way of drawing all of us closer to God in the hope for her special life to continue. We wanted a victory in the prayers that many were saying for her. Gary and I wanted her dedicated to God in a special way. It was appropriate for her great-grandfather, Pop, to christen her, and for her Aunt Suzie and Uncle Tom to be her god- parents. Susan wrote in her diary about the christening.

10/13/79

A lot has happened since I wrote last—

First of all, Ann Marie was christened Oct 6—and that was a lot of fun.

She wore the long white dress Mimmy made for her with all the hand tatting, and Pop christened her.

His first Great-Grand baby—

He did really well at containing his pride until the very end when he said to her "do you want to see all the people?" —and he held her up so we could all see her —Well—I can't blame him—

She was really good—and the fact that we finally discovered her long time yeast infection and had her on medication helped—

I held her at the alter and gave her to Pop—she looked like she might fuss—so I entertained her by making little faces and noises -- anything to keep her happy—Then Libby took her after it was over —it was a memorable occasion—

Libby and I talked for a long time yesterday about Ann Marie and her problems—

What she will have to face in life.

How tragic it seems in part and yet how blessed she is to be able to live through all of this.

Her life doesn't have to be tragic—already it seems to me that her life is triumphant that she has now and will continue to have victory over her handicap—and I really believe someday soon we'll be saying "What handicap?" "She's perfectly normal."

I think any of us would be willing to have the surgery for her—I wish I could—but God has settled my heart about this—I know He will continue to protect her—because He loves her.

Psalm 139 —A Psalm for Ann Marie

His promises have convicted me time after time—

And what other people have done has been wonderful. Debbie Holley said we must storm the heavens with her name— and we sure did and have and are continuing to do —almost every day I pray for her to gain weight.

We've all prayed for her so much. Tom usually prays for her at night—I just want to remember all of this—

I'll never forget the first time I saw her—Libby said "she looks better today" but I secretly thought she might die in my arms she was so tiny and weak— I came home and cried for three day— I couldn't get my mind off of her little face. She was real—not just Libby's baby—she really was a person struggling to survive—It's unbelievable that was just three months ago—and now she's so strong and determined—and cute—How can she be so cute and funny? I can't get over it.

In October, Gary told me something he had known for a couple of months. Air Force doctors had found a lump in Gary's throat. It was a tumor on his thyroid and there was a ten percent chance of it being cancerous. He had kept it to himself because he knew the stress I was under with Ann Marie. The doctors were waiting for test results. If it did not shrink, he would have to have surgery in February to remove the tumor.

During November and December, Ann Marie continued to gain strength and weight. Her diuretic was reduced from three times a day to twice a day, then to once a day. She started eating cereal and egg yolks. Her length was catching up for her age. In January, she weighed between ten and eleven pounds. The doctors were amazed at how well she was doing. "She is a social child, looking good," doctors commented. By January she was on solid foods. I was relieved that she would not go off to college with her case of Similac.

February brought a climax to what had been building up over the past six months. God had been working on many hearts. He had been healing broken hearts and binding up their wounds. He had set the stage for a dramatic "valentine of His love." A church had been praying for the heart of a little girl, and for healing of her parents' hearts.

CHAPTER SIX

First Miracle

But for you who fear My Name,
the sun of righteousness shall rise,
with healing in its wing;
and you shall go forth
and skip about like calves from the stall.
Malachi 4:2 (NAS)

Expect a miracle to happen in this place.
Expect a miracle to happen by God's grace.
And through a miracle, He will show His power.
Expect a miracle, this very hour.
Expect a Miracle — by Randy Mayfield
©Ramay Music — Used with permission

February brought the news that Gary would have thyroid surgery on February 14. Happy Valentines Day! I just knew it would probably be cancer. I thought I would lose my child, and be a widow all in that year. That cold hard winter in St. Louis drove me deeper into depression.

Susan and Tom were in a prayer group, which met every Friday night. Bob and Delores Fenn, Dr. Bill and Joyce Flannagan, Randy and Sharon Mayfield, and Eric and Ellen Schmidt were in the prayer group. On Friday, February 1, 1980, Susan visited Ann Marie and me. Later that evening she asked the prayer group to pray. Her diary records the events.

Prayers for Gary — Lord heal him.

2/1/80

Tonight at prayer group Eric Schmidt prayed for Gary to be healed— also Ann Marie— We prayed in faith Lord knowing you have heard our prayers.

Soon you'll be seven months old! That's great!

I spent the day with you today— and you are more precious than ever! You have a sweet disposition and you never cry without a good reason— you've become a very happy and easily contented baby.

Today you had a little real breakfast along with your milk— your mother put you in your walker—and put some toast and bananas in your tray—you gummed the toast to death—

You're so interested in faces—and people. Your mother and I talked today and you silently watched us with great intent.

Your mother was sad because your father has to have an operation. We prayed about it, and we prayed for you too. Your mother cried. She prayed for you to be healed and to grow up into a beautiful Christian woman. She prayed that she would always be a good mother to you and raise you in love. She loves you very much. You smile all the time.

"He heals the broken hearted and binds up their wounds." Psalm 147:3

I was facing Ann Marie's six-month cardiac checkup at St. Louis Children's Hospital (SLCH) by myself, because Gary would still be recovering from surgery at Scott AFB Hospital. On Tuesday, February 12, I had to take Ann Marie for heart x-rays and an EKG at Scott AFB.

Dr. Cathy Henry wanted us to bring the EKG and x-rays with us when we had our visit at SLCH on Saturday.

Gary went in for thyroid surgery on Thursday, February 14. John Splinter came to Scott AFB to wait with me during the surgery. John was once again taking on the role as our pastor. The good news came a few hours later that the tumor and half of Gary's thyroid were successfully removed. There did not seem to be any cancer present. He would be on thyroid medication for the rest of his life.

John and I went to the recovery room. Gary was just beginning to come around from the anesthetic. He was trying to talk. He had remained composed about the surgery until that moment.

His hidden fear was exposed as he cried, "Am I OK?"

John took his hand and said, "Hey, Gary, buddy, this is John Splinter. You are OK. Do you hear me? You're OK."

We had a prayer right there for Gary and thanked the Lord for the good news. I was so thankful John had come to be with us and reassure Gary. Gary was going to have to stay a few more days before he could come home.

Saturday, February 16, I got Ann Marie up and dressed. I took the heart x-rays and EKG with me and we headed off to St. Louis Children's Hospital. Dr. Cathy Henry began to examine Ann Marie with her stethoscope. She listened to Ann's heart. She looked at the x-rays. She looked at the EKG. She left the room and went to get Dr. Arnold Strauss. He came in and did the same thing she had just done. They talked about the x-rays and EKG.

Then he turned to me and said, "Mrs. Grunick, something is blocking the holes in Ann Marie's heart. We do not know what is happening, but it is helping her to live and grow. The holes appear to be closing. The x-rays show her heart is smaller. We are going to take her off her diuretic. She may not need open-heart surgery. Let's wait until she is fifteen months old and do another cardiac catheterization on her to see what is happening."

After Dr. Strauss left the room, Dr. Cathy Henry told me, "I have only seen this happen twice; once to a pastor's child, and now to Ann Marie. I have checked my medical books, and this is very unusual with holes as big as Ann Marie's."

I knew then in my heart, God had answered the prayers for Ann Marie. Coming home, I immediately called Aunt Susan to tell her the second good news of the week.

When she answered the phone, I said, "Susan, the doctors say something is blocking the holes in Ann Marie's heart! It is helping her to live! The holes may be closing!"

Susan replied, "I've been waiting for you to call. There is a man in our prayer group named Eric. He just told me last night, that Tuesday while you were having the x-rays made of Ann Marie's heart, he was praying for her. While he was praying, he had a vision of the Lord's hands going around her heart and healing it. Will you come to my church tomorrow morning and meet Eric and tell him what the doctor's have said?"

I had not been in church for ten years. I called Gary's mother and asked her if she would watch Ann Marie while I went to church with Susan the next day. On Sunday morning, February 17, I met Susan in front of Central Presbyterian Church. That morning was a very unusual morning worship service. Central Presbyterian had just gotten new hymnals and the service was a hymn singing worship service. As I sat in the pew with Susan, I looked up into the choir loft. There sat Dr. Cathy Henry, Ann Marie's cardiologist. She was a Christian. I was sure that she must know Susan since they both sang in the choir together. She must have known about the prayers for Ann Marie.

After church I met Eric, the man who had prayed and had the vision. When I told him what the doctors had said the day before, he was unable to talk and began to cry. It was a confirmation to Eric; God had answered his prayers and the vision had been real. I was very touched by this man praying for us and by his tears.

I had never been in a church that really prayed. Not like this kind of praying. I could not believe Eric had prayed for someone he did not even know. John and Marcia Splinter were at church and came to give me a hug. They were glad to see me at church and told me to come back next week with Gary. They thought we would like to hear a sermon preached instead of the hymns. I liked Susan's church. They were friendly and something was different about their commitment to God. When this church prayed, God heard and answered their prayers. I knew He had answered with a miracle. He heals the broken hearted and binds up their wounds.

Susan had written to Ann Marie the day before.

Dearest Ann Marie   2/16/80

The Lord has heard our prayers —all of them! He is faithful.

He loves you very much. He loves your father and mother too. Your father is well and will come home from the hospital tomorrow.

And what joyous news for all of us today to hear that your holes are mending — That your little body is being healed!

Eric Schmidt told me today of his prayers Tuesday for you when the Holy Spirit commanded him to pray and he saw a vision of hands around your little heart.

You are truly an angel sent to us to prove the love, power and glory of the Lord. Your very being is proof. Your face reminds me continually of His love and mercy.

Gary and I began to attend Central Presbyterian Church the next Sunday. It was a tall gray stone traditional building. The sanctuary was long and narrow with a balcony, and more seating in the two alcoves off to each side of the altar. Stained glass windows surrounded the pews. A pipe organ commanded attention at the front of the church where the choir sat. There was a dark wooden railing around the altar with two praying angels carved at the front handrails. Two dark wood pulpits stood opposite each other. The largest pulpit on the left side of the altar was reserved for the senior pastor, Dr. Andrew Jumper, to deliver the sermon. The smaller pulpit, on the right side, was for announcements, prayers, and scripture readings by an associate pastor.

My original impression of the church being a highbrow rich Presbyterian church was not accurate once we came to know the people and the ministries of the church. It was true that there were some very wealthy members. However, we found those blessed with wealth were also very generous and gracious. They used their wealth to further the Kingdom of God, sensitive to needs of others and supporting worthwhile ministries. Our attraction to the church was a genuine loving, caring congregation that showed us what the "Body of Christ" should be. This church took Bible study, prayer, tithing, fellowship, and evangelism/missions seriously.

Tom and Susan took us to their Sunday school class. Dr. Bill Flannagan, associate pastor, was teaching on "The Revelation." I knew Revelation was the last book in the Bible. I knew Genesis was the first book, and in the middle were Matthew, Mark, Luke, and John. I had no idea what the Bible said, or where to find any scripture verse. To begin in one of the most difficult to understand books of the Bible was part of God's plan. I was surprised the Bible said Jesus is coming back. There will be a Second Coming; a day when God's Judgment will come. There is a future to God's purpose and will for my life here on earth.

Dr. Flannagan had been praying for months for Ann Marie and us. He knew whom we were when we walked into his class. He shook our hands and told us he had been praying for Ann Marie. A few weeks after we started his class, Dr. Flannagan gave his testimony. He was saved several years before as the pastor of a large church in Mississippi during a Lay Renewal event. The day he had walked the aisle, he quit playing church and started preaching the Truth from the pulpit. His humility to confess, as a pastor, he had been outside of the Will of God for his life was a powerful testimony.

The director of evangelism just happened to be Bob Fenn. Bob had set into place several ministries in the church to bring in unbelievers, and "romance" new members. Church members willing to help us integrate into the church and make friendships immediately welcomed us. Within a few weeks, a couple visited us with a cassette tape from Dr. Andy Jumper. The tape welcomed us and explained the responsibilities of church membership and the plan of salvation. I began to understand how sin came into the world in the Garden of Eden. Dr. Jumper explained that there is sickness, birth defects, and death on earth because when Adam and Eve sinned in the Garden, all nature and man fell into sin. I realized I was a sinner who needed a Savior. Jesus Christ came as God in the flesh the first time, as a baby born to die on a cross for my sin. If I believed that Jesus died for my sin, and resurrected from the dead, I would be saved from the penalty of sin just as if I had never sinned. The penalty for sin is eternal death in hell away from God. If I believed, I would receive abundant life now on earth through the power of His Holy Spirit in a personal relationship with Jesus Christ to do His will. If I believed, I would receive eternal life in heaven in a glorified body to worship and serve God forever. The Jesus that could heal the same today as He did when He walked on the earth in the New Testament was becoming real to me. Each Sunday as Dr. Jumper would preach an evangelical message, I began to understand what truth the Bible contained and the purpose of God's Church. The Holy Spirit had drawn us to a place where we experienced His love and grace through His Church called the "Body of Christ." A place where we could hear the Word of God preached in truth. His Church loved us, and let God heal our broken hearts.

By April 1980, Gary and I decided we wanted to become members of Central Presbyterian Church. For the first time in my life, I understood the true meaning of Easter. We came forward on the last hymn April 13, 1980, and I professed Jesus as my Savior and Lord. Gary did what he calls, in military terms, an "about face" in his walk with the Lord. It was a very emotional moment for us. We walked up to Bill Flannagan at the altar with tears streaming down our faces. Dr. Flannagan moved to tears because of all the prayers for us, welcomed our membership.

John Splinter came crying and grabbed us with a big hug. He was saying, "We have been praying so long for this day!"

Many in the congregation rejoiced to see their prayers answered that day. I believe a great cloud of witnesses in heaven rejoiced to see their prayers answered also.

Susan had written letters to Ann Marie in her diary.

Dearest Ann Marie   4/3/80

It's been a while since I wrote. You are growing so fast and looking so happy and healthy. This Sunday you will go with us to church because it is Easter. Mom bought you a beautiful outfit to wear. A pretty pink dress and white bonnet. You'll look precious as always.

Ann Marie, I hope someday you will understand all about Easter and what it really means. I know as you grow up you will search for many answers to life, but they all begin and end with Jesus and what happened at Easter. I will never be able to make you believe. You must find that in your own heart, and someday it will be between you and Jesus, but I pray that you will believe in Him when the decision is at hand. He loves us so much, and He is so wonderful to have died for us, and to have healed your heart.

I love you little one! You are more important to me than you'll ever know!

Love,

Aunt Susan

Prayers for Ann Marie   4/26/80

Claiming the promise in Psalm 147:3

"He heals the broken hearted,

binding up their wounds."

Picturing her heart being mended by the Holy Spirit.

Picturing her healthy and full of healing.

Picturing her with the extra weight she needs.

Picturing Ann Marie and her parents in the arms of the Lord, who is healing them now.

Dear Ann Marie,   *4/29/80*

I love you very much. I can never tell you how much I love you. I love you as if you were my own child and sometimes I wish you were. I miss you when I'm away from you and I think about you everyday! I put you in Jesus' hands because I know that as much as I love you, He loves you even more, and His Holy Spirit is at work in your little body right now—healing your tiny heart. Someday I pray you will decide to invite God's Holy Spirit to live in your healed heart.

Central Presbyterian invited us to a special dinner, held every six months in the fellowship hall, for new members. After the dinner, about seventy-five new members met with the staff of the church highlighting the various ministries. Dr. Jumper then took us all on a tour of the church including every office and hallway. He even took us up into the hidden sound booth where Randy Mayfield made copies of the Sunday sermons on cassette tapes available to the congregation. The newest members sat together at one special Sunday worship service. The women received a flower corsage and each family stood for an introduction to the congregation. Membership in the Church as the "Bride of Christ" is a covenant relationship, just like marriage. Being appreciated as new members, encouraged us to participate in membership and find a ministry. We were learning how to love and care for one another by being loved and cared for by others.

We joined the prayer group Susan and Tom went to on Friday nights. The first time we went, Eric Schmidt led a Bible study, and then we began to share prayer requests and pray. We were completely out of our league with those who were there praying. These were the most powerful prayer warriors I have ever known in my life; a grand group of saints storming the Throne of Heaven in Jesus Name. Gary and I were afraid to open our mouths.

I remember just saying, "Lord, help us. Amen."

Our Lord was putting us on the fast track of learning from the best. His plan for our lives was to get to the meat of ministry, because He knew the time was short for learning. He had more places for us to go. He was giving us a story to share with others.

In the spring, a church Family Weekend Retreat took place at Trout Lodge near the Ozarks. Susan and Tom told us we were going as their guests. We would share a cabin and they would not take "no" for an answer. We were able to make more friends on the retreat and build upon other relationships. The retreat theme focused on "Strengthening Family Relationships." On Saturday night, there was a time to come forward if you wanted to be "filled with the Holy Spirit." Gary and I just sat there and watched as almost everyone came forward. We were thinking we had just come forward and accepted Jesus Christ the month before, what was this "filling of the Holy Spirit?" When many who we knew as strong Christians went forward, we decided we did not want to be the only ones sitting down when the music stopped. We moved forward for prayer. We felt it was an act of obedience to the Lord. There were tears, but in our new faith we did not know what to expect.

For this reason, I bow my knees before the Father,
from whom every family in heaven and on earth derives its name,
that He would grant you, according to the riches of His glory,
to be strengthened with power through His Spirit in the inner man;
so that Christ may dwell in your hearts through faith;
and that you, being rooted and grounded in love,
may be able to comprehend with all the saints
what is the breadth and length and height and depth,
and to know the love of Christ which surpasses knowledge,
that you may be filled up to all the fullness of God.
Ephesians 3:14-19 (NAS)

Susan wrote in her journal.   *5/24/80*

What a wonderful month this has been for us. Libby and Gary have grown tremendously in their faith. They have joined Central Presbyterian and love it and the people.

We all went on a family retreat and it was super for everyone. Ann Marie was the center of much attention and of many prayers. Dr. Jumper laid hands on her and prayed for her. Gary and Libby also received many prayers and much love.

Gary gave his testimony at Young Life, and Libby and Gary are starting with the Friday night Bible Study.

Libby and I continue the picture prayers for Ann Marie—claiming God's promise to heal her heart. I've been secretly praying for her appetite to increase and Libby keeps telling me how much more she's been eating lately—almost to the day I started praying for it.

Ann Marie is sweet and eager to learn. She smiles so easily and seems to know no fear!

I began to attend the young mother's circle which met every week, making friends with several young women in the church, developing a bond and support system. Weekly we would have Bible study, prayer, and a mission project. A telephone prayer chain kept us in touch during the week. All of the "circles of women" in the church would meet together monthly for a special lunch in the fellowship hall and an invited speaker would give a challenging message from the Bible.

The church believed every member should have a ministry based on his or her spiritual gifts. We were encouraged to try several ministries. Our first service was in the children's nursery every few months. Eventually, I came to be the liaison between the young mothers and the staff nursery director. It was a beginning in women's ministry for me. Mothers could bring concerns to me, and I would then anonymously share them with the nursery director. I will never forget the lessons learned. If young mothers are not happy with the childcare in the church nursery, no one is happy. It is probably one of the most crucial ministries in the church. It is a trust that must be honored and secure.

With a growing desire to understand the Bible, I spent hours reading and asking the Holy Spirit to teach me. The words, once too hard to understand, began to come together in a way I could see how God was working in my life. I would talk to the Lord about everything.

Thanking Him because He had chosen to reach me through Ann Marie's heart defect and the prayers said for our healing. Gary and I had come together in this new walk of faith. I was confident the cardiac catheterization scheduled for October would reveal the truth. There had been a miracle performed. God had chosen to do this miracle when He could have chosen Ann Marie's death. His grace was amazing to me.

During the summer, Gary and I went to Frontier Ranch in Colorado with the Young Life group. We were no longer just "crowd control." John Splinter was giving us real counseling responsibilities with the youth. One of the girls in my cabin was dealing with several physical and mental disabilities. It was a very difficult week for her to fit into the group. My heart broke for her as she tried to make friends. I mentored her and challenged the other girls to reach out to her. By the end of the week, we had all undergone a transformation about how we judge and look at others.

Ann Marie spent the week with Aunt Susan. Ann Marie was cutting her teeth and had started biting those she loved. She bit Susan in the grocery store one day. It was a way of her expressing emotion. She was not biting to be mean, but it was part of her hug. Instead of kissing, she would bite. She stopped biting when I showed her how it felt by biting her back. She was a very compliant child and could hardly stand it when we disciplined her. She would hang her head and cry at the slightest raising of our voice. To have to discipline her, with all that sweetness looking back at me, would tear me apart.

Bob Fenn had organized another ministry at Central Presbyterian called "Knife and Fork Evangelism." The idea was to help members of the church mix in small group fellowship with a casual dinner in a home. The host couple would invite two or three other couples for dinner along with a "target couple." The "target couple" would be new members needing to find common relationships with other members of the church. We were invited, not knowing that we were the "target couple," to a dinner where we met Jay and Carol Barrington. As we shared with them our experience with Ann Marie and her heart defect, they shared what we had in common. Jay and Carol also had a son with a heart defect born just before Ann Marie. Their faith in the Lord had been strong, but their beloved baby son had died from his heart defect. I realized that could have been our experience. Our faith in God was encouraged by their testimony, because God had graciously chosen to heal Ann Marie.

One Sunday evening, Eric Schmidt talked to us about having Ann Marie anointed with oil in a prayer service for healing. It sounded very strange to us, but Eric said it was scriptural.

He said, "In the book of James, the Bible says if anyone is sick they should call for the elders and be anointed with oil and pray for healing."

He told us there was nothing magic about the oil, but it would be an act of obedience to God's Word. We thought about it for a couple of months. Finally, in September during a Sunday evening vespers service, Dr. Bill Flannagan announced there would be a prayer service held for healing and anointing with oil in the small chapel. Gary and I looked at each other and headed for the nursery to get Ann Marie. We knew what we needed to do.

Susan recorded the event. *9/10/80*

Sunday night we anointed you with oil—something that Eric had suggested several months back. It happened after the Vespers Service in the little chapel and the elders led by Bill Flannagan did the anointing.

It was a very important moment for us all, partly because it was fulfilling the command for the sick, but also because it was a tremendous step of obedience on the part of your father and mother.

Sometimes I think the act of faithful obedience is what engages the power of healing. We praise the Lord because He has shown us the way to wholeness and Holiness.

You even said "AMEN!" during the anointing and subsequent request for healing. By the way, "Amen" means, "so be it!"

It was true that Ann Marie, who was just starting to say a few words, blurted out a very loud "AMEN!" after Bill Flannagan had prayed. Susan and I were being very serious about what was happening, but when Ann Marie just shouted the "Amen," we began to giggle. Then she did it again, and we could hardly keep the laughter in. She was learning how to pray early in life.

In October, Susan went on a Lay Renewal to North Carolina.

Dearest Ann Marie,   10/2/80

It has been a week since I saw you last. I've been away in the mean time on a renewal in Brevard N.C. I understand from Momma that your favorite words now are "Oh, Baby!" I will see you tomorrow and I can't wait. While I was in Brevard, I had the whole Lay Team pray with me for you. We all agreed in the Name of Jesus that you would be healed.

I think it's so important to understand that the work concerning your healing was done a long time ago when Jesus died for you on the cross. If you had been the only person alive, He would have poured out His Blood for you. With that act of sacrifice, He acquired your healing. "With His stripes we were healed." Isaiah 53. So we are praising Him and thanking Him because your little body is receiving that healing—meant for you!

Love in Jesus, Aunt Susan

A cardiac catheterization was scheduled for October 8, 1980, when Ann Marie was fifteen months old. We took her to St. Louis Children's two days before for several other tests. The medical team expressed concerns because she was still so small, weighing only 15 pounds 4 ounces. She was socially and mentally progressing; able to count to four and she would ask, "What's that?" as she would point to everything in sight. Her physical motor development was delayed. She could not sit up alone until seven months old, and did not start walking until the day we went for the catheterization. Bone density and thyroid tests explored other possible medical problems.

The reason for Ann's heart defect could not be certain. Rubella titers done on both Ann Marie and I had been elevated, indicating possibly I had been exposed to the three day measles in the first three months of pregnancy. Another factor was lead poisoning from the paint on the garage we had refurbished might have affected my early pregnancy. There were some medications and multi-vitamins I had taken early in pregnancy that could have been responsible. I had only been off the birth control pill two months when I got pregnant, and that may have contributed. The most likely reason was a family history of early childhood death and small weight babies. Counseled that future children would be likely to have a birth defect, medical staff advised us not have more children.

Spending the night in Ann Marie's hospital room, my spirit was rejoicing that the next morning would bring medical confirmation a miracle had happened. I opened my Bible searching through scripture, asking the Holy Spirit to speak to my spirit about how to pray. Late into the night, I prayed over Ann Marie as she slept. I found myself worshipping the Lord for showing His mercy and goodness in this situation. He had planned from the foundation of the world for us to be the parents of this little girl. He had brought us through tragedy to triumph according to His purpose for our lives. There in the early hours of the morning, His Holy Spirit began to intercede for me with groanings too deep for words. It was a sign from the Lord that He hears the prayers of our hearts even when we are without words. Thank you, Lord, for causing all things to work together for good. I love You, and know I am called according to Your purpose. Amen.

For in hope we have been saved,
but hope that is seen is not hope,
for why does one also hope for what he sees?
But if we hope for what we do not see,
with perseverance we wait eagerly for it.
And in the same way the Spirit also helps our weakness;
for we do not know how to pray as we should,
but the Spirit Himself intercedes for us
with groanings too deep for words;
and He who searches the hearts

knows what the mind of the Spirit is,
because He intercedes for the saints
according to the will of God.
And we know that God causes all things
to work together for good to those who love God,
to those who are called according to His purpose.
Romans 8:24 -28 (NAS)

CHAPTER SEVEN

I Am A Miracle!

What shall I render to the LORD
for all His benefits toward me?
I shall lift up the cup of salvation
and call upon the name of the LORD.
I shall pay my vows to the LORD,
Oh may it be in the presence of all His people.
Psalms 116:12-14 (NAS)

Aunt Susan was in the room with us for the news of the catheterization. She wanted to hear it with us firsthand. Praise the Lord for His miracle hand of healing! The cardiac catheterization proved medically what we had all hoped for spiritually. The ASD hole in Ann's heart had closed completely. The VSD hole was considerably smaller and expected to continue closing. There was some concern about two small muscle bundles developing in the lower right heart chamber, which could enlarge and fill the chamber requiring open-heart surgery. The decision was to watch the muscle bundles and have another cardiac catheterization sometime between four and five years old. It was a victory in prayer power to hear Dr. Hartmann give us the diagnosis, when he had said fifteen months earlier that Ann Marie would die. She would live. She was a miracle. She was a promise from God.

Dearest Ann Marie   10/8/80

The past three days have been very difficult for you and I
hope all the tears you have shed will be completely forgotten!

Although it's been hard (and we knew it would be) it has been a time of proof to those who would not believe. The Lord has heard our prayers. We knew that long ago, but now the doctors must admit that the holes are closing. The smallest one now normal. The large one much smaller and on the way to being closed.

I know the Lord will continue this process and we have claimed your complete healing, so He will also take care of your muscle build up. The Lord has had a very busy year with you and your mother and father. He has been healing three hearts and binding them to His heart. And He will continue!

You were so groggy when you came out of surgery and yet you knew they were doing tests on you. You squirmed and cried all the way through it even though you could not focus your eyes. Your father was somewhat concerned about the discoloration around your mouth until he found out it was grape juice!

You were supposed to stay in ICU recovery for three hours, but you were awake in 45 minutes. So we took you back upstairs to your room. You are very smart. The doctor said so, because you know exactly when someone is ready to do something to you.

It's amazing you cried for 5 minutes when the nurse held the thermometer under your arm this afternoon, but you thought it was funny when I chewed on your feet (which I am sure hurt much worse). But you know whom you trust and you don't want the others with their stethoscopes and crazy gadgets near you.

I love you munchkin,

Susie

The next months Ann Marie became a little girl with blue sneakers and a ponytail. She was no longer a sick baby. Her personality was very social and life was exciting for her. She loved to talk, and dance and sing songs. She would play "Bullfrogs and Butterflies -- Both Been Born-Again" and "I Am a Promise" over and over again on her little blue record player. Her favorite record was Aunt Susie's new recording of Christian songs dedicated to Ann Marie, including "I Heard About a Man," and "His Eye Is On the Sparrow." Her word for music was "Susic." Ann loved tea parties, although she called it coffee. Fried chicken legs and green beans were her favorite foods.

We continued to do the Young Life club, and John asked me to teach the book of Romans to the Sunday evening teenage girls' Bible study. I worked hard all week preparing the materials and typing out the lessons for the teenage girls. As I studied, I was learning doctrinal concepts I could apply with my testimony. I was much more comfortable teaching these teenagers the Word of God than I was doing skits. Gary enjoyed the fun parts of Young Life club and was always coming up with crazy ways to make the kids laugh and participate. One night, he gave his testimony at the club meeting. The impact was powerful on the kids. Now they knew the story of our baby, and could relate to being part of our lives. They were growing to love Ann Marie, too.

When Ann Marie had been in the hospital for her catheterization, she wanted to ride in a red wagon that was in the playroom on the Cardiology floor. We would pile it with a pillow and blankets and her "Baby Grunick" doll. Then we would put her in the red wagon with high wooden sides and take a ride around the hospital ward a couple of times a day. That Christmas, my dad gave Ann Marie her very own red wagon. Susan wrote about the red wagon.

> *I remember at Christmas when Grandpa gave you the red wagon. You hadn't even seen a wagon in 2 months since you'd been in the hospital, and when you saw it you said, "WAGON!" Everyone screamed with surprise and delight at your brilliance. But you got scared when we screamed and you started to cry. It took Grandpa a good 20 minutes to get you near the wagon after that.*

It was my first Christmas as a Christian, and my heart thrilled with the true meaning of the birth of Jesus Christ in the words of the Christmas carols. Growing up, every Christmas morning we had to wait until my dad put "Joy to the World" on the stereo before we could get out of bed and open our presents. Now, for the first time, I could understand all the verses of the beautiful Christmas hymns.

I had come to know the Prince of Peace who has clothed me in His Righteousness. Jesus who came in the flesh to walk this earth, with healing in His hands, laid down His glory in heaven to die for my sins. His Holy Spirit had given me light to see, and life "born again" in a second birth. The power of the second birth meant victory over death in risen eternal life. I could sing with the angels in heaven, "Glory to the new born King."

Over the Christmas holidays, Ann Marie stayed with my parents, while Gary and I went skiing with the St. Louis Young Life Club to Monarch, Colorado. It was a long twenty-hour nonstop trip in a tour bus. After sleeping all night on the bus, we finally arrived at a McDonald's for breakfast. That was the first sign one of the students had brought the flu bug with her on the trip. She did not make it off the bus, just to the steps of the bus where John Splinter was standing in his new Christmas sweater. The flu made the rounds during the rest of the week.

Once again, I had a girl in my group who really struggled to fit in with the other girls. She was a large girl who had trouble getting up off her skis when she would fall. She was too heavy for me to pick up, so I taught her how to use her poles and skis to get up off the ground. I gave her a few hours of private lessons. At the end of the week, she had improved her self-esteem by learning to ski. The skiing was great; the food was lousy. Kids who hated the food and refused to drink enough fluids found out how quickly altitude sickness can hit. Fortunately, Gary and I dodged the bullet with all the sickness going around.

In the spring of 1981, Bob Fenn approached Gary and me about going on our first Lay Renewal to give our testimony at First Presbyterian Church in Hannibal, Missouri. We knew we had a beautiful story to tell. We should have understood the spiritual warfare headed towards us. A two by three-foot brass rubbing picture depicting Revelation Twelve suddenly fell off our dining room wall as we were heading out the door for the trip. We had made the brass rubbing in Westminster Abbey while visiting London. The frame cracked and glass shattered everywhere. The "dragon of old" in the brass rubbing was about to wage war with those who hold to the testimony of Jesus.

Hannibal was a two-hour drive to the setting for Mark Twain's books about Tom Sawyer and Huckleberry Finn. We arrived at the church on Saturday afternoon during the end of the twenty-four hour prayer vigil for the event. Walking into the church sanctuary was a trip back in time. This was the church where Samuel Clemens, also known as Mark Twain, had attended as a young boy. Samuel Clemens had left church and become an atheist in later years.

At the team meeting, we learned this church had participated in a Lay Renewal five years before with another organization, and it had split the church. There was a great deal of concern about that happening again. Our prayers and continual focus were to be on healing those split relationships and bringing the church back together.

By Sunday morning, Gary and I were struggling to get along. We had come on the team to witness and instead we were at war with each other. The problem had developed over Bob Fenn asking me to give my testimony, without Gary, at a worship service. Gary was to speak at the men's luncheon on how his faith had influenced his life as a husband, father, and in the workplace. Gary was angry I was going to get to give the testimony, and he would have to deal with a real issue. It was a very central issue and he was struggling with it.

The deeper problem was we had a beautiful testimony of Ann Marie's miracle healing, but our marriage was in big trouble. The first ten years of marriage, we had settled into a habit of putting each other down, and taking each other for granted. We left open the possibility that we could get divorced if things got worse. Ann Marie's birth defect and our coming to the Lord had changed us in a vertical relationship with God, but had stressed out our relationship with each other. We were at a breaking point and had not even realized there was a problem.

By Wednesday of the Lay Renewal, I was in tears with Susan in the bedroom of the house where she was staying. Susan and I knelt down at the side of the bed together and prayed for the Holy Spirit to heal this marriage. After all the things Ann Marie had been through, she needed parents who loved each other. Gary was at the men's luncheon speaking while we were praying. When Gary and I met back at the church that afternoon, he was so angry he told me to get in the car. We pealed out of the church parking lot and headed to a nearby park. We just sat in the car yelling and screaming at each other. Finally, we both broke down and cried as the Holy Spirit made us listen to each other and how all the years of hurt had been both of our faults. I had not wanted to submit to Gary as my husband. He was hurting because of my rebellion and lack of support. I was hurting from his lack of expressing love and care for me. We knew at that moment there was more the Lord wanted from us than a beautiful testimony of Ann's life.

The final evening as Bob Fenn had the altar call, many in the church who had suffered broken relationships for the last five years came to each other in forgiveness and love. Gary and I came forward and rededicated our marriage to our Lord. God wanted all of us. He could not use us until we had surrendered everything to Him. There was more God had to teach us. We needed to recognize the sacred covenant we had made to each other in our marriage vows. A covenant only death could separate. We began a long process of growing together in a deeper marriage relationship.

The next few months would test our marriage commitment. Gary was promoted to Major one year below the zone. His selection for Air Command and Staff College (ACSC) in residence meant that he was in the top ten percent of officers promoted to Major. Only the "cream of the crop" went to ACSC at Maxwell AFB for grooming in command and staff positions. If he accepted the promotion, he would have to stay in the Air Force for two more years, and we would move to Montgomery, Alabama, by the end of summer.

Gary felt the Lord held our future in His hands. Gary saw this as a chance to become missionaries at the government's expense. We had already been in the Air Force over seven years. By the time Air Command and Staff College would be over, we would be almost halfway to retirement. He wanted to make the Air Force a career for at least twenty years and then consider retirement. The other factor was Ann Marie's heart condition. It would be almost impossible to get health insurance on her pre-existing condition if we left the Air Force.

I was devastated we would have to move from St. Louis and our Christian friends, family, and prayer support. I could not image leaving our wonderful church. I hated moving every two or three years with the Air Force. I had planned on us settling in St. Louis and getting out of the military. I wanted Gary to get a job with a fine law firm in St. Louis and begin making money. Ann's heart doctors were in St. Louis. How could we keep moving her all over the world if she needed further treatment? I seriously thought I would be leaving Jesus in St. Louis. I knew for sure, Jesus could not possibly be in Montgomery, Alabama! I cried for three months over this horrible situation.

Finally, I realized Gary is the spiritual head of our family. If God was telling him to go to Montgomery, Alabama, I had better get ready and go with him. If I did not straighten up, my husband would be gone and so would my marriage. God was giving me the choice, but the consequences of me not submitting to God's will and not trusting Him to lead Gary in our future could destroy our marriage and family. I was also learning Jesus is in all true believers and me. He is there no matter where I go or where He sends me. Montgomery, Alabama, was just the beginning of where He was going to send me.

Still, saying good-bye to all of our dear friends and family was difficult. We decided to enjoy each day left in St. Louis. We would get the family together as much as possible. Ann Marie had a way of entertaining us all.

Dear Ann Marie,   *5/27/81*

You came for dinner tonight with your mother and father; grandpa and grandma; and Uncle Freddie. We had a good time at dinner and afterwards, we went up to the park where you sat in the swings and also on the horse and the duck. You loved it.

You've taken to calling me "Susan" the past two days instead of "Susie," and you're calling your mother "Libby." Your father fed you ice cream and strawberries tonight and you loved them. And you kept eating more and more until you began to gag! We were afraid you were going to throw it all up, but you kept smiling at us even while you were gagging and your eyes were watering. It made us laugh, so you smiled and gagged some more. Then you put on your little yellow nightgown and played with the ladybug magnets on the fridge.

You gave me a big wet kiss goodbye!

Love, Aunt Susan

Spring brought the Annual Central Family Retreat at Trout Lodge. Several of the older girls had been praying for Ann Marie and taking care of her at church. One of Ann's new friends, Betsy, made a puppet out of felt, yarn, and scrap material. Betsy gave the puppet to Ann Marie on the family retreat. The puppet's mouth could move open and shut with a hand stuck inside of the body and up into the head. When we asked Ann Marie what to name the puppet, she said, "Betsy Puppet." Such a good friend was Betsy Puppet, that after a few years her nose wore a hole in it from talking so much to Ann Marie.

There were other puppets on this family retreat. The Central youth did a puppet show for the families. One puppet resembled church staff member, Randy Mayfield, who sings contemporary Christian music. Randy had a chest and head full of black curly hair and so did the puppet. The puppet's name was Randy Mudfly. We laughed so hard at the puppet show, except for Ann Marie. She was afraid of the puppet and hid her face.

Susan wrote about something else that happened on this family retreat.

Dear Ann Marie,   5/26/81

We had a very nice visit today although you were pretty tired and took a two hour nap after lunch. We've had some really happy times these past few months. We went on the Family Retreat again this year and it was so much fun to be with you and your Mom and Dad. You really enjoyed it and squealed a lot with delight when we first got to our cabin because you were so excited!

Betsy baby-sat for you and you love her as much as she loves you! You talked a lot about Kermit the Frog and Big Bird. You also got to see the ponies, and you almost fell out of the boat with Mommie.

You really liked the puppet show the first night, so we were excited for you to see it the next night—but the first puppet was gruff and he yelled right at the beginning—you almost passed out with fear. You hid your face in your hands and wouldn't look for 15 minutes. You got very white and quiet!

Your Daddy had a lot of fun with you on the retreat. He took very special care of you and on the last day, when no one was there to help, he fell while he was carrying you. He twisted his ankle and fell down so hard that he tore his jeans and made his knee bleed. But he held on to you the whole time and kept you from hitting the ground. You weren't hurt at all!

That's how Jesus is with us! He is like our Father—only in Heaven—but He came to earth for a while and He died on the cross for us. Kind of like your Dad taking all the hurt of the fall so that you wouldn't have to be hurt yourself. Then He sent His Holy Spirit to come and live in our hearts when we believe in Him.

Just think of how much your earthly father loves you, and multiply it by a thousand! That's still not as much as Jesus loves you! It's hard to believe!

Love, Aunt Susie

Betsy

Betsy is a puppet with pink felt skin and a little round nose. She has brown scraggly hair and a ragged looking dress with all sorts of colors that don't really match. When Betsy was made, her makers took one look at the finished product and said, "Yuk! Let's pitch her!" But a sweet young lady named Betsy said, "Wait, I know a little girl who just might like her. This little girl is full of love and of course this puppet surely needs a lot of love!" So that's how Betsy came to live with Ann Marie. Ann Marie didn't seem to notice that Betsy wasn't pretty, she just put her little arms around her and said, "I love you! Come stay with me!"

That was how Ann Marie would respond to people. She did not care what they looked like on the outside. She had a gift of freely giving them love and friendship. She had a way of getting into their hearts.

When summer came, we put our house on the market for sale. We knew that the chances of ever coming back to St. Louis before we retired were very small. The market was flat in the summer of 1981. We had several open houses and a few bids. When we got a call from the "Sisters of St. Joseph" looking for a home to rent for four nuns, we took them up on the offer. Everyone in the street was delighted because we were the only Protestants in the neighborhood. What better renters could we ask for? They would pay the rent on time, and four nuns were certainly not going to damage the property.

The rest of the summer we spent at the Central Presbyterian retreat center called Centreat. There were two swimming pools, one pool for adults and a beautiful kiddy pool with a fountain in the middle. Every Sunday night Centreat would have a vespers service outside. Church families would barbeque dinner and eat together at picnic tables. We would arrive early Sunday afternoon to swim or play tennis before dinner and vespers at sunset. It was a beautiful time to fellowship and worship together.

Dear Ann Marie,   6/16/81

I saw you at Centreat Sunday. You loved the swimming and you looked so cute. When you got out you were so cold, your lips turned purple! You're full of spunk and mischief, but also full of hugs and kisses. Sometimes you get this determined look on your face. You jut your chin and lip out and go for it -- whatever it is. Mommie is good with you. She loves you and plays with you and laughs with you, but she also makes you mind which is good, too. I gave you a little terry swim suit today. Sort of a pre-birthday gift. It "fits perfectly" as you put it. "Perfect" you said when you saw it in the mirror! Today when you left you told me for the first time, "I love you." And you giggled.

Susan and Ann Marie celebrated their birthdays on July 8. The days were growing closer to our leaving for Montgomery. We were cherishing these last few days together with those we had grown to love and depend on. Susan wrote about some of the summer moments.

Dear Annie,   7/14/81

Much has happened as usual, and it is too hard to believe that in a month you will be gone. I haven't thought of it because I can't bear to. What will I do without your happy little face. We will all be so sad and you won't be able to understand our tears until later. We had a very nice vacation together out in Colorado. We spent the week at Trail West where we hiked and swam and looked for rubies. You had a lot of fun with your Grandparents and also all the little children who were there.

You had such a long ride out there and back though. I know it was very difficult for you to sit in that car seat for 8 hours a day! You got to the point that whenever we stopped to rest you would get out of the car and let out a scream of frustration!! Poor kid!

One night while you were with me at Trail West, I put you to bed and you said your prayers with me. You asked me to pray for Mommie, Daddy, Tom, Megan, Mimmy and Pop, and Big Bird. I had a little trouble with Big Bird, but you were so sweet. You would think for a minute really hard and then as a person came to mind, you would smile like a light had gone on and you would tell me who to pray for.

You're still basically a sweet, unselfish little girl. You're the type of person people fall in love with. All the children at Trail West loved you, because you are so doll-like and cute. One day we walked past a number of older children who were playing and they literally stopped their play to rush over and see "Ann Marie." You were delighted!

We also had a birthday last week. It was at your house and you were very excited about it. Both sets of Grandparents were there, also Mimmy and Pop and Great-Grandma Grunick. Plus Tom and I and Mom and Dad. It was like Christmas in July for you. Everyone brought super gifts and your mother made a beautiful cake with clowns and balloons on it. We blew out the candles together and sang Happy Birthday several times. You were overwhelmed with all the gifts including every fairy tale ever written. Plus a Big Wheels in pink and blue decor, a table and chair set, and of course, Kermit and Miss Piggy. You were delighted that they had come to live with you, and you took turns riding the frog and the pig on the bike.

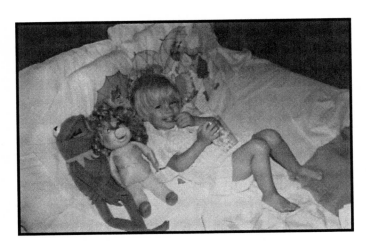

At one point you stopped and looked at me. You came running across the room and put your head in my lap and said, "Oooooh Susie, Happy Birthday!"

God Bless you sweetie, Love, Aunt Susie

Dearest Ann Marie,   *8/4/81*

I weep as I write now, because I know soon you will be gone and I won't be able to just hop in the car and come over. I will miss you and your parents. Your mother and I were talking today about how we are best friends to one another as well as sisters and this is true. There isn't anyone else who is as close to me as your mother, where friends are concerned. I have many friends, but none I talk with and share with like your mother. She has been a wonderful friend to me and I thank God that she is my sister!

We had a little going away party for you and Mommie today out at Centreat. We had a cake and the ladies from Young Life and your mother's circle came to say "goodbye." Your mother got some nice gifts which you helped to open. Then we went swimming and we swam all afternoon. You and I had a great time playing in the water. You are so affectionate—lots of hugs and sitting on my lap. We "flew" around the pool and really enjoyed ourselves. Before we went swimming, I played with you for a while in your room and you sat in your swing and named everyone in the family. I thought about how full your life has been with relatives. Grandparents, aunts, uncles, and I hoped inside that it won't be too much of a shock to suddenly lose that surrounding of love. Although you will be loved wherever you go!

Remember, Ann Marie, as you grow and learn about life, both the good and the bad, that things are different for you than they are for the world in general. You fall under the hand and protection of God and that makes a difference in the out come in life! Anyone can have this protection, but there are few who believe in it, and that is the key. You must believe in it -- In Him. He is on the side of the believer and He will cause the course of your life to fit into His plan -- and His plan is always good. I pray for your future, for the happiness you are to experience as you grow.

I love you,   Aunt Susie

<u>The Truth About You.</u>
Psalms 124:1 (NAS)
Had it not been the LORD who was on our side.
Where would we be?

Psalms 124:8 (NAS)
Our help is in the name of the LORD
who made Heaven and Earth.
His name is Jesus Christ.

<u>To be thought of when you wake up in the middle of the night!</u>
Psalms 91:5-7; 11-13 (NAS)
You will not be afraid of the terror by night,
Or of the arrow that flies by day;
Of the pestilence that stalks in darkness,
Or of the destruction that lays waste at noon.
A thousand may fall at your side,
And ten thousand at your right hand;
But it shall not approach you....
For He will give His angels charge concerning you,
To guard you in all your ways.
They will bear you up in their hands,
Lest you strike your foot against a stone.
You will tread upon the lion and cobra,
The young lion and the serpent you will trample down.

Psalms 127:3 (NAS)
Behold, children are a gift of the LORD,
The fruit of the womb is a reward.

I Am A Miracle!

This little child is a miracle
A tiny face with smiling eyes
A turned up mouth— ready to kiss
Blonde hair fixed in a ponytail
And hands full of something all the time,
A chicken bone, a frog, or barrette.
Feet that jump and tap and dance.
Legs so delicate climb and run
Arms that open wide for a hug
And the words "God bless you" with every sneeze.
A soul that knew it would survive
A heart that truly fought the battle
A little girl so busy with life
That she doesn't remember the Valley of Death.
A life so precious to all those around
More so because it seemed we might lose her.
A little life that stands up in living proof
The face, hands, feet and smile all shout for Joy—
"I am a miracle!"
For the child bears the imprint of God's Hand.
Susan Werner©8/14/81

CHAPTER EIGHT

Tribes of Every Nation

After these things,
I looked and behold, a great multitude,
which no one could count,
from every nation and all tribes and peoples and tongues,
standing before the throne and before the Lamb,
clothed in white robes,
and palm branches were in their hands;
and they cry out with a loud voice, saying,
'Salvation to our God, who sits on the throne,
and to the Lamb.'
Revelation 7:9-10 (NAS)

"Oh Susannah! Oh, don't you cry for me!
For I come from Alabama
with a banjo on my knee!"[1]

We prepared Ann Marie for the move to Montgomery, Alabama, by making it a new adventure. She was excited about staying one night in a hotel with a swimming pool. All the way down the road from St. Louis to Montgomery, we sang "Oh Susannah."

Arriving in Montgomery, we spent a few days with our friends Mike and Pam, and their cat, Wendy. Mike was a judge on the Second Circuit Trial Judiciary at Maxwell AFB. We had become friends at Dover AFB when Mike and Pam had taken us on our first ski trip to Blue Knob, Pennsylvania. Six years later, we were catching up on their tour in the Philippines and our tour to Germany. However, there had been changes in our lives that we knew would keep us from gaining that close relationship again. Obviously, Gary and I had become Christians. It had brought a reversal of priorities in our lives that Mike and Pam were not inclined to appreciate. The addition of a two-year-old child complicated the relationship even more.

This would be a time of moving from saving faith to testing faith. Our salvation experience would have to set us apart, and keep us from going back to old habits, which could easily ensnare us. Would we be faithful to live the change Jesus had woven into our lives as a tapestry of grace? Could we lovingly give the testimony of our Lord to old and new friends?

> This would be a time of moving from saving faith to testing faith.

I knew we were going to the Deep South, but I never realized the Civil War was not really over in the minds of many Southerners. It had been the "War of Northern Aggression." The "Flag of Dixie" still waved over the State Capital in Montgomery, Alabama. One of our going away gifts was a little book entitled, "How to Speak Southern." Montgomery was not just a Southern accent; it was a completely new culture. We were "fixin" to learn a few things about Southern hospitality. A new multi-colored thread was weaving into the tapestry.

Tall dark green pines, white magnolia blossoms, and pink azaleas charmed the landscape of this lovely old capital of the South. Southern attitude dripped with polite hospitality and manners. Barefoot children always said, "Yes, sir" and "No, ma'am." Sonny's Country Barbeque served the best flavors of Southern pulled pork, cornbread, and grits. Once we got past the giant flashing electric blue catfish sign outside of Ezell's Catfish Cabin, Ann Marie could eat twenty-four shrimp with hush puppies at one sitting. Ice tea (pronounced - soo-wait-tay) was cold and sweet. Dessert was always a choice of two-inch high pie topped with meringue or whipped cream. Surely, this was a little taste of what heaven might be like.

Montgomery was full of rental homes available for military students who passed through the Air University sometime during their air force career. We were able to find a nice home to rent for one year, just down the street from Mike and Pam. For a very reasonable price, we rented three bedrooms, two baths, and a large dark paneled family room with a fireplace. The kitchen wallpaper was in shocking orange because the owner had gone to the University of Auburn. Above the kitchen counter was a cut out opening for passing food through to the family room. Across the front of the home, an attractive living room/dining room with shuttered windows faced the street. The best part was the backyard. A large covered patio ran the full length of the back of the house complete with built-in gas grill, a picnic table, and firewood. In the fenced backyard were apple and pecan trees just ripe for picking. The first week, after unpacking the pots and pans, Ann Marie and I made applesauce from the apples off our backyard trees. It was all part of finding the blessing God had for us in Montgomery, Alabama.

Locating a church was no problem. Bob Fenn had prepared the way by giving us the name of the church we should attend. He recommended Memorial Presbyterian Church on Court Street. We were to look for the tallest couple in the church, Ron and Anne Knox. The first Sunday, Ron and Anne were easy to spot as we looked out over the congregation. Ron was an elder/trustee for the church, and Anne was the president of the women of the church. They knew we were coming and immediately took us into their lives by inviting us for lunch. They quickly became adopted grandparents to Ann Marie.

The young minister was Reverend William E. Dudley, who had first served the church in the late 1960s as the youth minister. He had been called back to be the senior pastor at Memorial Presbyterian, and was dearly loved by the entire congregation. Bill visited Gary and me a few weeks after moving into our new home. Ann Marie helped me bake apple muffins and serve coffee. It was a lovely visit until I noticed a giant cockroach crawling up the wing-backed chair in which Reverend Dudley was sitting. Staring at the cockroach, I watched the big black bug peak over the upper edge of the chair and wiggle antennae. I began to pray it would not crawl onto the pastor's shoulder before the visit was over. Although living in Montgomery, Bill Dudley was probably used to the size of the cockroaches in the South. I had never seen bugs that big. These critters could fly; and this one decided to take off to another room in answer to my prayers.

Our experience at Memorial Presbyterian was part of the blessing God had planned for our lives, by giving us new Christian friendships and allowing us to blossom in ministry. Reverend Dudley, and Ron and Anne Knox were very attentive to involve us in ministry as soon as possible. They had a great deal of respect for Bob Fenn and Central Presbyterian Church in St. Louis. Memorial Presbyterian had been involved with Lay Renewal Ministries in the past years. Since we had the experience of our first Lay Renewal at Hannibal, Missouri, and had come from Bob Fenn's church, we were asked to be on the Strengthening of the Church Council as co-directors of group ministries. We brought several ideas from Central Presbyterian Church. Our Young Life background equipped us to be church youth counselors, and we began serving with the youth group program.

The church was growing and having a dynamic impact on the community. It had a citywide congregation, marked by both young and old, known as the "Presbyterians on Court Street." The church treasured the experience of military members and knew the time was short to use us before we would be moving on to our next assignment. Memorial considered the military members as missionaries who move around the world in the service of our country. Many in the military returned for a second tour of duty, or for retirement in Montgomery. They found Memorial to be an oasis of rest and refreshment. The military members left Memorial richer through their work, fellowship, and spiritual growth. Many gave generously of their time and great ability by serving in every position within the life of the congregation.[2]

A place of worship is a special place, where Christians attach significance to the buildings in which we gather regularly to praise God, and listen to His will for our lives. Memorial Presbyterian Church was such a place of worship. The Gothic designed church, was constructed with Briarhill stone in 1947, and on five acres of land donated by the Bellingrath family. The gray stone sanctuary edifice, completed in 1954, rose high to a point of the cross towering above a bell tower. A beautiful terraced azalea garden and stone fountain connected the education building to the sanctuary and fellowship hall.[3]

Inside the church the old, old, story was in the ministry of color, which the Willet windows displayed as sunlight moved through the stained glass prisms. Each window was a teaching ministry of the Word of God. Ten large nave windows depicted "I Am" statements of Jesus Christ. High in the balcony windows, two north windows represented the Minor Prophets of Habakkuk and Joel. The two south windows portrayed Isaiah and Jeremiah. Creation windows ran the full length of the facade. Twenty-three clerestory windows depicted Christian vocations while the five chapel windows reflected on the prayer life of our Lord. The grandest window of all was The Rose Window high above the chancel. The circular deep blue and red Rose Window drew all attention to the doctrine of the Trinity. The Trefoil of three intersecting circles forming a central triangle reminded the worshipper of the Godhead: Father, Son, and Holy Spirit.[4] Many of the windows were given in memory of loved ones who seemed to hover as a great cloud of witnesses celebrating their resurrected lives.

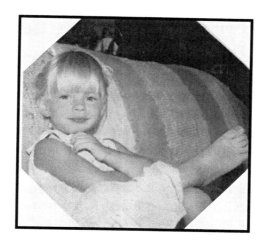

Ann Marie found her place in the two-year old Sunday school classroom with Mrs. Clara Birchfield. Ann Marie's leadership ability seemed to blossom forth especially in the social area. One Sunday morning as we picked her up after church service, she was standing in the middle of the two-year-old classroom on a chair. With her hands waving in the air to gain attention from the other children, she said, "OK kids, let's all go to McDonald's for lunch now!" How many children actually talked their parents into McDonald's we never knew. It was one of those moments where we knew that our child obviously did not have low self-esteem, and would be used to challenge and lead others on to bigger and better things. We did go to McDonald's for lunch that day.

As Gary and I began to work with the youth in the church, we came to know and love them each in a special way. A few have remained close through all the years that we have followed their lives from graduation to marriage. Some have had children and some are no longer with us on Earth. That is part of the story of the tapestry.

Scott and Cindy Gosnell were in the youth group. Their dad, Col. Wayne Gosnell, was on the staff of the Air War College, and an elder at Memorial Presbyterian. We had a great deal of respect for Col. Gosnell as we witnessed his faith both at church and in the Air Force. Scott and Cindy were also leadership quality in the youth group. We became great friends with the Gosnell family. Ann Marie would call Mrs. JoAnn Gosnell just plain "Gosnell."

Ann would say, "Come on Gosnell, let's go play!" Jo Ann thought it was so cute no matter how hard we tried to get Ann Marie to call her Mrs. Gosnell.

One of the special youth was a high school senior, David Stowe. David's mother had died tragically in a drowning accident. Rev. Bill and Jakie Dudley had taken David into their home to live. They had one daughter, Elizabeth, who loved to baby-sit for Ann.

When it came time for Youth Sunday, we needed some seniors to give their testimonies. Gary and I picked Cindy Gosnell and David Stowe to share with the congregation. Cindy did a beautiful job of being vulnerable. She told how at age twelve, she had wanted to go forward after communicants' class to become a member of the church, but she was not sure in her heart that she was a Christian. When the whole class came forward on the final Sunday of class to join the church, she had remained seated because she felt it was a more serious decision than just being a member of a church. She wanted to make sure if she went forward, that she had made a commitment to Christ. It was a convicting testimony of how many times children are led to make a commitment they do not understand, or are not ready for, because of peer pressure or parents' expectations. Later as a teenager, Cindy had made a serious personal commitment to Christ.

Then it was David Stowe's turn to share his testimony. The testimony had been a secret we kept from Bill and Jakie Dudley. David stood to tell the tragic story of his life. He spoke about how grateful he was to Rev. and Mrs. Dudley for taking him into a Christian home and showing him Christian love at a time when he was all alone. He publicly thanked them for modeling the life of Christ. Rev. Dudley was sitting in a chair on the altar platform with tears streaming down his face, and then had to preach the morning sermon. Eventually, Bill and Jakie adopted David as their own son. Elizabeth gained an older brother as well as a brother-in-Christ. Everyone was delighted a few months later when Jakie and Bill announced that they were expecting another baby, even though they were both in their early 40s. Clay Dudley was born soon after we left Montgomery.

Someone else was expecting a baby. Aunt Susan had come to visit us in Montgomery in the early autumn. She had missed Ann Marie so much, that she and Tom had decided to have their own child. Elizabeth Ann Werner, named after her Aunt Libby, was born on March 24, 1982.

Ann Marie and I decided to fly to St. Louis for Easter and the birth of baby Elizabeth Ann. The day before we flew to St. Louis was Good Friday. Ann Marie had watched a movie on television that evening about the life and death of Jesus Christ. She was grieved by the crucifixion scene and cried huge tears for Jesus. The next day our plane landed in St. Louis and Grandma Statler picked us up at the airport.

We hardly got into the car before Ann Marie started telling Grandma about the Jesus story. When Ann got to the crucifixion, she raised her voice most dramatically and said, "And then you know what they did Grandma? They just took this crown of thorns and SHOVED IT DOWN on His head! They just SHOVED IT DOWN, Grandma!"

Her little two-year-old hands smashing her blonde hair to her head as she tried to make Grandma understand how that must have hurt Jesus. Her hazel eyes were wide open and teeth clinched with the drama of pain and anger.

She wanted Grandma to know what had happened. It was a moment of realization for us all about Easter. Ann Marie's heart was broken by what she saw happen to Jesus on the Cross. She was learning to sense good from evil. She was beginning to understand the cost of her salvation. She was also learning to love a new cousin who would now take Aunt Susan's affections. She would have to learn to share the center of attention in the family with this new baby.

Our assignment to Montgomery, Alabama, was more than growing in Christian ministry at our church. The military life called for a commitment to defend our country's freedom, even at the cost of lives. Gary was attending Air Command and Staff College (ACSC) for the grooming of future command and staff officers in the Air Force. Officers who would one day hold command positions that may be responsible for sending military personnel into harms way and risking their lives.

The ACSC class had three wings, divided into twelve seminar groups. Each of the thirty-six seminars had two foreign military officers, seventeen U.S. Air Force officers, a few civilian personnel, and one student from another branch of the U.S. military. This select group of men and women included majors involved in the last years of the Vietnam War. Among the six-hundred students were F-4 aerial combat pilots who had shot down communist MIG jet fighters in Vietnam. Other pilots had flown B-52 bombers shot down over Vietnam, becoming POWs. Any given night in the smoke-filled O-Club bar, you could witness the controversial arguments between Air Force C-130 pilots and the fighter "top-guns" as to which one was the bravest or most useful in our military forces. Without hearing a word of the conversations, just watching the hand motions that represented two airplanes, anyone could follow the combat action from across the room.

Sixty-eight foreign military officers from Africa, South America, Europe, and the Middle East were selected to attend ACSC, because of their potential to become the future military commanders in their countries. Libyan President Mu'ammar Ghadaffi was one of the known former dropouts of the Air Command and Staff College. The atmosphere of freedom allowed the collegiality between these foreign officers. Tribes and tongues from Jordan, Egypt, Syria, Kuwait, Saudi Arabia, and Israel, nine years after the 1973 "Seven Day War," conversed with each other in the hallways. People who had fought on both sides of that war in the Middle East sat together in class. When Argentina invaded the Falkland Islands during the school year, and England was at war with Argentina, the seminar discussions became very interesting. The students received Intel briefings every week on military situations around the world.

Project Warrior was the theme for the school year. Top military brass concerned that the image of the military had gone too far with a management style, desired to head back toward a leadership style. An entourage of legendary speakers lecturing in the Blue Room auditorium each day became exhilarating for colleagues. Politically correct responses to sensitive issues had not come in to play yet. A special form had to be filed if a student had an objection to something said during a lecture or class. A non-attribution policy protected a speaker from being quoted or used as a basis to question another speaker. During classes and lectures, confidentiality was honored.

The Class of 1982 started a tradition, which became a legacy known as "The Gathering of Eagles." During the year over a dozen famous aviators were the first Eagles to gather and share personal experiences through interviews and panel discussions at the Air University. Their expertise spanned aviation history from World War I to the Space Age. General Chuck Yeager, the first man with the right stuff to fly faster than the speed of sound, exchanged aerial combat stories with a German WW II fighter ace on the auditorium stage. Brig. Gen. Paul Tibbets related the events of dropping the first atomic bomb on Hiroshima, Japan, on August 6, 1945, from his B-29 bomber, which he named after his mother, Enola Gay.

For a few days, the wives exchanged places with their husbands by attending classes and lectures. Seminars for military spouses helped to prepare them for the career progression and responsibilities that lay ahead for the family. One spouse briefing about "Meeting the Media" was given with the possibility that a military member or spouse might be telephoned at home or in the office to give a statement to the media. After being briefed on interview preparation and guidelines of "do and don't," the military spouse was advised that if "Sixty-Minutes calls —Hang up!"

ACSC was more than studying, classes, and lectures. Social and sporting events included the whole family in this unique year-long experience. Hopper Lodge was the place to gather and barbeque under the covered pavilion with an open fire pit. While seminar friends enjoyed a game of baseball, the children ran around the playground. Wives exchanged recipes and child rearing techniques. A lifetime of friendships woven into military careers opened a worldview of the past, present, and future.

In the military, a "dining-in" is for the military members only. Spouses attend a "dining-out." Several "dining-outs" held in the Grand Ballroom of the Maxwell Officers' Club required wives to wear long formal gowns, and the military to squeeze into mess dresses dripping with gold braid and rows of medals on their chest. These dinners usually began with everyone standing to toast the President of the United States, Heads of State, and the Chief of Staff of the Air Force. The proper protocol and other "rules" printed in the program demanded observance. Infractions of the rules could lead to a trip to the "grog bowl," which was a concoction of various liquors and beverages. Smoking was permitted only when "the smoking lamp is lit." The junior ranking officer often filled the position of Mr. Vice. The President of the Mess was normally a more senior officer appointed for the evening. A good-natured bantering went back and forth between Mr. Vice and the President of the Mess, providing a great deal of amusement and laughter before the evening ended. It all added to the spirit and charm of the evening.[5]

A special "dining-out" dinner with the Canadian Air Force encouraged relationships between the U.S. and its northern neighbor. Waiting for the dinner chimes to be sounded, we would circle the open bar area for conversation, juggling a drink in one hand and light hors d'oeuvres in the other. Flown in from Washington, D.C., the U.S. President's own "Strolling Strings" serenaded us throughout the room as we dined on steak, twice-baked potatoes, salad, mixed vegetables, hard dinner rolls, and cheesecake. The Canadians were quite a wild bunch, as they started throwing unraveling toilet paper and hard rolls across the ballroom during dinner. It all came to a loud thumping halt when a roll of toilet paper refused to unwind and hit the head table.

As the year ended, the 1982 ACSC Graduation Dinner began with an opening monologue by comedian Bob Hope. The class graduation gift to the Air University was an oil painting by William J. Reynolds of "Famous Events in the History of Air and Space Flight." Every ACSC student received a limited edition numbered lithograph of the painting personally autographed by sixteen of the Eagles. Through the years, as these most distinguished aviation pioneers have passed on, the numbered prints have become more and more valuable. Continuing the tradition, every ACSC graduating class has commissioned a "Great Moments in Aviation History" painting. The autographed lithographs from each painting have become valuable collectors' limited editions. In the following years, a non-profit organization, the International Association of Eagles (IAE), was established to further the study of aviation history, research, and scholarships in aviation. [6]

All of this grooming, refining, learning social graces, along with military traditions and protocol, prepared us for the next military assignment. We understood what would lie ahead for our little family was a great adventure in military life, wherever a Sovereign God had planned for us to serve our country and His Kingdom. We were developing a Christian worldview, with a heart for the tribes and tongues of all the nations to come to know Him as Savior and Lord.

CHAPTER NINE

Spiritual Warfare

Beloved, do not believe every spirit,
but test the spirits
to see whether they are from God;
because many false prophets
have gone out into the world.
By this you know the Spirit of God:
every spirit that confesses that Jesus Christ
has come in the flesh is from God;
and every spirit that does not confess Jesus
is not from God;
and this is the spirit of the antichrist,
of which you have heard that it is coming,
and now it is already in the world.
You are from God, little children,
and have overcome them;
because greater is He who is in you
than he who is in the world.
I John 4:1-4 (NAS)

Orders for our next assignment came in the early spring of 1982, just before graduation from ACSC. Little Rock AFB would be getting a new staff judge advocate (SJA) at the base legal office when Gary arrived to fill the position. He would be the staff lawyer for two wing commanders and the base commander. Under Gary's direct command were six air force JAG attorneys and a staff of non-commissioned officers. Little Rock AFB had a Military Airlift Command Wing (MAC) and a Strategic Air Command Wing (SAC). The MAC Wing consisted of C-130 aircraft. SAC Wing maintained the underground missile silos in case of a nuclear attack on the United States.

The new position as SJA brought with it command and staff responsibilities. It would require leadership, mentoring, social grace, highly visible presence on the air base, and the opportunity to share our faith in a dynamic way. It also brought the occasion to use our home for entertaining and ministry.

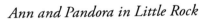

Ann and Pandora in Little Rock

As we searched for the right home to rent in Little Rock, one stood out among all the rest. It was like a dream home to us. An architect had designed, built, and lived in the beautiful home we chose to rent. Surrounded by tall white pines, our home on Foxboro Cove was a combination of brick, stone, and tutor masonry. The heavy pine door entrance opened to a two-story glass atrium. Approaching the curving driveway from the street, the glass hallway allowed visitors to see straight through the front of the home with an open staircase and into the backyard wooden deck. To the left of the front door was a sunken family room with a vaulted beamed ceiling. Across the front end of the family room, a gray stone fireplace rose to meet the ceiling beams. Sliding glass doors opened onto the deck, which stepped down to a backyard complete with a sandbox and a small tree house. The right side of the front door led to the dining room, living room, powder room, kitchen, laundry room, and two-car garage.

Winding up the front hallway staircase were the three upstairs bedrooms and two baths. Our master bedroom spanned the whole front of the second floor level, with windows looking out over the white pine trees and curving stone driveway. A special wiring option allowed us to turn on all the outside floodlights with the flick of a switch from our bedside. Any noise in the middle of the night alerted a sudden blaze of lighting around the whole house. A beige marble tiled master bathroom connected to the master bedroom.

Ann Marie had her own bedroom in the back of the house on the second floor. She had graduated to a trundle bed, which allowed overnight friends to sleep in a pullout bed. She had a large double sink bathroom next to her bedroom. The guest bedroom was at the top of the staircase, with a window that looked down onto the back deck.

Christmas Angel 1983

This architectural aspiration was a delight to decorate for Christmas. It was time to buy new Christmas decorations for such a grand home. The vaulted ceiling in the family room accommodated a large Christmas tree next to the fireplace. Three white artificial doves on the tree branches appeared as if they were looking for a peck at red holly berries or candy red apples. Surrounding the doves were white and red ornaments, white lace ribbons, and small white lights. I draped the glass atrium stairs with evergreen garland and bells woven out of basket reeds. Flowing from inside each bell were red apples and a small white doves perched with open wings along the staircase. Tiny white lights entwined into the garland, glowed through the two-story glass from the front entrance. In each window of the home, one single electric candle lit up the wintry night. Small snow dusted wreaths with red ribbons encircled the crystal chandelier in the dining room. A large door mantel of bells, red apples, and a white dove greeted visitors.

We knew that God had given us this beautiful place to use for His ministry and Kingdom. As we began to look for a church home, we felt that many churches in the area did not welcome new members. After being at Memorial Presbyterian, it was difficult to realize the Lord was leading us to a different experience. The opportunities for us to minister were wide-open at the air base chapel. The Vice-Wing Commander and his wife were very strong Christians involved at the chapel. Feeling needed and welcomed helped us look at the military chapel as our mission field.

Only a few months after our arrival, a chaplain's wife visited me one afternoon. She had spotted our eagerness to be involved in ministry, and was sitting in my family room explaining the need for a spiritual life director for the Protestant Women of the Chapel (PWOC). The position involved leading the monthly meetings by giving a devotional, organizing and maintaining the telephone prayer chain, and directing a weekly Bible study. I told her I would pray about it, and get back with her in a few days. The opportunity was somewhat overwhelming, but I knew that prayer and Bible study were the areas of ministry where I felt pulled to use my spiritual gifts. I had not been heavily involved in women's ministry, since most of our time was with youth ministry; but I knew as a mother, I had a platform to give my testimony. The difficult part would be publicly speaking each month and coming up with something to say in the devotional.

As I prayed through what the Lord would have me do, not only did He show me what Bible study to direct, but after a few days, I had written before me on a sheet of paper themes for the monthly messages! I was surprised at the clarity of plan lying before me. The Bible study would be *What Happens When Women Pray!* by Evelyn Christenson. It would be a basic introduction to the women on the power of prayer. I should have known that Satan would thwart the plan every step of the way. He would throw the fiery darts to burst my happy Christian ministry bubble. Spiritual warfare was the next lesson the Lord would teach me as He continued to conform me to His image in my growing walk of faith.

The first deadly dart was the denial of any room or space to hold a weekly women's Bible study in the chapel facilities. Now I knew why I had such a big house; of course, the Lord needed it for women's Bible study.

Flaming dart number two. No childcare would be available through the PWOC. This was not a problem! The women would bring their children to our home and they could all play upstairs in Ann's room. Naively, I thought they would all behave as sweetly as my own child, and just stay up there—getting along and not breaking her toys!

The first Bible study lesson went very well. I had not counted on some of the women and their children loving it so much that they stayed for lunch to continue talking. I noticed that some of the enlisted wives had not had much food to eat for a few days. It was a treat for them to have bread, meat, and cheese with chips. The kids were happy with peanut butter and jelly sandwiches and milk.

The second week's lesson emphasized the need to be a believer if the Lord was to answer your prayers; since the first prayer to the Lord is the one of salvation. When pressed on the issue, "Are you saved?" one enlisted wife broke into tears that she was a Jew married to a protestant airman. They attended chapel because of his religious background. She wanted to pray the prayer of salvation and become a Christian believer. One chaplain's wife, who was attending the Bible study, took her and a few of us into the living room to lead her to the Lord. She was a large over-weight woman with very low self-esteem. She had no concept of outer-beauty with her short-cropped hair, white T-shirt and jean cover-alls. She wore no make-up or jewelry. As the tears rolled down her checks kneeling beside my blue couch, I watched an abused, angry, young woman, become born-again into the Kingdom of God. She arose from kneeling on the carpet with a smile of excitement. Satan was not going to be happy with this defection from his camp to the one of eternal life.

Within a few days, I received a call to come to the chaplain's office. I was reprimanded for holding the Bible study in my own home. Someone was not at all happy with the fact that I had fed lunch to some of the wives and children, "keeping them there for hours." The final issue came down to "what did I think I was doing, leading women to Jesus Christ! No one had that authority except an ordained chaplain." They "had seen the trouble Bible-thumping fundamentalists caused by cramming the Bible down the throat of unsuspecting people."

I should have known when I could not have a room in the chapel or childcare support that the intention was to keep women from studying the Bible. The intimidation of women who studied the Word of God was obvious. When I responded that the need for a chapel room to have the Bible study and childcare had been requested and denied us, the chaplain realized who had been the one keeping us out of the chapel. This did not seem to surprise him, and within the week, he found a room for us to meet in and childcare provided.

The attacks continued with the prayer chain ministry. The prayer chain had been one very long list of names and telephone numbers. It had become clumsy and ineffective at getting the prayer requests through to the last person on the list. I began to understand that prayer requests seemed to stop somewhere in the middle of the chain, and were not passed on. The Bible study book *What Happens When Women Pray!* gave an outline of how to organize a telephone prayer chain. We needed rules of confidentiality, and keeping the prayer chain from becoming a gossip chain. After much prayer and tracing back where the problems were with the chain, the Lord revealed the solution. I divided the chain into two chains with the evident cause of the constipation at the end of the first chain. This left her with no one to pass the prayers on to, which is what she was not doing in the first place. The miracle was that she was the exact middle of the chain, so there was no need to rearrange the names, just divide and conquer. With the wheels greased, the prayer chain combined with the study on women praying took on a power beyond expectation. Women were learning to pray with excitement and taking the responsibility seriously.

Many times, we prayed for healing, husbands, children, jobs, new assignments, and salvation of family members. As I would record the requests in a prayer journal, Ann Marie and I would sit and pray each morning for those in need. I knew the prayer chain had reached the importance of prayer when I received a call at 2:30 a.m. to pray for the brother of one of the women. He had tried to commit suicide and was not expected to live. He was on the operating table at that moment. Struggling to get out of bed and wondering what to do about a middle of the night call, I called the Assembly of God chaplain's wife, Janet Carlson. Their family was used to 2:30 a.m. phone calls, just like the SJA. Janet and I decided to call only two friends on the chain that we were comfortable waking up. I knelt on the stairway and prayed for this young brother for half an hour or more. The next morning the news came. He pulled through the surgery and was expected to live. He had another chance at life. Prayer for his salvation was in order.

Chaplain Gary Carlson and his wife, Janet, had become very good friends to us over the first year at Little Rock. Capt. Gary Carlson was the youth chaplain who guided our youth events, and we worked along side him as adult counselors to the teenagers in the chapel. The Carlson's blonde headed daughter, Christina, was close to Ann Marie's age; and the little girls would play together every chance they could get. Their son, Michael, would tag along for company. One day, we were having a chapel potluck when Ann Marie and Christina decided to go to the restroom on their own. They were big enough that the two of them could push the door open, but they could not reach the handle to open it and get out. The Catholic Chaplain, Father Caine came in the fellowship hall and asked Janet to check out the ladies' room. He thought there might be someone who needed help in there. I went with Janet to check things out.

When we got to the door, we could hear the girls pounding on it and yelling at the top of their lungs, "Help! Help! Let us out! Somebody, help us! We're stuck in here!"

After that frightening event, the girls would stick their shoe in the door to hold it open so they could get out.

Janet Carlson had started teaching the Women's Bible Study. One morning she was teaching on the baptism of Jesus Christ. She referred to His baptism as immersion under the water. I found this frustrating, especially when she talked about the need for a believer's baptism. I had been "sprinkled" as an infant by my grandfather. I had heard the story of how Pop had dipped a red rose in the baptistery and touched it to my head. Now Janet was meddling with my comfort zone on baptism. We agreed that baptism does not save you; but she continued to teach about obedience to be dipped completely under the water as a sign of being buried with Christ and raised to new life as a Christian.

The Holy Spirit began to deal with me so strongly on this issue of believer's baptism that I could not find any peace as I argued back with the Lord. For a few weeks, I continued to justify my baptism experience. If baptism did not save me, why would I need to be double baptized? How would I explain to my extended family a second baptism without them thinking that the first infant baptism was not good enough by my very own grandfather? However, the Holy Spirit would not let me go.

A strange thing began to happen to me physically; I began to loose my voice. I thought about how Zechariah had lost his voice when he had not believed God about the birth of John the Baptist. I knew one of the real fears I had about getting dunked was what I would look like as an adult woman with wet hair and running mascara, coming up out of the water in a dripping white gown. The chapel did not have a baptistery, and who would arrange the baptism in another church?

The Spirit convicted me with this thought, *Libby, I bled and died publicly on the Cross for your sins, can't you at least publicly get your hair and makeup wet for me?*

I hardly could speak by the time I made the phone call to Gary Carlson about my need to obey the Holy Spirit in believer's baptism. Chaplain Carlson was very gracious with the idea, and already scheduled another baptism of a young boy for the next Saturday at the Assembly of God Church. He would be delighted for me to join the occasion for my own baptism. It would be just a few family members and friends of the young boy. In obedience to God's Word, I was immersed while my husband and daughter watched along with a few friends and neighbors. Little did I know, my obedience so deeply moved one of those neighbors that he started on a spiritual journey culminating in his own salvation and baptism two years later.

My biggest challenge in spiritual warfare came when a highly controversial political activist was asked to speak at a PWOC monthly meeting. His dubious qualifications included running a meal ministry, best known for its sweet potato pies. I was to give the monthly devotion that evening before the main speaker's message. I prayed for the scripture text and message for weeks. As I stood to read the scripture with the notorious speaker sitting on the front row, my knees were shaking and my throat was tight. How could I have been so bold to stand there and lay out this scripture text?

> *Beloved, do not believe every spirit,*
> *but test the spirits to see whether they are from God;*
> *because many false prophets*
> *have gone out into the world.*
> *By this you know the Spirit of God:*
> *every spirit that confesses that*
> *Jesus Christ has come in the flesh is from God;*
> *and every spirit that does not confess Jesus*
> *is not from God;*
> *and this is the spirit of the antichrist,*
> *of which you have heard that it is coming,*
> *and now it is already in the world.*
> *You are from God, little children,*
> *and have overcome them;*
> *because greater is He who is in you*
> *than he who is in the world.*
> I John 4:1-4 (NAS)

The application of the lesson was simple: Truth vs. Counterfeit. My illustration was about bank tellers who learn how to detect counterfeit money by only handling real money. As soon as their fingers touch a counterfeit bill, it does not feel right and they can detect it immediately. If we are familiar with the scriptures and handling truth, as soon as we see or hear a counterfeit spirit we will know it.

The point apparently touched the main speaker. For a moment after I sat down, I thought that he was unable to stand up. When he finally stood to speak, he slowly said, "I wish I knew all that this young lady has spoken about. I wish I knew the Holy Spirit and His power." Then, as if a hand had grabbed him by the throat, his self-righteous attitude bucked him up by his bootstraps. He proceeded to praise himself for the rest of the evening, bragging on his goodness and his works of kindness. Some women were entertained. They presented him with a sweet potato pie.

Time came in the spring of 1983 for the PWOC to host the World Day of Prayer service and luncheon. One of my responsibilities as spiritual director was to plan this event. I needed a speaker and a singer. My first choice was a pastor's wife from Central Presbyterian as the speaker, and Aunt Susan to do the music. They both consented to come and considered it an honor. Once again, I encountered problems as I learned that my budget was limited and would not pay for two honorariums. Susan agreed to sing without an honorarium just so she could come to Little Rock. As I continued to struggle with this constant confrontation, I found myself physically drained and emotionally depressed about thwarted plans of spiritual ministry.

In late winter, Gary had an opportunity to attend a conference in Albuquerque, New Mexico. Gary wanted me to go with him and spend a few days skiing after the conference. Needing to get away together, we decided to leave Ann Marie in St. Louis with Mom and Dad.

It was in a hotel room in Albuquerque that I turned on a Christian radio station. I remember the Christian speaker teaching:

No temptation has overtaken you,
but such as is common to man;
and God is faithful,
who will not allow you to be tempted
beyond what you are able,
but with the temptation will provide the way of escape also,
that you may be able to endure it.
I Corinthians 10:13 (NAS)

I knelt beside the hotel bed and began to cry out to the Lord about all the pain I was feeling in this spiritual warfare against the tools of the devil. I asked God to make it clear to me if I needed to resign from the PWOC Council, or for Him to remove the one causing this spiritual warfare. I could not endure this continual confrontation any longer. I felt a release of the burden when I arose from the bedside. Joy replaced my depression.

When we arrived back to Little Rock, the answer to my prayers greeted me. Orders had come from headquarters that the person who had been blocking ministry was moving from Little Rock AFB within a month! God provided the way of escape from this situation. He honored our faithfulness to pray and ask for His intervention. He broke this dark black thread in the tapestry of my life. He would replace it with golden ministry that would change lives for eternity. In spiritual warfare our offensive weapon is prayer.

With all prayer and petition pray at all times in the
Spirit, and with this in view, be on the alert with
all perseverance and petition for all the saints,
Ephesians 6:18 (NAS)

The Lord continued to answer my prayer far beyond what I was able to think or hope. A new senior protestant chaplain, Col. Ben Kelley came to the Little Rock AFB chapel. Chaplain Kelley had years of wisdom and experience as a full Colonel in the Air Force. He was a Southern Baptist, and fully supported Bible study and prayer in the Protestant Chapel. Things got even better than that! His wife Mary, was such a partner in ministry with him, and an encourager to everyone she met that we became great friends. When the Kelleys first arrived, they needed to find a home. The house two doors down the street from us was for sale, and I prayed that they might move into that beautiful home. During a meeting with Chaplain Kelley, I mentioned that there was a home for sale in our neighborhood. He assured me they had already found the perfect place and would be moving into it soon. As we talked about where they planned to live, I rejoiced to discover the home they had chosen was that very house just two doors down the street!

On the day Ben and Mary moved their belongings into the house as our neighbors, Ann Marie and I paid a visit with a little welcome dessert. Mary was so gracious to show us their beautiful things from all over the world. They had just come from an overseas assignment in Korea. Ann Marie was attracted to three little brass owls that were sitting on the fireplace mantel.

Mary reached over and said, "Would you like to have these?"

Ann was so delighted to have the gift, she said, "Can I call you Grandma Kelley?"

So, from that day on, Ben and Mary Kelley became Ann Marie's "Grandpa and Grandma Kelley." Two silver-white threads, intertwined with love wrapped themselves around us. Delightful joy bound us together in serving God. Encouragement, vision, and ministry brought healing to a chapel.

Gary and I became so involved with chapel ministry, that Ann Marie found herself spending hours in the childcare center. We were busy being youth counselors, singing in the choir, and teaching Sunday school. I continued women's ministry, and Gary became chair of the protestant chapel council.

Our duties as SJA and commander's wife included hosting visiting dignitaries and officers' wives functions. The demands on Gary were critical to legal issues on the air base. Environmental hazards from the Titan missile silos in the field; competed with court-martials; and notifying next of kin when one of our C-130s crashed in Texas. Then there were alerts, exercises, inspections, and the invasion of Grenada in October 1983.

Ann Marie had her own schedule of activities. She was enrolled in pre-school three days a week, and had tap and ballet lessons once a week. In the fall of 1983, Grandma and Grandpa Statler came to see her dance recital. Of course, Ann was the smallest Groovy Chicken sporting her yellow sequined leotard with a gathered tulle-net tutu and a hat with a chicken beak coming out of the front at her forehead. Her second number was a tap dance to the song, "Hey, Big Spender!" Her class opened the song lying on their sides kicking one leg up in the air to the timing of the music. She strutted her stuff up on the stage. This costume was royal blue satin with white sequins and a big white plume in the side of her blonde hair piled on top of her head. Getting to put on mascara, blush, and lipstick made her think she had grown up far beyond her four years.

Life was busy, fun and exhausting. The prospect of another heart catheterization to check Ann's heart muscle bundles seemed to be part of routine doctor's visits, antibiotics for sinus infections, and strep throat. The happy, outgoing, giggly little girl may have been small for her age, but she was big in the hearts of those she touched.

Hey! Big Spender!   *Groovy Chicken*

CHAPTER TEN

"Peace Be With You!"

When therefore it was evening,
on that day, the first day of the week,
and when the doors were shut where the disciples were,
for fear of the Jews,
Jesus came and stood in their midst,
and said to them,
"Peace be with you."
And when He had said this,
He showed them both His hands and His side.
The disciples therefore rejoiced when they saw the Lord.
Jesus therefore said to them again,
"Peace be with you;
as the Father has sent Me, I also send you."
John 20:19-21 (NAS)

From the first weeks after my salvation, I had wanted the opportunity to attend a Bible study called Bible Study Fellowship (BSF). In Little Rock, I was able to start Bible Study Fellowship. For the three years I studied, "The Gospel of John," "Genesis," and "Matthew." I took extensive notes, never missed a week, and felt drawn to teach the Bible like the lecture leader, Marion Millet. Marion encouraged my teaching gift. I desired to know the truth and search the scriptures for answers to my questions. It was in BSF that I began to discern the difference between grace and works, light and darkness, the true gospel and the social gospel. God had woven into my life, a royal purple thread called Marion, a mature godly woman who had gone through the death of her precious husband. She ministered to me and patiently modeled

Christ-likeness for all those she taught. Marion attended Grace Bible Church, and her pastor Dr. Marlin Howe, was on daily Christian radio. I began to listen to his radio program and learn from him. His life thread would be waiting to catch us like a safety net when we would face a future tragedy and triumph.

Ann Marie had been going to the children's Bible Study Fellowship (BSF) and learning more about the Bible and Jesus. One day she had stunned her children's BSF teacher, Miss Ruby, with the reality of something the teacher had mentally assented to, but not taken so deeply into her heart. When Miss Ruby had asked a question of the children's group, expecting the answer to be "God," Ann Marie had answered, "Jesus." Miss Ruby gently corrected the "Jesus" answer to be "God."

Ann Marie directly and boldly stated, "But Miss Ruby, Jesus is God!"

Miss Ruby confided in me after class, that Ann Marie's serious pronouncement had been a convicting witness to her. On the way home, I congratulated Ann Marie on her bold statement that Jesus is God.

Her reply was, "Mom, I know that Jesus is God, but who is the Holy Spirit?"

After almost driving off the road with the astonishment that this tiny four-year old would be thinking such theological questions, I attempted to answer her without too much detail. I determined to find a better way to explain the Holy Spirit to Ann Marie. What I found was a small children's book, *Who is the Holy Spirit?* written by Carolyn Nystrom. I sat down one evening with Ann Marie in her bedroom and read the children's book to her. There beside her bed, Ann Marie knelt and prayed for Jesus to be her Lord and Savior, and His Holy Spirit to guide her life. She would tell everyone, "Jesus is in my heart!"

Ann Marie's spiritual heart was healthy, but her physical heart was developing another problem. We had taken Ann Marie to St Louis Children's Hospital in February 1983 for a follow-up visit with her pediatric cardiologist, Dr. Arnold Strauss. It had been almost two years since he had seen her. At that time, Dr. Strauss discussed with us in detail the situation. The letter he wrote to her air force pediatrician, Dr. Hilbert, outlined the plan of action for her continued treatment.

I have discussed the situation with Mrs. Grunick in some detail. It has been our experience with multiple follow-up catheterizations in patients with right ventricular muscle bundles, that these tend to progress with age. We recommend surgery routinely in any patient with a gradient within the right ventricle of greater than 50mmHg or, of course, if the ventricular septal defect shows a greater than 2:1 pulmonary to systemic blood flow ratio. In view of Ann Marie's continued findings suggesting right ventricular outflow tract obstruction, I feel she should undergo repeat cardiac catheterization and angiocardiography some time in the next six months to a year in order to determine whether she has progressed to the point whether surgery would be recommended. The reason for this is solely that prior to going to school, I believe that it would be important to know in which direction she appears to be progressing, i.e., whether her obstruction is stable or worsening. Obviously a decision concerning surgery will rest on the catheterization findings.

Although Ann Marie was growing and gaining strength, she needed continued follow-up on the muscle bundles, which had developed at a valve in her heart. We knew that our Lord had healed Ann Marie's two holes in her heart. Now we were praying and hoping that another cardiac catheterization would give us a good report that her muscle bundle problems were stable and no open-heart surgery would be necessary. On November 28, 1983, Ann was admitted to St. Louis Children's Hospital for a third cardiac catheterization. She was discharged December 1, 1983. Dr. Strauss wrote the findings and recommendations to Dr. Hilbert.

It is evident that there has been progressive obstruction in this little girl. Our criteria for operation of this condition is a gradient of 50 mmHg or greater. Accordingly, we advised the Grunicks that we recommended surgery to relieve this obstruction. We told them we felt it should be

*done within the next year, and they stated they would like
to have it done in April 1984.*

Arnold W. Strauss, M.D.

Professor of Pediatrics and Biochemistry

Director, Pediatric Cardiology

Ann Marie had experienced one miracle healing, but God can heal through the hands of doctors and nurses. We were coming to a point in our walk of faith to trust Ann Marie's physical needs to The Great Physician knowing that she was His child and He held her in His hands. If He chose to use surgeons here on earth, we would pray for wisdom for those who cared for her and for Him to be glorified in this situation. The open-heart surgery dates were set for the end of April.

In the meantime, we had another event to concentrate on which we expected would bring many others into the Kingdom of God. In the fall of 1983, we approached Chaplain Kelley about the possibility of having the first lay renewal event in the Air Force. As we shared the idea with him, he consented to work with us to form a team within the chapel membership to host the lay renewal, and have Bob Fenn bring in an outside team to do the ministry. The dates of April 14-18 were chosen to be just before Ann Marie's open-heart surgery. The publicity team picked the theme:

Growing Together -- A Celebration of Faith
*But grow in the grace,
and knowledge of our Lord and Savior Jesus Christ.
To Him be all glory both now,
and to the day of eternity. Amen.*
II Peter 3:18 (NAS)

Once we had done one lay renewal with Bob Fenn, it was in our blood. In Montgomery, Alabama, we went on two lay renewals. The first was at Chattanooga Valley Presbyterian Church, in Flintstone, Georgia. On the lay team of the second renewal in Cedartown, Georgia, we met Tino Wallenda Zoppe of the famous circus act — The Flying Wallendas. Tino is the grandson of the great Karl Wallenda, who created the "Seven-Person Pyramid" on the high wire. On January 31, 1962, Karl Wallenda was part of the "Seven-Person Pyramid" at the State Fair in Detroit when the lead man slipped on the wire causing it to topple. Three men fell to the floor from the wire, killing two of them and paralyzing the third, Mario Wallenda. Grandfather Karl Wallenda had a cracked pelvis and double hernia, but continued to perform the next evening to prove "The Show Must Go On!" Karl later fell to his death in March 1978, while walking the high wire in San Juan, Puerto Rico, at the age of seventy-three.[1]

When we first met Karl's grandson, Tino Wallenda Zoppe, we were amazed that this famous circus performer could be such a committed Christian. We were just as surprised at his humble spirit and polite demeanor, considering his reputation as one of The Flying Wallendas. Tino seemed to gravitate toward us after we gave our testimony at the Sunday morning worship service. We had taken Ann Marie with us to the lay renewal and she was a few years younger than Tino's oldest daughter, Alida. Little did we know that a bond of friendship would form from that meeting which would last through the next thirty years and beyond into eternity. This was a glittering, exotic silver thread, which would weave itself in and out of circumstances far beyond our imagination.

There was such a connection of the Spirit, that in future years, when Ann Marie would say, "I've been thinking of The Wallendas today," they would call us long distance just to say, "Hello! We are coming to visit you." However, that would be in another time and place in the tapestry.

Bob Fenn brought together a team of thirty people from all over the country to share their faith at the air base renewal. We rejoiced when Aunt Susan Werner agreed to come and do the music. The Flying Wallendas were a special addition to the team along with several friends from Central Presbyterian in St. Louis, and Memorial Presbyterian in Montgomery.

There was much prayer, planning, and work done before this Celebration of Faith. Prayer was the key. Bob Fenn came and shared with the chapel team about the necessity of four to six months of prayer and planning before such an event. For it to have a lasting effect on people's lives for the Kingdom of God the renewal was bathed regularly in prayer; otherwise, it would be just a "spiritual bubble bath lasting a few days." We started praying for one another with prayer cards placed in the Sunday bulletin. An intercessory prayer group formed to pray for those who attended chapel regularly; for the team that would come from all across the country; for the chaplains; for the air base; and for the impact this event would have on lives all around the world. Finally, a prayer vigil kicked off the Celebration of Faith with prayer warriors coming to the chapel every fifteen minutes to pray, even throughout the night for the twenty-four hours before the Lay Renewal Event started.

This part of the tapestry would reach far into eternity..

The military is continually on the move, and for this brief moment in time, the Celebration of Faith would touch those men, women, and children on Little Rock Air Force Base. Whatever effect it would have on their lives, they would take with them as they traveled to other military assignments. God would spread the gospel through His government paid missionaries as He reassigned them throughout the world. What happened during those few days on Little Rock AFB spread like seeds scattered in the wind planted in other lives. This part of the tapestry of faith would reach far into eternity, and anchor us as chosen people and a royal priesthood.

Part of the ministry of the lay renewal was to place the visiting team in private homes of those who needed a special one-on-one witness for a few days. The plan was to "peel the onion" and not use the same old people for all of the jobs, but to get down to those who might be on the outer edge of fellowship with the chapel or the Lord. Chapel members were asked to help with housing, meals, special events, publicity, prayer, and whatever they could do to have ownership of the event; because the more people involved in the planning and prayer, the greater the success of the event. The excitement was building and when the lay ministry team finally arrived for the event, everyone was ready to enjoy the blessing of the testimonies, preaching, and singing.

Team members strategically placed in homes found one-on-one ministry to several families. One single woman hosted a team couple.

Her style of dress seemed caught somewhere in the late 1960s, as if time had stopped and not moved forward in her life. When the team couple stayed in her home, they discovered that she had been driving a car several years before, when she was involved in an auto accident. Her only child, a daughter, died in the accident.   She had become bitter and angry with God for what had happened; and consequently, her husband had left her all alone in her grief. She showed them a special bedroom. It had been the little daughter's room, now a memorial to the child. She had become frozen in time, afraid to move on and live again with any joy or hope. During the Celebration of Faith, she began to experience God's grace and forgiveness in her life. Another team member shared his testimony of the death of his son in a car accident. She began to understand that she had let bitterness rule her life and all her relationships. She came forward at the end of a worship service and knelt to pray. As she rose with tears streaming down her cheeks, it was obvious she had experienced a changed life; filled with joy and excitement about her relationship with Jesus Christ. For years afterwards she would send us cards and letters about her walk with Jesus. She was able to move forward with a future committed in service to Him and the joy of knowing the Hope of Eternal Life.

Our greatest excitement was watching with hundreds of air force members, as Tino Wallenda walked a slender black thread of wire high above an open field next to the chapel. The Wallendas never use a net under the high wire. Gary had recruited several young airmen to help Tino set up the complex rigging for the skywalk performance. The hard work gave the young men ownership in the Sunday afternoon events. Several had invited friends and neighbors, to see the special performance; followed by a *Wendy's Where's The Beef?* Chili Supper. Tino, wearing a wireless microphone, shared his faith on the high wire thirty feet above the ground; riding a bike, skipping rope, standing on his head, and sitting on a chair.

Tino had brought his two daughters Alida and Andrea, along with his wife Olinka, who was pregnant with their third child. Every time the little girls were together with Ann Marie, they would hug and kiss and say, "Peace be with you!" It became their unique friendship of love as they would go around saying to everyone, "Peace be with you! Peace be with you!"

The chapel youth experienced an awesome spiritual growth led by a young Christian recording artist from Nashville, Tennessee, named Scott Roley. Scott played the guitar and harmonica while he sang Christian music which he had written. All of the youth invited friends and the group continued to grow larger each time they met.

We breezed through the renewal on a mountaintop spiritual high. Many lives changed for eternity through the sharing and fellowship of "The Celebration of Faith." Ann Marie walked around for days blessing everyone with the words, "Peace be with you!"

CHAPTER ELEVEN

Valley of the Shadow of Death

Even though I walk through the
valley of the shadow of death
I will fear no evil,
for Thou are with me;
Thy rod and Thy staff,
they comfort me.
Psalms 23:4 (NAS)

Two days after the Little Rock AFB Renewal, we packed our suitcases and headed to St. Louis for Easter Sunday and Ann Marie's open-heart surgery. God had poured out His blessing on us in a spiritual mountaintop experience, and we felt His peace and presence as we headed into what would be "The Valley of the Shadow of Death."

My dad, Fred, had struggled with his faith for several years after being in a liberal denomination and not hearing the Word of God preached with boldness and authority. On this Easter Sunday, he became particularly irritated about hearing the Resurrection Story. He began an argument with me about the Bible and its inerrancy and divine inspiration. He doubted that Jesus was divine or even resurrected from the dead. After several minutes of heated conversation in the living room about the subject, Ann Marie finally walked into the room and stood in front of Dad with her hands on her hips. She looked him straight in the eye and said, "Grandpa, the tomb was empty!" Then she turned and walked out. That ended the argument, at least for a while. Her childlike faith was such a conviction of the Truth that it echoed in the silence.

> *Truly I say to you,*
> *unless you are converted and become like children,*
> *you shall not enter the kingdom of heaven.*
> *Whoever then humbles himself as this child,*
> *he is the greatest in the kingdom of heaven.*
> Matthew 18:3-4 (NAS)

Tuesday, April 24, 1984, Ann Marie entered St. Louis Children's Hospital for the fourth time. Her 3 foot 2 inch frame weighed exactly twenty-five and a half pounds. She had slowly grown over her four years and nine months to reach the minimum weight for the doctors to fix her tiny heart. Her open-heart surgery would be Thursday morning, April 26.

St. Louis Children's had just opened a new beautiful building for patients. We were ushered to a brand new semi-private room with two hospital beds. Parents were encouraged to stay in the room with their child and to help with some of the treatment. The room had a large picture window overlooking Kingshighway and Forest Park. By lifting a window seat, which held pillows and blankets, the seat made into a bed for one parent. A reclining chair close to the door of the room folded down to make a bed for another patient's parent. The two patients and parents shared a bathroom in the room that included a shower. The facilities were so new that the operating room was not ready. Surgery would be in the connecting Barnes Hospital operating room.

Dr. Thomas Spray, one of the leading heart surgeons in the country, would perform Ann Marie's surgery. He stopped by to talk with us and answer any questions that we had about the procedure. Medical history was recorded, and several nurses and the social worker made sure we were comfortable and knew the routine and rules of the floor. We decided that I would spend the nights with Ann Marie, not wanting to leave her alone, while Gary stayed with my parents. I slept on the window seat, which seemed narrow and hard. Above my head was the air conditioning vent blowing directly on my face. I felt like construction dust was still in the air vent as I breathed it into my lungs.

Pre-op tests started early the next morning with blood tests, heart x-rays, an EKG, and a tour of the ICU where Ann would recover after surgery.

It was during the heart x-ray that Ann Marie asked the technician, "Can you see Jesus in my heart? He is in there!"

Then when the medical lab technician came to the room for the fifth time to take a vile of blood, because it kept clotting before they could get it to the lab, Ann Marie had enough of all the poking with a needle.

She started crying, "I won't have any blood left! No more! No more!"

I told the technician that he would have to make this one good, because she was not going through another stick to draw blood. She had been such a good patient all day long, trying to do whatever they had asked her to do. Assured this would be the last time to give a vile of blood, she stuck out her arm and her bottom lip with tears rolling down her cheeks and gave one more time.

Gary arrived at the hospital early Thursday morning to accompany us through the long underground tunnel into the Barnes Hospital Complex. Ann's long blonde hair was pulled back into a ponytail as she sat up on the rolling hospital bed holding on to her special baby doll she had named "Happy." She seemed excited and talked all the way down the hall to the small waiting room.

Then the reality of what we had come for began to set in as the doctor told me to lift Ann Marie off the hospital stretcher and hold her in my arms. I took her on my lap and turned her to look at me as I told her how much we loved her. As I held her, the nurse came behind her and gave her a shot in the buttocks. Ann began to scream wildly. The look in her eyes was frantic and glazed. Within a few seconds, she collapsed on my chest and fell strangely lifelessly asleep. The nurse placed her on the cart and rolled her off to surgery.

What really goes on during open-heart surgery is more than most parents want to know; when it is their beautiful little daughter going through a surgery that will leave her with a full chest scar from her lower throat down to just above her belly button. The surgery involves cutting the sternum (breastbone), suspending the heart in a pericardial cradle and placing the patient on a cardiopulmonary bypass machine while the body cools to 26°C. After repairing the heart, the body warms to 37°C.

Ann Marie had anomalous muscle bundles removed from her lower right ventricle. Examination revealed a 5-mm ventricular septal defect

(VSD) covered by the muscle bundles. A fibrous rim was present around this defect consistent with its attempted spontaneous closure. Two sutures closed the small VSD, and an oval shaped patch of Gore-Tex material placed in her heart enlarged the outflow tract. She came out of the surgery with her sternum wired together, and subcuticular sutures and steri-strips holding her chest tissues and skin closed. Her total time on the heart pump was one hour.[1]

At 8:25 a.m., Ann Marie had gone into the operating room for her surgery. I slipped into the women's restroom to kneel at the sink and pray. At 12 noon, her stretcher rolled into the ICU recovery room, and Dr. Spray reported to us that things went well during the surgery. Around 2:00 p.m., she began to awake. We were shocked to see her small body with all of the tubes and huge bandage across her chest. She was very groggy and pale. Gary and I visited her several times during the afternoon and evening. At 10:00 p.m., she was resting comfortably and we went to spend the night at Queeny Tower in a nice guest room next to Barnes Hospital. We all slept well that night thinking the worst was over.

I woke around 5:30 a.m. and made a trip down to the ICU. The nurse allowed me to hold Ann on my lap. As Ann lay there, trying so hard to wake up and see me, her little body would shake as if it had the jitters. Finally, she woke to say a few words, knowing that she was in my arms. At 12:00 noon on Friday, April 27, just twenty-four hours after her surgery, Ann Marie transferred to the seventh floor. Ann had lost almost two pounds, and she was encouraged to take small amounts of fluid and Tylenol for pain. That evening, both Dr. Spray and Dr. Strauss paid Ann Marie a visit. Everything looked good with her incision and progress. The surgery had been a success.

The second evening after surgery, Ann Marie cried much of the night keeping me and the staff busy trying to relieve her pain and make her comfortable. On Saturday morning, her nurse helped me prop her up in bed surrounded by several pillows. She was happy watching The Smurfs cartoons on the TV in her room.

Ann got my attention when she said, "I can't see!"

Thinking that I needed to turn the TV screen more toward her, I got up and adjusted it. When I turned to ask her if the TV screen was better, she had a strange look on her face. The left side of her face was drooping at the corner of her mouth with a grimace that was unusual. She held up her right arm and made a claw-like shaking gesture with her right hand.

The nurse said to me, "Does she do that very often?"

I replied, "Never."

The nurse said, "Watch to see if she does it again. I am going to get the doctor."

Before the nurse could return, Ann had the same seizure-like activity.

"Ann, Ann, Annie!" I was alarmed at what I was seeing.

Gary was standing by the bed and went out of the room to find the nurse who was looking for the doctor. When all three arrived back into the room, it became a flurry of activity checking Ann's heart and lungs, blood pressure, arm and leg reflexes, pupils, and responsiveness.

About that time, a man in a tuxedo and black top hat showed up with a bouquet of helium balloons for Ann Marie. Thinking the balloons would evoke a response from her, we tried to get her to take hold of the bouquet. She could not make a fist with her fingers to hold the balloons.

She began to cry, "No, No, Noey, Noey."

The nurse and doctor tried to get her to stand up, but her legs were weak and she would collapse when they would let go of her. Ann Marie would not or could not talk. She was limp in her right arm and leg and unresponsive. The doctor decided to do a CT scan on her immediately.

The stretcher arrived, and as we hurried through the hallways to the CT scan, I realized that Ann was not tracking or seeing anything that was happening. I suspected that she was blind. Outside in the waiting room, Gary and I held on to each other and prayed, knowing that something very wrong had happened to our little angel.

The doctors were very serious and unsure of exactly what had happened to Ann Marie. The results of the CT scan were inconclusive because the time interval had been too short for the appearance of an infarction on the scan. Something had happened inside of Ann Marie's heart to throw a blood clot that had traveled to her brain. Once it reached her brain, it had scattered throughout her brain damaging several areas. She was cortically blind; weak or paralyzed in her legs, arms and neck; unable to speak; and having difficulty swallowing. There was further concern regarding her bowel and bladder control. The findings seemed most compatible with a left hemisphere subcorticol stroke and seizure disorder. The prognosis given for her future was devastating: Ann Marie had massive brain damage and would probably remain in a vegetative state, institutionalized for the rest of her life. The beautiful blonde, charismatic little girl, we had brought to the hospital for a rather routine open-heart surgery, had been left empty of personality, strength, and the ability to communicate or see what was around her.

She cried, "No! No! Noey! Noey!" as she felt darkness and confusion, unable to move, see, or speak words.

Gary and I were devastated beyond anything we had ever experienced. Faith in our Lord Jesus had come to its greatest testing. We questioned how God could use Ann's life in such a special testimony, and then leave her lying helpless in a hospital bed. She had touched so many lives for the Kingdom, including our own. It was as if God had turned and left the universe, never to hear our cries of anguished heartbreak.

Faith in our Lord Jesus had come to its greatest testing.

My parents and Gary's parents had not come to visit Ann Marie on that Saturday after having been at the hospital during the surgery and thinking that everything had gone so well. We called them about the devastating prognosis. They wanted to come immediately, but we told them to wait. We just felt unable to deal with our own depression and grief, and could not handle watching them see their little granddaughter in such a helpless situation. We asked them to pray and to ask others to pray, and to call the rest of the family to pray.

The word of Ann Marie's "massive stroke" spread quickly throughout the churches we had been in during the prior four years of her life. Prayer warriors began lifting up prayers to the Throne of God, storming the gates of heaven for healing once again in this small child's body. In Montgomery, Alabama, the women's council was meeting at Memorial Presbyterian Church when the word came about Ann Marie. Breaking down crying, the president of the women Nancy Jackson led the circle of women in intercessory prayer on our behalf, and pleading for a second miracle in Ann's testimony. Little Rock Air Base Chapel was stunned and grieved over the news of her brain damage. The news reached Central Presbyterian Church in St. Louis through my sister, Susan. Prayer chains activated all over the United States.

That evening, Ann Marie was admitted to the Seventh Floor ICU, unresponsive to verbal stimulus, saying only "NO!" and thrashing about. An IV started to sedate and hydrate her. She was unable to eat or drink, and had no urinary output.

Susan arranged for us to spend the night at her house so we could be together and pray. When we arrived at Susan and Tom's house once again they were there to give us the spiritual support that we needed. We talked, prayed, and cried together. Time came for their two-year-old daughter Elizabeth to take a bath and go to bed. Elizabeth was everything that a two-year old could be physically, emotionally, and actively. She ran around the room singing, dancing, jumping, and laughing. The awareness hit me that Ann Marie would probably never be able to sing, jump, dance, or laugh again. The pain of losing Ann's physical and mental abilities with just a shell of a body was unbearable. As Gary and I lay in the guest bed together, we held each other and cried until we fell asleep in emotional and physical exhaustion.

Sunday morning came with the awakening consciousness that all this was not just a bad nightmare, but the true "Valley of the Shadow of Death." God once again held Ann Marie's life and death in His hands. If He chose to give her life, what would be the quality of that life? How long could such a life continue in bed, unable to move, speak, see, or eat? As parents, we refused to think about her death. Surely God must have heard the prayers on her behalf from those who had been interceding for her and us throughout the night.

We dressed to return to the hospital as early as possible, thankful for God's grace to give us some hours of sleep during the long night. Susan and Tom left to attend Central Presbyterian Church services with an update for those praying, and to call upon the pastors and elders for special prayer. When we arrived at the Seventh Floor ICU and came to Ann's bedside, she was unresponsive to her name or our voices.

Several doctors came to see her. Dr. Barber discussed with us in depth the prognosis of bilateral hemispheric involvement of an embolism with an unknown source or cause. They were all baffled at the reason for this "stroke" to occur and therefore had no other options but to observe Ann Marie for any further seizures or improvement. Her heart surgeon, Dr. Spray, came by for a visit and was devastated by the situation.

Dr. Strauss, who had been Ann Marie's pediatric cardiologist from her birth, came and knelt beside her bed and cried. He said, "We just don't know what happened. But my own children are praying for Ann Marie."

After church service at Central Presbyterian, Dr. Bill Flannagan and several elders of the church made plans to come to the hospital to pray and anoint Ann Marie with oil that evening. We agreed that it would be appropriate for them to come, and we asked permission from the ICU nurse to allow these men into the Intensive Care Unit. The head nurse said she was a member of Central Presbyterian and would be pleased to allow this special request.

While we waited for the elders to arrive later that evening, the phone rang at the ICU desk near Ann Marie's hospital bed. The nurse turned to me and said, "There is a phone call for you."

I took the phone and heard a familiar Southern drawl, "Libby, this is Bill Dudley."

To hear the voice of our pastor from Montgomery, Alabama, when we were in such need of spiritual support broke me to tears.

I said, "Bill, how did you know where to call, this phone is at the foot of Ann Marie's bed!"

He just said with a smile in his voice, "Pastors know how to get through to those who are in the hospital."

He asked how Ann Marie and we were doing. I told him the elders from Central Presbyterian, along with Dr. Bill Flannagan, were on their way to pray and anoint Ann Marie with oil. He assured me that all of Memorial Presbyterian was in prayer for us, and if there was anything they could do for us to call him. It was so good to hear his reassuring voice, and know that he cared about us. We had been gone for two years.

That evening, Bill Flannagan and several elders including Eric Schmidt, and Uncle Tom and Aunt Susan Werner, arrived at the ICU. We met in a small conference room to discuss Ann Marie's situation. The elders offered prayers on our behalf and anointed Gary and I with oil. Then we proceeded to Ann's bedside where she was lying helpless and unresponsive. As prayers were said for her, she began to become agitated and whimper. The anointing oil was more of a distraction for her, but Susan began to sing, "His Eye is on the Sparrow" as I patted and rocked her in my arms, and Ann calmed down into a restful sleep. The ICU nurse recorded in Ann Marie's medical records,

Church elders here; anointed and prayed for Ann.

As shadows of the night fell on St. Louis, the hearts of many remained in constant prayer for Ann and for our strength and peace. Gary and I refused to leave the hospital to spend the night elsewhere. With no accommodations in the ICU for parents, we located two blankets and a few pillows to rest on the firm cold vinyl couches in the parent's lounge. My heart was in my throat as I laid there in the darkness praying and searching through my mind for what the future might be like. As dreams floated in and out of my head, I suddenly woke with a gasping for air. The thought had hit me so suddenly and hard I could not catch my breath! *"What if Ann Marie never returned home again!"* The vision came of her beautiful bedroom full of dolls and toys, puzzles, stuffed animals, and a white and yellow trundle bed with fluffy pillows that she would never use or even be able to see again.

Breaking into a cold panicked sweat, the thought of Ann in a hospital bed for the rest of her life or death suddenly taking her away, stung me into awareness. I sat straight up on the hard couch and cried out in the darkness of the sterile unforgiving hospital room.

I prayed, *God, Oh God! No! Please No! You cannot let this happen! The Holy Name of Jesus is at stake in this situation! For Your Name's sake, and the testimony You have already given to Ann Marie's life, You can not let this continue!*

Tears flowed down my face as I sobbed, releasing my grief to the Lord with groanings too deep for words. My breathing became slower and fuller as I sensed the thoughts of trusting Jesus with everything. Slowly a peace came over me as the Holy Spirit began to intercede according to the Will of God. I knew that God the Father heard a prayer in the blackness of doubt and pain, and He would cause all of this to work together for good to the glory of His Name. I fell asleep comforted and assured that this black thread of the "Shadow of Death" would be broken. Jesus would anchor our hope deeper in Him.

In the dawn of first light, hope awoke in me with the excitement of what God would do. I walked to the ICU where Ann was restlessly sleeping. Gazing at her petite body lying helplessly paralyzed and rigged with tubes and an IV needle, I touched her right arm. Her index finger flicked at my touch as a sign of Hope.

Monday morning brought both grandmothers to the hospital after they had patiently waited in misery for two days to see their granddaughter. They were not prepared for her condition, but were determined to help with Ann Marie's care to give us a break from the constant vigil at her side. Ann Marie sensed that her grandmothers were in the room, and turned her head to the sound of her name, but did not respond to any other verbal comments. The "mothering instinct" took over, and in a courageous effort to get some solid food into Ann's stomach, both grandmothers set about on a plan to coax her into taking small amounts of juice through a straw, and tiny bites of Jell-O. Gary's mom had brought a Child Craft book of poetry from her home, which she always read to Ann. After reading some of Ann's favorite poems, she left the book with us at the hospital and went home late morning to fix lunch for Gary's dad.

By 11:30 a.m., Ann Marie had voided in the diaper that she now wore, a good sign that her kidneys and bladder were functioning again. The doctor decided to remove the IV in order to do another EEG, and then transfer Ann out of ICU back to a room on the Seventh Floor East. At lunch when a plate of macaroni and mashed potatoes came, Mom and I coaxed Ann Marie into eating by telling her if she would eat, then the IV would stay out of her arm. As Mom would lift the spoon to touch her lips, Ann's mouth would fly open like a little baby bird and in would go the food. She struggled to chew and swallow, sometimes drooling out of the side of her lips. She was starving for real food, but there was no other acknowledgement or communication from her for the next few hours as she fell asleep.

Late afternoon, Mom was ready to go home. She walked to the door of the hospital room, anguished about what she would tell Grandpa when arriving home. As she looked back at her granddaughter lying helpless in the bed, Ann's eyes seemed to be looking at her as if to say, *Goodbye, Grandma.*

Mom walked back into the room to the bed, and bent down to kiss Ann Marie good-bye and said, "Grandma has to go home now and make dinner for Grandpa. I love you Annie."

As Grandma kissed her, Ann Marie smiled. Gary and I saw the weak smile and started jumping around the room yelling, "She smiled! She smiled! Did you see her? She smiled!"

Ann made a little giggle and then started to whimper. It was a tiny smile, but a life-size ray of hope.

Gary went down the hospital corridor to a pay phone to call his Little Rock office. While he was out of the room, I noticed that Ann Marie's eyes were following the movement of the silver helium balloon bouquet blown by the air duct at the window seat. The bright sun shining through the window was reflecting off the silver foil, casting a prism on the wall.

I said, "Do you see the balloons?" She smiled again. I said, "You see the balloons!" "You can see!" She smiled again.

Then she opened her mouth and said, "Aaaatttt Sssssahh. Aaaaannnttttsssaaa. Annntt Sssuuuzzzzeeee!"

I cried, "Aunt Susie? You want Aunt Susie!" She smiled.

I jumped up, "I'm going to call Aunt Susan!"

When I dialed the phone in the hospital room I exclaimed, "Susan! Your niece is asking for you!"

Susan's reply was an excited scream, "I have just been lying flat on the floor praying and crying out to God to give us a sign that Ann will be alright!"

I told Susan, "Well, when Mom was leaving this afternoon and kissed Ann, she smiled. Then I noticed her looking at the balloons in the air, and Ann said Aunt Susie!"

Susan replied, "Praise God, I know she is going to be alright! Libby, God has a plan for all of this. We just have to pray and trust Him!"

The next day, Ann Marie had more of a breakthrough in her communication skills, when my Mom visited and started reading to Ann poems from the Child Craft book. One of her favorite poems "Little Bug, Little Bug" brought delighted giggles and attempts to speak. The words would come out of Ann Marie's mouth, but they did not make sense. She could not say what she was thinking, and the confused responses would make her giggle even more instead of crying. After a few hours of working on speaking, Ann Marie began to make sense with a few words. It would be a long hard road, but her determination continued to give us hope that she would not give up on getting better.

Physically, Ann was still paralyzed and unresponsive to Dr. Deuel pinching her on the foot. Even though we could hear bowel sounds in her intestines, she had not had a bowel movement since the stroke. Doctors were concern about her bowels becoming paralyzed or impacted. Over the next days, several suppositories, Colace syrup, enemas, manual digital examinations, prune juice, and painful tears finally produced a few small hard stools to relieve the pressure and start her bowels working normally. Ann began taking anti-seizure medication called Dilantin. The doctor ordered another EEG to see if there had been any improvement since the last EEG on Monday. Her heart surgery incision was healing nicely, and what had been one of our worst concerns about a permanent chest scar seemed to grow dim in light of her neurological status and future.

To do an EEG, electrodes had to be stuck on Ann's body and head with a sticky jelly. The second EEG results indicated a moderate to severely abnormal EEG. The left side of Ann Marie's brain was showing greater slowing sending signals to the right side of her body as the brain waves crossed below her neck. This was causing her right side to be weaker than her left side in her arms and legs.

All of that sticky goop in her hair made Ann uncomfortable and she looked like a wet cat. I asked a nurse to come and shampoo the mess out of Ann's hair, but a few hours later, the nurse had not responded. After the first EEG on Monday, Mom had gone with a nurse to help wash Ann's hair in a sink around the corner from the nurse's station. We decided to take Ann Marie back to that area again, put her on the counter with her head over the sink and wash her hair with baby shampoo. One nurse was very displeased and she wanted to know what we were doing. We explained that no nurse had responded after several hours, so we had proceeded to wash Ann's hair. The nurse was upset because there was a refrigerator within six feet of the sink. I was not exactly sure what the problem was with the nurse, but I was getting tired of the situation and constant stress.

One nurse had a habit of coming in the room and talking in front of Ann Marie about her condition, as if Ann could not hear or understand. Ann was too young to understand everything that was going on, but she could hear, and it frightened her. What may have seemed routine care to the nursing staff was far from routine to us. We began to understand that a child in a hospital situation should never be left alone without a parent or relative. The staff can make mistakes; no child has the ability or authority to be their own advocate.

Bob Fenn had been on a lay renewal in a church in Harrison, Ohio. He asked that church to be in prayer for Ann's recovery and healing. Hearing of Ann's improvement, he wanted to see the answer to the prayers. He paid a visit early in the week, while Gary was performing a puppet show with Burt and Ernie dolls and Betsy puppet at the foot of the bed to keep Ann Marie entertained. Seeing Ann Marie's progress and responsiveness to the puppet show confirmed what Bob had heard. As Bob rose from a chair to leave the room, he was very hopeful that we were once again witnessing a miracle answer to obedient prayers.

He turned to Gary and me and said, "God is Sovereign. He is still on the Throne."

We were encouraged that God had something very special in mind for the testimony of our daughter. God was not finished with her or us. We realized that we could have lost Ann Marie through all of this, but God was giving her back to us for a purpose. She was the most important responsibility we had as parents. She was twice a miracle.

On Thursday, Ann ate a good breakfast after sleeping well and not needing any Tylenol for eight hours. She started physical therapy to evaluate her range of motion and physical ability. She was already getting stiff in her right heel cord and her head would flop forward when propped up in a sitting position. She could not roll over or lift her arms to wipe her nose when she sneezed. The physical therapist gave me a list of range of motion exercises to start doing with Ann. The activities seemed so simple; I wondered how this would ever help her move again. What I did not know was that physical and occupational therapists are God's angels sent to perform miracles that help restore disabled bodies back to health.

Friday, May 4, brought the cardiologists in for a look at what was going on with Ann's recovery. From a heart surgery standpoint, she was nearing the point of discharge. Resources for neurology, P.T., O.T., and speech therapy near Little Rock were being set up so we could go home.

Improving day by day, Ann was using more words and smiling more often. She had particularly remembered a phrase of words from her friends The Flying Wallendas. Dr. Spray, her heart surgeon, came by for a visit with Ann.

When he walked into the room, he asked, "How is she doing?"

We replied, "Say something for the doctor, Ann Marie."

She said, "Peeassse Beeah Witha Yoooou!"

He said, "What did she say?"

Again, Ann said, "Peace be with you!" He turned with tears in his eyes and left the room.

There was still some needed neurological evaluation on Ann Marie, and it would take most of the next week to do the testing. Gary had to get back to work in Little Rock after being gone for two weeks. He was prosecuting a murder trial at the air base, and did not plan for our trip to St. Louis Children's Hospital to keep him longer than two weeks from work. On Sunday, after spending the morning at the hospital with us, he drove back to Little Rock alone to return the next weekend and bring us home.

The next week, Ann had another CT scan, EEG, and x-ray. Physical therapy continued, accompanied by occupational and speech therapy evaluations. I received instructions on how to carry Ann Marie and position her in bed. The therapist made foot and hand splints for her to wear when she slept, to keep her feet and hands from atrophying in a curled-up position. She was strapped onto a standing board with a neck collar and raised into a standing position for up to an hour at a time, while the speech therapist tested her verbal responses. Every session more "homework" to do with P.T., O.T., and speech therapy kept us busy. Ann really began to do well and smiled when she finally had a bowel movement on her own after a week and a half! She began to eat and gain weight.

Although Ann was trying very hard, it was obvious that there was some brain damage. Recovery would be slow. I was in a state of denial about the test results with speech therapy. Even though Ann was beginning to say words and phrases in a very slow monotone voice, she still had trouble recognizing objects and calling them by the correct name. I had not understood all of the nuances in speech and communicative disorders.

Learning colors, numbers, and the alphabet again was progressing with increasing recall. But how does the brain process long and short-term memory? How do you re-teach a brain to organize daily tasks, or use good judgment in a dangerous situation? How do you help eyes that were blind to track words across a written page; or stiff fingers to hold a pencil and draw a picture, or write a letter again? Can legs ever crawl, stand, walk, and run when the body is too weak to hold up its head? The task that lay ahead was a mystery. If we had known just how difficult it would be, we may have given up the first week. God's grace continued to encourage us to keep trying; bonding us closer to each other and our Lord with healing everyday.

Chapter Twelve

"Do You Want To Be Made Well?"

And great multitudes came to Him,
bringing with them
the lame, crippled, blind, dumb,
and many others,
and they laid them down at His feet;
and He healed them,
so that the multitude marveled as they saw
the dumb speaking,
the crippled restored,
and the lame walking,
and the blind seeing;
and they glorified the God of Israel.
Matthew 15:30-31 (NAS)

After completing several medical tests, St. Louis Children's Hospital made sure that continual care would be provided for us once we were back in Little Rock, Arkansas. Contact was made with Little Rock Children's Hospital for continuation of physical, occupational, and speech therapy. The Little Rock School System was notified of Ann's special needs for fall placement in a kindergarten class for children with communicative disorders. We were given a follow-up date to return to St. Louis in three months, and a list of further testing to be done in Little Rock by the air base hospital.

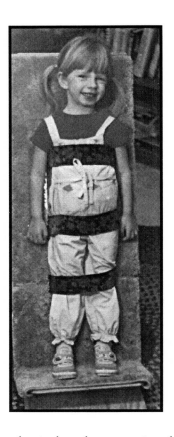

After a 9:30 a.m. physical and occupational therapy session, the long awaited discharge from St. Louis Children's Hospital came on Thursday, May 10, 1984. My parents came to take us to their home until Gary could come from Little Rock that weekend. Mom and Dad went to the therapy session to see how Ann was progressing. Sensing the opportunity to help Ann continue to gain strength, Dad asked for the information on how to construct a standing board. Being an aerospace design engineer, Dad was able to build the simple standing board within twenty-four hours of Ann's hospital discharge, and we began using it by Saturday. We would carefully lay Ann Marie flat on the long board with her feet resting at the end against a small platform. Then she would be strapped onto the board with Velcro straps across her legs, waist, and chest. Slowly, we would raise the board to a standing position, and prop it up in a notched frame. Ann Marie was able to bear weight on her legs without falling over, causing her muscles to strengthen each day. Since Ann was not able to hold her head up, or hold a spoon to eat, Dad also constructed a head/neck support to fit into the back of a highchair, which allowed Ann to sit up as we fed her without her falling sideways, or forward.

We took the standing board and head support back to Little Rock. When we got back home, I was running a fever of 102°F with a sinus infection and cough. On Monday, I called Mom, and she flew down to Little Rock the next day. I drove to the air base hospital. Seeing the dark circles under my eyes, the doctor prescribed medication and bed rest. Knowing Mom could take care of everything, I fell into bed totally exhausted by the events of the previous month. Mom stayed for several days doing laundry, cooking, cleaning bathrooms, and allowing me the extra rest I needed.

The word of our arrival back home brought "Grandma and Grandpa Kelley" up the street for a visit. When they saw Ann Marie's condition, they were speechless with tears. It was worse than they had expected, and we had to explain that she was actually much better than before. The Kelleys went to work seeking help from the chapel members. We needed some way to transport Ann Marie around the house and outside. Carrying her everywhere was exhausting, even though she only weighed twenty-four pounds. A family on the air base heard of our need, and offered the use of a special stroller with head and shoulder supports. It was a perfect fit for Ann's small body.

A list of women volunteers from the air base chapel formed to go with me for Ann Marie's physical and occupational therapy. I knew I was able to drive the half hour to Little Rock Children's Hospital three times a week; but it was such a comfort to know that others were willing to come along side us to help, pray, lift our spirits, and minister to our needs. We were not alone. The trips to therapy also helped the women to understand the painful process Ann was undergoing learning to move again. It gave them an invested interest in seeing her get better and knowing how to pray for us.

When they would ask me what I needed them to do, I could not think clearly enough to answer. I felt very humbled by the offer of help, and struggled with my pride. One day a friend appeared at my front door with a large bowl of strawberries. It was a simple gift, but it made me realize the pleasure others received by being of service. I was wearing out, and they needed the opportunity to minister to us using their special spiritual gifts. I was learning what the gift of mercy felt like and they were learning how to use it.

At the end of May, The Flying Wallendas came through Little Rock for Tino Wallenda to walk across the Arkansas River on a high wire. We made contact with them and explained how Ann Marie was doing. Tino wanted us to come down to the "walk" and watch him cross the river. After using the wireless microphone at the air base chapel Celebration of Faith, Tino had decided to try it again while broadcasting to a Christian radio station in Little Rock.

Just before he set his foot out on the high wire for the first step, he said, "I would like to dedicate this walk to a special little girl, Ann Marie Grunick. Ann has just suffered a stroke which has set her back physically, but we are praying for the Lord to heal her."

What a privilege and encouragement we received from that event as Tino gracefully glided across a raging river in a testimony to our Lord.

Between the three times a week therapy sessions, I would pack up our towels and swimming suits and head for the Little Rock base swimming pool. The fresh air, warm water and hot sun had a tremendous healing effect on Ann Marie's tight muscles. She could move in the water with a freedom that gravity would not allow outside of the pool. Floating in the shallow end of the pool, she would move her arms and kick her legs for increased range of motion. Her blonde hair lightened with sun streaks and her skin darkened a deep brown with all the sunshine. Her appetite increased with exercise along with her muscle strength. Sometimes she would attempt to walk in the water, but her falls were softened, as she went under water and came up laughing.

There were times when the entire struggle over what to expect from her body got to Ann Marie. She was determined to walk again, but the progress was physically and mentally painful. When she would become depressed over her physical disabilities, we would put a record on the stereo, and Gary would pick her up in his arms and dance around the room with her. He would sing to her and kiss her. Then he would hold her tightly and do a little dip backwards with her. It made her giggle and smile.

One day, Ann just broke down sobbing while lying on the couch. As we talked to her, she shared what one of her deepest fears had been. Our German shepherd, Pandora, started limping and gradually became unable to walk in her hind legs. Suffering from hip dysplasia and a tumor on her back, Pandora had undergone surgery, but had not recovered her ability to walk after six months of us carrying the dog around. When Pandora began to lose bowel and bladder control in the house, we had taken the dog to the vet to be put "to sleep." Pandora was twelve years old, and had "gone to heaven" just a few weeks before Ann's open-heart surgery. Ann Marie was afraid that, if she did not learn to walk again, we would put her "to sleep" like Pandora! It was difficult to explain to Ann that she was not the same thing as a dog. We assured her that we would not put her "to sleep," but every night she prayed for Pandora in heaven to be able to run again.

Ann was determined that she would walk again. Not only did she want to walk again, but also to run, dance, and ride a bike. As her P.T. and O.T. continued through the summer months, she learned to roll over, and then push herself up to sit. Then she began to crawl everywhere, and finally started pulling herself up to hold on to furniture and take a few spastic steps with her skinny little legs. She tried to walk without holding on to a coffee table or the couch, but she would fall after a step or two. If I would hold on to her hands and arms over her head, and walk behind her for support, she would kick out her legs one at a time and desperately move forward. The first night she tried to walk to her bedroom after her bath while I held on to her, we all cheered as I tucked her into bed.

I said, "Ann Marie, you walked today!"

She said, "Tomorrow, I'm going to run!"

To watch the determination of this soon to be five-year old, learn like an infant to move again, was heart breaking and encouraging all in the same moment.

Ann Marie's fingers were very stiff and unable to move independently of each other. It was tough enough to pick up finger food with her hands, but impossible to grasp a spoon or fork and maneuver it to her mouth without dropping the food or eating utensil. We purchased a specially carved wooden spoon with a wide handle and deep bowl. By taping the spoon handle into her clinched fist, Ann began to learn how to scoop food up and into her mouth. Her arms and wrist were getting better directional control so that she did not stick the spoon in her nose or eye too often. She still lacked strength and coordination to use a knife to cut her food.

Before Ann Marie's open-heart surgery we had promised to buy her a bicycle after she came home from the hospital. At the time of the promise, we had no idea that she would come home so challenged physically that even sitting up was difficult. In June, we rewarded her continued effort to improve with a "Strawberry Shortcake" two-wheeler, complete with pink fringe on the handlebars and a front basket. She cried with glee at the sight of her new bike. Once we lifted Ann onto the bike seat, she could sit on it and hold on to the handlebars. The vision of her being able to one-day balance, pedal, hold on and steer the bike would dance in her eyes; but her body was not able to coordinate the dream. She would simply sit on the bike in the front yard with the kick-stand holding it up, training wheels helping to balance, going nowhere but places in her imagination.

Ann also wanted to sing again. She slowly began to practice "Jesus Loves Me." Her voice was extremely squeaky because the muscles needed exercise. She had to stop with each word and think what word came next and how to pronounce it. She prayed, *Lord, help me to remember the words!*

Gradually as she would rehearse the chorus, her memory and voice came back with the expression of the words. "Yess, Jaaesuss Lovess Meee! Yess, Jaaesuss Lovess Meee! Yess, Jaaesuss Lovess Meee! For the Bible Tellss Meee Sooooah!"

Ann Marie was turning five years old in July. When we would ask her how old she was, she would stop and think for a few seconds and then say, "Fiiive, nooo, fourr!"

We would ask, "When is your birthday?"

She would say "July. July 4, no July 8?"

For Ann Marie's fifth birthday, on July 8, Grandma and Grandpa Statler were coming to visit, bringing Aunt Susan and little Elizabeth. Ann decided that she would surprise them by walking without help on her birthday. She got this idea from sitting in her beanbag chair in front of the television and watching the movie *Heidi* starring Shirley Temple. Ann was greatly encouraged by the part of the movie where

Clara gets out of her wheelchair and takes a few steps for her father. Finally on July 5, we were out in the yard practicing walking when Ann jerked away from me, took four or five steps, and stayed standing for several seconds. I was so shocked to see her not fall immediately; I knew that she had made a major breakthrough in coordination and balance. When the big birthday visit came, she gave my parents and Susan the best gift of all. She walked several steps for them. Susan and Ann would share their birthday party knowing that everyday the Lord was healing Ann Marie more and more.

Aunt Susan also had a surprise. After having gone through a difficult miscarriage the summer before, she was pregnant again. The new baby would be born in early January, just at the time of Uncle Fred's birthday.

During worship service at Little Rock Chapel one summer Sunday night after Ann had started walking steadily, Chaplain Kelley requested anyone to come forward who had a praise to share. Ann Marie sitting in her little stroller in the aisle began to move out of it. She told me she wanted to go up there and say something. I helped her out and walked behind her as she struggled up to the front of the Chapel holding on to pews for balance.

Silently all eyes were on her as she took the microphone and told everyone, "Jesus is healing me. He is making me well. Jesus is in my heart!" There was not a dry eye in the sanctuary that evening.

During that hot August summer of the 1984 Olympic Games in Los Angeles, California, Ann would sit in her brown beanbag chair and watch the television coverage of Carl Lewis and Florence Griffith Joyner in the track and field Olympic competition. Thinking that someday she would get good enough to win an Olympic gold medal, she would wobble out the front door, bend down in a starting stance, and tell me to "toot-pow" the sound of a starting gun.

When I would say, "Ready, Set, TOOT—POW—GO!" she would take off running across the yard in a spastic jerky run, falling, then getting back up; reaching the evergreen trees at the end of the yard and turning back to the finish line. All the neighbors would watch her run like a newborn fawn struggling to get her legs under her body; but she was determined to press on toward the goal and prize.

*Do you not know that those who run in a race all run,
but only one receives the prize?
Run in such a way that you may win.
And everyone who competes in the games
exercises self-control in all things.
They then do it to receive a perishable wreath,
but we an imperishable.*
I Corinthians 9:24-25 (NAS)

> Was our God big enough to get us through this trial?.

One of those neighbors, Tom, was a teenage boy who lived next door to us. His older sister Kit had been a babysitter for Ann. Kit had gotten married in early summer, and her wedding was the first time for Ann Marie to make a public appearance since returning from the hospital. Tom saw us in the yard one day and walked over to talk. He had a tender heart seeing the struggle Ann was having and commented that he did not know how we could endure it. I took the moment to witness to Tom about our faith in Jesus Christ. I explained how He had healed Ann's heart as an infant and was continuing to heal her body each day. I testified about the Sovereignty of God in all things; and how a personal relationship with Jesus helps to deal with difficulties in life. The opportunity to share with Tom continued to develop over the next several weeks, as he would stop by to talk about religious things. I had become so aware that many people were watching to see if our God was big enough to get us through this trial. Tom was another thread in the tapestry God was weaving in this difficult situation.

Cato Elementary School was several miles away, but designated as the best facility to mainstream students with disabilities.[1] Ann Marie attended a kindergarten class with Miss Paula and Miss Lori, who were speech therapist teachers; and five other boy students who needed special education. A special school bus would pick Ann up at our driveway at 7:15 a.m., and bring her back home at 2:30 p.m. She received physical and occupational therapy on a regular basis at school. Therapy at Little Rock Children's Hospital ended with only occasional follow-ups. Since Ann had outgrown the standing board that Grandpa had made, we donated it to the Little Rock Children's Hospital for other children to use. Ann had learned to walk and run, although she easily fell over when bumped, especially if she was carrying her lunchbox. Her two teachers grew to love her along with her classmates, who encouraged one another with their individual struggles in life.

As the summer ended, it became clearer that our time at the Little Rock air base chapel needed to end. Our responsibilities at the chapel had been more than a full time ministry before Ann's hospitalization. Now with ministry gearing back up in the fall, pressure was mounting for us to resume our commitments. We realized that most of our time doing ministry in the past had left Ann Marie in the air base childcare center. The Lord had made it very clear that He had given us a child to parent and raise in the nurture and admonition of the Lord. We could have lost her, and now she needed us to be there for her. She also needed to be in a supportive Sunday school environment. The chapel had been a great mission field to do ministry, but a kaleidoscope of religious beliefs and doctrines. We were exhausted and needed care during this healing process. We wanted a church home where we could bring others into a secure fellowship, and know they would hear sound doctrine and teaching.

We decided to go to Grace Bible Church in Little Rock where Dr. Marlin Howe was the pastor. I had talked with Marlin on the phone several times over the previous year after having scheduled him as a women's chapel speaker. Since he had been encouraging us to visit, the decision to join the church delighted him. His expository teaching from the pulpit was powerful. The congregation immediately took us into their fellowship and hearts. The safety net of love had caught us before we could be hurt in a spiritual fall of ministry burnout.

On Sunday evenings, Ann Marie started AWANAS as a little "Sparky" and earned jewels for her crown badge by memorizing scripture each week with other five-year olds. We helped chaperone the youth group, but did not have near the responsibilities of leadership as in the past. One week we invited our teenage neighbor Tom to attend a youth event with us. He felt so welcomed that he began to attend church. His life changed by hearing the Word preached, and he grew to love the Lord deeply. He became a golden thread of joy out of a dark shadow in our lives, continuing to share his faith and encourage us through years of letters, e-mails and special cards. Tom is always a reminder of how God has used our circumstances for His good.

Grace Bible was a growing church, but without a choir. A soloist or small group provided music each week. Someone had heard me sing a two-line solo at a Christmas concert on the air base and decided that I needed to be a regular soloist at Grace Bible Church. My career as a "Christian singer" began with the Cynthia Clawson favorite "I Heard About a Man." I had to wonder at God's grace and humor, since that was the song I first heard the day I met Bob Fenn; and Aunt Susan had recorded the song on her own record album she had dedicated to Ann Marie. My untrained voice would have paled in comparison with Cynthia Clawson or Susan Werner, but I sang from my heart because the message was about "The Man" who raised the cripple up and made the blind to see.

Some of my dearest friends, who had been in Bible study at the chapel with me, were attending Grace Bible Church. I was surprised to see one friend and her husband attending worship. My friend had asked us to pray for her husband's salvation two years before. When he appeared in the baptismal tank one Sunday for Marlin Howe to immerse him, I had to tell him about our prayers over the two years for his salvation. His answer completed a part of the tapestry for me. He told me that he had been at my baptism as a neighbor of the little boy immersed by Chaplain Carlson. When he saw my obedience in believer's baptism, knowing that I was a Christian, the Holy Spirit convicted him to seek the Lord. My baptism had been a witness to him and an answer to our continued prayers for his salvation.

Healing had also begun in the Presbyterian faith when two reformed denominations, the United Presbyterian Church and the Presbyterian Church U.S., united in the 195th General Assembly in 1983. The newly formed denomination became The Presbyterian Church (USA). Presbyterian churches had been losing members and the General Assembly set out on a five-year plan for evangelism and spiritual renewal called "New Age Dawning."[2] In November 1984, we were asked by Bob Fenn to attend the "Presbyterian Congress on Renewal" being held from January 7-10, 1985, in Dallas, Texas. Nearly 6,000 people gathered in the Dallas Convention Center for this historic event to pray for the renewal of the Presbyterian Church (USA) through the lay people, and worshipping the Lord with Bible study and singing. The worship was awesome as thousands of voices stood to sing great hymns like "All Hail the Power of Jesus' Name" and "Great Is Thy Faithfulness."

The daily schedule offered over two-hundred workshops. The highlight of the conference for us was hearing and meeting two of the keynote speakers: Dr. Lloyd John Ogilvie and Dr. Leighton Ford. Dr. Ogilvie was the pastor of First Presbyterian Church in Hollywood, California, and preached on the weekly television program *Let God Love You*. He had written over a dozen books at that time, and would become the Chaplain of the United States Senate. On the evening he took the platform, he called the Presbyterian Church a denomination that is ill and needs healing. In the words of Jesus, "Do you want to be made well?" Dr Ogilvie challenged the Church to surrender to the "leadership of the Father who is calling to 'Come home—come all the way home.'"[3] The hope of healing a grand reformed denomination after years of separation and disagreement lay in the answer to the question. Would factions of the church demand their own way, or submit to the leadership of God the Father, in the power of His Holy Spirit to heal the Body of Christ?

Gary and I attended one of Dr. Ogilvie's "Preaching Seminars." The moment he entered a large room, charisma exuded from his presence and words. He gave his testimony in a very vulnerable way and shared how he prepared for sermons in a three year preaching plan. He talked about preaching styles, praying, and preaching in the power of the Holy Spirit for the purpose of changed lives, and discerning your listening congregation. We bought several of his books, which helped us with our prayer life and walk of faith.

Another keynote speaker was Dr. Leighton Ford, evangelist Presbyterian brother-in-law to Billy Graham, and an accomplished author and conference speaker. His book, *Sandy—A Heart for God,* is the story of his son Sandy, who died in 1981, while undergoing open-heart surgery at age twenty-one. [4] This one book ministered to me in the months after Ann Marie's heart surgery. In later years, it would come back to my hands to read and re-read, as a thread of the testimony of Sandy with blue eyes and golden hair, inspiring and encouraging me to tell the story of my own daughter.

While we were in Dallas at the Congress on Renewal word reached us that Aunt Susan had delivered her baby on January 8. Upon hearing that the new baby was a brother named David, Elizabeth said, "But I wanted a Rachel!"

As winter continued into the 1985 New Year, we formed friendships in our new church with several of the deacon families. They had planned a ski trip to Winter Park, Colorado, and asked if we would like to come with them. We jumped at the chance to take Ann and see if she could learn to ski. We caravanned with eight vehicles for the twenty-hour drive.

Winter Park is known for its accommodations for disabled skiers. Gary and I witnessed several skiers with only one leg flying down the slopes with special equipment. Other blind skiers were amazingly following an instructor who would yell out to them to turn right or turn left down the slope.

Ann was in a ski kindergarten each day for the week, while we skied some of the most delightfully groomed slopes in the Rocky Mountains. At the end of the week, Ann Marie could do a "pizza wedge" also known as the "snow plow," coming to a stop at the end of a short slope. She was continuing to face the physical challenges of recovery. She wanted to be made well, and with the help of our Lord, she was giving it all the effort possible.

In April 1985 during Spring break, one year after heart-surgery, we returned to St. Louis Children's Hospital for a follow-up visit. We walked into the hallway where one of the doctors, who had seen Ann Marie during her heart-surgery, was sitting on the floor rolling a large ball to another child. The ball rolled passed the doctor to where Ann Marie was standing. When the doctor turned and saw Ann Marie, he recognized her. She walked up to the ball and gave it a big kick back to him.

He said, "Well, Ann Marie! It is so good to see you! What a surprise to see you kick the ball! You just made my day!"

As we entered the doctor's office, he confided to us that he never thought Ann would be able to walk again. He was witnessing the testimony of a child who "wanted to be made well." In the days to come, Ann would humbly tell others that Jesus was healing her heart.

Yes, Jesus Loves Me!

CHAPTER THIRTEEN

Fix'n to Go

Thou art my hiding place;
Thou dost preserve me from trouble;
Thou dost surround me with songs of deliverance.
I will instruct you
and teach you in the way which you should go;
I will counsel you with My eye upon you.
Psalms 32:7-8 (NAS)

Our three years at Little Rock Air Force Base had been a maturing experience in our walk of faith. Deep friendships had developed from the struggles we faced with the help of people God had woven into the tapestry of our lives. We knew that no air force assignment lasts forever, and good-byes are always just around the next corner. To leave some of our dearest friends and prayer partners tore at our hearts and souls. Our only consolation was knowing that we would meet again, either somewhere else on earth or in eternity.

In the summer of 1985, Gary's JAG career brought a promotion to Lt. Col., moving us on to the next assignment. Orders came to go back to Montgomery, Alabama, as the Chief Circuit Defense Counsel for the Second Circuit Trial Judiciary. Gary would be commander for all the defense attorneys assigned to the Air Force in the Southeast United States and Panama. He would be traveling to nineteen air bases in seven states, inspecting offices and mentoring twenty-five defense counsels and twenty-two paralegals. The Second Circuit Trial Judiciary offices at Maxwell AFB, Alabama, also included a staff of circuit defense attorneys under Gary's command; the Chief Circuit Prosecutor and his prosecuting attorneys; and the Chief Judge with several circuit trial judges. Most of the air bases handled their own court-martial trials, but if a major case came to trial and a senior officer was involved as the accused, Gary served as the special defense counsel. If a case had several defendants, Gary and his defense attorneys handled the clients.

At least we knew where we were "fix'n to go," and what church we would be attending. Looking forward to seeing old friends we had left in Montgomery helped ease the pain of leaving Little Rock. However, we would learn that you can never go back to how things were, because things never stay the same. We had grown spiritually in our walk through the "Valley of the Shadow of Death," and Memorial Church was experiencing growing pains with the uniting of the two Presbyterian denominations.

We contacted Col. and Mrs. Gosnell, who were still at Air Command and Staff School in Montgomery, and made plans to stay with them until we could find a home to rent. Wayne Gosnell was retiring from the Air Force that summer and becoming the first regional coordinator for Lay Renewal Ministries. Their daughter Cindy, who had been in our youth group as a senior nearly four years before, had fallen in love with a guy named Matt. The wedding would take place toward the end of summer.

The Gosnells also wanted us to come with them to the annual Family Life Conference in Montreat, North Carolina, and stay in a cabin with some other Memorial families. At the Family Life Conference we met new friends who had come into leadership roles during the three years we had been gone. All of the children Ann's age had grown from toddlers to school age. Many of the former youth were married or at college. One evening after a group dinner, Ann was outside on the lawn trying to keep up with the other children kicking a ball. She still had a slight limp and her arm and hand movements were jerky when she would run. As I stood watching her, two boys were being very gentle and patient with her. Rev. Bill Dudley walked up next to me and watched Ann for a while.

Then Bill said, "She surely has come a long way from when I talked to you on the phone in the hospital. It is an answer to prayers."

I said, "Yes, it has been a hard year. We almost lost her, but God has been good to heal her."

Living that summer with the Gosnells, Ann Marie looked forward to Cindy and Matt's wedding. Matt was at the house almost everyday before the wedding, and he would play around with Ann tickling her and giving her special attention. Cindy had asked Ann Marie to hand out the little birdseed bags at the wedding. We helped fill the colored net circles with birdseed and tie them up in ribbons. Ann was to carry a basket filled with the bags and give each guest one to open and throw as the bride and groom left the church. The evening of the wedding Ann Marie wore a long white dress that Grandma Statler had made for her. I fixed her blonde hair high on top of her head and pinned silk dogwood blossoms and ribbons into her curls.

It was a beautiful wedding in the gray stone church on Court Street, followed by a grand reception of food and dancing. Several of the little girls got on the stage and danced while Ms. Jessie Creech played the piano. Ann Marie was right in the middle of the stage dancing and took a bow.

We found a home to rent just a few blocks from the Gosnells. It was on the corner of Winchester and Aimee Drive, up the street from a playground and running track at Vaughn Park. The large ranch house sat on a slight hill with a big front yard. The mother-in-law floor plan separated our master bedroom on the kitchen side of the house from the two other bedrooms off the large family room with a fireplace. In the front of the house was a formal dining room and living room. The three-car garage was converted into a finished playroom with carpet and a wall of mirrors. Ann could put all of her toys in the playroom and still have room to dance. Off the playroom was the laundry room and outside was a carport, walled patio and banana trees. The master bedroom had an outside door to a tall wooden fenced patio; the perfect place for the hot tub we bought. No one could see through or over the fence. We spent many hours as a family relaxing in the warm tub. It was wonderful therapy for loosening and strengthening Ann's muscles.

We had been in our new home a few weeks, when one evening Ann Marie turned to me while sitting in her beanbag chair in front of the television and said, "Mom, I am so lonely. I want either a brother or a sister or a dog."

I replied, "We can get a dog!"

Some friends in Memorial Church just happened to have a female dog with brand new puppies. They were six-week-old "cocka-daucha-poo" puppies. A mixture of cocker spaniel, dachshund, and poodle; we thought they were international with Spanish, German, and French heritage. When we went to see the puppies, one little black one walked right up to Ann Marie. He was not the most beautiful or biggest; in fact, he was the smallest and had wavy hair instead of curly poodle hair. Nevertheless, he was friendly and noticed Ann Marie, instead of just wallowing around with the other puppies.

Ann said, "I think he wants me to take him home!"

He was the one she picked. We decided to name him Winchester because we lived on the corner of Winchester and Aimee Drive. Since he was a male dog, Aimee was not a good name; but Winchester sounded important, for a Southern gentlemen dog.

Winchester immediately made friends with the dog next door named Rebel. Rebel's owners were Col. and Mrs. Frank Mizell. Col. Mizell served as an Air Force JAG, but was retired. They were in their later years of life and enjoyed having us as neighbors. Col. Mizell would tell stories of how it was during World War II to practice law in the Air Force. We would often visit at each other's homes. Evelyn Mizell invited me to a neighborhood Bible study led by Mrs. Nellie Wade. Nellie lived across the street and was well into her nineties, but still teaching the Bible. Nellie's daughter lived a few streets away and often came and checked on her parents. Nellie also had a very nice grandson named Charles, who was a year older than Ann Marie.

Shortly after arriving in Montgomery, I received a phone call from Bill Dudley's neighbor, Patty Williams. Patty was starting Bible Study Fellowship for the first time in Montgomery. She would be the lecture leader, and Bill had told her that I had been in BSF in Little Rock. She wanted my help with forming the new BSF group. I was delighted to help her and consented to become the treasurer. Patty allowed me to give my testimony to each of the new classes during the next year.

The end of August brought the start of first grade for Ann Marie. In Little Rock Pulaski County School District, Public Law— "Education for All Handicapped Children Act of 1975, P. L. 94-142"[1] served us extremely well. We expected the same service in the Montgomery County School District. We found things worked a little differently in the State of Alabama known for "states rights."

Ann Marie had to undergo a series of tests to determine provided services. After a tiring day of testing, the Alabama State Department of Education approved Ann for placement in the Individual Education Program (IEP). She received transportation by a special school bus to an elementary school several miles away. The selected public school was for children with disabilities, because there were no steps to enter the school door, and wheelchairs could have access.

Ann started first grade on August 28, 1985, exhibiting trust, openness, and eagerness to learn. Just sixteen months earlier, she had suffered her devastating massive stroke. She was excited about school. Although she still struggled with some physical coordination, she signed up to be on a cheerleading team with other first and second grade girls. Football and cheerleading start in the early years of life in Alabama, and sports competitions become quite a significant part of higher education. Being so petite, Ann was more of a mascot in her purple and white pleated cheerleading skirt and monogrammed top. Learning the cheers and jumping helped her coordination and physical strength. If success in life was based on looking cute and having beautiful long blonde hair, Ann would have had it made.

September 17, three weeks into the school year, was our first scheduled IEP meeting. By the time of our first real contact with school administration and teachers to communicate medical history and needs, Ann Marie was already beginning to lose the race of keeping up in class. When we expected adapted physical education, occupational, physical, and speech therapy, special equipment and modifications in the classroom, the teachers and principal agreed and assigned a resource teacher.

However, by October 18, there had been no therapy and the classroom teachers would continually forget to make the modifications or grasp the extent of Ann Marie's physical and learning disabilities. Gary and I addressed these continual frustrations by requesting reports on testing evaluations and compliance with the Federal Law for physical and occupational therapy. The administration scheduled a special meeting for October 29.

We did not enjoy pressuring the school to comply; but there were twenty-nine children with disabilities, who needed an advocate. God provided us with the exact person to help us with this problem and support us at the October 29 meeting. Debbie Curtain, a physical therapist, was married to the Chief Circuit Prosecutor in the Second Trial Judiciary. Debbie was willing to attend the meeting with us, and address Ann Marie receiving the needed therapy and educational modifications. As a response to "our therapist" attending the meeting, the school also invited the physical therapist from Maxwell AFB Elementary School. We made the point clear that we were losing confidence in the Special Education Program services, and federal law and funds required the school district to provide the services. The agreement was that therapy be given to Ann Marie and the other twenty-nine children. After the meeting, the therapist from Maxwell AFB confided to us that she did not know how we did it, but she had never been allowed in that school before.

We had won the battle but not the war. Ann Marie received an evaluation the next week from physical and occupational therapists. Gross motor skill testing showed Ann had low muscle tone; inconsistent motor responses with instability; and an ataxic gait able to gallop, but unable to skip. Her fine motor skills indicated difficulty cutting with scissors; and unable to draw a square, "x," or triangle. Her visual motor accuracy was poor and arm movements were often stiff due to fixing in the shoulder and elbow. Visual tracking was inconsistent; and difficulties noted in tracking diagonals and circular movements. Classroom modifications were recommended and placement in adaptive physical education class.

Ann Marie's first report card came home with a "B" in Reading, but "starred" as "below grade level." We questioned how she could have a "B" in reading and be considered "below grade level" in her first semester of first grade. Kindergarten was not required in Montgomery. How can a child know how to read the first six weeks of first grade? The resource teacher responded with a note that the "below grade level" was given to all students who were in the low group in reading. The principal of the school had checked with the assistant superintendent on this procedure, and he said there was no need to "label" any first graders! At his request, the school administration removed the words "below grade level" from Ann's and all report cards!

A few weeks into the second semester, I attended a parents' visiting day held at school. I was stunned by what I found happening in Ann's math class. The class was learning to count by ten using beans. Ann Marie was struggling to keep her beans on her desk as her jerking arm movements knocked several beans to the floor. Then the teacher called Ann Marie to the front of the classroom to an over-head projector. While Ann had to stand on tiptoes to look into the light, she struggled to move some Indian feathers made of construction paper to count by tens. The teacher helped her fingers move the small pieces of paper feathers around the projection screen. The children in the class began to chant, "Ann cheats! Ann cheats!"

I was so angry that the teacher had allowed this taunting. Then I almost rose through the roof when the teacher turned to the class and said, "Well, we all cheat sometimes."

Ann sat down beside me with tears in her eyes and said, "Mommy, I cheated!"

I said, "No Ann. The teacher helped you. That is what she is here to do."

After class, I had a very frank discussion about the incident with this teacher. I told her that as a Christian family, we do not tolerate cheating. What she had allowed the class to do to Ann Marie was unprofessional. I also recommended that she allow Ann to use an abacus for counting instead of beans that end up all over the floor. The math teacher did not know what an abacus was!

I pointed to a large abacus she had in the corner of the classroom, and said, "That is an abacus! It is an instrument for making calculations by sliding beaded counters along rods."

Finally four months into the school year, at a December 19 meeting in the principal's office, paperwork was signed listing "Modifications for Handicapped Students." Several modifications were made in Ann's schoolwork requirements, reducing the amount of work and increasing the amount of time to complete work. She was given preferential seating to allow her to move in and out of the room without tripping and falling over table and chair legs. Pencil and scissor grips were to be supplied; along with a special footrest to stabilize her balance when sitting at her desk, since her tiny legs could not reach the floor. Her papers were to be taped to the desk. A pencil tied to a string around her neck would keep her from having to pick it up off the floor when her gross arm movements knocked it off the desk. We finally had something in writing for handicapping conditions. However, there was a strong hint at this meeting that students with handicaps like Ann Marie's, were pulling the SAT test scores down for Montgomery and the State of Alabama. Competition had erased the reason to teach. The school seemed to have lost the vision to see children grow and bloom into the knowledge of who they are and can be.

The week before Christmas break, Ann Marie came home from school and sneezed just as she reached the front doorstep. Her inability to maintain her balance threw her to the ground, scattering her books and lunchbox.

When I reached the front door and helped her up, she announced, "I just wish I was dead. I want to kill myself!"

I knew then that the school battle was taking too big of a toll on Ann Marie. She had been trying so very hard, but was not receiving the encouragement and praise on which she thrived from teachers. Criticism easily crushed her spirit, and the other children often made fun of her and left her out. Ann had come such a long way. It was painful to experience this attitude change of being a failure. We could not let it continue, and began to pray about changing to a private Christian school.

I had shared with my neighborhood Bible study group, BSF group, and several friends at church about our prayers for moving Ann Marie to a Christian school. Mrs. Nellie Wade told me of the wonderful private school which her grandson Charles attended. Two women in my BSF group spoke of the same school, along with several members of our church.

After the fifth person told me, "You should try Gray Wilson School. It is great!" I realized that the Lord was answering the prayer. I gave the Gray Wilson School a phone call. Mrs. Gray Wilson answered the phone. In her pleasant Southern drawl she gave me directions and information. Her little schoolhouse was located on Walnut Street among several specialty shops just down the street from the Burger

King where the schoolchildren went every Friday for lunch. Gray had been teaching for several years, and was a remarkable fine Christian woman. She suggested that I bring Ann Marie to her school the next day to try it.

I had never thought my child would attend a private school, but the public school system had let us down. Ann Marie had not missed one day of first grade until that day, but it was worth the try. Ann eagerly got up the next day for me to drive her to the new school.

Gray Wilson School was for kindergarten through third grade. Gray taught the combined kindergarten-first grade class of ten students in the front rooms of the school. Diane Gibson had the second-third grade class of twelve in a larger room in the back. The kitchen separated the classes, and a large backyard was the playground. Gray explained to me that every morning class began with the pledge of allegiance and then prayer request time. Since Ann would be in the combined kindergarten-first grade, no one would know at which level she was working. She could progress at her own speed. Gray would not tolerate any misbehavior, or making fun of other children. Anyone who needed discipline would receive a warning, and if that did not work, they would get a "loving" which meant a trip to the bathroom and a paddling across Gray's knee. Then she would say, "I did this to you because I love you, and want you to grow up to be a special child of God." Of course, neither of us expected that Ann Marie would be receiving that kind of loving.

I picked Ann Marie up from her first day at Gray Wilson School to find her still excited and eager to show me what she had learned. In just one day, using flash cards, she had learned all of her addition tables through the number ten. She had learned the "nine's table" with the reminder that "nine added to a number is one less than that number made into a teen." Four months in the Montgomery Public Schools had not taught her this much. She was overjoyed knowing she was able to learn math. She wanted to stay at Gray Wilson School and never go back to public school.

The next day I went to the public elementary school and requested Ann Marie's files for transfer to Gray Wilson School. The hostility that met me in the public school office was hardly concealed. When I told them the name of the transfer school, they questioned what that little private school could give Ann Marie that the State of Alabama could not give her. Physical and occupational therapy would not be provided in such a little private school.

I replied, "Ann Marie may not receive therapy, but she will receive love and encouragement at Gray Wilson School. Right now, Ann needs to feel love not failure."

The assistant principal said, "Mrs. Grunick, Ann Marie will never be able to write properly. I know, because my own daughter had a brain injury accident. It has been years and she has never been able to write."

I replied, "Well, I am sorry for your daughter, but if your daughter had received the kind of therapy that I expected Ann Marie to receive here, maybe she could write. I have watched Ann Marie come this far and I will not give up on her."

I took the files and exited the school door. Later, I learned that one of the disabled students had moved out of his wheelchair and learned to walk using a walker because of our insistence that the therapist be allowed in the public school.

Mrs. Gray Wilson had several techniques for teaching and expectations of her students. She always said, "Use it or lose it!" She had the children continually review what they had learned, so they would not forget or lose what they were building on in knowledge. The class memorized and recited the class poem "The Daffodils" by William Wordsworth. When Mrs. Wilson wanted them to impress visitors, she would gather all her little children together, and off they would go with the first verse in a unison Southern drawl boldly working to a crescendo. Finally, with the back of their hand lifted across their forehead and speaking almost in a dreamy whisper they ended with the final words.

Ann Marie decided that she wanted to be a writer. She loved the poems and began to write a few on her own, including one that won Honorable Mention in the Montgomery County Christmas Poem Contest. At the ceremony, Ann received from Mayor Emory Fomer, a certificate for framing, a silver dollar, and a bronze medal on a ribbon around her neck. The most excitement was that it snowed that day in Montgomery, Alabama. It was only a powdery dusting, but they closed Maxwell Air Force Base and let the schools out.

CHRISTMAS
By: Ann Marie Grunick
Gray Wilson School   December 15, 1987
Baby Jesus lies down in the hay.
He once was a little baby,
He'll be a carpenter some day.
The angels said, "Go and see this Child,
Down in the manger lay."
He will become the King of Kings,
And His birthday is Christmas Day.
I lay my head to sleep on Christmas Eve.
He died on the Cross for me.
He died on the Cross for history.
He heals the blind to see.

Nevertheless, Ann's handwriting skills remained a problem to read what she had written. Gray tried all sorts of thing to help Ann hold her pencil correctly and build the strength in her tiny fingers. Mrs. Wilson resorted to putting a small amount of Elmer's glue between Ann Marie's index finger and thumb to keep the pencil stable in a pincer grasp. Slowly Ann Marie would trace over the alphabet as she concentrated on drawing perfectly formed letters.   After three or four months of practice, there seemed to be some improvement, but Ann would become frustrated and erase more than she usually accomplished.

I picked Ann up from school one afternoon and Gray Wilson wanted to talk with me. She acknowledged that Ann was trying so very hard and things were progressing slowly.

She said, "I really want to see Ann Marie's handwriting improve and I think we have had enough patience and practice. I believe it is time to ask God for another miracle. Would it be possible for you to contact the elders of your church and ask them to anoint Ann with oil and pray for her handwriting to improve?"

I thought for a second about how we could arrange this anointing at our church.

Then Gray said, "I would like to have the anointing here at school with all of the students participating in the prayer and expectation of this miracle."

The idea that we would bring elders to school, openly explain the anointing process, and pray with the students was a stark contrast to our public school experience.

I said, "Are you sure you want to do this at school with the kids?"

Mrs. Wilson said, "Of course! It will be a lesson in faith for them, and an encouragement for Ann Marie to know they are praying and supporting her. I expect a miracle to happen!"

I went home and called Col. Wayne Gosnell and asked if he could set up a time when a few of the elders from Memorial Presbyterian could come to the school and anoint Ann Marie with oil and pray. Wayne was excited at the possibility of ministering to Ann Marie.

Within a few days, the afternoon time was set for the anointing service. With all of the children gathered into the front room seated on chairs, Elder Wayne Gosnell, along with two other elders, explained the anointing process. They would place Ann Marie on a small chair in front of the elders and children. Based on the Bible scripture from James 5:14-16, they would mark a small cross on Ann Marie's forehead using anointing oil. Then they would pray for her continued healing. Before the anointing took place, Wayne asked if there were any questions from the children about what was happening and why they were anointing Ann with oil.

One boy raised his hand and asked, "Are you using 30 or 40 weight motor oil?"

With a smile and holding back a laugh, Wayne explained that the oil was not motor oil, but the kind of oil you would use for cooking in the kitchen like vegetable or olive oil.

The next question followed the oil explanation, "Will the oil burn and cook her?"

As Wayne explained that the oil would not be hot and would not burn, it became obvious it was a good thing to let the children ask questions and participate in the service. The anointing took place as the elders led in a prayer time. The seriousness of the moment weighed heavily on Ann Marie's classmates. They were invited to pray for Ann if they felt led. Several of the children prayed for her healing and for her handwriting to improve.

One special friend prayed, "God, I thank you that Ann Marie did not die when she had her heart surgery. Heal her in Jesus Name. Amen!"

Ann Marie raised her head with renewed hope and encouragement. She had found a treasure in the golden friendships of love at Gray Wilson School.

A few weeks later, I was at the school to pick Ann Marie up. One of the boys stopped to tell me his observations. He said, "Mrs. Grunick, I sit next to Ann Marie in school, and you know, her handwriting is getting better!"

I replied, "Well, why do you think that is happening?"

He responded, "Oh! It is the Lord! He is healing her!"

The Flying Wallendas came for several weeks to Montgomery for the 1987 Alabama State Fair. We made contact and brought them to Gray Wilson School to perform for the students and share their testimony. Such a special relationship developed with the school that The Wallendas held a free performance one afternoon at the State Fair just for the kids. Gray Wilson asked Tino to come and preach at her church on the next Sunday morning. Gray had talked her pastor into letting Tino preach without the approval of the Official Board. Several of the Board Members attended the church service with a frown and sat with arms across their chest. When Tino finished comparing balancing on the high wire by focusing on one central point and the

Christian walk fixing our eyes on Jesus Christ, the frowns had turned to smiles. The Chairman of the Board approached Tino after church and confessed that he had come to church with an angry attitude that a circus performer would stand in the pulpit, but he praised the Lord for the message given that morning.

For the next two and a half years, Ann attended Gray Wilson School making steady progress completing second grade. She made life-long friendships with many of the children. One friend Eve Holley continued to write to Ann Marie and send pictures for several years. The discipline and training Ann learned in these early school years would enable her to face trials and new situations with boldness in the future. The relationship she developed with her Lord, and the foundation laid for her continuing walk of faith and witness, blessed all of those she touched.

Many times, she would ask me, "Mom, how much do you love me?"

I would stretch my arms wide and say, "Ann Marie, I love you more than anything in the whole world!"

Ann would say, "No Mom, you must love God more than anything else! If you put anything before God, it is your idol!"

She had learned that in Gray Wilson School. It was a hard lesson for me to learn not to make my only beautiful child an idol.

Memorial Presbyterian continued to open ministry doors for us. The Women of the Church (WOC) at Memorial Presbyterian asked me to become the vice president of the women's council. This meant placing each woman in a "circle group." These circles met once a month in different homes for Bible study, took on responsibilities for church service, and hosted monthly meetings of the entire Women of the Church. The Christmas Cookie Tea held in the mansion of a prominent church member was one of the special events for the WOC. Decorating the chosen home usually was a daylong process of fine Williamsburg Christmas decorations strung and hung from one room to another by a large committee of churchwomen. Engraved invitations sent out weeks in advance, especially welcomed the new women members of the church as our guests of honor. Silver trays filled with hundreds of different cookies were brought for the event, each carefully baked by hostesses who subscribed to *Southern Living*

Magazine. Large silver punch bowls and silver tea services poured forth the wassail, eggnog, or spiced tea and coffee to wash down the delightful sampling of goodies.

Along with serving on the women's council came added experience in ministry with women in the church. Several of the older women took me under their wing to encourage and mentor me. In the summer of 1986, I attended a Precept Bible Study on *Covenant* held at our church. I had never experienced this kind of in-depth inductive Bible study before. I found in doing the homework, class discussion, and watching the videotape of Kay Arthur, I wanted to continue the study method.

I spoke with the class Precept leader, Brenda, and she invited me to attend a fall Precept training workshop in Chattanooga, Tennessee. Brenda and I drove to Chattanooga and stayed at the Precept Ministries Ranch. For the four days of training, Betsy Bird lectured and trained about one-hundred and fifty students during the day. In the evening, Kay Arthur lectured "live" while the TV cameras in the studio cut a videotape for the II Peter Precept Bible Study. As I sat in the beautiful lecture hall surrounded by awesome teaching and hearts hungry to learn the Word of God, tears streamed down my face with the blessing of finding a ministry that not only was changing my life; but God would use to touch other lives through me for years to come. I knew that God had called me to a teaching ministry of women. Precept was the tool God would use to open that door all over the world.

I started teaching *Hebrews* within the next few weeks. Though I stood in front of the class with shaky knees, I had a confidence that came from doing what God had purposed in my life. The next summer study was *Lord, I Want to Know You! A Study of the Names of God.* This life changing study was as powerful as the *Covenant* study, and I saw many students gain deep understanding of the character, and attributes of God. Together we learned Biblical truths that would sustain us in difficult times that lay ahead.

Gary and I loved coordinating large events and finding the gifted people to do various ministries. To cast a vision for how to accomplish a goal and then turn God's people loose to do their best; and seeing their eyes brighten and smiles glow once they had found a purpose for serving the Lord in ministry, delighted our hearts. When Col. Wayne

Gosnell had retired from the Air Force, he became an area director for Lay Renewal Ministries. Wayne asked Gary and me to work with him planning a Regional Family Life Conference at Huntington College in Montgomery. We helped with transportation, facilities, and program coordination. Several hundred people attended the Conference from various local churches. The main platform speaker was Franklin Graham, son of Billy Graham. During the Sunday morning worship service we gave our testimony just before Franklin Graham preached the sermon. His scripture on Jonathan's crippled son Mephibosheth fit perfectly with our testimony.

Our education pastor Ray Stover challenged our Sunday school class to find someone in the church we felt particularly drawn to and begin to mentor them in their faith walk. We were to write their name on a piece of paper and begin to pray about how we would minister to them. When Gary and I compared our selected names, Gary had written down Steve Tomberlin, and I had written down his wife Billie Tomberlin.

Steve and Billie were relatively new members we had met in the Fellowship Garden one Sunday morning. In getting to know them, we found out that they had two sweet little daughters Mary and Melissa, who were close to Ann Marie's age. Our relationship began to develop with Sunday lunches, and visiting each other's homes while the girls played together. Billie came to my Bible study, and we developed a close friendship. Steve and Gary had a great time kidding around and talking sports. Steve had been hesitant to get involved in church until our friendship developed.

Steve had an older brother Jim, who was a Baptist pastor in New Mexico. Steve asked us to pray for Jim and his two children, Christina and Jared. Jim's wife had died of breast cancer, but he had found a new love and was planning to marry again. Our prayers for Jim, his new wife Deryl, and the children would stretch as threads of love in our tapestry of faith farther than we could have known.

In the spring of 1986, Memorial Presbyterian decided to have a Lay Renewal—Celebration of Faith on February 21-25, 1987. Gary and I were on the planning committee. One of our responsibilities was to set up a hosting committee for the visiting team members. We asked Steve and Billie Tomberlin if they would take the job. Steve and

Billie hosted completely and graciously. They supplied snacks, fresh fruit, cold and hot drinks, Kleenex, Tylenol, breath mints, and various other necessities for the team. They became more involved in the Lay Renewal and ministry of the church. Their faith and commitment to the Lord grew deeper.

Several others in the church took on responsibilities and ministry that they had never been involved in before. Having "ownership" in a ministry bigger than themselves gave them a picture of service and belonging to the family of God. Working together on committees strengthened the bonds of friendship and caring among the congregation. We tried to reach as many members as possible from all areas of the community in the planning of the event, so that it would be a successful and lasting experience of growth for the church. Plans included a Kick-off Celebration Feast and Concert, a Sonny Frye Country Breakfast (with grits), a women's luncheon at the Capital City Country Club, a men's luncheon at the Maxwell AFB Officers' Club, an Air Force General's wife hosting a morning women's coffee, an afternoon tea at John Knox Manor, morning Bible study, evening afterglows, and worship services every night.

Our friend Randy Mayfield came and led the youth activities with "Mayfield Madness." Ann Marie had a crush on Randy and loved it when he would imitate Elvis Presley. Randy had prayed for Ann when she was born, and would continue to be a fun part of the tapestry of Ann's life making her feel like a special princess.

We were thrilled my sister Susan Werner would be part of our own lay renewal, knowing that her singing would be touching and memorable. She had already won many hearts in Montgomery, including Dr. Bill Dudley, when she performed a Vesper Concert in 1981 on a visit to see us during Air Command and Staff College. For years afterwards, Bill Dudley would call her to do the music at special conferences in Montreat, North Carolina, because of her wide range and sensitive interpretation of sacred music.

Dr. David Chadwick came to Montgomery from Charlotte, North Carolina, as the visiting preacher. We first met Dr. Chadwick on a lay renewal in April 1986, at Clairmont Presbyterian Church in Decatur, Georgia. His preaching and teaching challenged us to walk in greater holiness, and represent the name of Christ in a manner worthy of a Christian. Later we were lay renewal team members with David Chadwick, Susan Werner, and Tino Wallenda at Trinity Presbyterian Church, Clearwater, Florida, in November of 1987.

When David Chadwick approached the platform to preach in Florida, he tripped on a step almost throwing his over six foot tall body across the floor. Gaining his composer, he stood behind the pulpit microphone and announced that he just wanted everyone to know that he always falls prostrate before the Lord prior to preaching the Word of God.

Over the three years we lived in Montgomery, our lives were full of ministry and mentoring. We gained much experience in church leadership and planning conferences. Gary served as a deacon and chairman of the evangelism committee. He also traveled several times a month visiting his defense counsel offices in the Southeastern United States and Panama. We hosted several Air Force functions, including an Area Defense Counsel Conference at Patrick Air Force Base, Florida.

Ann Marie grew stronger in her faith and continued recovery from her stroke. She would listen to my Precept videotapes of Kay Arthur, go into her bedroom, lay her Bible on her bed and "preach" to her dolls and stuffed animals.

One day, Ann asked me a startling question, "Mommy, when will my scar heal?"

She was referring to the long chest scar left from her open-heart surgery. It had been over three years since the surgery.

I replied, "Well, Ann Marie, your scar is healed. But, you know Jesus has scars from His crucifixion. When you get to heaven, you can compare your scar with Jesus."

In the spring of 1988, we were "fix'n to go" back to Germany. Only this time we would go with Ann Marie. This time we would go as Christians. This time we would see a Sovereign God tear down a Wall that divided a nation; and open the Gate of Freedom to Eastern Europe for the Gospel of Jesus Christ. Little did we know that God had prepared us in Montgomery for what we would face in Germany. The picture was taking shape of His planned purpose for our lives in the colored threads He had been weaving as the tapestry of grace.

CHAPTER FOURTEEN

A Light Shines In the Darkness

Daniel answered and said,
"Let the name of God be blessed forever and ever,
for wisdom and power belong to Him.
And it is He who changes the times and the epochs;
He removes kings and establishes kings;
He gives wisdom to wise men,
and knowledge to men of understanding.
It is He who reveals the profound and hidden things;
He knows what is in the darkness,
and the light dwells with Him."
Daniel 2:20-22 (NAS)

During the dark night of November 9, 1938, known as *Kristallnacht* (The Night of Crystal), the rampage of Nazi SS and Hitler's youth stormed German neighborhoods leaving behind the mark of tragic death and violence across Germany. Broken glass glittered streets with the gutted destruction of 7,500 businesses and 177 synagogues belonging to ninety-one Jews who were killed and hundreds more who were injured.[1]

In an *Anschluss*, German Chancellor Adolph Hitler had annexed his homeland of Austria into the Third Reich. Within a few months after *Kristallnacht*, in March of 1939, the German military marched unopposed into vulnerable Czechoslovakia while Italy seized the tiny Balkan state of Albania.

By August 1939, Germany was ready to launch the Nazi *blitzkrieg* (lightning war) invading neighboring Poland. World War II began on September 1, 1939, when the Nazi war machine crushed Polish forces.

177

Britain and France along with the Commonwealth of Nations declared war on Germany.

In the spring of 1940, Germany pushed northward into Denmark and Norway without resistance, continuing into tiny Luxembourg, crossing the borders of Belgium and the Netherlands. Within months, Germany raced toward the English Channel outflanking the Maginot Line and collapsing France. Turning eastward, German troops invaded and destroyed much of Eastern Russia.

On June 22, 1941, the Soviet Union allied with Great Britain against the Axis powers of Germany and Italy.

On December 7, 1941, Japanese bombs surprised the United States military ships and planes stationed at Pearl Harbor in the Pacific Ocean; leading President Franklin Delano Roosevelt to declare war against Japan, and throwing the United States into a double fronted conflict. The aggression of the Axis Powers could not be ignored. The whole world was at war.

Two and a half years later, after dark periods of battle in the Pacific, North Africa, the Russian front, throughout Italy, and even to the shores of the United States; Allied forces landed on the shores of Northern France on "D-Day," June 6, 1944. The invasion of German-held France was a plan that helped change the tide of World War II. Allied forces began a race toward the Rhine during the summer of 1944, clearing most of France and Belgium. Allied airpower brought tremendous destruction of transportation systems and industry in cities like Frankfurt, Mainz, and Berlin.

On the eastern front, Soviet armies swept through the Baltic States, Poland, Belorussia, and Ukraine. Russian forces seized Romania, Finland, and Bulgaria; then continuing the push toward the West, entered East Prussia and Czechoslovakia in January 1945. Germany lost eastern Germany in February 1945. Berlin lay in ruins falling to the Russian armies after Hitler's suicide on April 30, 1945. The Western Allies had smashed through the Siegfried Line, crossed the Rhine, and overrun western Germany. Germany surrendered unconditionally in May 1945. Tragically, nearly six million Jews died, systematically exterminated in concentration camps by Nazi forces.

For a few more months the Allies fought on the Pacific front. To bring a quick end to the war and save lives, the United States dropped the atomic bomb on the Japanese cities, Hiroshima and Nagasaki. Japan surrendered in August 1945.

It had been the largest and most costly war in history. Entire cities lay in rubble or totally wiped out. The dropping of the atomic bomb on Japan demonstrated the destructive threat posed to humanity by nuclear weapons. Death had come to tens of millions and left millions homeless. The world lay in physical and moral devastation. Even with the birth of the United Nations, the consequences and degradation of victims left a politically unstable situation.[2]

The Cold War began between the Western powers and the Communist-bloc nations. Hostilities between the USSR and the United States emerged from the postwar conflict, particularly over the division of Germany into two countries. As part of the Yalta Conference in February 1945, the country of Germany and the city of Berlin were divided into four zones among Great Britain, France, the United States, and the USSR. Sir Winston Churchill came to Fulton, Missouri in 1946 and warned of the threat of Communist aggression behind the Iron Curtain of Soviet States.

No arrangements existed for access to Berlin, and in June 1948, West Berlin became an isolated island of freedom 110 miles deep within the Soviet zone of East Germany. The Soviet Union hoped that the Allies would abandoned their occupation of West Berlin, when the Soviets blockaded all railroad, highway, and water traffic through East Germany to West Berlin. However, aid came in an unprecedented attempt by the United States, Great Britain, and France, to supply West Berlin with food and fuel, known as the Berlin Airlift. From June 1948 to September 1949, in a round-the-clock airlift, some 272,000 flights were made into the Berlin Templehof Airport in three-minute intervals. More than two million tons of coal for heating and supplies were delivered to over two million West Berliners. The Berlin Airlift succeeded when the failed Soviet blockade lifted on May 12, 1949. The borders reopened, and the Allies held on to the western part of Berlin.

One of the many C-54 Skymaster transport pilots who helped sustain the thirteen month Berlin Airlift, was Colonel Gail S. Halvorsen; known to the children of West Berlin as "Uncle Wiggle Wings," or the "Candy Bomber." On one of Col. Halvorsen's first flights into Berlin, he began rocking his airplane's wings and waving to the children near the runway. One day, he started dropping small parachutes made from handkerchiefs carrying candy and chewing gum to the children. Each day they would wait near the runway to watch for the candy to float out of the sky. For his humanitarian actions during the Airlift, he received the 1948 Cheney Trophy for "Operation Little Vittles."[3] Rhein Main Air Base in Frankfurt, Germany, honored him by naming the U.S. Air Force base elementary school Halverson Elementary. Every American child attending the school would hear the story of "The Candy Bomber," and how Rhein Main had been one of three air corridors used to supply the Berlin Airlift.

Seventy-nine airmen lost their lives during the airlift. On July 10, 1951, at Templehof Airport the citizens of West Berlin dedicated a memorial to the Luftbruecke Air Bridge which supplied the city. A replica of the memorial was dedicated at Rhein Main Air Base in July 1985, as a reminder of the lessons learned from this humanitarian gesture.

Between 1945 and 1961, about four million people fled East Germany crossing into West Berlin. On August 13, 1961, the East German communists began to build a wall of cement and barbed wire between East and West Berlin. An Iron Curtain of reinforced dark silence stretched between East and West Germany. Guard towers built into The Wall overlooked a no-mans-land controlled with attack dogs and dotted by land mines. Over the next twenty-eight years, eighty people were shot to death by East German border guards as they tried to flee to freedom over the concrete Wall. From windows of tall apartment buildings, East Berliners could gaze into the flourishing West, but they were imprisoned and cut-off by the ugly gray Wall that kept them from crossing to freedom.[4]

In 1949, The United States signed an agreement with eleven other European nations to form the North Atlantic Treaty Organization (NATO). As a reaction and balance to NATO, the communist bloc formed the Warsaw Treaty Organization in 1955. The Cold War spread worldwide during the next two decades into China, Taiwan, Asia, Africa, and Latin America. The ideological differences between communism and democracy heated up in the Korean Conflict during the early 1950s, the Cuban Missile Crisis of 1962, and the Vietnam War during the late 1960s and into the early 1970s. Ideological differences extended into a power struggle between the United States and the Soviet Union for military occupation, an arms race of nuclear proliferation, and competition in space exploration and missile capability.[5]

In the beginning years of the Cold War, U.S. Presidents Truman, Eisenhower, and Kennedy faced the terror and threats of Soviet Premiers Stalin and Khrushchev. For over thirty years, world leaders came and went on both sides of the conflict. In the early 1980s, President Ronald Reagan referred to the socialist system as "The Evil Empire," and began escalating the nuclear arms race and increasing the size of the U.S. military strength.

Times and epochs are held in the wisdom and power of God Almighty. A turn of events was about to happen in history that could only come from the Sovereign Hand of God. What was hidden in the darkness behind the communist Iron Curtain was a ray of hope for truth and the power of freedom; an answer to the prayers of persecuted Christians meeting secretly in homes and small churches throughout the Soviet controlled nations. In the fullness of time, God raised up a new leader.

In 1985, a man named Mikhail Gorbachev rose to become a light in the darkness of the Soviet Union. When Gorbachev was appointed General Secretary of the Soviet Communist Party, he began a program of political economic and social openness, and restructuring called *glasnost* and *perestroika*. He allowed greater freedom of expression, released political prisoners, allowed increased emigration, and attacked corruption. The Cold War began to thaw as relations improved between Reagan and Gorbachev in a series of summit talks from 1985-1988. During these talks in 1987, the two world leaders signed an Intermediate Nuclear Forces (INF) arms limitation treaty.[6]

So it was, into the historical involvement between these two men who sought to beat their "swords into plowshares," that Gary, Ann Marie and I flew over the Berlin Airlift Memorial and Halverson Elementary School into Rhein Main AB, West Germany. Landing on the runway of Frankfurt International Airport on July 6, 1988, and looking out the left window of the airplane, the words stumbled out of my husband's mouth.

"There is a Soviet Aeroflot plane sitting on the U.S. air base side of the runway! What are Russians doing on a U.S. air base?"

We had arrived at our next air force assignment in Frankfurt, West Germany, on the same day as the first Soviet inspection team had begun implementation of the INF Treaty. Entering the Rhein Main Gateway Hotel, the tightness of security and tension over possible contact between American and Russian personnel was frightening and inconvenient. Three types of identification were required to enter the hotel lobby. Some elevators were blocked off for "INF Team Use Only." The finest steakhouse restaurant in the hotel was reserved for the INF team, and we were abruptly turned away at the door. Seeking somewhere to eat dinner, we were cordoned-off into a pizza section of the cafeteria to avoid speaking or looking at "the communists." We were warned not to use the stairwell, except in an emergency, since the Russians were sleeping in the rooms below our officers' suite. But the greatest tension was over the hotel cleaning crew that included refugees from Afghanistan!

All of this commotion over the Russians coming to an American air base continued outside the confines of the Rhein Main Gateway Hotel. When the Soviet INF team went by bus to the Base Exchange for a little shopping before returning to the "dark side" of the world, they were overwhelmed with the amount of cars on the BX parking lot.

Thinking that the Americans had staged the appearance of so many automobiles on the parking lot, the Soviets asked the Base Commander, "How long did it take for you to get this many cars here?"

Once inside the Base Exchange, they were shocked to see vast amounts of goods available out in the open on shelves. Many could not resist the temptation to "pocket" some merchandise, since Soviet stores only had limited rationed amounts and payment had to be made before customers could even touch the product. The experience of seeing firsthand the results of democracy, freedom, and economic wealth, stung the conscience of the INF team. They began to realize that they had been lied to, not by the Americans, but by their own government about what was on the other side of The Wall. During the next several months, the Soviet INF team would fly into Rhein Main unannounced to see if the cars were still on the BX parking lot, and to do a little shopping while confirming the progress of the INF

Treaty. These top Soviet officials in the communist government were beginning to see the advantages of *glasnost* (openness) and *perestroika* (restructuring). A flame of revolution was beginning to smolder which would thaw the Cold War and change the history of all of Europe.

The red threads of communism were starting to unravel before our eyes during those first few weeks in Germany. The breathless tension of security issues added to our stress of culture shock in a foreign country and the anxiety of an overseas move. Having arrived in Frankfurt without a car or housing, Gary immediately began the task of getting us transportation and a place to live. The first day at work, Gary met his boss, Col. David Williams, the Wing Commander. Col. Williams insisted that his Staff Judge Advocate must live on the air base in Gateway Gardens housing. He wanted Gary available immediately incase of an emergency. We were put on the base housing waiting list and within a week, we were shown a third floor, three bedrooms, one bathroom, officer's stairwell apartment in the building next-door to the Commanders' duplex. Having left several thousand pounds of our household goods in storage, we decided our smaller overseas shipment could squeeze into the cozy 1,506 square foot space.

Looking out our dining room picture window at the Frankfurt International Airport runway, we could watch a plane land every seventy seconds. Behind our apartment, we could hear Frankfurt Autobahn 5 and Autobahn 3 intersect without speed limits. The sooty air and noise pollution was horrific. My white lace curtains turned gray from jet fuel and automobile exhaust.

There was a waiting period of several days before telephone service installation. Calling back to the U.S. was so expensive that we reserved our calling to special holidays and emergencies, since one half hour calling home would cost one-hundred dollars. After calling collect to my parents to tell them we arrived in Germany, they received a bill for seven minutes of time costing $16.19. We could read one newspaper in English, *The Stars and Stripes* and watch one American TV station, the Armed Forces Network (AFN). At 8:00 a.m., we could watch *Nightline*, then at noon, *CNN* news. The morning *Today Show* was televised at 4:00 p.m., and *CBS Evening News* came on at 6:00 p.m. Local AFN news about what was happening in the U.S. military showed at 7:00 p.m. The rest of the television watching was an assortment of reruns from all of the major U.S. networks ranging from *Moonlighting,* *L.A. Law,* and *Growing Pains,* to *Mr. Rogers.*

In the winter, the apartment was heated with radiators that stuck out from the wall. The third floor rooms could get so warm from the steam heat that a few windows left cracked open even in freezing weather kept the air circulating. In the summer months, no air conditioning was available in most of Europe. Windows without screens were flung wide-open to allow the flies, noise, and pollution full entrance.

Eight families lived in our spiral stairwell. The walls and floors were thin enough to hear the neighbors. We all shared the laundry facilities in the basement with four washers and dryers. Each family was assigned a half day of the week to do their laundry, leaving the nights and weekends on a first come basis. Once every eight weeks it was our responsibility to scrub and clean the outside stairwell steps from top to bottom. Every family had a place outside at the back of the building with common picnic tables and their barbecue grill. We carried all of our groceries up three flights of steps. Winchester went up and down the same flight of stairs to "go outside." Gary and I started losing weight, and Ann Marie gained strength and coordination in her legs climbing the steps.

Separating the Frankfurt Autobahns from our backyard was a ten-foot high chain- link fence with two more feet of barbed wire. A thirty-foot high concrete barrier not only kept the sound of the autobahn out, but also kept a terrorist from throwing a bomb into the commander's home or coming onto the air base from the autobahn. Armed security police and guard dogs regularly patrolled the back barrier around the commander's duplex and our stairwell. At night, a security patrol officer with a machine gun, stood guard outside Ann Marie's bedroom window watching the road and wooded area.

The eight-car garage would shelter one of our cars with the second car left out in the weather on the parking lot. Our van, shipped by boat, would not be in country for a few weeks. We rented a small car for temporary transportation. Gary's German attorney advisor, Ernst, began looking in the local newspapers for used cars and making phone calls negotiating in German. He found a used, four-year old, 1984 powder blue Mercedes 280SE, with automatic transmission and a sunroof for the price of five-thousand dollars. Delighted with the condition of the car, we paid cash. Most Germans drove a Mercedes, Audi, BMW, or Volkswagen. Ernst drove a French Citron "Duck." He was a member of the German "Duck Club." He would spend his lunch hour polishing the "Duck."

Ernst, a German attorney, had been in the Rhein Main Legal Office for many years as a liaison for the German government. He repeatedly told the story to visitors of the morning he was sitting in his office chair and got up to get a file from the filing cabinet. Within moments of moving out of his chair away from the window, a car bomb had gone off outside on the Rhein Main Headquarters parking lot. A large metal pipe came blowing through his office window and would have taken his head off if he had been sitting in his chair.

The infamous Bader Meinhoff Gang had planted the car bomb, using fake cardboard license plates and a stolen military identification card to get on the air base. Security tightened at the entrance gates after the bombing. Every driver and passenger was required to show multiple types of ID before passing the gate guard. Sometimes mirrors were placed underneath entering cars, and bomb-sniffing dogs walked around randomly selected automobiles. Many times security police checked out a package or a briefcase left sitting unattended in or outside a building. During high security threats, tall metal scaffolding was erected in front of the main gate, with an armed security police officer facing the long line of cars waiting to enter the air base. The armed SP was nicknamed "Target One."

The first week on the job, Gary came home one night and said, "Well, we won't be going to church at the air base chapel. I have to court-martial one of the chaplains."

We began looking for an American church off the air base. There was one European Baptist Convention (EBC) church just outside the main gate in the village of Walldorf named "Rhein Valley Baptist Church." Our first Sunday in Germany also happened to be the first Sunday for the new pastor of Rhein Valley Baptist. Pastor Race Lariscy, and his wife Linda, had flown into the Frankfurt Airport one hour after we arrived. Although I was not sure I wanted to become a Baptist, Linda and Race immediately sought out our friendship after the first worship service. Knowing that we had not established relationships in the church, and feeling a common ground in a new overseas assignment, we developed a bonding relationship of trust and ministry together. We became Baptists.

Ann Marie had turned nine years old, and asked if Pastor Race could baptize her. Pastor Lariscy was impressed with Ann's answers to his interview, and mature spiritual understanding of her testimony. Rhein Valley Baptist met in the upstairs meeting hall over a Mexican restaurant and did not have a baptistery. Race secured the facilities of a local German Baptist church. Ann was the first baptism for the new pastor after arriving in West Germany. Not understanding the German instructions, Race had not figured out how to warm the water first and they both went in shivering, but came out smiling.

Race Lariscy had gone through melanoma, a deadly form of cancer, a few years earlier. Although he and Linda were in their mid-thirties, because of chemo and radiation treatment for the cancer, having any children was unlikely. So, they adopted all the children of the church as their own, and especially enjoyed being with Ann Marie.

In late summer, just before Ann was to start third grade at Halverson Elementary, we planned a trip to the Netherlands with Race and Linda. Gary had to remain on the air base because of work responsibilities. Loading up our big Ford Econoline van, I drove Ann Marie, the Lariscys, and two summer youth interns to Holland. Within a few hours, we entered the land of tulips, windmills, canals, and dikes, for a few fun days staying on the Clara Maria Cheese Farm in Amstelveen just outside of Amsterdam. We had rented a small cottage on the countryside farm that offered a farmer's breakfast. Tulip fields spread right up to the cottage walls. We watched the making of a variety of cheeses; from the milking of the cows, to separating the curds from the whey, to packaging and aging the fine cheese products. We toured the *Bloemenveiling of Aalsmeer* where fourteen million flowers and one million potted plants go on auction each day, in the largest flower market in the world. In Amsterdam, known as the "Venice of the North," we rode on a canal boat to view the old shops and homes after shopping for blue and white delft porcelain trinkets. Ann Marie bought wooden shoes and found them too uncomfortable for walking. She preferred to wear a Dutch neckerchief tied with a small wooden shoe scarf ring.

Our most memorable tour in Amsterdam was Anne Frank's House. Now a museum, the building tells the story of the hiding place of eight

Jewish refugees during World War II. On July 6, 1942, the Frank family moved into the blacked-out annex of Otto Frank's herb and spice business to seek refuge from the Gestapo rounding up Jews for slave labor. Four other refugees later joined them in the hiding place. Thirteen-year-old Anne Frank wrote in her diary, describing the daily events of life in two upper floors and an attic annex hidden behind a hinged bookcase. After two years of hiding, Nazi police discovered the group of eight on August 4, 1944, and sent them to several German concentrations camps. Anne and her older sister, Margot, both died of typhus in March of 1945 in Bergen-Belsen Camp. Two months later, the Allies liberated Holland. Anne had died just three months before her sixteenth birthday. Only her father, Otto Frank, survived the Auschwitz death camp to return to the secret annex and discover Anne's diary. In 1947, Otto Frank published *The Secret Annex—The Diary of Anne Frank* based on Anne's writings. It became one of the most widely read books in the world.[7] Ann Marie was inspired to become a writer just like Anne Frank.

Ann Marie went off to third grade walking the half mile to Halverson Elementary School. We had visited with her teacher Mrs. Kemmitt the week before school started to make sure Ann was comfortable with finding her room and teacher. Mrs. Kemmitt was so sensitive about Ann's self-esteem and her educational needs. She called her "a little lady" when speaking about her achievements in the classroom. Physical and occupational therapy testing found Ann to be at a five-year-old level of physical ability. P.T. and O.T. sessions were arranged through the DOD Exceptional Family Member system. Everyone on the school staff wanted to see Ann succeed in her new school environment because she was such a pleasure to work with. Ann started taking gymnastics and ballet at the American Youth Center after school to help her physically and socially. She also brought a jump rope home from gym class and spent several hours determined to learn how to jump it.

Ann Marie had made friends with Amanda Few at an office picnic. Amanda and Ann Marie were born on the same day; and became "kindred spirits" as they walked around the playground together. They loved spending the night at each other's homes. Amanda lived off-base and wanted to live on-base. Ann thought that it would be great to live on the German economy like Amanda.

New neighbors moved in downstairs shortly after we settled in our apartment. Lt. Col. Dale and Vera Oderman had two teenage daughters Karen and Terri; and one son Robbie, who was two days younger than Ann Marie. We immediately developed a close relationship with the family since they were very serious about their Christian faith.

Robbie loved animals, but did not have a pet of his own. He would hear Winchester's dog tags rattle coming down the stairs and suddenly open his apartment door to escort us on our walks. He was more than willing to dog-sit if we went on vacations and trips. Robbie did start collecting snails in a bucket and feeding them lettuce. Gary told Robbie about a nice clear plastic container we had seen at the *Werkauf* department store. Immediately, Robbie took his money to the store and gave the snails a new see-through home. The snails must have been happy because in a few days they had laid snail eggs. Robbie was excited when he showed us the eggs and snails wiggling up the sides of the container. We congratulated him on being a father!

Karen and Terri were sweet role models for Ann Marie. Having two Christian teenage girls as babysitters living downstairs came in handy when Gary and I had social functions. The Oderman family decided to join Rhein Valley Baptist Church after we took them there one Sunday. It was the beginning of another treasured friendship. A tapestry weaving of God's providence bringing us together in Christian love.

Time at Rhein Main was filled with distinguished visitors and guests who came through the Gateway of Europe at Frankfurt Airport. Gary and I quickly learned where the historical points of interest were in the immediate area, and what were the best restaurants and shopping trips. Our favorite Saturday morning excursion was to drive out the back gate down a winding forest road to the Schwanheim car ferry landing. After a brief crossing of the Main River, we parked at the city of Hoechst, known for its ancient porcelain collection and modern pharmacological factory. Walking into the ancient town was like stepping back centuries in time. Restored half-timbered buildings surround a beautiful medieval town square hosting a 600-year-old tradition of unique Gasthaus restaurants, apple wine taverns, and an open-air market. The oldest church (9th Century) in Frankfurt and one of the very first churches in all of Germany, Justinuskirche—The Church of St. Justinian, raises high above the town wall with fine columned arcades. The Old Town Hall was rebuilt after a fire in 1586. The three-winged Balongaro Palace surrounded by a moat lies situated in a double-terraced garden that opens onto the river. The Palace has a splendid chapel and richly decorated ballroom.

The Hoechst market was open on Saturday to the public. Produce stands of fruits and vegetables, flowers, and baked goods, made it a delight to shop on Saturday mornings. Ann Marie always carried 2 Deutsch Marks (DM) to buy a large salted pretzel, and a Coke.

After only three months in Germany, the first distinguished visitor arrived for inspection of the Rhein Main Legal Office and the new Staff Judge Advocate. Gary and I had spent several weeks planning the social events for the two-day visit when Maj. Gen. Moorehouse, Deputy T-JAG, and his team would be on base. This visit could be a career maker or buster for Gary and his officers. Carefully, we checked out recommended restaurants to hold our office dinner. We found the perfect place for a medieval celebration.

We started the special visit by meeting in the Wine Stube of the Gateway Hotel for a little wine and cheese tasting allowing the group of thirty-five to gather for the start of our evening of sightseeing and dining. A big blue air force bus transported the group off base to the ancient town of Dreieichenhain. In the cool evening temperature, we worked up an appetite walking the Romanesque cobblestone streets of the old ivy-covered walled city. The castle grounds with a stone bridge over an ancient moat called forth visions of Charlemagne and his royal hunting parties.

As the sun set behind the half-timbered gatehouse, we reloaded the blue bus for a drive to our dinner reservations and "Munching with Maidens." The Alter Burg Muehler Restaurant with a large upstairs private party room offered lively dining. Lovely maidens in authentic German costume served a six-course meal, while a minstrel playing a violin serenaded guests with medieval music. The meal started with a bitter drink of *mead*, followed by dark hard bread spread with a seasoned lard called *smalz*. The third course was a strange *Congealed Chicken Salad*. The tasty soup course of *Lentil Soup and Bratwurst* was served with no spoon and had to be drunk from the bowl. The main course was delicious *Roast Wild Boar with Dumplings and Red Cabbage. Gingerbread in Rum Sauce* topped the night, making a lasting impression on the guests.

Every time the General turned around, "two star license plates" distinguished the car or helicopter waiting for him. Briefings in the wing conference room went smoothly the next day like icing on the cake. As a farewell gift, Gary gave General Moorehouse a limited edition memorial medal coin commemorating the Berlin Airlift from Rhein Main Air Base.

Word about the visit had traveled to HQ USAFE at Ramstein Air Base. They were still talking about how Gary's office "watered the eyes" of the Inspection Team the next week when Gary went to a SJA Conference. The future of everyone's career seemed assured. However, it was the first of many more visits from JAG commanders who wanted to hear the briefing and get the "royal treatment."

Rhein Main's historical legacy and strategic location, five miles south of Frankfurt, made it unique among all the other USAFE air bases. Rhein Main Air Base was home to the 435th Tactical Airlift Wing, the only Military Airlift Command base in Europe. The C-130E Hercules aircraft flew in support of allied combat units throughout Europe transporting personnel and supplies. The 2nd Aeromedical Evacuation Squadron and the 55th Aeromedical Airlift Squadron provided medical airlift in Europe to two military hospitals. The US Army Hospital in

Frankfurt was ten miles north, and the USAF hospital at Wiesbaden was twenty-one miles west.

In October 1988, out of the silence of the night, a medical evacuation plane landed on the Rhein Main runway at 2:00 a.m. It was bringing a hostage on his way home to freedom and the Wiesbaden Hospital for treatment and examination. Several more hostages and refugees would slip through the night on the wings of freedom over the next two years at the Gateway to Europe.

We had the opportunity to attend a Baptist Missions Conference held in Wiesbaden in October of 1988. Pastors and missionaries from Europe, and the Soviet Union came together to encourage each other in their Christian faith. We were amazed to hear a Russian pastor, Srgei Nikolaev, from St. Petersburg, speak in English about his faith dealing with the poor medical and living conditions in the Russian city. Hospitals were using sewing thread for stitching patient's wounds, and no pain medication was available. Operating rooms had to re-use hospital bed sheets, needles, syringes, and bandages without sterilization. Baptist women were volunteering in the hospitals. The women's concern for the patients impressed the communist government; their kindness was breaking down the walls.

From the many conference attendees, three pastors from Poland came to speak at Rhein Valley Baptist church on the following Sunday morning. Race Lariscy asked Gary to host the Polish pastors and arrange for brunch at the Rhein Main Officers' Club on Sunday. After church service, we escorted the men to our van and drove toward the air base. Passing through the security checkpoint at the main gate, they sat silently with smiling faces full of excitement. Once we passed onto the base, they exclaimed how they would tell their family and friends in Poland about their first trip onto a US military base.

Sunday brunch at the O-Club could impress even the most sophisticated guest, but when these three Polish gentlemen entered the chandeliered formal ballroom, their eyes bugged out and jaws dropped. Before them spread long linen covered tables filled with delicious foods and beverages accessible in an "all you can eat" buffet line for the price of $5. The choice of food ranged from: fresh Belgian waffles covered in whipped cream and strawberries, melons, bacon, eggs, sausage, biscuits, and oatmeal. Then came carved roast beef, stroganoff, mashed potatoes, gravy, fried chicken, hash browns, glazed carrots, green beans, baked fish, and caviar. On to a salad bar, and a Champaign fountain surrounded by a variety of desserts including cheesecake, fruit cobblers, and ice cream. Never in all their days under communist rule had they been treated to such a royal meal. They must have thought it was just like heaven.

They praised Mikhail Gorbachev and said, "Who would have believed three years ago that we could be sitting here and talking and eating with you!"

A prayer began to rise up in our hearts for God to open the door in communist countries for freedom of Christian worship as we bonded with these men.

That men may know that Thou,
whose name alone is Jehovah,
art the Most High over all the earth.
Psalms 83:18 (KJV)

CHAPTER FIFTEEN

Fall of the Wall

For Thou dost save an afflicted people;
but haughty eyes Thou dost abase.
For Thou dost light my lamp;
the Lord my God illumines my darkness.
For by Thee I can run upon a troop;
and by my God I can leap over a wall.
As for God, His way is blameless;
the word of the Lord is tried;
He is a shield to all who take refuge in Him.
For who is God, but the Lord?
And who is a rock, except our God,
the God who girds me with strength,
and makes my way blameless?
Psalms 18:27-32 (NAS)

"Mr. Gorbachev, tear down this wall!"
President Ronald Reagan
June 12, 1987
During a speech at the Brandenburg Gate, West Berlin
750th Anniversary of the City of Berlin, Germany

Every day of our lives at Rhein Main contained a sense of adventure exploring the past, grasping the present, and excited about the future. We felt inextricably mixed into historical events happening all around us. What an opportunity to show Ann Marie a worldview of all the cultures and capitals of Europe.

Our heart for international people and missions continued to grow with ministry opportunities. Gary became a deacon at Rhein Valley

Baptist. Race was encouraged to have Gary and two other men come on the deacon board and help establish a new vision for the direction of ministry. Vera Oderman and I organized a new fellowship ministry called "Salt Shakers." Small groups of church members met once a month in different homes for dinner and friendship. Gary and I began working with the young singles in the church. Being single and overseas can be lonely, so we organized ski trips, tours, lunches, dinners out to eat, and time together in homes.

We started teaching an adult Sunday school class at Rhein Valley Baptist on prayer and progressed to a study in the Epistles of the *One Another's* by Gene Getz. As we taught, our class grew. Beginning in a small room behind the choir loft, we soon were using several pews in the worship center. I had written our next study on *Covenant* taken from the study material by Precept Ministries to fit into a short Sunday school hour. As the pieces of the puzzle began to fit together of God's covenant promises, the twenty-five adults gained excitement and understanding.

One deacon told me, "I have been in Sunday school for thirty-six years, and I have never learned what you are teaching me! But I know that it is true, because it is in the Word of God!"

One afternoon, after picking up our mail from the base mailroom, I was walking along the sidewalk reading the newsletter from Memorial Presbyterian Church. I stopped in my tracks as I read the news of the death of David Stowe. The young man, who was in our Montgomery youth group, went on to medical school and married a physical therapist. He was killed in a tragic bicycling accident. My thoughts went to his new wife who was bicycling with him when he lost control and fell over the edge of a mountain road. Then I thought of Bill and Jakie Dudley as they grieved the loss of an adopted son of promise. David's testimony of faith played repeatedly in my mind for days. Our family grieved over the loss of his life, but rejoiced he had come to know the Lord in his teenage years and had shared the story with us.

In the early spring of 1989, we began to pursue the idea with Pastor Race Laricsy of having a Lay Renewal in Rhein Valley Baptist Church. He warmed up to the idea after talking with Joe Schluchter, director of Lay Renewal Events, in St. Louis, Missouri. Joe recommended our dear friend from Montgomery, Alabama, Wayne Gosnell, to be the visiting team coordinator for the renewal event. Since Wayne was a retired Air Force Colonel, he would understand the military environment in which most of the church members lived. We were delighted to have Wayne and Jo come and visit us, and lead the team. To give enough time for travel arrangements, and several months of prayer and preparation, the dates were set for November 4-7, 1989. Little did we know the significance those dates would have in history.

Several other events took place during the spring months of 1989 which encouraged relationships and challenged others. Ann Marie's third grade teacher Mrs. Kemmitt announced that she and her military husband would be moving back to the States in April. I was worried about Mrs. Kemmitt's replacement after having the comfort of such an understanding teacher working with Ann every day.

I turned to the Lord in prayer asking Him to send another special teacher to Ann's class. His answer to my prayers was Mrs. McMillan. Vickie McMillan was very interested in Ann Marie's health and educational concerns. The first day of school she called me and gave me her home phone number in case I ever needed to call her. Then as an extra blessing, Mrs. McMillan came to Rhein Valley Baptist Church. She and her husband had just come to Germany and were looking for a new church. Not only was she a great teacher, but she was a Christian too!

I began tutoring three-second grade students in Reading at Halverson Elementary three mornings a week. Gary was elected to the school board advisory council to help advise the school on special issues and policies. I continued through the next school year to help with special needs children. Volunteering in the school helped me to establish relationships with other teachers and the administration, allowing better communication at school meetings addressing Ann Marie's needs. The school administration saw us as supportive parents who wanted to help, not criticize the school.

At a January meeting the following year, I was having a particularly difficult time with one of the caseworkers about Ann's written Individual Education Program (IEP). The caseworker had not bothered to follow Ann's medical history and thought that our meeting was unnecessary. Earlier in the fall, she had insisted that Ann did not need a special eye examination for perception problems and the school nurse could do the exam. Ann Marie's occupational therapist reacted to the situation by personally calling the eye doctor at the Exceptional Family Member Department (EFMD) and setting up an appointment for Ann. The EFMD eye doctor diagnosed Ann with ocular motor dysfunction and prescribed glasses and eye exercises.

At the January meeting, the caseworker had taken an eight page IEP and reduced it down to a half page. The classroom teachers, guidance counselor, gym teacher, O.T., P.T., and Assistant Principal all came to my aid at the meeting when I insisted that the IEP for the next year have all classroom modifications in writing. We would be moving to a new school, and I wanted it written out for the next teacher and school to know what to expect in the Individual Educational Program. I refused to sign the paperwork until the caseworker had listed everything from the year before. After the Assistant Principal instructed the caseworker to comply with my request and the meeting adjourned, the Assistant Principal walked out with me. She patted me on the back, and thanked me for all of the time I had given to the school as a volunteer.

During spring break, we took advantage of staying in Austria at our favorite place, Gasthof Zur Post; returning to the familiar place of our early skiing days in the 1970s. We had spent our Christmas vacation there a few months before, when all three of us had gotten new skis and boots. After a week of ski lessons in December, Ann Marie had come home with a silver medal in the children's ski races. Ann loved the hotel where she had her own little room with a single bed covered in a down comforter and feather pillow. She could easily go down the stairs on her own to the fireplace lounge, order a hot chocolate, and put it on our "tab" for the week. By the second visit in the spring, she was learning how to go on the "bunny hill" rope tow and come down the hill with some important ski moves.

In April, I was able to attend another Precept Training in the Taunus Mountains of Frankfurt with several Precept leaders from all over Europe. Three women from England flew into the Frankfurt Airport for the training and I volunteered to drive them to the conference. It was such an encouragement to share several days together studying God's Word. I came home more excited than ever to teach another Precept class, and began to pray for the opportunity to use my teaching gift. The Youth Sunday school class needed a teacher, so I taught them,

Lord, I Want to Know You! A Study of the Names of God. They loved learning to study scripture and knowing the character, nature, and attributes of God in His Name.

Our first year at Rhein Main was swirling to an end. More changes, special events and visits began to appear on the summer horizon. A new Wing Commander and Base Commander were welcomed to Rhein Main Air Base in May 1989. Col. and Mrs. John Handy moved into the Wing Commander's duplex next-door to our stairwell apartments. They had hardly gotten over jet lag when the new president of the United States, George H.W. Bush and his wife, Barbara, flew into Rhein Main Air Base paying a visit to the troops on May 31, for Memorial Day. Standing outside on the tarmac, there were Secret Service men watching the crowd all around us. Gary put Ann Marie up on his shoulders so she could see the President and First Lady. At the end of the President's speech to the troops, he and Mrs. Bush moved off the platform and began shaking hands with those closest to the ropes. Ann Marie bent forward over Gary's shoulders and Mrs. Bush shook her hand. Ann Marie suddenly had a new role model. Later Ann would read a biography of Barbara Bush and write an essay about the First Lady.

The sparks of a revolution in Eastern Europe had sprung up in various forms and in several countries during the previous three decades. Soviet tanks rolled over each attempt for freedom. The revolution smoldered, waiting for a fresh wind to fan it into unsuppressed flames of freedom. The opening came when the Iron Curtain was breached, and authorities looked the other way. On May 2, 1989, Hungarian guards snipped a hole about one-hundred yards wide in the Iron Curtain along the border with Austria. By the end of August, thousands of East Germans had paid a visit to their Hungarian friends, and found their way through the barrier. Czechoslovak and Polish authorities began to let special trains pass out of the Soviet bloc, while lines of cars filled with fleeing people crossed into free Western Germany and Austria. Hundreds of thousands of East Germans fled westward via Poland, Hungary, and Czechoslovakia.

The opportunity came for us to take Ann Marie to see the Berlin Wall in August before school started. Many of our friends had successfully driven their cars through Checkpoint Alpha, entering into

East Germany, and Checkpoint Bravo, entering West Berlin. The final destination, Checkpoint Charlie, opened into communist East Berlin. Shopping opportunities and bargains in East Berlin were worth the stress of border guards and checkpoints. A private vehicle could hold more purchases than a pedestrian, or a suitcase on an airplane. Craig and Sandy Koontz had made several successful trips and put their firsthand information in a brochure called *Driving to Berlin*.[1] The information was available to those who had expressed an interest in driving, but did not want to make a side trip to the *Gulag* (Soviet prison camp).

Before making a trip across the communist borders, Gary had to get flag orders from his unit and a leave slip specifically authorizing travel into West and East Berlin. The flag orders had to be letter perfect. All the information recorded exactly the way it was on our military ID cards, USAEUR vehicle registration, and passports; including spacing, periods, and commas. Any variation in numbers or letters would stop the trip at the first border crossing or delay us for hours. We had a briefing on the situation by the Office of Secret Investigations (OSI) about several things not to do, and some things we needed to do during the trip.

Deciding to take the Mercedes because is would be faster to drive, and not as obviously American as our Ford Econoline van; we headed north on Autobahns 5 and 7, on August 18, 1989. We exited towards Braunschweig to connect with the Berlin Autobahn. As we approached the Allied Checkpoint Alpha at Helmstedt, we stopped at the BP gas station about one mile away. A full tank of gas was needed once crossing into East Germany because stopping or getting off the Autobahn was forbidden. BP accepted the ESSO gas coupons, which were rationed to US Armed Forces in Europe. At the Checkpoint Alpha building, Gary took all the paperwork, auto registration, flag orders, ID cards, and leave/pass slip into the office, along with the odometer reading of our car. While US Army personnel checked the paperwork and gave Gary a very detailed briefing on driving in the East, including an instruction book with pictures, directions, and emergency forms, Ann Marie and I used the nice restrooms. We heard the restrooms in the East had no toilet paper and did not flush.

After leaving Checkpoint Alpha, we proceeded through the border fortifications to the Soviet checkpoint. A young Soviet troop was waiting to check all of the paperwork. Gary stopped the car, got out as directed and walked up to the soldier. The Soviet soldier saluted Gary, and Gary returned the salute handing him the paperwork package. The soldier then motioned Gary to a small building where the paperwork slid into a small slot in the wall. Ann and I remained in the car trying not to make eye contact with the Soviet guard who was walking around our car and recording the license number. We had been afraid to speak to anyone, but he smiled at Ann and said, "Hello." She blushed and lowered her eyes with a slight smile on her face. After a few minutes, the paperwork reappeared from the slot in the wall. Gary had to return to the outside guard with the papers and have them checked again for a time stamp placed on them. The guard also checked all of the numbers and letters again to make sure nothing had moved around on the papers while they were behind the secret wall. He gave the papers back to Gary and saluted. Once we were together in the car, as we drove by the guard he saluted once again. Gary made sure to return the salute as directed.

Following the instructions to the letter along with the military traffic signs, we prayed to get through East Germany safely to Checkpoint Bravo. The speed limit was 100 kilometers per hour (60 mph). There were numerous radar traps; if you arrived earlier than the two and a half hours expected, the Soviets would make you wait at the other end until the time when you would have cleared the Checkpoint driving the speed limit. If you were late, they would come out looking for you on the road. Reaching the Soviet checkpoint, Gary repeated the same procedures. Of course, the Soviets were concerned we had picked up an East German and might smuggle them into free West Berlin. Breathing a sigh of relief and needing to use the bathroom again, we moved on to US Checkpoint Bravo, where we showed the paperwork, including recording the odometer reading and turning in the travel book.

Berlin, the divided city, was a lesson of stark contrasts. The West had everything to offer in the shops. The East offered only the bare necessities of a meager existence. American and Soviet soldiers spent hours staring at each other with guns pointed across the barrier.

Entering West Berlin, we found Templehof Air Base. After checking in to The Columbia House, we made the short trip toward Checkpoint Charlie to see The Wall.

In front of us stood the bright colored graffiti on the spray painted concrete slab that had separated families for decades. A daily reminder that the city, country, and the continent, divided by a nuclear stalemate, kept people apart instead of united.

Ann Marie had one determination in her mind. Armed with a colored red marker, she reached out and wrote on the rough concrete,

Mr. Gorbachev, tear down this wall!

Ann placed some Christian stickers near her writing. I engraved my Bible verse with the red marker,

You shall know the Truth, and the Truth shall make you free!

Looking up at the tall apartment building on the East side of The Wall, my eyes caught a glimpse of a woman's figure in a dark window. As our eyes seemed to meet, she reached up and pulled her window shade down.

The next morning we set off for the adventure of crossing in our car to visit historical sites, shop for bargains, and eat cheaply in East Berlin. Gary was required to put on his Class A military uniform, minus the nametag, before entering the East side of Berlin. The big black and white sign posted at the checkpoint warned, *You Are Leaving the American Sector.* Once again, all the paperwork was shown, while we remained in the car at Checkpoint Charlie. Reaching the East German guardhouse, Ann and I were to hold our passports up to the passenger window against the glass. Gary's uniform allowed him to cross without showing his passport. Clearing the Soviet guard post, we headed down Friedrich St., to the corner of Unter den Linden. To the left we glanced at the golden Quadriga gleaming on the roof of the Brandenburg Gate, built between 1788 and 1791. The Peace Goddess Eirene—Victoria waved her scepter in a chariot pulled by four white horses above the gate. The Unter den Linden Avenue had been Hitler's favorite parade route for the fascists to march through the victory gate. On August 13, 1961, with the construction of the Berlin Wall, the

Gate closed off and became part of the "no-man's-land" between East and West Berlin. It symbolized the divided city. [2]

Passing the Soviet Embassy, we turned right onto Unter den Linden Avenue facing the statue of Frederick the Great, "Old Fritz" standing 46 feet high across the street from the Prussian Library with five million volumes of books. We approached Bebel Platz, which was the scene of the 1933 Nazi book burning next to the beautiful Opera House. Across the street stood the old Royal National Library where Lenin worked in 1895, and next to it Humboldt University where Marx was a student and Einstein worked on his theories of relativity.[3]

Farther down the avenue, we stopped to videotape the snap-kick goose-stepping in the hourly changing of the guard at Neue Wache, the Memorial to Victims of Fascism and Militarism, where an eternal flame burns inside the monument. As the guard marched forward toward us, he seemed to grimace as if to high kick us out of the way before sharply turning on his heels just inches in front of the camera lens.

Back in the car we turned down Holzmarktstr looking for a place to eat. We spotted the New Centrum department store on Koppen Strasse at the East train station, which had originally been part of the Orient Express route. Parking our car, we entered the large department store and took an escalator to the upper floor where there was a dining room. Going through the cafeteria line, we picked out sandwiches and dessert. I came to the soda fountain machine, placed my glass under the spout and selected a cola drink by pushing the button. As I waited for the drink to fill the glass, I happened to leave my hand on the top of the small drink machine. An East German woman who was working behind the counter in "customer service" approached me with a glare and yelled, *Neyet, Neyet!* as she slapped my hand off the machine. I was shocked to have been touched in such a rude manner. She pointed to the sign that said in German, "Only push the button once!" I had only pushed the button once. She thought I had held the button, and would find a continual stream of cola flowing over my glass. There was no apology from her to this American when she realized that my glass filled perfectly to the top.

Having exchanged our dollars for East Deutsche Marks before crossing The Wall, the smallest bill we had was a 100 East DM. Our total bill came to around 10 East DM. Exiting to the cash register, another frustrated East German man grumbled and snorted resenting the rich Americans, as he tried to make change for our 100 East DM. We quickly ate and left for more sightseeing and shopping.

Gary was very self-conscious in his military uniform as East Germans would crane their necks and stare at us. We soon found that I could accomplish much more shopping by leaving the guy in the U.S. Air Force uniform outside on the street. Entering a clothes boutique, I found a limited number of dresses all the same color and style. Black or gray were the two choices. However, I did find a black knit skirt and blouse in my size. Speaking German, I asked the overly aggressive saleswoman if I might try the dress on in a dressing room.

"This dress is too small for you!" was her angry reply in German, as she noticed Gary peeking in the doorway to the shop.

My second experience with "customer service" made me determined to buy the dress, whether it fit or not. I expressed that the dress was my size and my strong desire to buy the dress. She grabbed it from my hands. Marching to a back room, she came out without the dress and walked to the antiquated cash register. Hand writing out a bill of sale for me, she demanded that I pay for the dress before I could see it again. I gave her the 150 East German Marks, which was the equivalent of $15 in U.S. currency. Turning to a small slot in the wall behind her, she received the dress carefully folded through the hole in the wall. Then she wrapped it in cheap tissue paper and handed it to me with the bill of sale straight pinned to the paper.

We proceeded down the street checking off our list of things to buy. Stopping in a music shop on Strausberger Platz, Ann Marie bought a glockenspiel for $8. In a jewelry store, Gary found a wristwatch made in Russia for $10. My treasure from East Berlin was a Samovar teapot for making Russian tea. At the Schonhauser Allee Featherbed Factory, which was only open Tuesdays and Thursdays after 3:00 p.m., we purchased two blue down comforters for Aunt Susan's children, Elizabeth and David. Many times, we would ask about an item in the display case of a store, only to be told that the quota for the day had already been sold and to come back tomorrow. The communist work ethic had left competition and customer service dead in East German society.

We headed to Alexander Platz for dinner at the 365-meter tall TV tower, also known as "The Pope's Revenge." The Telecafe revolved around the city panorama once every hour while guests dined on the best food in Eastern Europe. As we waited in line below the tower to go up the tower elevator, a small boy was standing behind us in line with his mother and father. He noticed Gary's uniform and asked in German where we lived. I replied to him that we lived in Frankfurt.

His face squinted up at us as he asked, "Frankfurt a.d. Oder?"

I replied, "Nein, A.M. Main!"

Realizing that we were not from the East German city of Frankfurt on the Oder River, but from the West German city of Frankfurt on the Main River, he gasped and covered his mouth. His parents laughed as he hid his face behind his mother's skirt.

In late August of 1989, Gary was promoted to "Full-bird Colonel" along with our downstairs neighbor Dale Oderman. The promotion party at the O'Club was very nice, especially since all six of the Colonel "selectees" pooled their money and threw one big bash for all their family and friends. General Moorehouse had been on the promotion board to select the Colonels. We realized how very important that evening of "Munching with Maidens" had been when we first arrived at Rhein Main.

Besides receiving many cards of congratulations from commanders, colonels, and generals in the Air Force, the best part of the new promotion was reserved parking spots on any air base in the world. The promotion did cause a problem with our staying at Rhein Main in a Lt. Col. position. Another move would be coming sometime in the next year. We still had more of Europe to see, and began hoping for a consecutive overseas assignment to HQ Ramstein AB, Germany.

It had always been in the back of my mind that another breast lump might occur. During a routine self-examination, I found another lump. When I visited the doctor at Wiesbaden Medical Center, he suspected three lumps in my right breast. He thought they were probably a reoccurrence of the fibro-cystic disease, and ordered a mammogram. He decided to remove the lumps and surgery was scheduled for September 27, 1989.

All summer I had been looking forward to one historical event. "Frankfurter Night" honoring the Fortieth Anniversary of the Berlin Airlift and Veteran's Reunion scheduled for September 26, 1989. Gary was on the board of directors for the Luftbruecke Chapter of the Airlift Association; I had a new pink lace dress, and Ann had a babysitter. The doctor seemed to understand the importance of the event, and let me be admitted to the hospital for blood work and pre-op tests, then sent home on an overnight pass until 6 a.m. the next morning for surgery. My restriction was no alcoholic beverages or food after 9 p.m.

The opening Berlin Airlift Memorial Ceremony was at Rhein Main Air Base at 1500 hours (3 p.m.) in front of the massive concrete monument that is an exact replica of the one which stands at Tempelhof Airport in Berlin. The half-arched monument was flanked by two of the aircraft that flew in the Berlin Airlift, a McDonnell-Douglas C-47 "Gooney-bird" and a C-54 Skymaster. Surrounded by a beautifully landscaped garden, the national anthems of Germany, France, Great Britain, and the United States played during the posting of the colors. Several of the veterans who helped fly "Operation Vittles" had returned for this celebration. For many of them, it was their first time back to German soil after leaving forty years before. Lt. Col. Gary J. Phipps, President of the Luftbruecke Chapter of the Airlift Association, gave welcoming remarks. He was followed by two keynote speakers; Dr. Friedrich Zimmerman, Minister of Transportation, Federal Republic of Germany; and Maj. Gen. William H. Sistrunk, Commander, 322 Airlift Division, Military Airlift Command and Deputy Chief of Staff for Airlift, US Air Forces in Europe. The conclusion of the ceremony was the presentation of a wreath at the foot of the memorial and a benediction.[4]

That evening a blue air force bus picked us up in front of the wing commander's home and took us to the "Frankfurter Night" veteran's reunion. As we waited for the bus, Mrs. Handy asked me about the lovely plastic hospital bracelet accessorizing my pink lace dress. After explaining to her that I was "on leave" from Wiesbaden Hospital to return for surgery the next morning, she turned and told her husband, the wing commander. Their immediate assurance of prayers for my surgery was sincerely gracious.

Upon arriving at the Frankfurt Officers' Club, we entered the Grand Ballroom and found our assigned seats. Gary and I were hosting one of the many round tables of guests from Germany, England, and US airlift veterans. Our place tags put us on opposite sides of the table with four guests on each side of us. My seat was between two veterans who seemed to be in their early seventies. The one to my left continually smiled while patting my leg. It was an overwhelming evening for both of us!

A Hessian specialty buffet was served at 8 p.m., after welcoming remarks. The six-course meal started with potato soup *Frankfurter Style*. It continued with the cold dishes including smoked trout with creamed horseradish, choice of *Hessian* sausages with mustard, jellied pork in onion-marinade, and boiled eggs in herb sauce. The salads followed as a selection of potato salad with bacon, *Hessian* sausage salad, and coleslaw-cucumber-bean-herring salad. Then we were served the hot dishes of braised breast of beef, shoulder and knuckle of pork, *Hessian Butcher Platter* with smoked loin of pork and roasted sausages, potato cake with stewed apples and cranberries, and sauerkraut with mashed potatoes. The fifth course was two cheese selections of *Siebkas* with cumin and chives, and *Handkas* with marinated onions, and homemade bread. Dessert was the best with strawberry cream *Kronberg Style*, *Sabayon* of apple wine, pudding with sauce *Bishop-Frankfurter* style, and pancake with plums and cinnamon.[5] The difficulty was eating something I wanted, but without alcohol and before 9 p.m.

General T. R. Milton, USAF (Ret.) the distinguished guest speaker, had served during WW II with the Eighth Air Force in England flying B-17 aircraft. After returning to the United States in 1945, he was reassigned to Europe in 1948, as Chief of Staff for the Combined Airlift Task Force, directing operations for the Berlin Airlift. His extensive forty-year military career started with enlistment in the regular Army in 1934. He retired in July 1974, as United States Representative to the NATO Military Committee with the rank of four-star General. He was a delightful and historical speaker regarding the intrigue of the Berlin Airlift and the bravery of those who struggled to keep freedom alive.[6]

Five o'clock in the morning came too quickly after getting home around midnight from the veteran's reunion. Gary and I quickly dressed and drove the half-hour back to Wiesbaden Hospital for my "three-lumpectomy." Lt. Col. David Brown was my surgeon. He did a beautiful cosmetic job of removing all three lumps, which turned out to be benign fibroid tumors. As I regained consciousness around noon, he was talking with Gary beside my bed about what he removed. Noticing that I was awake, he took out his ink pen and began to draw on the paper bed sheet, beside my head, a diagram of the surgery site.

Then his words burned into my head, "You are a garden for growing these kinds of fibroid tumors. You will probably have more. Keep up your self-examinations."

I was able to leave the hospital within the next hour, as soon as I could stand and walk. When we arrived home, waiting for me was a beautiful bouquet of flowers from Col. and Mrs. Handy. Later in the afternoon, Mickey Handy called to see if I needed anything. I was very appreciative of her thoughtfulness and concern.

During the months leading up to November 1989, we had been working with several committees at Rhein Valley Chapel in preparation for the Lay Renewal Celebration of Faith. Many of the military members had opened their homes to host the visiting team members. The visiting team was excited to be coming for the first Lay Renewal in Germany. Col. Wayne Gosnell and JoAnn arrived from Montgomery, Alabama, to coordinate the Lay Renewal Team. Randy Mayfield came to lead our youth group and praise music. Allen and Sue Schaefer flew in with Joe and Peggy Schluchter from Central Presbyterian in

St. Louis. Phillip and Anne Jung came from Mobile, Alabama, for the children's ministry and stayed with us. The visiting pastor was Jack Oats from Clairmont Presbyterian Church in Atlanta, Georgia. We had been to his church in 1986, on a Lay Renewal Team. All of the events of the Renewal came together Nov. 4-7, 1989, to build and strengthen the members of Rhein Valley Baptist Church. Race and Linda appreciated the growing support and love they felt among the congregation.

After the Renewal, some of the visiting team members were staying in Europe to do traveling. Allen and Sue Schaefer were not returning home for a few days, and asked Gary what they could see in the area around Frankfurt. Gary suggested they take the train thirty minutes west to the Wiesbaden/Mainz area. The Mainz Cathedral contained a copy of the Gutenberg Bible printed in 1456. Allen and Sue took the tour of Mainz Cathedral on November 8. Allen felt the need to bow at the altar of the cathedral and pray for Germany. He prayed that God would shake the nation of Germany from top to bottom, so the country where the Protestant Reformation was born would return to the Lord. The next day, November 9, 1989, God answered Allen's prayer for Germany. There was such a shaking from top to bottom; it could have only come from God. In fact, in years to come, Allen Schaefer would take credit for "The Fall of The Wall!" However, he was really only one of many who had lifted prayers to the Lord.

For two years, regular Monday night prayer for peace meetings had attracted young people in Leipzig, East Germany, at the Saint Nicolas Church. The crowds had surged to three-hundred thousand by November 1989. On the night of Nov. 9, 1989, fifty-one years to the exact date after *Kristallnacht—The Night of Crystal*, the "handwriting was on The Wall." It started with a very odd announcement during a press conference by Guenter Schabowski, the communist official in charge of the Berlin Capital. He was giving a briefing about the communist reforms and travel restrictions. When asked about The Wall, he told reporters that freed travel had begun *ab sofort (*immediately). The news flashed during dinnertime in Berlin—*they are opening the borders!* Unsure of the vague announcement, East Berliners watched the 10 p.m. news show *Tagesthemen,* which broadcasted from West Berlin. When *Tagesthemen* reported people were coming across and

Checkpoint Charlie might open soon, hundreds of East Germans began to swarm at the Brandenburg Gate and checkpoints into West Berlin. The mass of people was too big to bully. Walking across the forbidden barrier and driving their strange little *Trabants* (East German made cars); they crowded into the once forbidden streets of West Berlin. At the Berlin Wall they came with hammers, chisels, and ropes. Pounding at The Wall they broke through it, dismantled it, and celebrated. East Germans woke the next morning to find the hated Wall had crumbled.

At Rhein Main Air Base, we stood in front of our television set and cried tears of unbelief that all the years of separation and torment had crumbled simply by a mistaken radio announcement. People surged across the forbidden boundary when the border guards thought it was an official order to open the checkpoints. Soon the West Germans were welcoming their brothers to freedom. For years, people had waived to each other from across the barricade, now they were meeting for the first time with sobs of joyful tears as they danced and sang in the street.

By January 1990, large slabs of The Wall sold as memorials for hard currency. In October of that year it was hard to find the short wall sections that remained standing. That same year, President Ronald Reagan and wife Nancy returned to Berlin to walk through the Brandenburg Gate into East Berlin where The Wall once stood.[7]

The Cold War was ending. Rapidly the Eastern bloc countries of the Soviet Union began to throw off their communist dictators. For some countries, like Hungary, it was a "velvet revolution." For other countries like Romania, it was a "bloody revolution." Other countries, like Yugoslavia and Czechoslovakia, were torn apart instead of uniting. The map of Europe changed several times in the next years.

There were still European countries and capitals for Ann Marie to see. We made a Thanksgiving trip to London, England, so Ann could do a special fourth grade report and slide show on English history. Flying into Heathrow Airport on Pan Am from Frankfurt, we took the underground to the Hotel Imperial. For four days, we walked or took the underground all over London, visiting the historical sites by day and London's theatre by night. Ann Marie was a trooper through it all, never complaining, always taking pictures and writing notes for her report. The highlight of our trip was the night we saw a new musical, *Les Misérables*, at the London theatre. Our seats were so high up in the balcony we needed binoculars to see the actors, but the music was spellbinding. Ann sat through the whole show entranced by the acting and singing. We bought the sound track and she memorized all of the songs. Her favorite song was "Castle on a Cloud," which the small child Cosette sings, dreaming of a place where no-one cries and she is loved very much.

Ann Marie was developing her own voice for solos at church. At Christmas the children's choir performed a musical drama called "Mary Had a Little Lamb." Ann Marie played the lead part of "Tiny," a lamb who sings to the baby Jesus in the manger. She invited her therapists and teachers to hear her debut. In the spring, Ann Marie sang her first solo for a morning worship service. She had practiced with Vera Oderman accompanying her on the piano. The congregation always remembered Ann Marie singing "I Love You, Lord" with all her heart. When she got to the lines, "...to worship You. Oh, my soul rejoice!" she closed her eyes and lifted her right arm up toward heaven. How far she had come to be able to stand, sing, and lift her hand in praise to Him!

As spring break approached, we made reservations for a trip to Rome, Italy. Morale dropped on the air base when an Operations Readiness Inspection (ORI) was scheduled during spring break. Gary would not be able to go on the Italy tour. We offered his seat to our good friend, Bonnie, a single schoolteacher in the US Army Frankfurt School. She had spring break off and was more than willing to travel with us. The tour bus was a double-decker with a flat front. When we got on the bus together, immediately we moved up the steps to the front upper deck. Ann Marie, Bonnie, and I had the best time sitting high above the cars in the seats in front of the huge glass window, looking down on the world as we traveled the German autobahn, the mountain passes of Switzerland, and into the countryside of Italy.

Our first stop was Florence, where we saw the Statue of David, and Ponte Vechio. Time in Florence was very limited as we continued to head south toward Rome. Once we reached the streets of Rome, the traffic was atrocious. Cars honking and traffic jams at every intersection. As we were driving in Rome, the bus had a minor accident with a car.

We were going through an intersection with a stoplight, when a car waiting at the red light rolled into the back wheel of the bus. Bonnie was in the bus toilet when we had the accident. Good thing the toilet was on the other side of the bus or she would have been sitting on the car! We laughed so hard thinking about her flying out of the restroom door; every time we looked at each other we started giggling.

The three of us had to share a hotel room in Rome for several days, but most of the time was sightseeing with the tour guide. From early morning wake up at 5:30 a.m. until midnight, our schedule was full of the romance of Italy. I only regretted that Gary was unable to experience the fun and food with us.

No trip to Rome would be complete without a visit to Vatican Square and St. Peter's Basilica where the bones of the Apostle Peter rest under the chancel area next to the Pieta. We marveled at the Michelangelo paintings on the ceiling of the Sistine Chapel. We walked around the Coliseum where once Christians were fed to the lions. We toured the Pantheon known for the worship of Greek gods. We heard lectures about Roman history at the Forum. Several times a day we traveled up and down the Appian Way. Ann Marie threw a coin backwards over her shoulder into the Trivi Fountain, wishing to return to Rome someday. However, the most remarkable part of the Rome tour was to the underground Catacombs. The vision of secret meetings of early Christians using the sign of the fish, and burying their dead in hollowed out graves in the narrow rock walkways was sobering.

We sampled the best Italian food, too. Ann Marie gained some pounds on that trip eating pizza, lasagna, and spaghetti. Our last night in Rome, we went to a very special restaurant named "Quo Vadis." Legend stated the restaurant was built on the site where the Apostle Peter was confronted with a vision of the Risen Lord. As the story goes, Peter was traveling the Appian Way to exit Rome and escape persecution and probable death. At this particular spot, Peter met the vision of Lord Jesus coming down the road entering Rome.

Peter stopped and asked Jesus, "Quo Vadis?" Meaning, "Where are you going?"

Jesus replied that He was going to Rome to be crucified in Peter's place. Peter, realizing he was not to leave Rome, turned back and was later arrested and crucified upside down.

One of the most beautiful days, we went to the Isle of Capri. The boat ride took almost two hours to reach the island shore, where turquoise-blue water deceived the depth of the ocean bottom. Tropical flowers and waterfalls caressed the sides of the steep white cliffs as they dropped off into the harbor of fishing boats. Lunch was pizza at an outside cafe looking at the quaint village shops winding down the hillside. Taking a hydrofoil from Capri, we arrived back to the mainland of Sorrento, Italy, in ten minutes, where we shopped for leather, cameos, and wood inlaid music boxes.

From there our bus wound through the rough terrain roads reaching the ancient ruins of Pompeii destroyed in AD 79, when the volcano of Mt. Vesuvius erupted. Our tour guide pointed out the excavation of the remains of Pompeii. Obviously, Pompeii had been a decadent society of orgies worshipping Roman gods. On the parking lot, Ann Marie reached down and picked up a little white tile from the ground. It looked like a small moonstone from ancient times. Carefully she put it in her coat pocket for her shadow box collection.

In August 1990, orders came for a move to Ramstein AB. We had a month to return to the U.S. and see our family before the move. There was one more thing to do before we left Rhein Main. Once every ten years, the town of Oberammergau, Germany, performs the world famous "Passion Play" during the summer months. Dating back to 1633, it has grown to attract thousands of visitors to see the stage performance. We purchased tickets a year in advance for July 8, 1990. It was a special eleventh birthday gift for Ann Marie. The next opportunity would not be until the year 2000 when Ann would be twenty-one years old. The play was in German, but we knew the story. The townspeople playing the parts did it magnificently. During the lunch intermission, we shopped at the craft shops known for fine religious woodcarvings, purchasing a few souvenirs. Ann Marie chose a woodcarving of a man's hand holding a small kneeling child.

I said, "Ann Marie, when you look at this carving, remember that from the time you were born, you have always been in the palm of God's hand. Nothing can ever touch you without first going through His fingers of love."

Chapter Sixteen

Romanian Rhapsody

When a stranger resides with you in your land,
you shall not do him wrong.
The stranger who resides with you
shall be to you as the native among you,
and you shall love him as yourself,
for you were aliens in the land of Egypt:
I am the LORD your God.
Leviticus 19:33-34 (NAS)

The pounding of the shuttle in our LORD's hand as He worked skillfully weaving the tapestry threads into our lives, thumped in our hearts. The tempo of the beat was increasing with excited expectation clearly revealing the picture of His purpose. A Romanian Rhapsody played to the rhythm, as if the song had always been in our souls ready to burst forth at the exact planned moment in time. His Holy Spirit drew us close and then spun the yarn so brilliant and colorful, that we gasped at a swirling glimpse of Eternity.

Reaching back to the young couple we had mentored in Alabama, Steve and Billie Tomberlin, God drew the connecting thread through the weaving frame and tied it to Steve's brother, Jim Tomberlin. Remembering prayers for Jim during the death of his first wife and new marriage to Deryl, we never imagined that Jim would become our pastor in Kaiserslautern, West Germany. One evening, when Jim was passing through the Frankfurt Airport, Race Lariscy had brought Jim to our apartment for dinner at Rhein Main Air Base. Immediately we bonded in our friendship with Jim, as he realized we were the couple who had mentored and become close friends with his brother and sister-in-law in Montgomery, Alabama.

When we received orders in the summer of 1990, to move 85 miles southwest to Ramstein Air Base, we knew God had led us to our next church home and place of service. Ramstein Air Base was part of the Kaiserslautern military community. USAFE was Command Headquarters for units stretching from Great Britain to Turkey. This 17th Air Force Base was also a NATO installation and Headquarters Allied Air Forces Central Europe. It was the home of two tactical fighter squadrons, the "Black Knights" and "Dragons." The 377th Combat Support Wing provided administrative and logistical support for all operations. Across the autobahn, three miles away was the US Army Second General Hospital in Landstuhl.[1]

Before making the move to Ramstein, we scheduled a trip back to the States. During those few weeks back in St. Louis, we experienced the death of my grandfather. Pop had been steadily weakening with Alzheimer's disease. It was as if he was waiting to see us one more time before giving way to this earthly life. We went to see him in the nursing home immediately upon our arrival. He was lying in a fetal position asleep, looking very disheveled, considering how clean-shaven and sharp he had appeared as a pastor in the pulpit. When we spoke to him, he awoke and looked dazed at us, but seemed to recognize Ann Marie. He smiled and then fell back asleep. Within the week, he slipped into a coma and stepped out into his eternal home with his Lord.

It was a difficult farewell for my family when we boarded the plane back to Germany. Nevertheless, we were looking forward to our new home. Gary's position as the Chief of Civil Law for all of United States Air Forces Europe did not require us to live on the air base. We had spent several months searching for an off-base home, and decided on a single-family home about ten minutes north of Ramstein in the town of Miesenbach. The two-story home was on a gravel drive surrounded with farmland and a view of six neighboring villages.

In August 1990, we found ourselves sitting in a church pew at Faith Baptist Church, spellbound by the testimony of two Romanians, Peter Vidu and Dinu Bulzesc. In April 1990, months after the Berlin Wall had fallen and Eastern Europe had collapsed, Pastor Jim Tomberlin and

Jerry Chambers, Minister of Music, had gone into western Romania and established a sister-church relationship with Second Baptist Church of Oradea, Romania. Peter Vidu, pastor of Second Baptist Church, and Dinu Bulzesc, professor of chemical engineering at the University of Timisoara, came to Faith Baptist Church in West Germany to encourage our Romanian partnership. This was the first trip for these two Romanians beyond the Iron Curtain into the freedom of Western Europe.

We were amazed to hear them speak English so well. Dinu had taken an English Bible, and by comparing the words with a Romanian Bible, he had learned the English language. We were all grateful that he had not learned the King James Version.

As Gary and I sat hearing the solemn testimonies of unwavering faith through torture, persecution, and threat of death, the reality of the fellowship of suffering gripped our hearts. Peter and Dinu spoke about how God had allowed the "communist experiment," so all the world would know that turning away from God and toward the philosophy of man is a failure and not a true way of life. As they spoke about the history of Romania, they explained Roman Christians, who were persecuted and exiled from Rome after Christ's death, founded their country. During the Romanian Revolution in December 1989, the communist Red Star was ripped out of the Romanian flag and a hole was left there. Peter and Dinu said the hole in Romania's heart needed to be filled with Jesus Christ. The Holy Spirit knit our souls to these Romanians that evening as a treasured gift of friendship in the love of Christ. We would never see mission work the same way again.

Major Steve Kahne, chair of the Romanian mission committee, had encouraged anyone interested in the Romanian mission to get in on what God was doing in Eastern Europe. We signed up that night to be on the Romanian mission committee. Gary had the task of "prayer and planning." We began praying as if there was no planning, and planning as if there was no praying.

Two sisters in our church, Carolyn and Kathy McCoy, gave testimony about adopting a Romanian boy named Luke. Kathy McCoy was an Army captain assigned to the Exceptional Family Member Department (EFMD) to provide physical therapy services to military children at Ramstein Grade School. Another couple, Steve and Sue

Strait, also were adopting a little girl named Valerie. Sue Strait was the civilian occupational therapist assigned to the grade school. Both of the Romanian children were from horrible conditions in Romanian orphanages, where many of the children received injections of AIDS tainted blood or hepatitis. They were malnourished and desperately developmentally delayed.

The Lord began weaving another thread of connection into our lives with these two therapists. Ann Marie would soon become one of their hardest working patients. Three days a week after school, Kathy and Sue would take Ann Marie through exercises, motor skill drills, and challenges to develop greater strength and coordination. On Sundays, Carolyn McCoy would teach Ann Marie and the other young girls about missions in the Girls in Action (GA) class at church.

One Wednesday night at a church dinner, we sat with Steve and Sue Strait and their dark-eyed Romanian daughter, Valerie. Quietly and carefully, Valerie nibbled at her hot dog as she listened to our conversation. Suddenly, she turned to her new mother Sue, and with tears in her eyes, Valerie indicated that she desperately needed to use the restroom. Her fear was leaving part of her hot dog uneaten on her plate. In the Romanian orphanage, she had not had so much delicious food, but it would have disappeared if she left any on her plate. Sue Strait explained to her that her hot dog would be exactly where she left it upon her return to the table. Of course, to her delight it was still there untouched when she returned, able to finish her meal. The blessing she must have felt to be out of the stark bitterness of life in the orphanage was overwhelming for her and for us to understand.

High on a hill, the beautiful German home we rented in the village of Miesenbach sat surrounded by wheat fields. A gravel road led to a goat pen and into the forest with a game reserve for deer. The three-story single family home had five bedrooms and two bathrooms. Two large bedrooms and a bathroom were in the basement, with the laundry room and a storage room in the unfinished section. Ann Marie picked one bedroom for her canopy bed and dressers, and the other room for her toys and computer.

A glass front door on the main floor, led to a bright breakfast room giving a view of the stone patio. Off of the breakfast room, was the small galley kitchen with a picture window overlooking the flower garden. The spacious combined formal living and dining room, with one wall of windows and a French doorway, opened onto the patio above a strawberry patch. A side hallway passed our large bathroom and master bedroom leading to a cozy family room where we watched television.

Climbing the stairs to a third floor finished attic, were two small bedrooms with slanted ceilings. The attic windows looked out over all of the village terraces and farmland for miles around. A skylight in the roof opened with a crank allowing fresh air into the stairway. From the open skylight, you could stick your head out of the top of the roof and look down on the quiet green slopes of the village cemetery across the country road. We made one attic bedroom into a guest room with two twin beds. The other room became my sewing room with a trundle bed for extra guests.

Gary decided that God did not bless us with five bedrooms in this new home and not expect us to use them regularly for special guests. On August 26, three weeks after moving into our home, Gary mentioned to the pastor that we had extra bedrooms, if the church needed a place for someone to stay. On August 29, Pastor Jim Tomberlin called and asked if the Ashworth family from New Zealand could stay with us for four days. Gary, who has a way of inviting international people to our home, was delighted to accommodate the Ashworths. We rushed around for three days finishing the unpacking and curtain hanging, getting all of the bedrooms ready for our guests.

All five of the Ashworths arrived Saturday night, September 1. Lloyd and Judy had three children: Elizabeth, age eleven; Emma, age nine; and David, age seven. Lloyd was to preach all three services on Sunday morning. The girls slept with Ann Marie in her queen-size canopy-bed downstairs. Lloyd and Judy were upstairs in the twin beds, and David had the other upstairs bedroom with a trundle bed and sewing machine.

We had quite a houseful sharing two bathrooms the next morning getting ready for Sunday church services. Since Lloyd and Judy had to use our bathroom on the main floor, Lloyd came down the attic steps and spoke to Gary in the breakfast room.

Gary, having some difficulty understanding Lloyd's New Zealand accent, thought that Lloyd had said, "May I share?"

Gary answered, "Yes!" thinking that Lloyd was about to give some fabulous testimony of his life.

Lloyd turned and walked off into the hallway toward our bathroom. Suddenly turning around and somewhat flustered Lloyd said to Gary, "Your wife is in the share!"

Gary realizing that Lloyd had really said, "May I shower?" answered, "Well, we don't share the shower!"

That morning during all three worship services, Lloyd told the whole congregation the funny story of sharing the shower.

The next day was Labor Day. Gary was off work, and we loaded up our van taking the Ashworths through the winding vineyard roads to Trier, the ancient Roman city on the Moselle River. Built over 2,000 years ago, Trier took us back to a time when the footsteps of the Gospel of Christ first reached into Germany's oldest city. The great Roman Gate of Porta Nigra revealed an enchanting city of Roman ruins and Christian cathedrals spreading out from the Market Cross of AD 958. The Caldarium captured our imagination of hot water baths, including The Imperial Thermae known to be one of the most spacious in the whole Roman Empire during the Fourth Century.

On the outskirts of the town, in the slope of the Petrisberg, three tiers of the Roman Amphitheatre built in AD 100 brought visions of gladiators and lions fighting to the death. At the foot of the Holy Cross Hill on the banks of the Moselle River, we visited the Basilica of St. Matthias. Built on the grounds of an ancient monastery, it stands on the site of the graves of Eucharius and Valerius, said to be the first Christian evangelists sent to Trier. The church was named after St. Matthias, whose tomb is reported to be in the nave of the church as the only grave of an apostle north of the Alps.[2]

The Ashworths were supposed to leave on Tuesday and go to the home of good friends who were just moving to Germany that week from England. When we visited the friends, who had arrived in country on Sunday, they had nothing in their new house. They would not even get a bed for another week! We invited the Ashworths to stay with us until September 10. The girls got along great, except that school had started for Ann Marie. Elizabeth and Emma would get up each morning and walk with Ann Marie to the school bus, and be waiting for her when she got off the bus in the afternoon. We had a great time getting to know the Ashworths during those ten days, in a friendship, which continued through the years in some unexpected partnerships.

Ramstein Elementary was the largest school in the Department of Defense outside the continental United States, serving more than twenty-one hundred children in grades K-6. Ramstein Elementary had two big buildings and several portable units just for the fifth and sixth grades. There were twenty-eight kids in Ann's class, and eleven fifth grade classes in the school. Ramstein was one of three elementary schools in the Kaiserslautern community.

The Friday before school started, Ann Marie and I went to find her classroom, so she would not get lost in the huge complex of buildings that sprawled across New York Avenue and up a steep hill. When we peeked into the open door of Ann's classroom, the teacher was in the room. We introduced ourselves and had a good visit with Mrs. Thelma Mease. She specialized in children with Individual Educational Programs (IEP), and she listened as I spoke of Ann Marie's history and special needs. She was ready for Ann Marie on the first day of school, and continued to nurture and love Ann throughout the school year.

The school bus situation was a different matter for Ann Marie. The first day of school the bus was late coming in the morning. It took off down the road before Ann could sit down and threw her backwards in the aisle. Then it was late coming home and when Ann got off, she was in tears. She said the bus had changed colors, which it had. It was a red and white bus when it picked her up and blue and white coming home. Mrs. Mease had helped Ann to find the bus. At first, they could not find the right bus out of so many buses. Thelma was running around in her high heels with Ann Marie trying to keep up, and Ann was afraid the bus would leave her. Just before the buses left, they found the right one. The next morning, Ann got on the bus and immediately sat in the front seat. Because she was the last stop before school, almost all the seats were taken. Eventually, I drove Ann to school and picked her up more than she rode the bus. It gave us time together to pray on the way to school.

219

Ann Marie had made a new friend before school started during a JAG office picnic. Allison Jackson was also in fifth grade at Ramstein, and her dad was in Gary's office. Allison had some health issues with asthma, so both of the girls tried to help each other in gym class. Ann Marie was so glad to meet someone to replace her friendships she had left at Rhein Main. Josh, a boy at church, was also in Ann's fifth grade class, and was friendly to Ann. When he found out about her open-heart surgery and stroke, he said he would look out for her at school. During the first week of school, Ann was the girl's line leader, and Josh was the boy's line leader. Ann came home giggling because Josh had reached over and put his baseball cap on her head when they were leaving the library. Josh was a very nice boy, and his parents were strong Christian leaders in our church.

Faith Baptist Church had a women's ministry called Renewal. Deryl Tomberlin had started the ministry with a few women. It had grown to over one-hundred women studying the Bible on Thursday mornings in small groups at church. Volunteers set up a children's ministry for the pre-school children during the same time called Kingdom Kids, and it had grown to over fifty children. Attending the Bible study, I began to know the women in the church. A few weeks into the study, I was asked to substitute teach for my leader, and sing a solo during the gathering time before we broke up into our study groups. After the choir director's wife heard me sing, I became a regular soloist at church. The next semester I taught the Precept course, *Lord, I Want to Know You!* I loved teaching Precept Bible studies to the women, and they enjoyed learning how to study the Bible with the Inductive Bible Study method. God was continuing to develop my teaching gifts to women, and deepen my faith in His Word.

The fall of the Berlin Wall had brought many changes to our military mission. Our reason for being a NATO force against communism was fading as the European borders opened to freedom. During the Cold War, a troop train had run regularly between Frankfurt and Berlin carrying military troops and families through the East German communist countryside to and from their West Berlin assignment. Less than a year after the Berlin Wall had fallen, there was hardly a trace of the horrible scar, which had once separated a nation. Citizens from the East and West freely traveled throughout the European countries. There was no need for the troop train, and the decision to stop the transportation ended the Cold War Era. Friday, September 28, 1990, we booked a VIP cabin for one of the last trips running the long rail system. Gary and I had a bedroom suite with a private bathroom on the train. Ann Marie was bunking in an adjoining suite with a couple of young girls. We traveled all night on the special train arriving the next morning at the Berlin *Bahnhof* train station.

Ron, the Air Force SJA for Berlin, met us at the train station. He was a single guy, who was more than helpful in hosting us around the New Berlin. Things had certainly changed from our trip the year before. Now the West Berliners were rude to Americans. Without a need for our occupation of West Berlin, they were ready for the troops to leave. As we traveled into former Soviet East Berlin, the people were gracious and thankful for our American part in the fall of communism.

We went to where Checkpoint Charlie had been. The spot where we had written on The Wall the year before was completely gone. People were traveling back and forth with no restrictions. The Soviet Checkpoint had been completely gutted and vandalized. Windows were broken and wiring pulled loose. Checkpoint Charlie was moved out of the area, and given to the German government as a museum.

At the Brandenburg Gate, tables of souvenirs lined the walkway. Soviet soldiers had laid down their uniforms, asking for asylum so they did not have to go back to Russia. We were able to purchase some Soviet hats and medals. Ann Marie bought a blue Soviet Navy barrette with a Russian pin. Gary purchased two military hats, one Soviet Army and the other an East German headdress. There would never be an East German Army under Soviet influence again. East German Deutsch Marks were obsolete, and there was talk of a new European currency called the Euro Dollar.

Wanting a piece of The Wall, Ron drove to the area of Potsdam where a section was still standing. Ron had brought spray paint and helped Ann Marie spray her name on the concrete slab. We took a few whacks with a hammer at the remains, collecting some small samples. Then Ron took a picture of the three of us stepping through a hole in a section of The Wall. Ann Marie held up two fingers in the "V" for victory sign. It made a great photo for our Christmas cards that year and a reminder of how different the world had become with the spread of freedom.

The next morning, we visited the most famous landmark in West Berlin, the Emperor Wilhelm Memorial Church dedicated in 1895. The bombed out tower of the church was left as a reminder of the devastation of WW II. Two things became clear in the Memorial Hall of the Old Tower at the destroyed church: this site is both an admonition against war and destruction, and a call to reconciliation in Jesus Christ. Sixteen large photos of the church and the city destroyed in the bombing attack during the night of November 22, 1943, reflect the suffering people in that terrible period. At the end of the series of pictures, the figure of Christ stands with the quotation:

We beseech you on behalf of Christ, be reconciled to God.
II Corinthians 6:20

On the opposite side of the Hall, a stone plaque petitions:

Forgive us our sins, for we ourselves forgive
everyone who sins against us.

The most amazing part of the church was the cross of nails next to the statue of Christ. The nails came from the English Coventry Cathedral, consumed by fire when the church was reduced to ashes by a German bombing attack on November 14, 1940. The Coventry congregation erected a cross, made of charred roof beams on the altar of the destroyed church. Behind the altar are scratched the words:

Father, forgive.

223

Using the nails collected from the ashes, the cross of nails was brought from England to the Memorial Hall in West Berlin on January 7, 1987. Today the cross of nails has become a symbol of worldwide efforts at reconciliation begun by two churches reaching across years of hatred, and painful suffering to offer forgiveness and healing.[3]

The hope of reconciliation offered by the Emperor Wilhelm Memorial Church was a sharp contrast to our afternoon tour of the East Berlin Pergamum Museum. In the early 1900s, German archeologists had excavated several historical artifacts. Adolph Hitler, in his obsession with collecting such antiquities, had huge monuments moved and reassembled in this Berlin museum. The name of the museum comes from the altar in the Temple of Pergamum originally built in Turkey between 180-160 B.C. In the Book of Revelation, this altar is referred to as the "seat of Satan." Hitler had moved the "seat of Satan" to Berlin in the early 1930s foretelling world events. A section of the wall of Babylon, and the Gate of Ishtar from Iraq, which Nebuchadnezzar built from 605-562 B.C., are also on display in the museum. Oppression swirled around the demonic symbols of Hitler's legacy to Europe. Physical freedom had not brought spiritual freedom to this part of East Berlin. Spiritual bondage and cultural decadence were replacing a hole in The Wall.

A ray of spiritual revival shone through an open door in western Romania. Our Romanian committee had been working very hard to supply necessities to the pastors of Second Baptist Church in Oradea, Romania. A supply truck headed through Austria, Hungary, and into Romania on October 31, 1990. Our committee chair, Steve Kahne, drove a van to escort the supply truck, while those of us in Germany prayed for Operation Raven. When he returned from the trip, Steve told us about some of the things that happened while in Romania. Arriving at the Austrian border, it was closed to all truck traffic because October 31 was All Saints Day! He made plans to meet the truck in Romania the next day at 6:00 p.m. Steve said the plan was full of holes, especially because they forgot, crossing into Romania they would lose an hour. They needed to be headed back home by 6:00 p.m. the next day. The truck waited at the border and went through early, before midnight, along with hundreds of other trucks backed up at the border. Steve, traveling on ahead in a van, decided to go to the church about 4:00 p.m. for some picture taking with the Romanian pastor. Steve began to cry as he told us that when they drove up to the church, the truck pulled up two hours early! They were able to unload the truck and start back home right on schedule.

During the time Steve was waiting, he went shopping in Romania with the pastor, Peter Vidu, but there was nothing to buy. One fabric store had seven bolts of fabric. The bread in the bakery was molded and hard. A dress store had racks full of the same dress and the fabric felt like paper. The pastor's wife Geta said that if you washed a dress once it would fall apart. Cans of vegetables had blown the lids with botulism, and the coffee was rancid. Geta worked half a day to buy a pound of butter. She worked two weeks to earn enough money to take public transportation for one month. Peter's total salary went to pay for their heat and telephone bill.

It was a time when the Western church needed to minister physically and spiritually to our Christian brothers and sisters in Romania. There were some churches in the U.S. offering to help by sending money or people. Steve told of one doctor from Colorado who was organizing a group of doctors to go into Romania. The problem was the burden on the Romanian people to feed and house the missionaries. In Oradea, there was no meat in the city. Under the dictator, Nicolae Ceausescu, farmland was sprayed with dangerous chemicals so they could not safely grow produce for several years. The orphanages were full of children given up by parents who could not feed them. Steve said it gave the word *suffering* a new meaning. Many pastors suffered in prison under the Communist regime. After such oppression by the secret police, it was difficult to trust neighbors.

With Europe experiencing the new freedom to travel across open borders, one night brought strangers to our door. Faith Baptist Church had a ministry called "dinners for six." Our first dinner, we had two couples come to our home. Just after dessert, there was a knock at our front door. Gary answered it. Standing on our doorstep in the cold and dark was an old woman and middle-aged man. They had been trying to find someone home across the road from us, but they were not speaking German! Gary finally began, through sign language, to understand their problem. He invited them in out of the cold. The man could speak some English. They had driven two days from Poland to find the people across the road not home! They were so cold and tired. The old woman had the phone number of a person in the next village of Landstuhl. We called the phone number, and fortunately those people were home and could speak English. They said they would be at our home in thirty minutes to pick up the Polish strangers.

I insisted that the man and old woman come into the dining room and sit down after they used our restroom. I offered them some leftover soup from dinner, but they said "No." I made them a cup of tea and served them some dessert. They did not want to inconvenience our company or us, but it was too cold to wait outdoors.

They sat at our table with our church friends as we tried to understand their situation. The man said that he had worked two years in Chicago and learned some English, but it must have been years before since he did not understand much of what we were asking him. When the Landstuhl man arrived in thirty minutes, he explained that the old woman had been a "nanny" for his wife and for her brother, the man who lived across the road from us, when they were small children. The middle-aged man was her son, born in Landstuhl. In 1945, she and her son were sent to Poland after the war as refugees. For two years the family had been working on papers for them to come to Germany, and now they had made the trip. The neighbors across the road had gone out of town, because they had not expected the visitors for one or two days. To think of all the years of separation between these two families, and finally they were free to be together again, made us sober at how many other relationships had suffered from the Cold War. When the strangers left our home, the man took my hand, kissed it, and thanked us so much for helping them. Maybe they were really angels!

Other world events where beginning to replace the end of the Cold War. In August 1990, the Iraqi dictator Saddam Hussein invaded Kuwait, a small country south of the Iraq border, and annexed it. President George Bush and the United Nations had drawn a line in the desert sand. Saddam was given a time limit to remove his military by January 15, or the U.S. and a coalition of U.N. troops would remove the Iraqi military.

During the months leading up to the deadline, several of our friends at Rhein Main and Ramstein deployed to Saudi Arabia as a troop build-up in the event an attack was necessary. Our Rhein Main neighbor, Col. Dale Oderman went to Saudi. The security around all of our German military installations tightened. By Christmas 1990, Operation Desert Shield had an APO address in Saudi for cards and letters, and a war to liberate Kuwait was on the horizon.

At the January 9, 1991, Officers' Wives Club luncheon, General Oaks addressed the wives seated in the grand ballroom of the O-Club on Ramstein Air Base. The scenario of events he projected gave us indigestion, as we squirmed in our over-stuffed chairs. His estimate of the number of casualties, if we met the enemy in the desert, stunned our senses. Thousands of wounded would be evacuated to Landstuhl Army Hospital and other field hospitals all over Europe. Preparation had been made with medical equipment and hospital beds waiting for casualties evacuated out of the Gulf.

Each of us knew someone or had a loved one already poised in Saudi for the conflict. The Deputy SJA's wife was sitting across the table from me. Her face went white with the information, since her husband was to report to an undisclosed location within a few days. Another JAG wife had been without her husband since November when he went to Saudi for at least six months. Those whose spouses were still in Germany had felt the tension building at the military installations. Fighter pilots were flying more sorties and special ops missions as the time grew closer to the deadline. Then Gen. Oaks asked us, as officers' wives, to volunteer to supply food, shelter, money, clothing, and medical services to service members! An added sacrifice would be preparing extra guest rooms in our homes for the expected relatives coming from the U.S. to visit their wounded sons, daughters, and spouses.

Gen. Oaks told of some of the torture of Kuwaiti citizens, especially those helping Westerners. Saddam had to be stopped in Kuwait, or he would move into Saudi Arabia and strangle the world's oil supply. For the countries of Eastern Europe, just coming out of economic deprivation and into freedom, it would have meant their death. The freedom of more than Kuwait was ultimately at stake if Saddam went unchecked. Our hopes and prayers were that the preparation of our service members would be enough to stop Saddam, and no shot would be fired.

With the threat of terrorist action on U.S. military installations, there was talk of closing base schools, the HQ building, and not having church, in order to protect us from gathering in large groups of Americans. Many of the children were having dangerous psychological reactions to one or both parents being sent to war. Spouses had to cope with living in a foreign country to raise children, while husbands and wives went off to war. For many the stress was so devastating that they returned to the United States. It was a very grim picture of events.

The following week would be the deadline for Operation Desert Shield to become Operation Desert Storm. It was also the week of the fifth grade ski trip to Austria. Gary and I had volunteered to go as chaperones for the weeklong trip, but Gary was not able to take leave with the January 15 deadline during the ski week. Most of the male chaperones had to cancel coming on the trip, but we did manage to bring a couple of fathers to keep an eye on the boys. Several moms, teachers, fifth graders, and a few dads headed to Austria on tour buses wondering what the world would be like when we returned home.

Ann Marie had improved her skiing during our family Christmas vacation to Zur Post for a week. She won a silver medal in the ski races and was ready to keep up with most of the kids in her class. The fifth grade ski trip was exhausting for me as a chaperone. I was constantly helping fifth graders adjust their ski boots, strap their skis on, picking kids up out of snow banks, and making sure they got where they needed to be without being left behind. We slept in a hotel reserved for the whole group. The food was horrible, and the kids complained and would not eat. The ski instructor for Ann Marie's group was a mess. He was a young punk who seemed to be drunk most of the day. He would yell at the kids and leave them lying in the snow if they fell down. The whole experience was a setback for Ann in skiing technique. We did bond with the five girls I chaperoned. One afternoon, we decided to ski without the abusive instructor, stop for some hot chocolate, and take time to visit the ice sculpture contest in the market place.

On the morning of January 17, 1991, I woke up in the small Austrian hotel room to the sound of my transistor radio crackling the news that coalition fighter jets had bombed Baghdad at 3:00 a.m. Immediately, I dressed and rushed out of the room into the hallway. Everyone seemed asleep. I went down the stairs. There I ran into two of the male chaperones. I told them the news. They excitedly ran up the steps to call back to their military stations. Coming back up the steps, I met Mrs. Mease and told her. Being a Christian woman, she began to pray right there in the hallway. I went back into the bedroom, fell to my knees, and began praying for our service members, families, nation, President, and for victory in Desert Storm. It seemed that one of the safest places we could be was right there in a little ski village in Austria, but our families where feeling the shock waves of separation in a time of war.

Arriving back at Ramstein, military personnel had gone into high alert. Gary spent much of his day in the headquarters bunker as some of the war effort was directed from Germany. We watched CNN news daily. High-tech equipment with night-vision systems and precision-guided weapons, launched from U.S. warships in the gulf or allied aircraft, took out biological, chemical, and nuclear weapons facilities in Iraq.[4] My dad was delighted to see aircraft and equipment, that he had spent his lifetime designing, working to win the war. Air strike pictures from aircraft cameras followed targeted buildings through crosshairs dead centered on hanger doors and roof vents until the impact took the buildings out.

On February 24, a major ground attack by coalition forces, including U.S. Army troops stationed in Germany, launched into Iraq and Kuwait. The television broadcast pictures of thousands of Iraqi soldiers laying down their weapons and surrendering in tears to coalition troops. Hussein ordered his troops out of Kuwait, and the 100-hour ground attack ended on February 28, 1991.

Although thousands of civilians in Iraq and Kuwait probably died in the Persian Gulf War of 1991, only about 370 coalition troops died. Even though a cease-fire agreement was formally accepted on April 6 by Iraq, Hussein failed to fulfill the terms of the agreement. Because Saddam Hussein continued to rule in Iraq, the U.S. and coalition members would have to establish aircraft patrols of a Northern "no-fly zone," make weapons inspections, and enforce trade embargoes with Iraq for several years to come.[5]

During the Gulf War, other events seemed to dictate our personal lives. Ann Marie qualified to receive services from the Exceptional Family Member Department at Landstuhl Army Hospital. Her first appointment with Dr. Butler was the week after the fifth grade ski trip. Dr. Butler was very concerned about Ann Marie's ability to integrate socially with her peers, especially when Ann's teacher reported that some of the kids in the class were the meanest she had experienced in seventeen years of teaching. We went through several months of appointments and counseling to help develop a plan for Ann Marie's sustained educational and physical needs at school and at home.

Romania continued to be on our hearts during the cold winter months of 1991. A chance for Gary to experience the Romanian Rhapsody first hand came on February 14. The medical supply mission had come together with doctors from Colorado flying into Vienna, Austria. Dr. Bill and Harriet Bathman from "In Touch Mission International" were flying into Frankfurt, Germany. Our mission was to pick up a supply truck to carry the medical equipment, some office supplies, and a new windshield for the Romanian church van. The supply truck needed a couple of drivers to escort the Bathman's van to Vienna to pick up the doctors and then into Romania. It was a window of opportunity our church could not pass up to help our sister church in Oradea. Gary crawled out of the Ramstein war bunker long enough to make the twenty-hour drive in the truck, unload the supplies in Romania and head back to Germany three hours later.

Vance Clarke accompanied Gary and a German man, whose church loaned the use of the green seven-ton cargo truck. Alternating drivers, they carefully drove through the night following Bill and Harriet's van in a blinding snowstorm to Vienna. After loading the doctors and medical supplies, they traveled on to the Romanian border where they met Pastor Peter Vidu and several of the church deacons driving the church van minus a windshield. The cold February wind sucked through the open windshield of the church van driving down the road to the church. Immediately, church members who helped to unload the supplies surrounded the truck. The windshield was unloaded from the truck and installed into a gapping hole of the church van's front window within three hours.

One smiling teenager came to help and spoke perfect English. Gary was wondering where this American kid had come from in Romania. Talking to the fifteen-year old in English, Gary discovered that Adonis was the son of Peter and Geta Vidu. He had learned English in school, and was reading *Mere Christianity* in English! He also loved the Chicago Bulls basketball team.

Dr. Nicolae Gheorghita, a Romanian endocrinologist and pastor, had started a Christian clinic in Oradea to supply outpatient services and prescription drugs to the church members. The doctors from Colorado stayed in Romania for a few more days to perform much needed minor surgery on several of those who could not afford medical care. By donating their services, the doctors were able to correct some conditions, which could have become life threatening if left untreated.

For Gary, the time in Romania was only a few hours before returning to Germany, but it had the most dramatic effect on him. Every time Gary started to tell me about the people he met in Romania, he started to weep. The dirty smoke-filled sky choked out the few hours of winter sunlight. Electrical power was at such a shortage that homes were heated only every other day. On the opposite days, when there was not heat, running water pumped into homes. A water supply kept in bathtubs was used to wash dishes and flush toilets, but warm clothing and blankets were the only source of heat for some. Gary saw people truly deprived of the most basic needs, but their tested faith resulted in a spirit of hope and joy. They were so thankful for the sister-church relationship with their Christian friends in Germany.

Back in Germany, I had discovered another breast lump. I was particularly depressed because it seemed to be at one of the spots where Dr. Brown had removed the last three lumps. I called the prayer chain for prayer, and Pastor Jim Tomberlin immediately called me. His concern was prompted by losing his first wife to breast cancer. He urged me to get it looked at immediately. I went to the Ramstein Clinic for an examination. The doctor referred me to the Wiesbaden Surgical Clinic where I saw Dr. Brown again. However, because of the Gulf War, dependent surgeries that were not an emergency would have to be performed in a German hospital or put on hold. Dr. Brown suspected the lump might be scar tissue from the previous surgery, and suggested I return in three months. I did not want to go to a German hospital for surgery, so I waited.

The Gulf War had brought our church members closer together in prayer and ministry. During Wednesday night prayer meeting, we continually lifted up those in our congregation who were on the battlefront or flying missions over Kuwait and Iraq. We were thankful for fewer casualties than expected and the quick victory. Our women's Renewal ministry was especially attentive to those women who were raising kids while dads were gone to war. Stories about new believers baptized in empty coffins in the Saudi desert gave fresh meaning to "buried with Christ, raised to newness of life."

One of the fighter pilots, upon returning from the Gulf War, gave testimony about the peace he had through our prayers. Even though he was flying above the war zone and realizing that the red lights flying up at him were anti-aircraft fire, he sensed God's protection in the battle. The military were back home by mid-March.

Calling upon our gift of hospitality, Jim Tomberlin asked if we would host Gerald Robison, who would be teaching the "Walk Through the Bible—Old Testament Seminar" at church March 1-4. Gerald was a pastor at Trinity Baptist Church in the Netherlands. We opened our upstairs bedroom to Gerald, and God wove another thread of the tapestry into our lives. Gerald's humorous and excellent gift of teaching God's Word held the entire congregation spellbound over the days he taught us the entire Old Testament outline with key words and hand motions.

Later that month we received a newsletter from our New Zealand friend Lloyd Ashworth about their family's arrival back home and a new mission's position he had accepted. Lloyd wrote:

> *Last night I had a brainwave...I'm going into the Tee shirt business and the first off the rack is going to say... "NO MATE, I'M NOT AN AUSTRALIAN!" I don't know how many times I denied being Aussie, while traveling through Europe. Even when I'd say, "close...try a bit more East," most would look blank.*

Lloyd's letter continued to tell of his acceptance of a new position in February 1991, as the New Zealand Executive Director of International Needs Network, a mission organization that does not send missionaries. Lloyd put it this way: a ministry "on the cutting edge of missiology, i.e., the training and releasing of national believers, to minister in their own countries and culture." We were glad to hear that he had landed on his feet after traveling for months before arriving home. Not thinking much more about International Needs, we continued in mission ministry at our church. Another thread was in the Hand of God for our future, but it would have to wait a few more years before He neatly wove the rest of the story of International Needs.

Faith Baptist Church had an outstanding fifty-member choir and choir director, Jerry Chambers. One of the highlights of being in choir was the fellowship among the choir members and Jerry. He was able to get the most out of us, because he expected it from us; but he also made choir a time of worship and fun. Throughout the year, Jerry would challenge us with new praise music and special concerts. From Christmas to Easter, we would work on memorizing all of the music and drama for an Easter Passion Play presented to the German community. After months of rehearsals, making scenery and costumes, our Easter musical drama, *I AM*, opened on Thursday, March 28, 1991, to a packed house. The community continued to fill the sanctuary for the Friday night performance, Saturday matinee, Saturday evening, and our final performance on Sunday, March 31.

Our Romanian committee chairman Steve Kahne played the part of Jesus. Steve was able to add much authenticity to the part, since he was born and raised a Jew, but had become "completed" as an adult believer in Christ. The costumed children had a brief stage entrance greeting Jesus with waving palm branches and singing "Hosanna! Loud Hosanna!" Ann Marie loved singing and waving her palm branch, dressed in her long costume robe.

Our large European Baptist church had contributed much to the German community during thirty years of gathering to worship and doing missions. With the fall of communism, many East Germans struggled with the western work ethic, and had become an economic burden on West Germany. The rudeness to Americans, which we had experienced in West Berlin, was progressing across all of West Germany. Strapped with financial and economic drain, the German government sent a tax bill to Faith Baptist Church for payment of all back taxes on church staff and employees for the last thirty years! The bill came to an estimated total of between 187,000-230,000 Deutsch Marks! In U.S. dollars, we needed to come up with about $100,000! If we did not pay the tax bill within thirty days of receiving it, the German government would send our pastor, church administrator, and financial secretary to jail! Jim Tomberlin asked Gary to help negotiate with the German attorney and tax investigators, because 95% of our congregation was U.S. military. Under the Status of Forces Agreement (SOFA) the U.S. military were tax-exempt in Germany. After several months of negotiations and letter writing to congressional representatives, senators, the U.S. Embassy, the German Baptist Union, and the European Baptist Convention; through political intervention the tax bill was reduced to $10,000. Members of the congregation sacrificially gave enough to cover the bill. The crisis was averted with the result of an even closer fellowship of suffering among us, and a witness of our faith to the tax investigators and German attorney.

Although Desert Storm was over, another situation had developed in Iraq which required further deployment of our USAFE troops. A Kurdish revolt against the Iraqi government failed, and about 1.5 million refugees fled to the mountains along the border with Turkey and Iran. The Kurdish population attempted to escape to the north into Turkey. They feared that Saddam Hussein would exterminate their entire population. Turkish officials refused to allow these desperate Kurds permission to cross the border into Turkey because of political concerns. The situation left hundreds of thousands of Kurds trapped on barren and rocky hillsides, vulnerable to the harsh elements and Saddam Hussein's forces. Each week, without necessities of water, food, and medical supplies, hundreds of Kurds were dying.

President George Bush made the decision to provide relief and protection for the Kurdish people. In early April 1991, "Operation Provide Comfort" was born. Maj. Gen. James L. Jamerson, the USAFE Deputy Chief of Staff for Operations, commanded the effort. After British and French cargo aircraft arrived the next day, he designated the organization as a Combined Task Force. Because of U.S. military air bases like Incirlik Air Base, in southern Turkey, less than forty-eight hours after receiving the orders, cargo and fighter aircraft re-deployed and began delivering humanitarian supplies. The task force dropped its first supplies to Kurdish refugees on April 7. For the protection of the Kurds, a U.S. led coalition force deployed into northern Iraq. In a few weeks, resettlement areas were constructed and a de-militarized zone established. By the end of the operation, July 24, the task force had delivered over 17,000 tons of supplies. On July 24, 1991, "Provide Comfort II" began as a show of force to deter new Iraqi attacks on the Kurds. It had only limited humanitarian aspects to its mission. More American and European forces were called upon over the next several years to maintain the "no-fly zone" in Northern Iraq until Provide Comfort II ended December 31, 1996.[6]

In April, I met Deryl Tomberlin for a Women's Renewal Leadership meeting. She had asked me to come early to Jim's office before the other leaders arrived. I almost fell off the couch when she told me that the Tomberlins had decided to leave Germany in July and move back to the U.S. Jim had been called to pastor a church in Colorado. Then, Deryl asked me if I would become the Director for the women's Renewal ministry. I had been teaching one of the Precept Bible Studies on *Covenant*. Now she was asking me to direct all of the Bible studies and large group time, organize a major women's retreat, coordinate with the Kid's Korner ministry, and fill her rather large shoes. I was overwhelmed and honored she would consider me capable of continuing the ministry she had birthed and grown. I was grieved that

Jim and Deryl would be leaving. After praying for a few days, I called her with my "yes" answer, but needed her wisdom and guidance in the few precious weeks before her departure. The women were so attached to her as the director; it would be difficult to change leadership without her support and recommendations.

When Jim announced from the pulpit that he would be leaving, it was a very emotional Sunday for our church. We had just gone through a tough time with the Gulf War and the tax issue. Every year about a third of our congregation rotated back to the States and a new third replaced them. For five years, the stability had been the Tomberlins. The church had grown to over 1,000 in attendance on Sunday mornings and a building program had started. I was on the pastor search committee. However, who could ever replace Jim and Deryl?

Gerald Robison came back to Faith Baptist the end of April for "Walk Through the Bible—New Testament." This time he brought his lovely wife Sharon to stay at our home with him. Of course, I was thinking he would make a great new pastor for our church. Gerald and Sharon understood the lifestyle and culture of Europe. Gerald had experienced the opening of Eastern Europe for the gospel. Moving from Holland to Germany would be quick and inexpensive compared to bringing a pastor overseas from the U.S. Nevertheless, our search committee had a long way to go before the right man was selected as pastor. It was a long and painful process of waiting on the Lord to bring His man at the right time.

Back in St. Louis, Aunt Susan and Uncle Tom were on the mission committee for Central Presbyterian Church. Because of our involvement with the Romanian church, they had presented Central's mission committee with the possibility of a trip to Romania. The committee approved the mission and planning began for the trip to be late June through early July. Susan and Randy Mayfield helped to raise $11,000 in funds for the trip and humanitarian supplies by singing concerts in several American churches. Romanian Pastor Peter Vidu selected several Romanian churches for them to sing and minister in during their mission visit. Randy and Susan learned some of the worship music in the Romanian language. Tom would bring a "word of greeting" to the Romanian congregations from American Christian brothers and sisters. Faith Baptist worked to collect clothing, humanitarian, and non-perishable food, then loaded the seven-ton green truck to take on the Romanian trip. The mission committee purchased white-boards and several single beds for a new seminary building in Oradea.

> *What use is it, my brethren, if a man says he has faith, but he has no works? Can that faith save him? If a brother or sister is without clothing and in need of daily food, and one of you says to them, "Go in peace, be warmed and be filled," and yet you do not give them what is necessary for their body, what use is that? Even so faith, if it has no works, is dead, being by itself.* James 2:14-17 (NAS)

On June 17, 1991, Susan, Tom, Elizabeth, and David Werner arrived at Frankfurt Airport for their European adventure including a trip to Romania. They had received their required shots, including a painful hepatitis vaccination. The Werners needed time to recover from jet lag and make sure all the arrangements to go into Romania were complete. Susan sang for our Thursday evening women's Renewal meeting, and three Sunday morning worship services, which increased awareness and prayer support for the trip. Humanitarian supplies poured in from the community that weekend.

"In Touch Mission International" requested help to purchase a van for the Romanian Second Baptist Church. Vance Clarke and Gary scoured the Germany countryside looking for a good used 15-passenger diesel van for approximately $7,000. Able to secure the type of van they wanted; they were delighted it had a built-in microphone system as an added accessory. The upholstery on the seats was dirty and stained, but Gary, Ann Marie, and I had a fun time using our upholstery shampoo machine to brighten the seats. Gary got the van insured and licensed for two couples from "In Touch Mission" to drive into Romania. Then they would give the van to Peter Vidu's church.

The actual trip into Romania was June 26-30, after Randy Mayfield arrived on June 24. We took Randy out to eat the evening he arrived. The Werners had gone on a day trip in our Mercedes to see the castles on the Rhine River. Dinner was just the four of us: Randy Mayfield, Ann Marie, Gary and I at a nice Italian restaurant. Randy played the part of his favorite character—Elvis Presley, and flirted with Ann Marie by calling her "Priscilla."

During the meal, he would turn to Ann and kiss her hand and say, "Cilla honey, would you like anything else to eat?"

Finally, Ann Marie leaned over to me and blushingly said, "Mom! Doesn't he know he is married?"

She had a crush on Randy from the time she was very little. She knew he had prayed for her when she was born with a heart defect. Race Lariscy had asked Randy to do a concert at Rhine Valley Baptist Church on July 4. Realizing that Ann Marie's birthday would be on July 8, Randy told her to get a party of girls together and bring them to Frankfurt for the concert. He would get free tickets, autograph a picture for them, and sing "Happy Birthday" to Ann.

Because of health concerns in Romania, Ann Marie and I stayed in Germany as prayer support and planned the birthday party. The Werner family wanted to take a vacation in Bavaria after Romania, so they drove our Mercedes to Vienna, Austria, and pick it up on the way home. Gary, Doug Sterk, and Vance Clarke were the designated drivers for the other vehicles on the Romanian trip. Traveling in our Mercedes, a rented white Ford transit van and the big green truck, the mission team took off headed first to Vienna, Austria. The Werners stayed with friends, Scott and Joan Holley, who had been living in Vienna doing ministry with Young Life and teaching in an Austrian school. Gary, Randy, Doug, and Vance stayed in an extra apartment in Vienna. The trip through Hungary and into Romania began the next morning.

Previous trips through Hungary had become difficult at the border crossings. The Hungarians were angry that humanitarian aid was traveling through their country into Romania without any benefit to Hungary. Oftentimes, they would delay the mission trucks or want the boxes of supplies opened for inspection. Sometimes they demanded payment of extra duty fees before allowing entrance to Hungary. To add to tensions, a new conflict between neighboring Yugoslavian factions had begun during the week.

The next morning, before leaving for the Hungarian border, Gary gave a travel briefing to the group. Knowing that Randy Mayfield is also a comedian, Gary reminded everyone that there should be no joking around at the border crossings. The guards were serious and the trip did not need any extra delays. There was a suggestion that the team chloroform Randy for the border crossing.

When the group arrived at the Hungarian border, the big green truck was leading the way with Vance Clarke, Doug Sterk, and Randy Mayfield sitting in the cab. Gary was following with the four Werners in the rental van. The Hungarian border guard approached the big green truck to ask for passports and paperwork. Vance Clarke handed him all three passports. Very carefully, the guard opened each passport and looked at the picture inside the front cover and then at the men in the truck cab to make sure they matched.

Opening the first passport the guard said, "Vance Clarke." He handed Vance back his passport.

Then he opened the second passport, "Doug Sterk" and handed the passport back.

Finally opening Randy's passport the guard smiled, looking at Randy's thick black hair and moustache, the guard said, "Saddam Hussein!"

They all started laughing so loud at the joke, that Gary could hear them in the van behind the truck. He was sure that Randy had made a joke, but then the guard waved them through with a smile. For years afterwards when Gary and Randy would minister together at a church, they would act out the Hungarian border crossing with Gary playing the part of the guard wearing his Soviet military hat, and Randy playing "Saddam Hussein!"

The second night, spent in the Tisza Hotel and Spa about 100 kilometers from Budapest in Szolnok, Hungary, offered a resort atmosphere. The spa and thermal spring adjoining the hotel resembled by-gone Turkish bathes, where hot medicinal water treated a variety of health conditions. The Tisza River flowed next to the romantic hotel. Legend says the river waters were held back, while Attila the Hun was buried in the riverbed, then the river was released to cover his grave.

Taking a stroll in the warm summer evening along the river, the mission team absorbed the sites and sounds of Szolnok. Sunset was not until 10 p.m., allowing the community to enjoy the outside entertainment in a carnival mood. People clad in European swimsuits relaxed in the warm water of a nearby outdoor pool. Driving bumper cars at the "Schwarzkopf Panzers" amusement ride, Hungarian children laughed and screamed as they rammed camouflaged tanks into each other.

Engraved archways, statues, and fountains surrounded the Tisza Hotel's regal architecture. Young couples holding hands sat at tables in the hotel's pleasant garden café, sipping wine and gazing into each other's eyes. Hungarian music serenaded the evening, as the team of Americans drifted off to sleep in their spacious hotel rooms.

Morning breakfast, served on the finest china and linen table setting, suggested European elegance. In the graceful dining room, crystal chandeliers hanging from the ceiling reflected the multi-colored Turkish rugs covering the floor. French doors leading to the garden hid behind white sheer curtains and long velvet swag draperies. The mission team enjoyed the last few hours of luxury before experiencing Romanian poverty.

Friday morning, driving in the rental van and green truck, the mission team headed out of Hungary for Romania. Approaching the Romanian border, the team was stunned to see large groups of people walking or riding bicycles on the road. The people were loaded down with shopping bags. They had walked ten miles from Romania into Hungary to shop for food and necessities for their family, because there was no food to buy in Romania. They were walking because there was a shortage of gasoline. Gasoline, rationed to five gallons a month, took two days of waiting in line to get to the pump. Gary was glad he had brought an extra five-gallon container of unleaded gas.

One member of the Baptist church was a Romanian border guard. He was alert to look for the big green seven-ton truck and white rental van, and quickly took care of the paperwork for the mission team crossing into Romania. Oradea, Romania, was a ten-mile drive past the border crossing. At the church, several strong deacons and youth met the team, and immediately unloaded the truck. Vance and Doug headed home to Germany in the green supply truck.

A deacon of the church managed the Băile Felix hotel and spa on the edge of town. The Werner family and Randy had rooms in the Băile Felix. Adonis Vidu was happy to see Gary's familiar face, and meet Randy Mayfield and the Werner family. David Werner became a new young friend to Adi Vidu. Peter and Geta insisted Gary stay at their home, with Adi more than willing to sleep on the floor or couch, if the Colonel wanted to sleep in his bed.

In the Bāile Felix lobby, Gary bought a bouquet of flowers to give to Geta Vidu. Gary had no Romanian money, so he pulled $4 in U.S. cash out of his pocket and gave it to the shopkeeper. The owner told Gary to wait there. Running into the back of the shop, he returned smiling with three more bouquets, and shook Gary's hand in appreciation for the money.

Second Baptist Church was located in the middle of the city of Oradea. The original church started with a small piece of property, squeezed onto a corner facing the street, and seated about 400 people. Needing more room, the congregation added 500 more seats without the communist government noticing. Taking a sharp 90° turn, a large annex to the sanctuary hid behind a wall on the property. Each week church members had brought empty buckets to church, filled them with construction dirt and carried them home. Then they began the construction of the annex behind the wall. The small street front of the church gave no hint that over 1,000 church members were packed into the church every Sunday.

Peter Vidu took the mission team to show them the newest construction projects. At the southern edge of Oradea, Gary, Randy, and the Werner family stared down into a large hole about ten feet deep. Bulldozers were digging out the new church basement. Buried in the earth were layers of bricks from previous antiquated construction. It looked like a great place for an archeological dig. Peter showed the plans for a grand church building and education center, which could seat nearly 3,000 people. Emmanuel Baptist Church was a dream of the future for this industrious congregation of believers.

There were other plans for the future. Catching the vision of an open door to make a difference in Romanian life, a new Christian orphanage was under construction southwest of the city. Several individual family units were in various phases of construction to house groups of orphans cared for by Christian couples. Knowing the tragic care Romanian orphans had received in the government institutions, this orphanage would raise children in a Christian home atmosphere. These children would not be adoptable, but cared for until they were adults able to be productive Christians in Romanian society.

The most exciting plan for the future was the construction of Emmanuel Bible Institute on eighteen acres of land just outside of Oradea. Under communism, seminary enrollments were non-existent and underground seminaries sought to fill the desperate need for pastors. At the time of the revolution in 1989, only one in ten churches had a pastor. The vision was that Emmanuel Bible Institute would train up strong Christian leaders to strengthen the church and to penetrate the Romanian society. Students receiving seminary training would come from Eastern European and Muslim countries, including Moldova, Ukraine, Russia, Siberia, Sudan, South Africa, and Kazakhstan.

Where there is no vision, the people perish.
Proverbs 29:18

On Saturday, the mission team went to the city of Timisoara. Here they visited the University Square where hundreds of Romanians, slaughtered by the military during the Revolution in 1989, were honored with a large cross in front of the Orthodox Church. It was on the steps of the Orthodox Church that women and children were shot down trying to get inside for protection. The Orthodox priests had locked the doors to keep political refugees from entering the safety of the church. Dinu Bulzesc, a professor at the Timisoara University was a witness to the massacre, and pointed out the bullet holes in the buildings. From this city, the Romanian Revolution spread, ending with the death of the dictator Nicolae Ceausescu and his wife Elena on Christmas Day 1989. For the first time in forty years Romanians openly celebrated Christmas. The headlines in the newspapers read: *Christ is born—Anti-Christ is dead!* The story of the Romanian Revolution rang in the hearts of the small mission team. Finally, they understood the sacrifice that was paid for freedom and faith by the Romanians.

Sunday morning worship began early in the Second Baptist Church of Oradea. As the congregation gathered, about 1,500 people packed into a sanctuary that could seat 900. They stood in the aisles, against the walls, and out into the street. After sitting for a while, some would get up and exchange their seat with another who had been standing. Susan and Randy sang for the worship service, but were very impressed with the church choir and director. Tom and Gary both gave a "word of greeting" from Central Presbyterian Church in St. Louis and Faith Baptist Church in Germany. After having done a Saturday night youth concert at the local Pentecostal church, Peter reminded Randy Mayfield about playing his guitar and singing for the Sunday Baptist worship.

Rolling his *r's* Peter said, "Not too rrrrhythmic, RRRandy!"

Following the morning worship service, Geta served a nice Romanian lunch. The team was thinking of taking a nap until Peter said, "We go now!"

Jumping in the van, Peter directed Gary to the small village church in Avram. After bouncing 6 miles down a gravel road, they were about to witness a Romanian baptism service. The church was packed with people surrounding the building and hanging through the windows. Susan and Randy were almost backed-up to the wall on the platform to sing. The baptism ceremony was a serious event in the life of the church. Dressed in white robes, the baptismal candidates were honored to have Americans present at the service. Loud speakers attached to the outside of the building broadcast the service for those who could not squeeze into the room.

Next it was on to a pastor ordination at the tiny village of Cuté Clete. An open sewer ran down the middle of the main road in the village, and 10–15 pigs weighing about 300 lbs. each were drinking out of the sewer. The pigs came running towards them when the team exited the van, and one pig lay down against the wheel of the van. Gary started calling to the pig to get up, because the pig was lying where Gary needed to open the trunk and put more gas in the van. The picture reminded the mission team of the Biblical scene of demon-possessed pigs.

Romanian pastor Josef Tson, who suffered severe persecution during the communist regime for his faith, was part of the ordination council. Peter had been careful about introducing Gary as a U.S. military member in the larger cities for security reasons. However, in the small village, Peter introduced Gary to the congregation as a Colonel in the U.S. Air Force. Tears started to run down the faces of the older women.

Gary turned to his interpreter and asked, "Why are the old women crying?"

The interpreter replied, "They have been waiting forty years for the American military to arrive! Today, you are here!"

After the ordination service, the church leaders invited the mission team to eat with them.

Upon seeing one of the pigs walk into the building where they were serving the food, Peter said, "No. We go now!"

Bumping back down the winding gravel road to Oradea, the team headed for a graduation ceremony at the School of Prophets. During the communist regime, the School of Prophets had been an underground Christian college and seminary. For the first time, the graduation was in the open. The vision of a future seminary for all of Eastern Europe, openly training men and women, would build on the foundation of this graduation class. Sunday ended with the exhausted team having done thirteen hours of ministry and four worship services before collapsing into bed.

On Monday morning prior to leaving their new Romanian friends, Gary gave Peter and Geta an envelope of money designated for the Vidu family expenses. Immediately Peter rushed out the door of their home and headed to the local furniture store. He bought a new bed for future guests who would be coming to visit them in this treasured sister-church relationship.

Driving about six miles past the Hungarian border, the mission team approached a strange police barricade on the road. After stopping for questioning, the security guards waived the team on down the road. One guard raised his thumb in the air, and yelled out to the Americans, "George Bush! Number One!"

Picking up our Mercedes in Vienna, Austria, the Werners drove to Bavaria for a few days of vacation. Gary took Randy to the Vienna train station to catch a train for Berlin. Unfortunately, while an exhausted Randy slept on the train, his video and camera equipment were stolen. We met up with Randy again in Frankfurt for the Rhein Valley concert. He made a special effort to welcome Ann Marie's birthday party and sang "Happy Birthday" to her as Elvis. The Werner family and Randy flew back to St. Louis, Missouri, on July 8 with Romania in their hearts.

On July 11, Gary left for Incirlik, Turkey, on an unaccompanied tour, as the Staff Judge Advocate for the Coalition Task Force of Operation Provide Comfort. The coalition forces integrated U.S., French, British, Italian, Dutch, and Turkish military. Gary's responsibilities included being legal counsel to the Coalition Task Force commander, General Jamerson, especially in negotiations with the Turkish government and writing rules of engagement in further Iraqi conflict. Gary earned his "spurs" taking regular helicopter flights with the 6th U.S. Army Cavalry over Iraq surveying the Kurdish camps and escorting dignitaries.

One day an entourage from the Green Party in Germany made an inspection trip to the headquarters of Provide Comfort. Upon seeing a large birdhouse on the camp premises, a German woman from the Green Party asked Gary, "Where are all the pretty birdies? Where are all the pretty white doves of peace for the birdhouse?"

Gary relayed the question to one of the Army colonels at the base command. The Colonel's reply was short and to the point. "Tell her, we ate them!"

A U.S. congressman, who was a Lt. Col. judge advocate in the Air National Guard Reserves, came to work for Gary in the Provide Comfort JAG office. Although the congressman said he wanted treatment like any other Lt. Col., Gary escorted him on a trip to the naval aircraft carrier, USS Forrestal. Sitting on the runway, the heat was reaching over 100°F inside the twin-engine plane.

Finally, Gary said to the pilot, "What are we waiting for?"

The pilot replied, "Sir, we're waiting for some congressman to show up."

Pointing with his right elbow to the uniformed congressman sitting next to him, Gary said, "He is right here!"

"Yes, sir!" the pilot responded. They were up and in the air immediately.

A tail hook landing on the deck of the carrier, receiving full honors coming on board, and spending the night in the Admiral's quarters, made the trip one of the highlights of the remote duty assignment for Gary. He was very impressed with the flight operations as Navy jets took off from the deck and landed caught in the tail hook.

With the end of the Gulf War, routine medical care for military dependents had resumed. I scheduled another appointment for a mammogram and a visit to the surgeon at Wiesbaden Hospital. Dr. Brown was not available for this consultation because he was in Turkey with Provide Comfort. I saw a female surgeon, Dr. Ohsiek, who thought my lump probably needed to come out. I was scheduled for a biopsy on August 7.

While Gary was on the aircraft carrier, he tried to make a phone call back to Germany. He got through just a few minutes after I had gone into surgery for my fifth breast lump removal. It was very difficult for me to face this surgery with my husband somewhere in the middle of the Persian Gulf. However, my cousin Debby was a surgical nurse at Wiesbaden Hospital. The Lord had placed her there to watch over me during surgery. My good friend and prayer partner Cathy Board took care of Ann Marie during my stay in the hospital. I was relieved to find the breast lump was scar tissue.

The doctor sent me home, and told me not to lift anything heavy for two weeks. Adonis Vidu came from Romania for a few weeks to do work around Faith Baptist Church and earn a little money. When he heard about my surgery, he came and mowed our lawn. I was humbled that Adi would come and help me when Gary was gone. Later, we learned that fifteen-year-old Adonis gave all of the money he earned that summer to help build the new Romanian church. It even surprised his parents!

Ann had been saving up her money for horse riding lessons. Dr. Butler, knowing that horse riding is therapeutic for stroke victims, referred Ann to a German riding stable in Landstuhl. Ann began private lessons in English saddle. Her horse, named Granada, was a 17-year-old tired and lazy brown Hanoverian mare. To our surprise, Ann Marie was able to get Granada to obey the German commands. The huge horse scared me, but Ann Marie gained confidence, and muscle strength in her legs and hands as she rode around the stable ring during lessons. I videotaped her riding and sent the tape to Gary in Turkey. Gary sent back pictures of his mid-eastern adventures.

Gary called home twice a week on the government phone line. He sent free postcards and letters to all of the family. Even though he missed us, he took advantage of the biblical history in Turkey and Iraq. One Sunday he went with his office on a trip to the Mediterranean Sea. For $1 he paddled out to a crusader's castle on an island near the ruins of a Roman city. One of the office lawyers went scuba diving in the deep blue water. It was so clear; he saw old urns on the bottom of the sea. On the way back to camp, they drove past Tarsus, hometown of the Apostle Paul. The next weekend, they visited Antioch. Turkey was a haven of unexcavated ruins and history.

Gary made several visits to the Solopi Turkish camp on the border with Iraq. In the middle of a hot, dusty desert, the Army troops slept in tents. The Air Force slept in air-conditioned tents. The "Always Ready—6th U.S. Cavalry—Six Shooters" would routinely fly AH64 Apache helicopters into Iraq. Flying with the Sixth Squadron over Iraq, Gary came very near the Kurdish city of Nineveh, where Jonah's grave is a shrine for both Christians and Muslims. The Iraqi name for Nineveh is Mosul where Saddam Hussein's northernmost palace rose out of the arid sand.

While Gary was eating seafood and sand in Turkey, Ann Marie started sixth grade. Mrs. Rhymes encouraged Ann Marie to write poems and articles for the class newspaper. Ann Marie published a short fable, submitting her manuscript to the Kaiserslautern District Young Authors' Conference and receiving a "Certificate of Recognition."

Bitsy Saves the Day
By: Ann Marie Grunick

Once upon a time, there was a puegolo that lived in Ming's Garden. Now this puegolo's name was Bitsy. Bitsy was a very smart but clumsy puegolo. Everybody made fun of her because she was so clumsy. Bitsy was a very pretty red animal. She liked to play in the garden with Honey the Rabbit, Ricky the Raccoon, and Melody the Giraffe. She also liked the swings in the garden.

But one day, she knocked down the swings, and the animals said, "Watch out you Clumsy!"

So Bitsy ran off thinking that no one liked her. Then she heard something in the bush.

"What could it be?" she said.

Then a dangerous rattlesnake slithered out of the bushes, and Bitsy jumped on top of the snake and killed the rattlesnake. All of the animals came out and saw what Bitsy had done.

The giraffe named Melody, and Honey the Rabbit lifted Bitsy up in the air and said, "Horray! Horray! Horray!" and they lived happily ever after in the garden.

As for the dangerous, fierce, poisonous rattlesnake, it died in the garden dead as could be and never awoke again.

MORAL OF THE STORY: You can't judge an animal by its cover.

With the start of the school year, my responsibilities as the Renewal women's ministry director were demanding. Some of the teachers from the previous years had moved back to the States during the summer months. With Deryl Tomberlin gone, I felt the burden of finding new committed teachers and leaders. Through prayer the Lord placed gifted women in the positions of Kid's Korner director, prayer chairman, greeter, treasurer, music director, publicity chairman, hostess, administrator, and retreat chairman. Six women accepted teaching positions and almost 90 women signed up as students. I continued to teach a Precept class with 19 women studying, *Lord, Is It Warfare? – Teach Me to Stand!* Our new leadership made plans for a spring retreat at the Potzberg Turm–Hotel in Fockelberg, Germany. By January, we added two evening classes to the Renewal ministry for working women.

I was also on the pastor search committee. The committee held weekly meetings, praying and reviewing applications from pastoral candidates. Our first meeting, we outlined the qualifications and expectations of the next pastor. Our model for a new pastor seemed to look a lot like Jim Tomberlin. Then we experienced Dr. Roy Fish. Dr. Fish had taken a four-month sabbatical as professor of evangelism at Southwestern Baptist Seminary to come to Faith Baptist as our interim pastor. Roy Fish was much older than Jim Tomberlin, and he had an expository Bible teaching style of preaching. He knew the Old Testament in such a way that even Tiglath-Pilezer—King of Assyria was interesting! (II Kings 15-16) The vision of our future pastor changed to look more like Dr. Roy Fish. Dr. Fish's wife Jean came with him to Germany and it was my privilege for her to attend my Precept class. We hosted Roy and Jean in our home for dinner, and they came to know Ann Marie's testimony of faith.

My brother, Fred, and his wife, Cathy, came to visit us the middle of September, after they spent a few days in Paris, France. Having never been to Europe before, everything was a great adventure for them, including the train ride from France to Landstuhl, Germany. Ann Marie's teacher let her take a few days off school, so we could travel with Fred and Cathy to Bavaria and stay in Austria. Since Gary was still in Turkey, I drove the big van while Fred navigated the map to Garmish, Berchesgaden, the Salzburg salt mines, Neuschwanstein, and Linderhof Castles. Cathy sat in the back of the van with Ann Marie and helped her do homework.

On Friday, September 20 at 5:00 p.m., I put Fred and Cathy on a tour bus for Italy. Then Ann Marie and I headed to Frankfurt to pick Gary up at 6:30 p.m. from the Rhein Main Airport. He had been gone for just over two months to Turkey. Driving onto the parking lot at the airport, several men in desert camouflage uniforms, tanned boots, and wide-brimmed hats were milling around the bus stop. One man seemed determined to approach our car. I just kept driving past him looking for a place to park.

Suddenly Ann Marie said, "MOM! That was DAD!"

Looking in the rear-view mirror, I finally recognized my husband running after the car with his suitcases. He had lost about twenty pounds, and was as tanned as the color of the "chocolate chips" in his desert camouflage uniform! I slammed on the brakes and backed the car up. It had not occurred to him why I would not recognize him, but he sure looked good to us.

Fred and Cathy returned from Italy on September 25. After we took a trip to the Black Forest and bought a coo-coo clock, they left for the States on September 28.

The next month was my time to take a trip. November 4-8, I went with two friends to Willingen, Germany, for the European Protestant Women of the Chapel Retreat. The guest speaker was my role model, and favorite Bible teacher, Kay Arthur. For five days I sat listening to Kay lecture on Philippians. She taught on having joy and a servant attitude in ministry. On November 6, Precept leaders were invited to come to Kay's hotel room for a very special time of sharing and fellowship. Kay let us in on a secret. Precept Ministries would soon be releasing an International Inductive Study Bible for use with the Precept courses. I ordered one of the first copies of the new Bible, which Kay personally autographed:

Libby dear –
Remember one thing is needful – don't neglect it,
and you'll always be prepared for every situation of life.
Luke 10:38-42
Love, Kay

During our church Christmas musical, Dr. Fish gave a message about the chrismon ornaments on the Christmas tree. As Dr. Fish sat in a rocking chair beside the tree, Ann Marie was one of a few children selected to sit at his feet and listen to the story. After Dr. Fish explained each Christian symbol, a child would take the ornament and place it on the tree. Ann Marie was the last child. Knowing that Ann's hands needed help, Dr. Fish and the other children gathered around the tree for her turn. Roy Fish placed his hand on Ann's hand to help her, and then the children bowed for prayer. Later that night, Ann Marie told me that when Dr. Fish touched her, she felt the Holy Spirit in his hand. She recognized Dr. Fish as a special man of God, sent to our congregation for a time of training and encouragement.

God continued to weave the Romanian tapestry in our lives with several more threads of friendship. Dr. Phil Roberts had served two military churches in Europe. He had also pastored five years at the International Baptist Church in Brussels, Belgium. In January of 1992, Phil Roberts headed to Oradea, Romania, as the Dean of Academics for the Institute of Biblical Studies at the newest and largest seminary in Eastern Europe.

> The tapestry swirled with a glimpse of Eternity.

Dr. Roberts needed a place to stay in Germany while organizing his travel into Romania. Steve Kahne asked if we could provide the accommodations for Phil to live with us from January 26 to February 2. We had one small problem; we had made ski reservations in Erphendorf, Austria, for January 25 through February 1. So, we made a deal with Dr. Roberts. We would leave the key to our house and Mercedes with Steve Kahne to give to Phil Roberts the day after we left for the ski trip. Dr. Roberts could live in our house while we were gone, provided he would dog-sit with Winchester. When we returned on Saturday, February 1, after a week of skiing, we met Phil Roberts for the first time when he greeted us at our front door. He had lived in our home for a week and become friends with Winchester before he ever met us. We had one night together before Phil headed out to set up his living quarters for his family in Romania.

Dr. Roberts returned to our home on February 14 with his family. His wife Anja, ten-year old daughter Naomi, and five-year old son Mark, had come from the U.S. to go to their new home in Romania. Before they left on February 18, we invited the Romanian committee to our home for a potluck dinner on February 17. That evening at our dining room table, the tapestry swirled with the glimpse of Eternity. Phil Roberts suggested that we consider bringing our choir to Romania to present the Easter musical drama in May. It seemed like an impossible plan to our choir director Jerry Chambers; but with God, all things are possible. It was one of those "what if" moments of exploring God's Will in ministry. Where could we perform such a drama in the former communist country? How would we get there with the choir, scenery, costumes, and sound equipment? What about the publicity and drama translated in the Romanian language? How much would all of this cost? Finally, Jerry's biggest concern—his wife Judy was expecting a baby around that time! However, it would be a great evangelism tool to present the Gospel in music and drama for the first time in forty years to the Romanians! We prayed about it.

When Jerry Chambers presented the idea of the trip to the choir that Wednesday night at choir practice, he thought the response would be weak. Instead, all of the choir members unanimously approved the idea with great enthusiasm. We envisioned being part of something bigger than we had ever known. Our Easter performance in Germany was only two months away, but the practices took on an excitement because this musical, "Behold the Man," would run longer than five Easter performances in mid-April.

The Lord was gracious to take care of all of the needs for the Romanian trip. The Romanian pastors were able to rent a former communist sports hall for three nights, on May 1–3, for the musical production at the cost of only $500. The hall would seat about 10,000 people! Jerry Chambers handled the details of publicity, sound systems, lighting, drama, and music. He and a group of ten men went into Oradea a few days early to set up the stage and production equipment. Gary took on the responsibilities of getting visas, transportation, hotel accommodations, and leading the choir bus for the trip; since he had made several trips into Romania and knew how to get to Oradea.

The forty-six members of the choir left the parking lot of Faith Baptist Church at midnight on April 29, 1992, in a large tour bus. Traveling all night, we arrived at our Hungarian hotel accommodations in Solnok the next afternoon. After a good nights sleep in the hotel, we awoke to find all of the streets surrounding the hotel filled with a flea market. The women in the choir were delighted to spend their money shopping for souvenirs. Gary was concerned that he could never herd the women back onto the bus to leave by 10:00 a.m. for Romania. After some delay, we loaded the bus for the Romanian border. To our surprise within a few miles outside of the city, medivac helicopters were evacuating the scene of a horrible traffic accident. Had it not been for the providential flea market, we could have been in the accident. The closer we got to the Romanian border the quieter the bus became. Realization of the living conditions struck those who had not seen such poverty in the Western European countries.

Upon reaching the border with Romania, our bus stopped to wait. Gary got out of the bus and approached the border guard to check our visas and passports. A smiling young man came bounding toward the bus waving his hands.

Looking out the front of the bus window, several of the women stood up and asked, "Who is the handsome young guy that looks like movie star Tom Cruise?"

As the young man jumped up the steps to the bus, he gave me a big hug! I introduced him to the choir as Adonis Vidu, son of the pastor. Adonis welcomed the choir to Romania, and guided us through the border to the former communist sports hall.

Adonis and his friend, George Pordea, slept several nights on cots in the sports hall as security guards for our sound equipment. Jerry and the support crew were happy to see us; our first performance would be in five hours. Several of the crew crawled around on the roof, covering large windows with black-out cloth. The auditorium needed to be dark for the drama, and the sun would not set until well into the performance.

The choir would be staying at the Bāile Felix, but Jerry, Gary, and I were to stay at the Vidu's home. Gary and I would get to use the new bed Peter had bought. Guiding the tour bus to the Bāile Felix hotel for lunch, our attention was drawn to a multitude of posters on every building and pole in the city of Oradea. Plastered everywhere were pictures of Jerry and the choir performing in Germany; with the promise to the Romanians that if they came to the free performance, they would see members of the U.S. military and families performing. When we reached the hotel, Romanian church members lined the entrance to greet us. The choir members received a fresh bouquet of flowers, with the Romanian custom of a kiss on each cheek.

Only a few hours before our first performance, we began rehearsal on the new stage in the sports hall. Working hard to get our bearings on cast movement and sound, we were amazed at how smoothly the plan had come together. Suddenly halfway through rehearsal, just before the crucifixion scene, all of the power in the auditorium shut down. On a darkened unfamiliar stage, the choir immediately hit their knees in prayer. We had come so far, it could all have been a total failure without lights and sound. While we knelt in prayer, Jerry crawled through the dark; grasping at cables, checking for a hot wire in the electrical system. Finding the problem, he changed the wire out and miraculously power was restored. The delay kept us from finishing the rehearsal. As we contemplated our first performance, we were unsure of how the cast would get Jesus off the cross and into the tomb in time for the resurrection. But, Romanians were lining up outside the hall and it was time to perform.

Quickly, we put on costumes and make-up in the sports hall restrooms, trying to avoid the overflowing toilets. Gary and I stationed ourselves outside the sports hall in costume to hand out programs translated into Romanian. As we looked out over the city, we were amazed to see lines of people walking from the adjoining neighborhoods and high-rises, headed toward the former communist sports hall. Old people, young families, people in military uniforms, couples on a date in their best clothes, were all streaming into the building to see the production. It was a big deal! It was free! The U.S. military had arrived!

At the first night's performance, 7,000 Romanians attended the musical drama of *Behold the Man*. Unlike anything that had happened in the performances in Germany, a most amazing event occurred during the first performance in Romania. When the character of Jesus stepped on the stage, the entire audience erupted in thunderous applause. It was a moment that sent chills through the choir at the outpouring of emotions from the grateful Romanians, as if they were saying - *we are no longer a communist country, we can become a Christian nation.*

One of the first night attendees was so enthusiastic over the performance, he went to everyone who lived in his building and made them sign a pledge that they would attend the second or third performance.

The Romanian pastors laughed that an old communist recruitment technique was helping spread the Gospel of Christ.

On the second night, 8,000 people filled the bleachers and chairs on the floor. The third night was a packed house of 10,000 spectators. In total 25,000 Romanians saw the life, death, and resurrection of Jesus

Christ in music and drama for the first time in this former communist country. At the end of each performance, several pastors explained the Gospel and gave an opportunity for people to respond. There was a great deal of emotion expressed by the crowds. During the finale, the choir left the stage singing to surround the crowd with our final song. Looking up into the tearful faces of a thankful people, our hearts filled with love for our new brothers and sisters in Christ. Every choir member returned home, changed by the Romanian Rhapsody.

After Sunday morning worship, Peter took the choir to the building site of the new church, Emmanuel Baptist. It had been ten months since Gary, Randy, and the Werners had stared down into the hole in the ground. Now, the building was taking shape. Walls were forming and scaffolding suggested staircases, platforms, and raised seating in the new sanctuary. As Peter stood in the middle of bricks and concrete mortar where the baptismal would be used for new believers, the choir and members of the Romanian church surrounded him. Together, we sang the praise song, "Give Thanks!"

Peter and Geta Vidu insisted that Jerry, Gary and I ride in their car on the way to the Romanian border to meet the choir bus coming from the hotel. It was time to say good-bye to our Romanian hosts. As we sat in the back seat of the car together, Geta asked me if I had children. I told her about Ann Marie and the miracles in her life. With tears streaming down her face, Geta tightly held onto my hand. Then Geta shared the story of another son, who had died from a brain tumor when he was five years old. She said, "His face grew radiant, like that of an angel, the day he died and went to Heaven."

As Peter Vidu said, "There will come a day in heaven, when we will rejoice together for our work on this side of eternity."

CHAPTER SEVENTEEN

Crosslink

Though the fig tree should not blossom,
and there be no fruit on the vines,
though the yield of the olive should fail,
and the fields produce no food,
though the flock should be cut off from the fold,
and there be no cattle in the stalls,
yet I will exult in the Lord,
I will rejoice in the God of my salvation.
The Lord GOD is my strength,
and He has made my feet like hinds' feet,
and makes me walk on my high places.
Habakkuk 3:17-19 (NAS)

Before our trip to Romania, we received military orders for our next assignment. We had tried to avoid any assignment in Washington, D.C., but after nearly twenty years in the Air Force, our time had come. Major General Moorehouse, had become The Judge Advocate General for the U.S. Air Force. Gen. Morehouse wanted Gary to sit as one of nine judges on the highest court in the military; the U.S. Air Force Court of Military Review in Washington, D.C. This military court reviews all court-martial cases on appeal, and is the military equivalent to the U.S. Supreme Court. Every U.S. Air Force legal office in the world would now have my husband's picture hanging on the wall. The judicial legal offices were at Bolling Airbase, across the Potomac River from the Washington National Airport and next to the U.S. Naval Station on the Maryland side of the beltway.

The week after our trip to Romania, Gary went back to the States for three weeks of Military Judges' School in Charlottesville, Virginia. During that time, he signed a lease on a two-story brick home in Annandale, Virginia, less than a mile from the Gallows Road exit off the Capital Beltway. Ann and I would have to wait until July to see the next home he had picked out for our family.

Our nation's Capitol sat on a hill, shinning like a jewel at night, but grinding careers to dust during the day. The news media captured it all with an inside the beltway mentality of rumors and political cartoons. We heard that it took two cups of coffee every morning to read the *Washington Post;* and if every member of the military wore their uniform, D.C. would look like an armed camp. Colonels were a dime a dozen, and had to wait in line with the rest of them. The shock of the cost of living, and long traffic commute was not encouraging, while we packed for our third move in four years. As we headed for fast-paced living in the most politically powerful city in the world, we took it as an opportunity to learn about our national heritage and governmental system.

While we waited for our household goods to cross the ocean, we spent a few weeks visiting family and friends. Departing Frankfurt on a Northwest Airlines flight on Friday, June 19, 1992, we arrived that evening in St. Louis. Jet lag and culture shock broke us into tears when Mom and Dad met us at the baggage claim area. It felt so good to be back on U.S. soil and home again. It had been a long and awesome four years in Europe. During that time, both Gary and I had turned forty-years old and then some! The little girl we had taken to Germany at age nine had grown into a young woman. Ann would become a teenager in just a few weeks. Even Winchester had settled down from puppy playing to becoming a lap dog.

On Monday, June 22, we had lunch with Bob Fenn at Lay Renewal Ministries. Bob and the staff wanted to talk to Gary about becoming the new Executive Director of LRM. Surprised that Bob wanted to retire and consider Gary for the position, we declined the invitation. Air Force retirement was still two years away for Gary, and filling Bob Fenn's shoes would be almost impossible.

We did not waste time getting back into the St. Louis culture. While we were in Germany, Grandpa Frazier had died in March of

1991, at the age of 100. My mom and her three brothers inherited over 100 acres of his farm property. We made a few trips to the farm to pick green beans, corn, cabbage, and tomatoes from the garden. Ann Marie did a little fishing from the pond and waded in the creek with cousins.

We went to the St. Louis Muny Opera, and we enjoyed a St. Louis Cardinals' baseball game at beautiful Busch Stadium. It was at the baseball game that Ann Marie announced that she thought Cardinal's player, Willie McGee, was such a handsome man! I thought she surely must have been looking at his heart, and humble spirit. Gary spoke at my parents' church about Romania. Their church had given money for the Romanian mission when the Werner family and Randy Mayfield had made the trip. Everyone was very excited to hear the news about twenty-five thousand Romanians filling the communist sports hall.

We could only bring one car back to the States from Germany, and the Mercedes did not meet the U.S. regulations to pass customs. We sold the Mercedes to Vance and Pam Clarke. They were delighted to drive it around Europe. Our Ford van would take a few more weeks in coming, and we needed two cars. Gary, and Ann Marie and I went car shopping in St. Louis. Well aware of the fact that our daughter would be driving our next car within three years, we allowed her input about the selection. On June 29, we purchased a new cherry red Chrysler LeBaron convertible with a black top. I was not sure if it was Ann Marie's comment, "It will look good with my hair!" or Gary's mid-life "Chrysler" that made the decision, but I went along for the ride! I would rather Gary had a red convertible, than a "red-head" as he approached age forty-five.

When we got home from shopping, something else was new! My brother Fred and wife Cathy had a new baby daughter. Olivia Rose was born the same day we bought the red convertible. When Fred had called us months earlier to tell us about Cathy's pregnancy, Ann Marie had said, "I think they are going to have a girl, and will name her Olivia Rose." What we did know was that Olivia Rose had been "made in Italy." Their trip to Europe the September before had produced more than a few souvenirs.

On Saturday, July 11, Gary and Winchester loaded up the mid-life "Chrysler," and headed for our new home in Washington, D.C. Gary needed to report for duty on Monday morning, and was excited to drive the new car on the two-day trip. Things were going fine on the drive until somewhere in Kentucky, Winchester stepped on the middle console and pressed the button with his paw to lower the top of the convertible. It took Gary a few seconds to realize what the buzzing noise was before he pushed Winchester back into the passenger side bucket seat. During the next week, Gary and Winchester slept in our empty house in Washington, D.C. on an inflatable queen mattress. Ann and I stayed in St. Louis because our furniture would not arrive until July 21.

On Monday evening, July 20, Ann and I flew into Dulles Airport from St. Louis. Gary met us at the airport in the red convertible. We were excited to see what kind of home he had chosen for us. We turned off the Beltway at Gallows Road, and headed down Holly Road. Gary explained that our house was at the end of a long private driveway with three other houses. He had met our neighbors on each side of our home. On the right side of us lived a Vietnamese family who had come to the U.S. on a small boat in 1972. They now owned two prominent Vietnamese restaurants in Alexandria, Virginia, and a new Mercedes. On the left of us lived Dr. and Mrs. Amighi and their college-age daughter, Roya. Dr. Amighi was a retired Iranian neurosurgeon, who had emigrated from Iran fifteen years before. He was a very devout Muslim, who prayed on his prayer rug several times a day. He also owned a Mercedes. It was the beginning of meeting people from all over the world in a city were English was a second language for much of the population.

Turning down the long driveway, Gary pulled up to a large two-story brick home, surrounded with 100-foot tall pine trees, holly bushes, and dark woods on an acre of land. The two-car garage was detached from the house, but connected to a covered breezeway. Opening the front door, we stepped into a spacious entrance hall at the bottom of a staircase to the second floor. On each side of the entrance hall were two large rooms with high ceilings and shiny dark hardwood floors. On the left was a sunken formal living room with windows overlooking the terraced front yard. A grand dining room with gold draperies and a Williamsburg chandelier was one-step up from the living room. On the right of the entrance hall, was a massive family room with a brick wood-burning fireplace. Windows across the back of the house and a French door revealed a concrete patio. The family room opened to a huge breakfast room and kitchen, which connected back into the dining room. On the backside of the staircase was a small powder room. A door in the kitchen led to a basement full of storage shelves, spiders, and an unfinished fireplace.

Upstairs were three fully carpeted bedrooms. Ann Marie picked one bedroom with windows looking over the driveway and front yard. The other front guestroom looked toward Dr. Amighi's home and flower garden. These two bedrooms shared a bathroom at the end of the hallway. The master bedroom, walk-in closet, and bathroom stretched the entire back of the house with a view of the woods, and connected to a small sitting room. The nicest convenience was the washer and dryer on the second floor laundry room. I would not have to go up and down the steps to do the laundry.

We slept the first night on air mattresses. The next morning our overseas household shipment arrived with our furniture. Since I had only seen the house in the dark the night before, I had to decide where the movers should place all the furniture. We were also receiving our storage shipment that week, which I had not seen in four years. It was a good thing there was a basement for storing extra dishes, lawn mowers, hoses, and tools. We had double of a few things with our storage delivery, but plenty of extra space to buy a few more pieces of furniture. Within a few weeks, things were unpacked and looking like home, just in time for the school year to start.

Luther Jackson Middle School on Gallows Road, first opening its doors in 1954 as Fairfax County's sole high school for black students, was five miles from our home. In 1965, it became an integrated middle school. In spite of the years of struggle for integration of public schools, Luther Jackson Middle School had one of the most diverse mixes in student population. In 1992, there were about 900 students at Luther Jackson Middle School, which consisted of only seventh and eighth grade. Over forty different languages spoken in the hallway represented some sixty countries.

Ann Marie could catch the school bus at the top of our private driveway on Holly Road. New student orientation was Friday, September 4, with the first day of school on Tuesday, September 8,

263

after Labor Day weekend. The day before orientation, I made an appointment with Mrs. Kyle, Ann Marie's guidance counselor. This would be the first year for Ann to have a different teacher for each class and switch rooms every study hour. I wanted to talk with Mrs. Kyle, and have her show Ann the building before the rush of students. Mrs. Kyle was very patient to escort us around the halls to each of the classrooms on Ann's schedule. She suggested that we modify Ann's locker with a lock and key instead of a combination lock. Her most valuable modification for Ann was to send a set of textbooks home, so Ann would not have to carry her textbooks back and forth.

Mrs. Kyle introduced us to the Principal, Dr. Michael Doran, who had a confident English accent. He immediately made friends with Ann, and welcomed her to Luther Jackson Middle School. We would soon realize that Dr. Doran tried to know every one of the nine-hundred students in his school and their parents.

Ann Marie was on the Explorers team. Seven teachers led the team with about two-hundred and fifty students. This helped the teachers to work together as they came to know the students during the school year. The team of teachers could share information about students and curriculum. They could collectively focus on a small section of the student population without having to teach all nine-hundred students. It allowed for healthy competition between all the school teams during spelling bees, fund-raising, reading contests, math competitions, and science projects. Camaraderie developed on the teams to help each other to be the best team. The school motto was "Building Futures Together." With forty different native languages represented in the school population, English as a second language was a challenge to many students. The student body was encouraged to celebrate their diverse backgrounds, and work toward fulfilling collective and individual potentials.

Within the first week of school, Gary and I had a meeting for an IEP evaluation with all of Ann's teachers, her guidance counselor, and the director of disabled student services. One of our immediate concerns was that Ann Marie had physical education the first period of the day at 8:05 a.m. She still struggled to make her fingers work buttons, zippers, and tie shoes. She was also slow moving physically and could lose balance if someone pushed her. As we explained Ann Marie's medical history and motor skill limitations to the teachers, they were compassionate and cooperative to help her excel in the classroom.

Her gym teacher, Coach Dave Muniz, was particularly responsive to her situation. He explained how he had worked with a variety of kids who had physical and mental limitations over a seventeen-year career teaching physical education. He promised to make Ann Marie his special project, to strengthen her arms and legs on the school's weight equipment. He would not let her be in any dangerous situation where she would be injured in gym class. Coach Muniz had already seen her determination to overcome adversities. He was not going to let her slip through the cracks or tolerate anyone making fun of her. To encourage Ann Marie, and help the other students in the gym class understand her extraordinary accomplishments, Coach Muniz asked Ann to give her testimony in gym class the next week. He made her feel special, and she witnessed to him and the class about the Lord. To keep the teacher/parent relationship progressing smoothly, I volunteered to help in the school nurse's office. The school staff was most appreciative of any parent volunteer.

We were greatly encouraged about Ann Marie's school situation. Every morning I would walk up the long driveway with Ann Marie to catch the bus. During our walk together, we would pray for her teachers, the school administration, and the kids in her classes. Ann Marie would always pray that she would find a good friend. I would send her off each morning with the blessing for "the Lord to be her strength and give her hinds' feet to walk in high places." Ann enjoyed being friendly to the international students, since she understood how difficult it is to live in a foreign country.

Since we had a new home and school, we needed to find a new church. Ann Marie would be old enough for youth group activities, so we wanted a church where some of the same kids from her school attended. Col. Charlie Heimburg, and his wife, Carolyn, had been stationed at Sembach Air Base, Germany, and attended Faith Baptist Church with us in Kaiserslautern. Col. Heimburg was one of the new appellate judges on the Court of Military Review with Gary. Stationed in Washington, D.C., before living in Germany, the Heimburgs had attended Columbia Baptist Church in Falls Church, Virginia. They had told us that although Neil Jones had been a good pastor, it was not until his small grandson had died that Neil's sermons had taken on a deeper understanding of faith. We visited other churches in the area, but kept returning to Columbia Baptist. One Saturday afternoon, Pastor Neil Jones called our home and encouraged the three of us to attend a Sunday evening class he taught to prospective new members. To receive a phone call from the Sr. Pastor of such a large church led us to that fellowship.

The next morning we attended Columbia Baptist. As we sat on a church pew waiting for the worship service to start, Ann Marie told me that a boy in her school named D.J. Campbell had been in her Sunday school class. I asked her what he looked like. She turned around to see if she could find him. Immediately, a young man coming down the aisle, spotted her, and scooted into the pew behind us. Ann Marie dropped her head, pressing her lips together in a smile. She bumped me with her left elbow, discreetly pointing to the back of our pew, her lips moved in a whisper, "That's him."

D.J. Campbell was a very friendly young man. He tapped Ann on the shoulder and said, "Hey, I didn't know you went to this church!" Ann just blushed.

I said, "Hello. We have only visited a few times; we are looking for a new church. Do you go here?"

D.J. explained that he grew up at Columbia Baptist Church and his dad was a deacon, and an usher. Since he was sitting alone, I asked him if he would like to sit with us. Ann Marie almost crawled under the pew.

D.J. said, "Sure!" and practically hopped over the back of the pew to sit right next to Ann Marie. He was very nice to share a hymnal with her. When church was over, he said he would see her at school the next day, and off he went. She began to breathe again, and look forward to school the next day. Now she had a friend.

Washington, D.C. offered the opportunity to observe our national government and history in detail. Before school started, we had taken a few days to travel to Williamsburg, Virginia. Gary and I had visited Williamsburg during our first Air Force assignment at Dover AFB. We were delighted to experience it again with Ann Marie. I booked a suite at the York Street Hotel Suites and purchased season passes with a military discount. The old colonial Williamsburg village was a charming as ever with the character re-enactments and horse drawn carts. The most delicious cream of peanut soup warms up an appetite, served in the King's Arms Tavern, by the glow of the fireplace. The best shrimp and lobster dish graced with pumpkin fritters melts in your mouth at Christiana Campbell's Tavern.

Our trip to Williamsburg was a time to check things out before my parents arrived the end of October for a week's visit. In preparation for my parents visit, I had looked into a White House Tour, and a scheduled visit with Missouri Senator, John Danforth, after a stop at the Capitol. My parents flew into Dulles Airport on Tuesday, October 27, 1992, having voted by absentee ballot in the up-coming presidential election. The next morning at 8:45 a.m., they were on a tour of the Bush White House. We ate lunch at the National Air and Space Museum cafeteria, after Dad pointed out the left control panel he had designed on the first Mercury spacecraft. Leaving The Mall area, I drove up Independence Avenue and parked behind the Library of Congress and the Supreme Court. Starting in the massive Rotunda surrounded by historical paintings, we toured the U.S. Capitol building. Although Mom and Dad were wearing out, we walked across the street to the Russell Senate building for a scheduled 3:00 p.m. appointment for pictures with Senator Danforth. Being a staunch Republican, my dad asked Senator Danforth what he thought about the up-coming elections. Senator Danforth's response was cautious about the re-election of President George Bush. The Senator indicated that the latest poll numbers were not good for the President. We were hoping that the poll numbers would be wrong.

I had sent the necessary security information weeks in advance, for a scheduled tour of the State Department. On Thursday morning, Mom, Dad, and I arrived with photo I.D. for our scheduled 9:30 a.m. tour. Not many people make the effort to get the security clearance to tour the State Department, but it is well worth the time. The tour included many of the diplomatic reception rooms used to entertain both foreign and American guests. The most impressive was the Benjamin Franklin State Dining Room, completed in 1985. The massive room has Corinthian columns surrounding the walls of gilded ornate plaster reflected in eight cut glass chandeliers. The Great Seal of the United States decorates the coffered cove in the center of the ceiling. The floor covered in a specially designed Savonnerie-style carpet, repeats the Great Seal of the United States woven into the center; along with the four important crops of the early Republic; the four seasons; and fifty stars representing the States of the Union.[1] The dining room balcony looks out over the magnificent layout of the city of Washington, D.C.

In the John Quincy Adams State Drawing Room is the original architect's table where Thomas Jefferson drafted the Declaration of Independence. On July 4, 1971, President Richard Nixon used the table in the East Room of the White House, when he signed the 26th Amendment, lowering the voting age to eighteen.[2]

After the State Department, we toured the National Cathedral, and then we visited Gary at his office on Bolling Air Force Base. By Friday, my parents needed a slower paced day, so we relaxed and picked Ann Marie up at school that afternoon. Mom and Dad were very impressed with the school and staff. However, Ann was somewhat embarrassed that her grandfather wanted to take pictures of her at the locker and outside the school.

Luther Jackson Middle School had teacher workdays on Monday before and Tuesday of the national election. Gary, Ann, and I took the long weekend for our second trip to Williamsburg with Mom and Dad. Staying again in the York Street Suites, we had confirmed reservations for dinner at Christiana Campbell's Tavern for Sunday night. We also took the time to visit the Jamestown settlement, which was nearby. My parents were great troopers throughout the hectic schedule of sightseeing, but were glad to relax in our new home during the off days.

We returned to Washington, D.C. in time to vote, and settle in on the couch with Mom, Dad, and Ann to watch the election results on the television in the living room. We watched until late into the night in disbelief that our country had elected Bill Clinton as the next President of the United States. Wednesday was a day of mourning at our house, especially as Gary and I considered who the next Commander-in-Chief would be. I put my disheartened parents on a flight back to St. Louis on Thursday morning. With depression setting in, Gary and I began to plan our military retirement within the next two years. After all, the President-elect had big plans for changing military policy, and he openly admitted "loathing" the military.

From the time Ann was two years old, she had a desire to play the piano. She would peck out notes on my parents' piano every time we would visit St. Louis. Since one of the lingering effects from her stroke was a continued stiffness in her finger movements, we decided that the challenge of playing the piano would be a therapeutic benefit. In mid-November, we purchased a new Kimball upright piano. Ann Marie enrolled in piano lessons with Pai Lin, her piano teacher from China, who would teach her how to use her left hand to play the lower notes. Ann's ability to play by ear became frustrated trying to track the notes on a written music script. She was challenged to read the music when we purchased an easy piano book with several songs from *Les Miserables*. Her favorite piece to play with her two thumbs and two index fingers was "Castle on a Cloud." A haunting melody frequently filled the house with memories of our visit to the London theatre.

Instead of driving back to St. Louis for the brief Thanksgiving holidays, we drove to Manteo, North Carolina, near Nags Head. Our dear friend, Bonnie, the single teacher in Frankfurt who went on our trip to Rome, had moved back home to Manteo to teach school. Manteo is located on the tiny island of Roanoke, the first English colony in 1584, between the mainland and the Outer Banks. Another historical first in the area was the "first flight" of the Wright brothers near Kitty Hawk and Kill Devil Hills. Although Bonnie had not married, she was a foster mother to a young eight-year old girl named, Jenny. Ann Marie and Jenny played together during the Thanksgiving holidays. They pretended to be sisters, since both wanted siblings. Bonnie cooked a fabulous turkey dinner for us, and her parents who lived next door. Gary especially enjoyed her fresh cooked collard greens from the garden seasoned with bacon. Before we left North Carolina, we made plans for Bonnie and Jenny to visit us in Washington, D.C. during Spring Break in mid-April. Ann was looking forward to Jenny seeing our home.

In Ann Marie's mind, if Jenny needed a new home and family, we should consider adopting her. All the way home Ann talked to us, trying to convince us that if we were Christians we would give Jenny a home. Gary and I did not want another child, especially the responsibility of a young girl who had come from an abusive family situation. During the next several weeks, Ann Marie continued to drop hints, some subtly and others not so subtle. In her Creative Writing class, Ann wrote a book about *The Loneliest Star,* and dedicated it to *Jenny – May she find her special home.* It was a book that not only reflected how Jenny probably felt about wanting to be picked to go to a special home, but also an allegory of Ann as the little girl who takes the loneliest star home. Although we got the message as parents, it still did not change our minds to add another child to our family. Jenny found her special home with another family.

THE LONELIEST STAR
By: Ann Grunick

THIS BOOK IS DEDICATED TO JENNY.
May She Find Her Special Home.

Once there was a star that was very lonely. This star waited on the store shelf day after day for someone to come and buy it. It wanted to get taken home for Christmas and be put on top of someone's Christmas tree. The star would watch all the people buy all the other stars, but not it! The star was very sad because people would come and say, "Look at all the beautiful stars," but would not buy the lonely star.

One day a little girl came into the store. The lonely star started to shine as bright as it could. The little girl saw how beautiful the star was. She bought it and took it home for Christmas.

As she took the star home in the car, it began to snow outside. When she got home with the star, she carefully put the star on top of the Christmas tree. The star was so happy to finally get to a home and be on top of a Christmas tree.

The next morning, the little girl was ill. She had the chicken pox! All she could do was stay inside and sleep and read. She wanted to go and play in the snow, but she could not go outside.

So the little star burst its heart to shine for her and made her feel better! Now the star knew why it had waited so long to be chosen in the store. It was meant to be in a very special home for Christmas.

The star watched as each day more gifts were placed under the tree. Finally, on Christmas day there was laughter, and singing as the family opened their gifts.

Every year the star was proud to be on the very top of the Christmas tree. Every year it would burst its heart to shine as the little girl grew older each Christmas. Then one year the little girl was gone. She was not in the house. The star missed her.

On Christmas day she came home. She brought with her a little baby. She had grown up and was a mother now. When it came time to take the tree down, the girl carefully took the star off the tree. She wrapped it up in a pretty box, and took it to her new home.

The next year the star was on top of the girl's tree shining brightly for her once again! The lonely star was never lonely again.

December brought many festivities for us to experience. One of the most famous Washington Christmas events is the lighting of the White House Christmas tree. Knowing that it would be the last time that President George and Barbara Bush would light the Christmas tree, we made plans as a family to be there. Thursday, December 10, 1992, Gary came home early from work to drive us down Arlington Highway across the Theodore Roosevelt Memorial Bridge to The Ellipse in front of the White House. The weather was cold and rainy. Local TV channels carried the pre-show, but the actual ceremony was televised nationwide. While we were huddled together under a big umbrella, the rain and wind started whipping through the crowd almost turning the umbrellas inside out. My bright red German loden coat must have caught the eye of Santa Claus. Before I realized who was touching my shoulder, there stood TV weatherman Willard Scott dressed as Santa laughing, "Ho! Ho! HO!" into my ear.

Following him was the local TV weatherman with a microphone asking me, "What kind of weather would it take for you to not be here tonight?"

I smiled and said, "Our family loves George and Barbara Bush. We wouldn't miss this tree lighting for anything!"

Putting his microphone down during a commercial break, the weatherman told me that he had been at a White House Press Christmas Party the night before, and expressed to President Bush his own disappointment in the election results. President Bush had responded that the nation wanted a change. We both agreed that the new president would definitely be a change. At 5:00 p.m., George and Barbara did the countdown and lit the massive Christmas tree in front of the White House. It was sad that the weather was so torrential, but then maybe it was a sign of things to come.

January 20, 1993, brought the Inauguration of President William Jefferson Clinton, a historical opportunity that we could not pass up. It was a freezing cold morning as we stood on Pennsylvania Avenue in the shadow of the Justice Department. Looking at the FBI - J. Edgar Hoover Building, we waited for the 42nd President of the United States to show up for his swearing in ceremony. Loud speakers above our heads broadcast the words he spoke as they traveled around the world simultaneously. Within the first five sentences, he spoke of change

– not for change sake – but change to preserve America's ideals. The Inaugural luncheon went late, throwing the Inaugural parade into the late afternoon. As the new president's limousine passed us, all we could see through the bulletproof glass were waving hands. After waiting hours in the cold as the parade passed, the sun started to set, and we headed for the warmth of the car. We had experienced our historical moment in time.

With the end of the Cold War, change was coming. The military was certainly in for a change, with troop drawdown and closing of military installations all over the world. "Don't ask – don't tell" would become the new policy in the military. Secretary of Defense Les Aspen refused to send the necessary armored vehicles at the request of military commanders in Somalia. Later, Hollywood would tell the October story in the movie *Black Hawk Down*. In November, when Bill Clinton went to the Vietnam War Memorial to lay a wreath on Veteran's Day, a group of Vietnam veterans stood at attention and upon command "about-faced" turning their backs on him. The high feelings of respect for the military after the Persian Gulf War seemed to have blown away like the dust of the Iraqi desert. We continued to feel drawn toward military retirement, but God had a few other things in mind for us to experience before we left Washington, D.C., and headed home to St. Louis.

In 1856, a group of seven men and women in the village of Falls Church, Virginia, began a Baptist Church in a home, later moving to a community building. On June 23, 1858, they dedicated Columbia Baptist Church's first church building located on Broad Street across from the Episcopal Falls Church. During the Civil War, the building served as a hospital. On October 18, 1864, Mosby's Rangers, fearing the political leadership of the Columbia Baptist pastor, killed Rev. John B. Read.

As the church struggled, it continued to grow. Columbia listed more than one-hundred members in 1902. In March of 1908, the women of the church contributed $100 to purchase property less than a mile from the old church. One-hundred-eighteen members held a dedication service of the new building on June 26, 1910. The new church built of stone added an educational wing in 1927. New construction and additions to the building continued over the next sixty years. Columbia also owned a mountaintop lodge in western Virginia, located on eight acres near the town of Winchester at Eagle Eyrie.

Senior Pastor, Neal Jones, had been the pastor since 1969, and would soon celebrate twenty-five years of service. His staff consisted of fifteen pastors and directors. The strength of this church lay in the encouragement of the laypeople to take a role of leadership in ministry. The church goal was "A Ministry for Every Member," based on the reminder that a church is not a building, but "a group of baptized believers, voluntarily associated in covenant relations, seeking to do the will of God and lovingly encouraging one another toward Christian maturity." Each of the over three-thousand members was invited to support the church and programs with regular contributions of time, talent, and financial support. In 1992, the annual church budget was approved at $3,550,065.

The unique position of Columbia Baptist meant not only sending members all over the world, but the world came to the Falls Church doors. Korean and Hispanic congregations met in a chapel area of the church, and both of these groups integrated in the life of the Church. Arabic and International Sunday School classes met on Sunday mornings. Columbia Baptist Church had become one of the great churches of the Commonwealth of Virginia and a leader in the metropolitan area of Washington, D.C.[3]

Columbia Baptist had several well-known members. Charles Colson, the founder and president of Prison Fellowship, was a member of Columbia Baptist. Pastor Neil Jones had baptized Charles Colson as a new believer after the Watergate Investigation had sent Mr. Colson to prison. In 1992, Charles Colson had just written a new book titled *The Body* which detailed insights and challenges to the people of God called to be the Church.[4] In the book, Colson used poignant stories about believers during the revolution in Timisoara, Romania, and the persecution of Christians in Eastern Europe. Again, we were convicted over the faith of our brothers and sisters in the Body of Christ, who had been willing to give their lives for the Kingdom of God.

Another famous member of Columbia Baptist was Washington Redskins football coach, Joe Gibbs. Coach Gibbs was a member of our Sunday school class, but usually had a football game to coach on Sunday during the season. He also was known for his Christian faith, and interest in racecar driving. After we became members of the church, Gary was asked to substitute teach our Sunday school class one Sunday. Amazingly, Joe and Pat Gibbs came that morning to class. Coach Gibbs laughed when Gary announced to the class that as the substitute teacher, he was not the "regular crew-chief." Gary had considered changing a team illustration in the lesson from baseball to football when he saw Joe Gibbs walk in the class, but decided to leave it as a baseball analogy. When class was over, Pat Gibbs thanked Gary for keeping it baseball, not football.

We were members of a large intergenerational Sunday school class. About one-hundred people attended our class every Sunday in the church gymnasium, as the education pastor Mark Brasler taught the Bible. The ages of the class members ranged from early 20's to almost ninety-years-old. The unique blending of generations gave wisdom, maturity, and vitality to the class discussions and fellowships. We had built-in "grandparents" for Ann Marie. One older couple, Roy and Lois Winston, graciously entertained the whole class every year at their summer cottage retreat on the Potomac River. Roy would take small groups out in his motorboat on the river, while Lois orchestrated the potluck lunch and children's outdoor games. Frequently, Roy and Lois would invite us to their McLean, Virginia, home for Sunday lunch. Their lovely backyard was lined with large azalea bushes and flower gardens. Lois made the flower arrangements for the church.

Although we found wonderful friendships in our adult Sunday school class, Ann was really struggling to fit into the church youth group. Several times she would come home from being with the youth, and tell me that she just could not seem to make friends with them. One evening, Gary and I decided to watch through the window in the door to the youth room and see what the problem was. Ann walked into the room and sat down in a chair next to a group of girls her age. When she sat down, one looked over at her, and then at the other girls. To our shock and frustration, all of the girls got up and moved their seats to another part of the room, leaving Ann Marie alone. My heart broke as I saw the rudeness. Ann Marie just hung her head fighting back the tears.

I scheduled an appointment that next week with the youth pastor. As I explained what we had witnessed, he seemed to brush it off as typical youth group dynamics. I began to tell him about Ann Marie's life, and how the Lord had healed her. I suggested that he give her a chance to give her testimony to the youth group, as Coach Muniz had done in gym class. He seemed somewhat distracted, and when I saw his eyes glaze over, I decided it was time to end the visit. He probably thought I was being overly sensitive to normal insecure youth behavior. However, some of the kids at Ann's school were friendlier than the "Christian" kids at church.

One Sunday morning in February of 1993, Josh McDowell was the guest speaker at our morning worship service. During an opening hymn, an usher approached the platform and handed Pastor Neil Jones a note. Neil immediately rushed out of the sanctuary, leaving Josh McDowell to continue with the service. Shortly before the end of the worship service, Neil reappeared looking very pale with disheveled hair. Standing in the pulpit, he asked if Mrs. Brenda Burchett was in the morning worship service. No one replied. He then announced that he had just returned from the scene of a terrible automobile accident a few blocks from the church. Three members of the Burchett family had died at the scene. Shock waves rippled across the sanctuary with cries of disbelief. Most of us had crossed the intersection that morning on our way to church.

Church member Dr. Wayne Burchett, who was also a Fairfax County elementary school principal, and his two daughters, Rena and Kara, were killed on their way to church. A driver of a stolen vehicle, fleeing police, had run a red light and smashed into their car. Mrs. Burchett had been feeling ill and not come with them to church that day. In one brief moment, Brenda Burchett had lost her husband and both of her precious children. A school district had lost a popular educator. Our church had lost treasured friends. The church and community searched for answers in the grief of such a tragedy. Only faith and hope could fill the emptiness of the loss of the three lives.

Located just minutes from the Beltway and Embassy Row, Columbia Baptist ministered to one-hundred and fifty embassy groups in Washington, D.C. One of the major ministries was teaching English as a second language to people in the community. Carol Soderquist headed the ESL ministry, "World Friends," to over one-hundred and ninety people from at least forty countries. She and husband Ron were members of our Sunday school class. Ron did Christian ministry at the Pentagon in a Bible study with some of the highest ranking military officers. Carol enlisted Gary as an ESL teacher for Wednesday and Thursday evening "World Friends" classes from 6:30 to 8:00 p.m. Daytime classes were on Wednesday and Thursday mornings from 9:30 to 11:30 for international students. During the English lessons, the students heard the Christian testimony of their teachers, memorized Bible scripture, and had the opportunity to watch the *Jesus* video. They also learned how to express everyday needs in English; like telephone conversation, reading maps, shopping for food and housing, reading a recipe, and emergency calls. The classes helped them to get jobs and become U.S. citizens.

Carol asked me to teach Precept Bible study to the ESL teachers on Thursdays from 11:30 a.m. to 12:30 p.m. while they ate lunch together. With a limited amount of time to teach, I started with *Lord, I Want to Know You!* The teachers were very responsive to the Bible study. I was surprised, since several teachers where highly educated. In appreciation of the study, Carol presented me with a drawing she had made of a strong tower. Written on each brick in the tower was a Name of God.

The Name of the Lord is a strong tower,
the righteous runs into it and is safe.
Proverbs 18:10 (NAS)

After serving nearly twenty-five years as the pastor, Neil Jones was very secure in his calling to ministry at Columbia Baptist Church. With a keen gift of discernment, he delighted in seeing the lay people of the church find a ministry and run with it. Always encouraging new ideas and ministries, each week over ninety-five events took place somewhere in the building. Columbia needed a custodial crew around the clock to clean, setup, and takedown the maze of rooms in the facility. A team of Vietnamese and Korean janitors kept the building secure and ready for service.

Pastor Jim Perdew, Minister of Missions, learned of our experience with mission ministry to Romania. Jim, a retired Navy chaplain, was encouraged when military families joined the church. He asked Gary to be part of the church mission committee, because the focus of international missions was a sister-church partnership with Moscow Baptist Church in Russia. Jim knew that Gary had experience with international missions into Romania and a sister-church relationship.

Lloyd Ashworth came to Washington, D.C. on Wednesday, June 9, 1993, for an overnight visit. We invited him to stay at our home, to catch-up on what was happening in our lives. He wanted the opportunity to meet with some of our church staff and share about his position with International Needs. Lloyd had toured most of the important attractions like the White House and Arlington Cemetery, but he had a fascination to tour the Pentagon.

Gary made the necessary arrangements for Lloyd to speak with our church mission committee after the church Wednesday night meal. Lloyd shared how International Needs (IN) supports indigenous Christian leaders and missionaries serving God in over thirty countries. Our particular interest was the ministry in Romania under the leadership of the Romanian IN Executive Director, Titi Bulzan. Romania IN was sponsoring 13 medical staff at the Bethesda Christian Clinic in Oradea, Romania. International Needs was also looking for sponsors of one-hundred and twenty children in the Caminul Felix Children's Home in Oradea. This was the same Christian orphanage, which we had seen built in 1991 by Second Baptist Church in Oradea.

The next day, after having lunch on the Potomac River, we drove the red convertible with the top down to the Pentagon for a tour. Lloyd had thought that a tour of the Pentagon would be off-limits for a "Kiwi." However, our little tourist group included visitors from Poland, Taiwan, and the Ukraine. As a young noncommissioned officer led our group through the maze of hallways explaining military history, he walked backwards facing us as he talked. Directing our attention to important office doorways, and pictures on the walls, we were led to the end of one hallway displaying two separate portraits under large gold letters, "Commander-in-Chief." Usually, only one portrait hangs under those gold letters; the NCO pointed to the separate pictures of Bill and Hillary Clinton and said, "Our Commanders-in-Chiefs."

Ann Marie finished seventh grade on June 24, 1993. She now sported the right of passage for every teenager, braces to correct her overbite. A routine scoliosis examination at school had indicated some curvature in her spine. A visit to Dr. Schrantz, the orthopedic surgeon at Bethesda Naval Hospital, had revealed a 15-degree curve in Ann Marie's spine. The follow-up visit would be in August to determine if the scoliosis was progressing.

We returned to Bethesda Naval Hospital for a scoliosis check on August 12. Dr. Schrantz viewed the new x-rays and was concerned that in the five months since he had seen Ann, her scoliosis had progressed to a twenty-degree curve. None of us wanted to think about Ann undergoing another major surgery to put a rod in her back. Our prayer was that she would not have much longer to continue growing taller. Although she would be short, when her growth stopped, then the curve should stop changing. The next appointment would be in January of 1994. If the curve progressed, then we would have to consider surgery.

Before Ann Marie started eighth grade on September 7, she and I decided to fly back to St. Louis for nine days, August 28 through September 6, to visit relatives and look for a new home. Gary and I had decided that Air Force retirement should be June 1994, so that Ann Marie could attend all four years of high school in the same school. Surrounded with grandparents, aunts, uncles, and cousins, she would gain from those relationships with her extended family. We had lived in so many homes in the twenty years of military life. I really wanted a home built the way I wanted it, not what someone else thought was "cute." Gary wanted me to look in St. Charles County across the Missouri River west of St. Louis. When we flew over the St. Louis area to land at Lambert Airport, the massive size of the "Flood of 1993" was astounding. At least we would know where the flood plain was in St. Charles, Missouri.

Mom drove us around the St. Charles area to several new housing developments she had found in the newspaper. Mom loved looking at display homes, and Ann Marie and I would go into each one trying to imagine what it would be like to live in the display model. St. Charles was one of the fastest growing counties in Missouri. It had been rich farmland, now sold off to land developers. Some of the back roads remained winding, hilly, and bumpy. One afternoon, after dipping up and down a particularly weaving road, I told Mom to stop the car. I had to get out because I was carsick. Practically falling out of the passenger door, I sat down on the street curb. After several minutes of breathing fresh air, I felt well enough to get back into the car. That is when my mom pointed to a realtor's sign in the front yard of the house we parked next too. She suggested we call the realtor's phone number and have her show us homes in St. Charles. Madeline Williams with Coldwell Banker was delighted to take us where we needed to go.

Madeline had several pre-owned homes on her list, and they were all very lovely. However, I had in my mind what I wanted. A brand new home built to my specification, including color of paint, flooring, cabinets, bathroom fixtures, lighting, and carpet. Madeline took us to a beautiful walkout ranch home with a finished basement, which was only two-years old. I loved the layout and wanted to buy it, but we would not be moving for another ten months. Madeline suggested that I talk with the builder, because he was building a new section of houses right down the street. I came back from St. Louis to Washington, D.C. with the exact floor plan that I wanted. In December, Gary could go with me, see the display, and pick a lot. Ann Marie could have the entire finished basement as her suite of rooms, and Gary could have an office for his legal work.

Ann Marie was happy to start back to Luther Jackson Middle School. She was on the Rising Stars team and once again had great teachers. Ann enjoyed chorus as one of her electives. She made several friends in her classes, and continued to reach out to those who were foreign or disadvantaged. She decided to be on the yearbook staff since she had a love of writing and journalism. Mrs. McNiff, her seventh grade math teacher, was the yearbook sponsor and enjoyed working with Ann again on the yearbook. Coach Muniz continued to challenge Ann five days a week on the weight equipment strengthening her arms and legs. Not only did the exercise help her to keep her balance and walk more stable, but also it strengthened her back muscles to stop the scoliosis.

I had been part of a telephone prayer chain directed by Lois Cox at Columbia Baptist Church. Lois wanted to start a women's Bible study on Tuesday mornings. She asked me to be her assistant teacher. After intense prayer, we gathered a class of godly women and began Bible study on September 28. Lois was an outstanding Bible teacher. I realized that much of the depth of her teaching came from her personal testing of faith in adversity. Five years before, Lois and Fred Cox had walked in faith through the death of their daughter, Michelle. A beautiful and active young woman, Michelle had developed pneumonia in the autumn before her freshman year of college. Through several weeks and then months of hospitalization, Michelle was unable to regain her strength and health. She had slipped into death just on the brink of the promises of young adulthood. Although Michelle's body had become weak, her faith had remained strong. I also realized that Lois still grieved the loss of her daughter very deeply. I could not imagine the pain she felt, and how she missed the treasured relationship that mothers and daughters have. I was even more thankful that Ann Marie had survived her medical traumas.

The end of September, the popular Christian music group TRUTH was coming to a church in Manassas, Virginia. Ann Marie wanted to go hear them in concert, because she knew that they were a favorite group of Adonis Vidu. TRUTH had ministered in Oradea, Romania, and given money to help build the new Emanuel Baptist Church. During the Friday night concert, the group sang a powerful song, "If You Could See Me Now," in memory of a member of TRUTH who had recently died. The song talked about walking streets of gold, standing tall and whole. The message was that if we could see what heaven is like, we would never want our loved ones to come back to earth.

That night, as Ann was getting ready for bed, she asked me a startling question, "Mom, what if I die before you do?"

I stood there stunned by her question, looking at her in her pink and white flannel nightgown as she crawled under her covers. I replied, "Ann, usually parents die before their children. I don't think that is going to happen."

She looked up at me from her pillow with searching eyes and said, "But Mom, it could happen."

Understanding that the question had come from the concert message and song, I quietly replied, "If that happens, Ann Marie, you just save me a seat, and I'll be there."

As I bent over to kiss her goodnight, she whispered, "O.K., Mom."

The next morning was a wedding day. One of the female NCOs in Gary's office, Naomi, was marrying Gregory in the Evangel Assembly Temple in Camp Spring, Maryland. Weddings excited Ann Marie, especially when she put on her new dress which I had found on sale. The pale pink layers of chiffon on the full skirt contrasted against the sleeveless black velvet top. A long-sleeved, open-front black velvet jacket covered her bare arms. A black velvet rhinestone studded belt cinched her waist. She could have been in the wedding instead of a guest. Receiving several compliments on how lovely she looked, the dress did reveal that she was developing a petite womanly figure.

Another door opened for us to do ministry with a special group of church members. One of the women in my ESL Precept class, Dr. Joan Stanton, was a professor at the University of Northern Virginia. She was coordinating a Singles Retreat at the Eagle Eyri Retreat Center for the single adults who were past college age. Joan enjoyed our Bible study so much, that she asked me to be the retreat speaker for the weekend of October 1-3, 1993. I consented to be part of the program, if Gary would also be part of the speaking program, and we could bring Ann Marie.

The theme for the weekend was "Spiritual Maturity." We arrived on Friday evening at the beautiful church retreat center in the western mountains near Winchester, Virginia. Autumn trees reflecting their colors of red, golden yellow and dusty orange surrounded the mountaintop lodge. A huge stone fireplace rising to an atrium ceiling welcomed us with the warmth of a log fire. As an introduction to the weekend, Gary and I gave our testimony to the group of singles that evening. Of course, they had the opportunity to meet Ann Marie and include her in their fellowship.

Larry Allison was an interesting single man, who could relate to Ann Marie's life experiences. Larry had several physical disabilities including life in a wheelchair. When 10:00 p.m. rolled around, Gary and I decided it was time for sleep. However, Ann Marie was having such a great time with the adults, who were teaching her to play a card game, she begged to stay up and continue the game. Larry was helping her hands coordinate the cards since he had a great deal of experience in the proper technique. She knew the bedroom was just down the hall, so we allowed her a growing experience to touch the lives of these single adults. Many of them would never have children, or missed the children they had left in a divorce. She finally came to bed around midnight, having experienced a little independence and acceptance.

The next morning, after Gary taught on the *One Another's of the Epistles* and I taught on *Oneness with the Father* from John Chapter 17; the singles group headed for a local apple farm. Ann Marie found a display of small sugar-pie pumpkins with faces painted on them. She picked out a little painted face pumpkin with singing notes coming out of the mouth. She kept the painted pumpkin in her room for months.

Tuesday, October 19, 1993, Peter and Geta Vidu had traveled to the U.S. to raise funds for their new Emanuel Baptist Church in Oradea. One of their stops was a meeting at the Southern Baptist Foreign Mission Board in Richmond, Virginia. Peter had called Gary, and asked if we could meet him and Geta in Richmond to escort them to the Foreign Mission Board meeting. He trusted us to give an American perspective to the project and help him with translation.

Gary and I left early in the morning for the drive to Richmond. Meeting the Vidu's at their hotel, we drove them to the Foreign Mission Board building. The new president of the Foreign Mission Board, Dr. Jerry A. Rankin, was moving into his new home that day, and unable to meet Peter and Geta Vidu. The Mission Board facilities were grand. Everyone seemed very welcoming as they escorted us around the various offices and into a small reception room. Several of the staff took a break to come into the room and share coffee, donuts, and fresh strawberries with us. They had a short ceremony where a staff person presented Peter with a special ink pen from the Foreign Mission Board, and told him to use it "to write to them sometime." As Peter opened his folder, thinking that it was his turn to present the pictures and vision of the new church building in Oradea, the staff excused themselves and went out of the room and back to work. One man offered to show us the Lottie Moon display room down the hall. We graciously followed him and walked through the information displays and history of missionary Lottie Moon, who died from starvation on her way home from China. The annual Christmas offering for International Missions is given in her memory. Then it was almost noon, and thinking that the opportunity would come over lunch to talk about the project in Romania, we waited for someone to offer to take us to a local restaurant. Escorting us to the front door, they thanked us for coming and seeing the Foreign Mission Board, and invited us to return sometime. Standing out on the sidewalk, the four of us looked at each other wondering where we might have lunch.

We drove around nearby streets and found a nice little restaurant for lunch. Once we ordered our food, the reality of what had happened set in. Peter and Geta had traveled all the way from Romania with such great hope of collaborating with the Southern Baptist Convention Foreign Mission Board. Gary and I had driven a couple of hours to Richmond to encourage and help. All we had was a grand tour, and an ink pen to write with sometime. Peter's disappointment was obvious. He pulled out his pictures and proposals he had worked so hard on for a presentation. Showing them to Gary and me, his heart was breaking that the opportunity had not come to make a connection in a partnership with the Southern Baptist Convention. It was a difficult moment for all of us. Knowing that God is Sovereign, we all had to wonder how the vision for a new church and seminary would ever come into being. The door of freedom might be open for only a short time, if the opportunity slipped away, the people would perish. We prayed together for strength, wisdom, and discernment to know how to proceed with the plans.

Although Central Presbyterian Church in St. Louis had not united with Romania after the Werners and Randy returned from their mission trip, they had a partnership with a church in the Ukraine. Tom Werner, as the chairman of the mission committee, had started a ministry in connection with the U.S. State Department of shipping large containers with humanitarian supplies to the Ukraine. Gary talked with Tom about the logistics of the State Department program. During the presidential administration of George H. W. Bush, *The Fund for Democracy and Development* was established. The State Department would deliver a forty-foot container, to an approved organization in the U.S., wanting to help former Soviet countries struggling with the transition from communism to becoming economically stable. Once filled with humanitarian supplies, the State Department would pick up the container and ship it free to any former Soviet Union destination. The only stipulation was that no religious materials, used clothing, or perishable goods could be sent at the government's expense.

Since the U.S. State Department was within a few miles of our church, Gary presented the idea to Neal Jones and the mission committee to start a Moscow Baptist Church container ministry. Neal was excited and encouraged Gary to investigate the procedures and cost. The mission committee was a little more skeptical that our church could fill a forty-foot container. Gary began the process of getting approval from the State Department, and information on the cost and customs regulations.

Columbia Baptist Church, in our nation's capital, had linked with the 5,000 members of Moscow Baptist Church, in Russia's capital. The opportunity opened when the walls of communism crumbled and fell. In March of 1989, at a brief Sunday morning meeting with two Baptist Union leaders from Moscow, a vision of where God might lead the two churches began to develop and expand into reality. By July 1989, in a business meeting, Columbia Baptist approved a proposal letter be sent to Moscow Baptist Church to establish the sister-church relationship. A year after the first meeting, Jim Perdew and three church members visited Moscow Baptist with a Baptist World Alliance study tour group. The partnership was established on the last Sunday in April 1990. Several exchanges of visits by pastors, choirs, and church leaders took place over the next two years. Seven Columbia ministers and church leaders provided training in education and computer programming in October 1992.

Pastor Neal Jones planned to travel to Moscow in September 1993, with five church members to lead in worship, provide training, and discuss plans for the future partnership. Putting the trip off until October because of political hostilities, they arrived during an uprising of Muscovites, who stormed the office of President Yeltsin for a few days. Conditions in Moscow were still deplorable with broken sidewalks, darkened streets filled with potholes, little food available in the stores, and crude medical care in the hospitals. One evening, as Neal Jones entered the elevator to go to the small apartment where he was staying in Moscow, he realized once the elevator door closed that there was no light bulb. Searching in the dark, he found the elevator panel of buttons. Unable to see which button to push, he continued to go up and down until the door opened on the right floor. Stumbling out of the elevator into a dimly lit hallway, he found his way to his room. Returning to Washington, D.C., Neil was even more determined to send supplies to Moscow in a container ministry.

Gary had been diligently working a plan for the Moscow container ministry, but he needed to give it a powerful name. Neil Jones preached a series of sermons called "Cross-Focus," which led Gary to consider a similar idea. Gary decided on the ministry name, *CrossLink*. The cross of Christ linked these two churches on opposite sides of the world through their faith. Joining in a sister-church relationship would strengthen both congregations for the Kingdom of God. Gary was further encouraged finding the definition of *cross-link* in the dictionary to mean—to join to, a crosswise connection, cross-linking increases strength and toughness.

The mission committee designated a $5,000 budget for *CrossLink* purchases. Gary contacted the commissary at Bolling Air Force Base for help with surplus canned goods. The commissary gave *CrossLink* several boxes of canned green beans and asparagus. One member of the mission committee saw the boxes of canned green beans and laughed that most Russians do not eat those "green sticks." He questioned how those few boxes would fill a forty-foot container.

Gary replied that the few boxes were simply the loaves and fishes that the Lord would multiply to fill the container.

Remembering the European Baptist Conference, we attended in Wiesbaden, Germany, where Dr. Srgei Nikolaev had spoken about using sewing thread to stitch wounds, washing out cloth bandages for reuse, and no pain medication, Gary knew medical supplies were a necessity. Dr. Barry Byer, a medical doctor, and Dr. Rod Murchie, a dentist, were members of our congregation. They both volunteered along with their wives, to help find, collect, or purchase needed nonperishable food, personal care items, medical equipment, and drugs for the shipment. Jann Murchie and I went to the local Price Club warehouse and purchased pallets of sugar, flour, rice, tea, dried beans, and several three-foot long rolls of summer sausage. We also purchased toothpaste, toothbrushes, soap, toilet paper, and shampoo.

Gary found a supplier, who sent a pallet load of children's chewable vitamins, along with two pallets of new hospital sheets. Another supplier sent a pallet of rice for a few hundred dollars. Dr. Barry Byer realized that he could find all sorts of new medical equipment and drugs which hospitals were willing to donate to a charitable cause. He would call up Fairfax Hospital and tell them what Arlington Hospital was donating, and then ask Fairfax Hospital what they would be willing to donate. One medical supply house sent a brand new examining table, a wheelchair, and boxes of sterile syringes and bandages. Dr. Rod Murchie found needed donations of dental tools and equipment for the shipment. A church member donated the use of his warehouse just a few blocks from the church to store the collected items. Gary, Ann Marie, and I spent one Saturday cleaning and sweeping out the dirt from the unused warehouse so that processing of donations could take place.

Ann Marie decided that her school could help with the *CrossLink* mission. Her Civics teacher Mrs. Grossman helped Ann organize a collection campaign for the students and teachers to donate personal hygiene items like soap, toothpaste, and toothbrushes. Ann worked hours collecting, sorting, and helping to pack boxes in the warehouse. She wrote in her Civics report that she felt like a missionary, and she wished that she could be there when the Russian people opened the container.

The name *CrossLink* caught on and people began to get excited about the mission. Our final source of supplies came from the members of Columbia Baptist Church. Thanksgiving weekend, we asked each family to bring a plastic grocery bag full of nonperishable food and personal care items, to place on the altar of the church during the worship services. The front of the church was full of donations by the end of the third service. Loading the bags into a truck, we carted them to the warehouse.

During the next week, a few members of the team collected boxes, sorted and labeled supplies. We sectioned off areas of the warehouse for similar items packed together in boxes. Jann Murchie and I made another run to Price Club with money given to purchase extra supplies. We bought canned hams, more summer sausages, and pasta. For the Russian children's Sunday school, we purchased school supplies of paper, pencils, crayons, ink pens, construction paper, watercolors, and scissors.

The State Department delivered the empty forty-foot container to the warehouse on Friday, December 4, 1993. Then on Saturday, our small *CrossLink* mission team packed, sealed, and inventoried the hundreds of boxes. Ann Marie worked with Dr. Byer inventorying boxes and taping them closed. Barry heard Ann Marie's testimony by mid-morning. As a medical doctor, he bonded with Ann and her life-story. Using a pushcart to move the boxes, Barry would tell Ann Marie to get on the cart while he pushed it around the warehouse collecting supplies and filling boxes.

Before we loaded the boxes into the forty-foot container, Neil Jones had an idea. Neil called all of the church deacons together for a Saturday morning breakfast and meeting. After the deacon meeting, he marched the deacons the few blocks over to the warehouse to see what was going on with the *CrossLink* container. Most of the deacons were shocked to see all of the boxes and the size of the container. They had not realized the magnitude of how God had supplied everything. Neil told each deacon to find a box and lay hands on it. Then he led all of us in prayer for the shipment and the blessing that it would bring to the Moscow Baptist Church. Several of the deacons realized what God was doing and decided to stay, helping load the container.

Later that week, on December 7, 1993, the State Department shipped the first *CrossLink* container on a two-month journey to Moscow Central Baptist Church. The forty-foot container with an estimated value of $130,000, filled with 18,800 lbs. of humanitarian and medical supplies, had cost the mission committee $5,000 to step out in faith. Our Lord had multiplied the loaves and fishes. However, this was just the beginning of what God would do through a ministry called *CrossLink*, which started with a few cans of green beans and asparagus.

Ann Marie had continued to attend and try to fit into the youth group at Columbia Baptist Church. She was particularly excited about the first campaign for "True Love Waits" introduced to the youth group during the month of November 1993. The final session of "True Love Waits" was a big pizza party in the fellowship hall where the youth would all sign their pledge cards to remain sexually pure until marriage. D.J. Campbell and his family sat at the same table with us. Although D.J. had remained friendly to Ann Marie, he was not ready to be involved in any serious relationship. Ann found that somewhat frustrating, since she really wanted a boyfriend. He and Ann signed their cards together and we all celebrated with pizza.

The next week, I took Ann Marie to purchase a "True Love Waits" ring for her to wear until her wedding day. When Ann Marie went to school wearing her ring, several of the kids at school asked her about her ring. She explained to them about the pledge of waiting until marriage to have sex, and that the ring was a symbol of the pledge. Five of the students at Luther Jackson, who did not even go to church, wanted to sign the pledge. Ann Marie got five cards from Allen Wilson and brought the cards to school. She began to look forward to the first week in February when Josh McDowell was coming back to Washington, D.C. Josh would hold a big *WHY WAIT?* Rally for area teenagers. Ann began to make a list of classmates that she wanted to invite to the Rally. She kept the list of eleven names in a notebook on her desk at home, and prayed for an opportunity to ask them to come to the event.

On December 23, 1993, we drove back to St. Louis for Christmas vacation and stayed at my parents' home. Our nephew Matt was studying to become a beautician. Deciding that she wanted short hair, Ann asked Matthew to cut her very long hair. I watched as Matt carefully took the scissors to Ann's beautiful long curls and snipped as they dropped to the floor. She took on the grown-up impression of being a mature young woman as the short hairstyle emerged around her checks and neckline. Grandpa cried when he saw her long hair gone. But, Ann was happy and giggled about the new look.

On December 29, 1993, Gary and I signed a contract to build our new home in St. Charles, Missouri, down the street from the house I had seen in August. We picked out the bricks, paint color, flooring, and fixtures. In January, the basement foundation would begin with expected completion of the house by the beginning of July. Ann Marie saw the lot we picked and met the two children who would be our neighbors. When we returned to Washington, D.C., Gary submitted his retirement paperwork six months in advance for the end of June. I began to shop with Ann Marie for accessories for our new home. Since her matching blue and pink bedroom curtains, sheets, and bedspread were almost eight-years old, I told Ann that she could have all new linens in her next bedroom. The finished basement would have a large bedroom and walk-in closet with adjoining bathroom. She could entertain and do her studying in the massive walkout basement den furnished with bookcases, desk, over-stuffed chairs, a couch, table, and a gas fireplace. Our three-bedroom ranch retirement home was around thirty-six hundred sq. feet including the finished basement.

CHAPTER EIGHTEEN

The Dream

For Thou didst form my inward parts;
Thou didst weave me in my mother's womb.
I will give thanks to Thee,
for I am fearfully and wonderfully made;
wonderful are Thy works,
and my soul knows it very well.
My frame was not hidden from Thee,
when I was made in secret,
and skillfully wrought in the depths of the earth.
Thine eyes have seen my unformed substance;
and in Thy book they were all written,
the days that were ordained for me,
when as yet there was not one of them.
Psalms 139:13-16 (NAS)

Ice storms had covered the eastern seaboard in the winter of 1993-94, closing schools for snow days week after week. It was beginning to look like those students in the Fairfax County school system would have to go extra days in June to make up the days of missed school. Our long driveway was so slick, that attempting to walk up it to catch the school bus, on days when there was school, was like ice-skating up hill. Taking one-step forward, sliding backwards several steps, and falling on hands and knees to stop the slide.

The Columbia Baptist youth group had planned a ski trip to Pennsylvania over the weekend for January 28-30. Leaving from the Falls Church parking lot on the evening of Friday, January 28, they planned to travel to the retreat center "Eagle Eyri" in Winchester, West

Virginia. Spending the night at the retreat lodge, on Saturday morning they would caravan in three church vans along the Pennsylvania Turnpike to Blue Knob Ski Resort for a day of skiing. Then on Sunday, the skiing would be at White Tail Ski Resort in Pennsylvania.

Gary and I decided to go as chaperones on the ski trip and help Ann establish some friendships, knowing that she was struggling with peer relationships in the youth group. Ann Marie had learned to ski in Austria, and had her own ski equipment. On our final ski trip in Austria, she had skied from the top of St. Johann down to the bottom, stopping for apple strudel and tea. We looked forward to skiing with her again. She needed the chance to show the other youth that she could excel physically in a sport.

The week before the ski trip, snow and ice began to melt on the roads in Washington, D.C. and Fairfax County. Ann Marie had an appointment on Monday, January 24, with the orthopedic surgeon at Bethesda Naval Hospital to check up on her scoliosis. Gary took off work because the roads were still snow covered, and he wanted to drive us to Maryland. I was thankful he was driving as we slipped backwards in the car trying to go forward to the next level on ice-covered steep ramps in the parking garage.

After early morning x-rays followed by lunch, we had the afternoon doctor's appointment. The nurse recorded vital statistics. Ann was fourteen-years and six-months old. In one year, she had gained about ten pounds, growing one and a fourth inches. She was still very petite at four-foot and ten-inches tall, weighing only eighty-five pounds. The examination of her spine x-rays revealed that Ann's scoliosis seemed to be more stabilized, showing the same twenty-degree curve in her spine as seen six months earlier. However, Dr. Schranz measured a leg length discrepancy of Ann's left leg being ¼ to ½ inch shorter than her right leg. Although the weight lifting exercises had improved her walking gait and sense of balance, her heel cords were tight. Dr. Schranz prescribed a small foam lift for Ann Marie to wear in her left shoe to even out her leg length. He also drew a diagram for a wooden wedge board to help stretch Ann's heel cords. She was to stand on the wedge against a wall for twenty minutes each day. I sent the diagram instructions to Dad to build the wedge board.

Ann Marie came home from the doctor's appointment depressed about doing more exercises and wearing a shoe lift. Disappointedly she said, "What else can go wrong with me, Mom?"

Wednesday evening a freezing rain started to fall again. The D.C. area highways froze-over. Traffic snarled around the Beltway. The weather conditions canceled school for Thursday and Friday. We were not sure whether the youth ski trip would happen, since the driving conditions were so dangerous.

All day on Friday, we waited to hear if the trip would go while I finished laundry so we could pack our clothes. Ann Marie wanted to wear a ski cap she bought in Austria, so we spent much of the morning looking for the hat in closets and dresser drawers. All of the looking led to more digging through baskets of toys, dolls, stuffed animals, games, and cleaning of closets. After lunch, I left Ann Marie to finish cleaning her room and laying out the clothes she needed to take on the trip. I vacuumed the house, dusted, and cleaned the bathrooms and kitchen. In mid-afternoon, I realized that Ann was still in her room with the door shut. I knocked and peeked in the door to see her sitting on her bed with all her dolls.

When I said, "Ann, what are you doing?"

She replied, "I'm saying good-bye to my dolls."

I said, "If you are going on this trip, you better finish cleaning the room, and get in the shower, or you will miss the trip."

Gary took off work early and arrived home around 3:00 p.m. We loaded the mini-van with suitcases, boots and skis, and then headed for the church. The warmer temperatures had turned the roads into mushy dirty snow and ice crystals. Snowplows had been able to clear most of the covered roadways. Meeting with the adults and youth at church the decision was to go ahead with the trip.

Two fifteen-passenger church vans would take the boys in one van and the girls in the other. A third van with a wheelchair lift would carry all of our suitcases and ski equipment. The youth pastor, Allen Wilson, would lead the way in the van with a lift. Gary decided to drive the girls in the church Ford van, since we had owned a Ford Econoline van for twelve years. Ron Rhodes would follow with the boys in a Dodge van. We had to wait for the Ford van returning from a men's retreat before loading and caravanning to Eagle Eyri. The sun was setting when the Ford van arrived, having just traveled the roads we were about to drive back to West Virginia. The driver got out of the van, pulled out a can of oil, and lifted the hood.

He poured the oil into the engine and said, "You be careful driving out there. I was sliding across the centerline of the road all the way home. Make sure you check the oil gauge. This van burns a lot of oil."

We loaded the thirteen girls. Gary got in the driver's seat. As I crawled into the front passenger's seat, my eyes locked onto the taped sign on the dashboard, *Remind Passengers to Wear Seat Belts.* I mentioned the seat belts to the girls, but most of the belts were pulled out between the back of the seat cushion. They were down under the seats on the floor and not accessible to be used. The girls moaned that they could not get the belts through the backs of the seat and did not want to wear them.

In the cold dusk of evening, we headed off the parking lot and into rush hour Washington, D.C. traffic. The roads were clear until we reached outside the Beltway. Melting snow was beginning to re-freeze on the pavement. As the night settled in, sleet began to fall pelting the windshield and shining off the headlights. Gary asked the girls to stop singing and laughing, so he could concentrate while he drove. There was some quiet protest from the back of the van. I prayed for angels to surround us and protect us. A few hours later, we arrived at the ice-covered parking lot of the retreat center. Gary and I were relieved to have made it safely.

I opened my door to step out of the van and realized the parking lot was a sheet of ice. The girls piled out of the side door, laughing, glad to be out of the cramped van. Ann Marie stood frozen at the van door looking down at the leap onto the ice. As I reached to help Ann down, a girl came from behind her and shoved her. Ann Marie came stumbling out of the door landing on her hands and knees. I bent down to help her up.

Ann had tears in her eyes and said, "Mom, I hurt my hands."

Helping her inside the building, I looked at her hands in the light. They were cut and bleeding from the sharp chunks of ice.

Giving her a hug, I said, "Let's find the restroom and wash your hands."

Inside the restroom, I carefully examined Ann's hands and washed the dirt and blood off with soap and warm water. She just stood there with tears of humiliation running down her cheeks. Anger began to rage in me about Ann being shoved and hurt by falling on the icy ground. The cuts on her hands were not nearly as deep as the wounds to her soul. The girl who shoved her probably did not realize how unsteady Ann was on her feet. However, to run off laughing and not say anything to Ann showed me how inconsiderate the girls were.

Drying Ann's tears and leaving the restroom, we began to look for the girls' dormitory and where to sleep. The girls' side of the retreat center had three rooms with four bunk beds each. As we went to each room, the girls would tell us that it was full. The twelve girls had already selected which four girls would go in each of the rooms. Then there was another very large room with about twenty bunk beds. The situation appeared to be that Ann Marie would not be sleeping with the other twelve girls, but she would have to sleep in the big room with me, Suzanne Wilson, Nancy Rhodes, and sixteen empty bunk beds. I found the youth pastor's wife, Suzanne, and explained the situation. I told her that I thought everyone should sleep together in the one big room leaving no one out, and the adults could watch over the room. She went to each of the three rooms and told the girls that they needed to move their things into the big room, because we were all sleeping together. There was once again some grumbling and protesting about having to gather up things and move. When the girls realized they had to move, they all rushed into the big room to pick which bed they wanted. Ann Marie had already picked her bed right in the middle of the room, surrounded with girls.

After getting the suitcases in the room and a few things unpacked, we headed to the main lodge room with a huge stone fireplace. Several of the boys helped gather wood and start a fire. The retreat staff served dinner from the kitchen. Gathering by the roaring fire after dinner, we sang and had a Bible study with the youth pastor. Allen spoke to the group about the words of Jesus in John, Chapter 14.

Do not let your hearts be troubled.
Believe in God,
believe also in me.

295

> *In My Father's house are many dwelling places;*
> *if it were not so,*
> *I would have told you;*
> *for I go to prepare a place for you.*
> *And if I go and prepare a place for you,*
> *I will come again, and receive you to Myself;*
> *that where I am, there you may be also.*
> *You know the way to where I am going.*
> John 14:1-4 (NAS)

Ann Marie sat with her Bible open, concentrating on every word the pastor spoke. Several of the kids were goofing around and passing notes. One boy was playing with a cigarette lighter. Gary reached over and took the lighter away from him after the kid set his sock on fire. My heart was so grieved with this group of kids. They were so undisciplined, self-centered, and rude. When the Bible study was over, we played a few games. The boys ran outside in the snow.

As most of the girls finally settled into a bed and began to talk, one of them decided they should have a prayer circle before sleeping. They began to go around the circle of bunk beds with each one taking a turn to pray. Some were praying silly things and giggling, and then before the whole circle could participate, one said "Amen" and ended the prayer time. They did not seem to realize that I was there, because I shocked them when I spoke up and exhorted them that prayer was a serious matter. I commended them for wanting to have such a prayer time. But, I pointed out that there were several in the room who had not had an opportunity to pray. If they were truly "Christian girls" they would consider the seriousness of prayer, and do the right thing by starting the prayer circle again, and allowing the rest of the circle to pray. Sobered by the warning, they began the prayer circle again with a much more solemn attitude. When Ann Marie prayed, she thanked the Lord for her friends who had come on the trip. She asked the Lord to bless them. Such innocent forgiveness for her "friends" broke my heart.

They were surprised to hear me join them in prayer. I thanked the Lord for giving us safe travel through the sleet and ice. I thanked Him for opening the door for each of the girls to come on the trip. I asked Him to use the trip to show us why He had allowed us to come and what we could learn about His Will in our lives. I asked that He would draw us closer together in friendships and ministering to each other. It was not a prayer my head wanted to pray. I was very angry about the behavior I had seen in the group. Nevertheless, what came out of my mouth even surprised me. It was only through the power of the Holy Spirit that such a prayer could even escape my lips. I did not know what a prophetic prayer it really was. This would be a retreat that none of the girls would ever forget. It would change all of our lives for eternity.

Turning out the lights, each one fell asleep. I lay on the hard plastic-covered mattress across the room from Ann Marie. I could not relax and let sleep come. Minutes ticked into hours, as the replay of events that evening kept circling through my mind. I knew I needed sleep in order to ski the next day. Finally, around 2:00 a.m., I got out of the bunk bed and went into the restroom. My face was beet-red; I was burning up from the heated room and anger over the situation of Ann Marie trying to be part of this youth group. I splashed cold water on my face and prayed for the Lord to give me wisdom and sleep. Returning to the sleeping room, I checked on Ann. She was sleeping soundly on her bottom bunk bed. I finally fell asleep.

Early the next morning we woke to sunshine and clear weather. Dressing for the ski slopes, everyone was excited about the day. Ann Marie needed help with her hair, so I heated up her electric curlers and fixed her hair and makeup. We took our time together getting dressed and talking while the other girls headed down to breakfast. I wanted Ann to look beautiful on this special day of skiing.

While I was curling Ann's hair she said, "Mom, I had a bad dream last night."

I said, "Really? What was it about?"

She took a deep breath, as if the memory was more than she wanted to revisit.

"I dreamed that I was water skiing and a big snake came up out of the water and bit me and ate me. I dreamed that I died!"

"Oh! Ann Marie! That is a bad dream! I think you are just nervous about skiing today. Don't worry. Everything will be all right. You already know how to ski. So you can just show the other girls how good you are at skiing. Come on now. Let's get to breakfast."

We walked down to breakfast and sat at a table with Gary, and Allen and Suzanne Wilson. During breakfast, I told Gary that Ann had a bad dream. When he asked what it was, I explained the dream. Allen and Gary just laughed.

Gary said, "Ann there are no snow snakes that are going to get you today! Let's go skiing!"

It was 8:30 a.m., time to load the vans and head off to Blue Knob Ski Resort. Coming out the front door of the retreat center, the sun was shining, but the walks and parking lot were frozen solid. Gary held his arm around Ann so she would not fall as they walked to the parking lot. Then he picked her up and put her inside the van. Allen decided to send one of the other men counselors, Nick, in our van with the girls. This meant more than a full load and four girls had to slide in together on the first seat behind Gary and me. At first, Ann Marie was sitting in the middle of the seat with another girl next to the left window behind Gary, and two other girls on Ann's right side behind my seat. Then one girl complained because she wanted to sit next to the girl at the window. Ann moved to the window seat and let the three other girls sit together. There were only three seat belts for the four girls, and the belts were all down under the seats. After the groaning the night before about seat belts and changing rooms, I decided not to mention the seat belt issue.

As we started down the road, it seemed to be clear and dry. We headed toward the highway and found even better roads. Conversation turned to skiing and what kind of previous experiences each girl had skiing. Most of the girls never skied before and were impressed that Ann had skied in Austria and Switzerland and won a racing medal.

About an hour down the road, following Allen and Suzanne's van and the boys in a van behind us, we turned off the main highway and on to a narrow winding road. I began to tell the story of my first time skiing. Actually, it was at Blue Knob where I first put on a pair of skis and realized that I did not know how to stop. As I told the story, everyone laughed. It had been almost twenty years since Gary and I skied the first time, and we were headed back to Blue Knob with our daughter.

Ann Marie asked me, "Mom, where was I when you skied that first time?"

Smiling, I replied, "Ann Marie you were only a twinkle in your Father's eye!"

I turned back around in the front seat to watch, since the road was getting more curves and I did not want to become carsick. Suddenly, as we came around a right-hand curve, the van seemed to slide across the road. Gary quickly steered in the opposite direction of the skid, but the tires were not responding to the correction.

I gasped, "Oh! Gary!"

I felt the van continue to turn around and then I closed my eyes as we headed backwards across the road again. I heard this terrible crunching sound of metal and glass breaking. Stunned, I opened my eyes. I realized we had stopped, but something was not right. I could see the smashed windshield in front of me, but somehow we were upside down. I saw daylight through the windshield and unsnapped my seat belt.

I called to Gary, "This way, come out this way."

I crawled out of the front windshield and helped Gary through the opening. Looking down I saw the girl who had changed seats with Ann. She was lying through the broken windshield crying, "Help me! Help me out!"

Gary and I reached down, took her by the arms and shoulders, and began to lift her up and out of the van. She seemed to be uninjured and able to stand on her own. It was then as the other girls began to crawl out of the van, I remembered Ann Marie was in there somewhere.

"Ann Marie! Ann Marie! Gary, where is Ann Marie?" I began to cry.

"She's here! She's over here!" Gary yelled.

He stood looking at her for a second and then he was gone to knock on a nearby door and call an ambulance.

I ran around the van and gasped at what my eyes saw, but my brain could not process. There lying on the road was my precious daughter. The upper half of her body was through the side window. From the waist down, she was pinned inside the van. She was lying face up with her eyes closed and arms folded across her stomach. She looked asleep, except blood was running out of her nose, mouth, and right ear.

Underneath her head, a puddle of blood was forming on the ground. Her breathing was slow and gurgling through the blood running out of her mouth.

From the depths of my soul I cried out, "No! Oh! God, No!"

I backed away for a moment and sat down feeling as if I would vomit.

Then I thought, *Go to her! She needs you! You are her Mom!*

I knew it was bad. Her injuries were clearly severe to her head and I knelt down next to her sobbing, praying for her. As I crouched there on the pavement soaked with motor oil and blood, someone brought a white scarf to put under her head and wipe her face. I lifted her head gently. My fingers touched a large hole in the back of her skull and I knew I had felt her brain. The right side of her face began to swell and turn blue as blood pooled under her skull and skin.

I cried out over and over, "Annie, Annie! Mommy loves you!"

The thought of dealing with massive brain damage gripped me with fear. Ann had come so far in her struggle to live after her stroke. The pain of her going through it again was unbearable.

I closed my eyes and prayed with all of my spirit to the Lord Jesus. It was a prayer of groaning too deep for words. I felt the Holy Spirit interceding in my prayer for God's Will in the situation. Suddenly, I was aware of being at the very Throne of God with an assurance that He was in control and sovereign over everything that was about to take place.

I felt His presence saying, *Trust Me in this. Let go of her. Let her come to Me.*

Allen had turned back around on the road in his van when he realized we were not following him anymore. He was stunned to come upon the accident in the roadway. The boys in the following van had seen us slide and roll into the side ditch. Ron Rhodes hit the brakes of his van just in time to avoid the patch of black ice on the road that had caused us to lose control. After doing a 180° spin on the road, the boys' van came to a stop with no one hurt. A gasoline tanker truck behind them came sliding around the curve and just missed hitting the boys' van head-on.

None of the other girls was seriously injured and all were able to get out of the van. Nick helped move all of the kids away from our van. D. J. Campbell had come to help from the boys' van. He tried to lift our van off Ann's body to get her lower body out of the window. The van would not move and he went away in tears. After several minutes, the ambulance came and an emergency rescue team began to cut Ann out of the van. Gary and I stepped away and prayed together with Allen. In our prayers as Ann's parents, we thanked the Lord for giving her to us for fourteen years, for her life testimony, and we gave her back to Him. She was always His from the beginning.

Ann was loaded into the ambulance.

The paramedic yelled, "Go! Go! We have to go! Send another ambulance for anyone else!"

Gary and I insisted on going with Ann in the ambulance to the hospital. Gary rode in the front seat with the ambulance driver; I rode in the back with Ann and the paramedics. I could not watch as they began to work on her body. I sat on the floor of the ambulance with my head down on my knees still praying. The wail of the siren droned as we sped down the road to a small hospital in nearby Bedford, Pennsylvania.

Arriving at the local hospital, Gary and I went into a small examining room to give necessary information about Ann Marie and her medical history. We used the adjoining restroom to wash the blood off our hands and faces. Both of us felt like vomiting from the shock of the situation. We examined each other for injuries. I had a cut under my right eye with small slivers of glass lodged in the skin. My hands were cut from pieces of the windshield scattering across the front seat. Glass littered my hair.

The roof caving in as the van rolled, had pinned Gary behind the steering wheel, shoving his head down to the seat belt buckle at his waist. Gary had been lifting weights for several months, which gave him strength to push his body away from the steering wheel and out of the van. The metal roof of the van had ripped open his ski suit making a cut down his back. Gary had another large cut in the back of his head, needing stitches.

Ann Marie had taken the brunt of the impact in the seat behind Gary. The three girls on her seat had their weight thrown against her tiny body. She had gone through the side window from the force. The other girls in the van had bumps and bruises, and a few needed stitches. One girl had a broken wrist.

Leaving the examining room, Gary located a telephone and called my parents in St. Louis. My mother was sitting in the kitchen writing in her journal when the phone rang, and she answered it that morning. In a shaking voice, Gary told her we had been in an accident. He explained that Ann was severely injured. He told Mom to start a prayer chain for Ann and to call everyone she knew to pray. Then with tears in his eyes, he handed the phone to me to talk. I could hardly speak to tell her the situation.

I just said, "Mom, pray. Please pray. It is really, really bad. I know Ann Marie has a hole in the back of her head."

The medical staff continued to work on Ann Marie while we waited outside the emergency room. Although Ann was unconscious, she responded by kicking one of the attendants when a catheter had been inserted. Her injuries were greater than the small Bedford Hospital could handle. Ann Marie was prepared for transport to Conemaugh Trauma Center in Johnstown, Pennsylvania. It would be forty-five minutes by ambulance, because fog was too thick over the mountains for a medical helicopter to come and airlift her. We would not be able to go with her. Technically, we were still patients and our injuries needed examination.

We entered the Emergency Room to see Ann Marie. There she lay, still unconscious. As I touched her leg, it was cold and hard. I felt death in her body. Her breathing was shallow, and I was not sure she could hear me. I moved close to her ear and softly spoke to her.

I whispered, "Annie, Mommy loves you. Daddy loves you. And, Jesus loves you. We will see you later."

Gary and I hugged each other, as paramedics transferred Ann to a stretcher and whisked her out the emergency room door. We both felt a total emptiness as we watched the ambulance back doors close and leave with the sirens blaring. She was totally in God's hands as we clung to each other for support.

Turning back to the emergency desk, a nurse approached us. My body was beginning to feel the pain of the accident as I discovered several other cuts on my hands. The nurse wanted to take head and spine x-rays of me because of my eye injury and pain across my chest. The seat belt had left a mark restraining me. Gary needed the back of his head sutured and his back bandaged. Seat belts saved our lives.

As I climbed up on the x-ray table, I thought about Ann flying down the road in the ambulance. I laid there looking up at the ceiling. I sensed a small flicker of light pass above my head. I had an amazing sensation that Ann Marie was watching me. After several minutes of waiting for the film to be developed, the x-ray technician came back with the results. I could get dressed; nothing else had shown up on the x-rays. I asked the female technician if she had any word about my daughter's condition.

She turned and in a surprised expression said, "Was that your daughter in the ambulance to Conemaugh?"

I could tell by the look on her face when I replied, "Yes" that she knew something, but would not tell me.

In the hallway outside the dressing room, Allen wanted to talk with Gary and me in a private conference room.

As we sat down, Allen's voice broke, "This is the hardest thing I have ever had to do in my life. We just received a phone call from Conemaugh Trauma Center. Ann Marie did not make it. She died in the ambulance on the way."

Father, I desire that they also, whom Thou hast given Me,
be with Me where I am...
John 17:24 (NAS)

CHAPTER NINETEEN

Out of the Crucible

The crucible is for silver and the furnace for gold,
and a man is tested by the praise accorded him.
Proverbs 27:21 (NAS)

THE WEAVER
My life is but a weaving
Between my Lord and me,
I cannot choose the colors
He worketh steadily.
Oftimes he weaveth sorrow,
And I in foolish pride
Forget He sees the upper
And I, the underside.
Not till the loom is silent
And the shuttles cease to fly,
Shall God unroll the canvas
And explain the reason why.
The dark threads are as needful
In the Weaver's skillful hand
As the threads of gold and silver
In the pattern He has planned.
Author Unknown

Our world stopped with Allen's words as Gary and I looked at each other trying to processes what "She didn't make it" meant. Crashing in on us was the reality that even though we had prayed at the scene of the accident giving Ann Marie back to our Lord, this time He had taken her home to be with Him. She had entered the Heavenly Sanctuary ahead of us; she would be saving us a seat. As I fell into Gary's arms, my mind was racing through the plans we had made for our future. Those plans suddenly shrunk into unimportance without our beautiful daughter to share them with us.

A strange thing escaped my lips, "We'll have to replace her!"

Then realizing that no one could ever replace what we had together with Ann, we looked at each other and said simultaneously, "But we can't ever replace her!"

My mind went to the vision of the new house we were building and the plans for Ann to have her own suite of rooms in the finished basement. She would never know that house or bedroom. The futility of retirement plans for her to attend four years of high school crumbled within our spirits. The desire to move so Ann would be surrounded with grandparents, aunts, uncles, and cousins, reverberated against the reality of telling them of her death and funeral arrangements.

After our meeting with Allen, we began the painful process of calling the necessary relatives. Gary called my parents again to tell them of Ann's death. He talked with my father and asked him to contact the local funeral home in St. Louis. Beginning the needed long-distance arrangements helped Dad to concentrate on supporting us. We would be bringing Ann Marie home to St. Louis for the funeral. Mom called the rest of my family, and Gary's sister Louise. Mom and Dad's church began planning a funeral dinner to be served at their home.

Calling Gary's parents was more difficult. Gary's mom, Laura, answered the phone. She was unprepared for what Gary was telling her. She screamed and dropped the phone. Gary's dad picked up the phone confused about what was wrong. Gary explained the situation to his dad. Don, in his typical personality, wanted to know whose fault the accident was.

It was a very painful moment for Gary to say, "It was an accident, Dad. It was no one's fault."

Just as Ann Marie's presence had briefly brushed past me on the x-ray table to say, *Good-bye, Mom,* she was waltzing across the heavens to touch the hearts of two other special people. Ann Marie had been looking forward to our move to St. Charles, because Gary's sister Donna had decided to move back to the area during the coming summer. Ann wanted to be a mentor to her little cousins, Robbie, Lara, and Anthony.

She wanted to tell them about Jesus and prayed for their salvation. She had even written a letter to Robbie about how they could be great friends, but she had not mailed it because Robbie did not know he was moving yet.

Donna was just waking up in California at the time of the accident. Going to work, Donna began to drive down the streets of Los Angeles, California. She turned on the car radio. A song, "No More Tears in Heaven," came on the radio station affecting Donna's emotions. She began to cry, sobbing for some unknown feeling of grief. She could not understand her sudden emotional response. Pulling the car over, she just sat and wept. Later at work, she would get the call of Ann Marie's passing.

Around the time of Ann Marie's death, Aunt Susan had been at Central Presbyterian Church for a wedding rehearsal. After she finished singing, Susan heard another group singing in the fellowship hall. She walked down the steps to see a group of men rehearsing for a Promise Keepers Conference. They sounded so good she asked the pastor who they were. He gave her a copy of their audio tape recording of praise songs. Susan left the church to go home, putting the tape into the car tape player. The first song was "The Battle Belongs to the Lord." Within the first few notes and words, Susan felt an overwhelming presence in the car with her. She believed the music had moved her to tears, until she reached her home.

When she entered the front hall, her eyes met her husband Tom's eyes as he was on the telephone calling the Central prayer chain. He began to tell her that there had been an accident, and Ann Marie was severely injured. Susan screamed and ran to her bedroom crying and praying. Within a few more hours, Tom received the phone call from my dad that Ann Marie had died. Tom handed the phone to Susan and let Dad tell her "Ann Marie didn't make it." Susan did not understand what he meant, but her legs gave out and she slid down the wall sobbing in a heap of groaning disbelief. Tom began to cry. Elizabeth and David came running into the room. Tom and Susan had to tell them that their cousin, Ann Marie died. Immediately Tom, Susan, Elizabeth, and David drove to Mom and Dad's home.

After calling the family, Gary and I went to an office in the Bedford Hospital to talk on the phone to personnel at Conemaugh Trauma

Center in Johnstown, Pennsylvania. Ann's body had been on the way to the trauma center when she died in the ambulance. Three times, she had stopped breathing, and the emergency paramedics had shocked her back to earth-life twice. What a struggle between the men of earth and the angels of heaven for Ann Marie. However, "The Battle Belongs To the Lord," and He has won the victory over death as the Sovereign Lord of the universe. All of Ann's days were written before there was yet one of them. It was her day, her time, to go home and see her Lord and Savior. Her battle was over. She had come out of the crucible and the refining fire of this earthly life. The testimony she left behind would reverberate in others' lives for years to come.

On the phone with Conemaugh Trauma Center, the voice at the other end of the line expressed sympathy for our loss.

Then the stranger's voice asked us the dreadful question, "Would you consider donating some of Ann's organs for transplant?"

The strange voice wanted us to donate her heart, but they could use her eyes too. I listened to the question still in shock that my daughter was gone from the earth, but her body still here. I explained to the medical personnel that Ann had open-heart surgery and her heart would not be what they had expected. She had a small Teflon patch at a valve and I doubted that they would want to put it into another patient. So we agreed to the donation of her eyes. Eyes she would not need anymore, but maybe someone else could use them to see the world she had left.

The patrolman at the scene of the accident wanted to talk with us about the police report. He explained the preliminary investigation showed why the van had skidded on the road. A nearby driveway was shoveled from snow the day before. The runoff of water from melting snow had frozen on the roadway during the night leaving a sheet of black ice on the right side of the road. When our tires hit the ice, they skidded on the road and then hit dry pavement causing the van to flip. What we would learn later, is that a fully loaded 15-passenger van is so unstable on the road that insurance companies would stop insuring them for churches in years to come. Many deaths result from sudden maneuvers to avoid accidents in these vans, causing them to flip even at low speeds.

Another phone call came into the hospital. Our pastor Neil Jones had talked to Allen and wanted to know what the church needed to do to help. I told him to have Lois Cox at our house when we got home that night. I knew that Lois had been through the death of her daughter Michelle, and would be able to minister to us.

The youth had not been told of Ann's death, and Neil Jones and Allen had decided to wait until they were all back at the church with their parents before they received the information. We were minus a church van to get the girls back home. A driver brought another church van to pick up the girls. All of the youth went to the retreat center to gather their belongings. Then they traveled back to Washington, D.C., to meet at the church with their parents.

The situation remained unresolved as to how we were going to get home. Gary and I needed to stay separate from the group and grieve privately. A young man from our church drove to the retreat center and picked up our clothing and suitcases. Then he came to the small Bedford Hospital to take us back to the church. We wanted to change out of the bloodstained ski suits we were wearing. The shock of what had happened seemed to remove us from reality as we searched for necessary clothing items in our suitcases out of the back of our driver's car trunk.

Quietly our chauffeur waited until we changed clothes in a hospital restroom and exited to take the long ride back to Washington, D.C. Gary and I sat in the backseat together, so we could hold each other and weep. As the car started to leave the parking lot, another unexpected fear came over us. Riding in a vehicle seemed dangerous and uncomfortable. The ride became even more stressful when cold rain began to pour down so hard that visibility was extremely limited.

Arriving at Columbia Baptist Church, we were whisked into the office of Pastor Neil Jones, where he hugged us as we cried. Neil sat and talked with us about the accident and Ann Marie. Neil understood our pain, because he had known the loss of his grandson a few years before. He helped us to remember the wonderful times we had with Ann. We talked about her helping to collect supplies and fill the *CrossLink* container. She felt like a missionary and wished she could be there when the Moscow Baptist Church opened the boxes.

Neil said, "I just received word from Pastor Ivan Korablev that the container arrived today in the Russian port. It is due for delivery to the Moscow Central Baptist Church on February 7 for unloading. I think Ann will see them open the boxes!"

We laughed a little about her growing pains, and her desire to be like the other kids. She would never have to want to be like them again. She would have real friends in heaven. We mentioned her desire for the eleven friends at school to come to the Josh McDowell *WHY WAIT?* Rally the next week. If we could get the names on Ann's list, Neil wanted the church to work on inviting those kids to the rally in memory of Ann Marie. Seeds of faith from her death would be planted in the lives of the eleven on her "Most Wanted" list.

Neil said, "The thing I remember about Ann is that her eyes were always looking to you, Libby. She watched you, as she tried to be like you in her life."

I was thinking *Ann had such a forgiving spirit. I wish I could be like her. She puts us all to shame!*

The funeral would be in St. Louis. Knowing that many of our military friends, church members, and Ann Marie's school friends would want to express their sympathy, we talked about a memorial service at Columbia Baptist in Washington, D.C. We set the date for Wednesday night, February 9. Neil and the staff would be in contact with us while we spent the next week in St. Louis.

Plans were in place for escorting us home and making sure that we had the necessary help to deal with the trauma, especially our first night. Knowing that neither of us would want to drive, Jim Perdew drove Gary home, and Jim's secretary drove me home in our van. Dr. Barry Byer and Lois Cox had gone earlier to our home. Lois Cox arrived first and went to our neighbor, Dr. Amighi, to get the house key. We had left Winchester with Dr. Amighi for the weekend. When Lois tried to explain to Dr. Amighi what had happened, he was confused about the strange woman at his door wanting our house key. Finally, he understood and went with her to our house bringing Winchester with him. When we arrived home, Lois, Dr. Byer, Dr. Amighi, and Winchester were there waiting for us.

We sat and talked in the living room. Lois was able to talk about what it is like to lose a child. Boldly, she told us that it would be the hardest thing we would ever go through. We could only get through it with the help of Jesus Christ. She explained what a privilege it is to be the parents of such a child, and know the same grief that God the Father felt for His only begotten Son. She spoke about the sacrifice of Jesus Christ on the Cross, and His resurrection giving us assurance that Michelle and Ann Marie are present with the Lord. Lois had gone through the suffering we were going to experience. God was using her trial to comfort and encourage us that we could also get through it.

Dr. Amighi listened carefully. I realized that the first seeds of faith from Ann Marie's death were being sown in our Islamic neighbor's heart. Understanding that we were speaking of spiritual things, of deep faith, of hope of eternal life, Dr. Amighi spoke respectfully of our daughter's life. As a neurosurgeon, Dr. Amighi understood Ann Marie's miracle recovery from her stroke. She had touched our neighbors with her gentle spirit and friendliness. Dr. Amighi said, Winchester had whined and howled for several hours that morning, as if the dog was grieving Ann's loss and knew that she would not return. Dr. Amighi felt that animals have a spiritual sense that we as humans do not recognize. He offered to take care of Winchester while we made the trip to St. Louis for Ann's funeral.

Gary had something on his mind he wanted to know. Why had we left the Pennsylvania Turnpike to take that small winding road? Where were we when we had the accident? He reached into his pocket and pulled out his wallet. Inside it was a folded piece of paper. It was the police report given to him at the scene of the accident. As he read the paper, he suddenly turned ashen.

Remembering Ann Marie's dream, he gasped, "We were on Snake Spring Road when we had the accident! The police report says Snake Spring Road."

The night before, Ann had dreamed a snake would eat her and she would die. The circumstances and the dream could not be a coincidence. We related the story of the dream to Barry, Lois, and Dr. Amighi so they could understand our astonishment.

Lois finally spoke, "I believe an Angel of the Lord gave Ann Marie that dream. God wanted Ann to tell you, so you would be assured; He is Sovereign in the number of our days. He is in control. It was her day to go home and be with Him."

Barry Byer had helped us unload our blood soaked ski clothes from the trunk of our van. Realizing the seriousness of our accident and trauma, Dr. Byer wanted to look at our injuries. Taking us into the kitchen, Barry carefully examined our cuts. We had not realized tiny glass particles were still in our hair, and he told us to be careful removing the glass. He was concerned about the cut in the back of Gary's head. He wanted Gary to see him to remove the stitches when we returned from the funeral trip to St. Louis. Dr. Byer offered to give us a sedative, but we did not think we needed one.

Lois said she could spend the night. Gary and I felt that we just needed to be alone, and begin making the necessary arrangements to fly to St. Louis the next day. Gary contacted Mortuary Affairs at Bolling AFB, and they arranged to transport Ann Marie's body from Pennsylvania to St. Louis. Gary also contacted his office to request leave from work to travel to St. Louis for the funeral and burial.

I ask Lois to go with me upstairs and help me pick out what to take for Ann Marie's funeral. I had no idea what the funeral home would need to prepare her body. I was dreading walking into her room and knowing that she would never be there again. As I turned the light on in her room, I realized how the Lord had even prepared this moment. We had cleaned everything in the room the day before, as we had tried to look for the ski hat Ann wanted to wear. All of her things were neatly in their place, the furniture dusted, and the carpet vacuumed. I remembered that she had even said "good-bye" to her dolls. In fact, I had cleaned the whole house the day before. Nothing was out of place. Even all of our clothes were clean, except what we had worn in the last twenty-four hours. The only thing missing in the bedroom, besides the child who lived there, was one of her pillows she had taken on the trip. The queen bed looked lopsided with a pillow missing. It was a reminder that she was missing. Ann Marie's things from the trip were to return from the retreat center to our home while we were in St. Louis.

Lois helped me go through possible clothing for Ann's body in the casket. We looked at the lovely pink chiffon dress with a black velvet jacket that Ann had worn to the wedding in September. I said to Lois, "Ann loved this dress. She wore it to a wedding."

Lois said, "Well, she is going to another wedding—The Marriage Feast of the Lamb of God."

Lois told me to pick out underwear, pantyhose, and jewelry to put on Ann's body. She said I should also take her make-up and curlers. I was so thankful that Lois knew exactly what I should take, since I would not be able to simply go home and get any missing items once we flew to St. Louis. As Lois left that evening, she said, "Call me if you need me to come back. I will come, even if it is the middle of the night."

After Lois, Barry, and Dr. Amighi left us alone, Mom called from St. Louis. We talked and cried on the phone. Gary had gotten flight reservations for the next afternoon to fly to St. Louis and my parents would be there to pick us up. When I told my mother about the party dress I had decided to put on Ann's body, she hesitated a moment before saying, "Libby, it is January. It is so cold outside. Why don't you pick out a nice blouse, sweater, and skirt for Ann to wear? I don't want her to be cold."

Going back into Ann's closet, I decided that her white blouse with a ruffle around the neck and red knit sweater would be a better idea. She had gotten a cute plaid kilt for Christmas to wear as a skirt. I laid her sweater and kilt on her bed. Winchester hopped up on the bed, laid down on top of her sweater, and whimpered. He would not get off her clothes. His eyes looked at me asking, *where is Ann?*

I did not realize how the Lord had even planned the change in what Ann would wear to her grave through my mother's suggestion. Later, I would find out that Ann would need the high-necked ruffled blouse to cover a tracheotomy performed in the ambulance. The low-cut party dress would not have covered her neck. She might be going to a wedding, but she would go in her warm Scottish kilt and red sweater with the white high-necked ruffled blouse. She would become part of the circle of some of her Scottish relatives who had gone on before as a great cloud of witnesses.

Trying to think through the necessary phone calls, I remembered that Ann Marie had a dental appointment for her braces the next week. It was almost 10 p.m., when I made a phone call to my friend Sandy White. The Whites lived in our neighborhood, and their son Geoff went to Luther Jackson Middle School with Ann Marie. Sandy and

I had become friends as volunteers at the middle school. Geoff had been a good friend to Ann, and taken care of Winchester for us a few times when we traveled. Sandy's daughter used the same orthodontist as Ann Marie, and I needed Sandy to call Dr. McGrath and tell him about Ann's death.

When Sandy answered the phone, I apologized for calling so late, but I had some bad news. While I told Sandy about the accident and Ann Marie's death, Geoff was watching local 10 p.m. TV news. As I was speaking, the local TV station was announcing to all of the Washington, D.C. area the news of Ann's death. Somehow, the station had gotten information from the church, and a school picture of Ann Marie flashed across the TV screen. It was an unbelievable moment for the White family and many of our friends to see Ann Marie's smiling face and hear the shocking details of her death coldly broadcast on their television screens. The public announcement invaded our private grief. The news tied in the church tragedies of the Burchett family deaths almost exactly a year before, and the brutal slaying of a Marine Corp. church member during a carjacking in June. Ann's death made those families revisit their nightmares.

The cold, dark, lonely silence of a home without a child encircled our upstairs bedroom as Gary and I tried to sleep. The day's events were a bad dream we wanted to wake-up from as they continued to play like a repeating video tape. Our sleep was restless even though we were exhausted. Finally, at 2 a.m. we both got up to talk and think through what else we needed to do. We went down to the kitchen for a cup of tea, and began making a list of people we needed to call and their phone numbers. At 2 a.m., we could only make one phone call. It was 10 a.m. on Sunday morning in Ramstein, Germany. We called Cathy and Carolyn McCoy in Germany to tell them the news of Ann's death. Carolyn and their Romanian son Luke had visited us in Washington, D.C. a few months before on a trip to the National Institute of Health; when Luke had a follow-up on his hepatitis condition. Cathy McCoy had been Ann's physical therapist at Ramstein Elementary School. She was devastated to hear about her former patient who had worked so hard at physical therapy. The McCoys carried the tragic news to our friends at Faith Baptist Church in Germany before our friends in the U.S. heard the news.

Gary and I tried to get a few more hours of sleep, knowing that it would be impossible for us to attend worship services the next morning and face the entire congregation. At 8 a.m. I called Lois Cox and asked if she would come back for the morning. We needed someone to answer phone calls we were starting to receive. The local Channel 4 TV station had called and wanted to come to our home and do an interview. Gary consented because he wanted to tell the testimony of Ann Marie's life and her impact on our faith. I was trying to pack our suitcases for our late afternoon plane trip to St. Louis. I quickly dressed, applied my make-up and fixed my hair. Within a half-hour of the phone call, the TV reporter and cameraman were filming the snow falling outside of our house and ringing our doorbell. As we sat on our big blue couch in the living room, the camera rolled while Gary explained that our faith in Jesus Christ gave us the strength to handle Ann Marie's death. The testimony went out over the airwaves to the tri-state area. More seeds of faith were planted as Gary explained our assurance we would see our daughter again in heaven.

The Washington Post called. Gary spoke with the reporter. Taking the risk religious references might not be reported correctly by the "politically correct liberal news media," Gary spoke plainly about Ann's triumph over her adversities in life through her faith in Jesus Christ. If the news media wanted a story, they were going to hear the "gospel story." We prayed the reporter would hear the truth over the phone line, and print it, spreading more seeds of faith.

There was only one church in St. Louis to take Ann Marie home for burial. It was the church where our testimony began with prayers for her healing fourteen years before. Susan and Tom contacted Central Presbyterian Church and arranged to have Ann Marie's funeral there. John Splinter was a pastor on the church staff, having graduated from doing Young Life ministry to singles ministry. John was at a conference in Vale, Colorado. Susan helped to track John down, and he consented to give the eulogy for Ann's funeral. Bob Fenn also agreed to give reflections about Ann Marie's life. Knowing that Aunt Susan would be too grieved to sing for Ann's funeral, we asked Randy Mayfield to sing.

Jim Perdew took us to Dulles Airport for our flight to St. Louis. He told us that Neil Jones had spoken of Ann Marie at the morning worship service. We asked him to watch for any television or newspaper articles on Ann's death. He would also stay in touch with us about the Memorial service arrangements. As we drove to the airport and talked about the new home we were planning on building, Jim connected another thread in the tapestry for our future. In December after signing the contract to build, we had toured a large Baptist church near our future home. Jim told us that his niece was the wife of a Baptist pastor at another church located near our new home. Jim had made a phone call to that church asking them to pray for us. The church was eager to minister to us anyway that they could.

Negotiating the Sunday evening airport lines and shuttle system at Dulles Airport was almost more than our raw nerves could handle. Out in the public, the realization came to us that "life goes on." We were moving through crowds of people with our silent pain. Yet, in the midst of all those rushing around us, we felt a peace and strength from the Lord. A protective circumference surrounded us, which allowed us to keep walking one-step in front of another. The prayers of the saints were holding us up. We were gaining a greater vision of things above, and the importance of spiritual reality compared to the wasted focus on temporal things on earth. Strapped into the airplane seats, ready for takeoff, exhaustion overcame our tired bodies and minds. Graciously, The Father had given us a time to rest. We were on the journey to bring Ann Marie home in body and say our final good-bye. We awoke upon landing at Lambert Field in St. Louis.

Mom and Dad were waiting at the airport gate as our plane unloaded. Our emotions broke into tears seeing them and holding each other. Gary's sister Donna was also flying into Lambert from Los Angeles with her eight-year-old daughter Lara. We walked to the airport gate where they would be arriving to meet their plane. Donna and Lara would stay with Gary's other sister, Louise, during the week. Donna had written her thoughts on a scrap of paper:

> *The last time my brother, sister and me were all together was when Ann was born. In 1979, she brought us together then as she has now.*
>
> *We do not expect our children to pass before we do, and that is what makes this so hard for us, her family. I can*

see a little bit of every one of us in her. A little bit of each of us died January 29, 1994.

Some of us feel guilt for the things we did not say or do. My guilt and sorrow comes from my children not getting to know Ann. Ann was to us a miracle. Our lives will not be as full without her. But we have to follow Ann's example and be as strong now as she was in her life.

Let us all take comfort in the fact that Ann had a wonderful life. She was too good for this world. I know she is at peace and will have no more tears in Heaven.

I will not say good-bye Ann Marie. You will live on forever in me and all your family.

Love, Aunt Donna

Gary's parents would not be making the trip from Arizona. Don was not able to walk because of extreme arthritis, and Laura needed to stay and take care of him. The last time Don and Laura had seen their grand-daughter, Ann Marie, was four years before when we were in St. Louis between moves. Gary's parents had come back to St. Louis when Don's mother was sick and dying. We had been in Williamsburg, when Louise called and left the message of Grandma Grunick's death. By the time we came home from Williamsburg and heard the phone message, the funeral was over. Now there would be another funeral without all of us being together.

When we arrived at my parents' home, my grandmother Mimmy was waiting there for us. Since the death of Pop, she had mellowed in her disposition. She had not been well enough to attend church regularly; but in listening to several taped sermons by Dr. Charles Stanley, she had developed a deeper understanding of God's Word. She reached out in tears to hug us as she grieved the death of her first-born great-grandchild. When Ann Marie had been paralyzed from her stroke, Mimmy had a vision of Ann dancing in her living room. The day came that Ann did dance for Mimmy, as she clapped her hands in joy to see her vision a reality. Now Mimmy told me of another vision she had.

Mimmy whispered, "I know Pop was standing there at the Gates of Heaven waiting for Ann Marie. He is showing her all around. They are together again."

I thought about the last time we had seen Pop before he died and how he had smiled, waking from unconsciousness and seeing Ann Marie standing by his bedside. It was comforting to think of them together with the Lord.

On Monday morning, Dad, Gary, and I met with John Hutchens, the director of Hutchens Mortuary. The funeral home was down the road from the Methodist church where Gary and I first met and were married. Mr. Hutchens graciously extended his condolences, and accepted the clothing and jewelry I had brought for Ann Marie's body. He explained that her body would arrive in St. Louis on an airplane that afternoon. He asked us about Ann Marie's life. We told him her testimony of healing and faith. The funeral of a young person is particularly difficult for a funeral home. We talked about visitation hours for Tuesday evening; the time of the funeral at Central Presbyterian; a spray of pink roses for the casket; newspaper obituaries; death certificates; and a limousine to transport all of the immediate family. Then John took us into a room of caskets. They were all beautiful; but the reality that our daughter would be laid to rest inside one with the lid closed and lowered into the ground was a bitter and painful moment. One casket stood out to both Gary and I. Even in the choice of her casket, we wanted it to speak of her testimony. The casket was dark polished wood with silver handles. Each corner was adorned with a silver sheaf of wheat. The wheat represented the harvest that would come from the death of this tiny seed of faith falling to the ground.

Truly, truly, I say to you,
unless a grain of wheat falls into the earth and dies,
it remains by itself alone;
but if it dies, it bears much fruit.
He who loves his life loses it,
and he who hates his life in the world
shall keep it to life eternal.
John 12:24-25 (NAS)

As we worked through the details of the funeral, the question came as to where we would bury Ann Marie. Although my parents had extra plots in a St. Louis cemetery; John Hutchens recommended that we consider Jefferson Barracks National Cemetery, as part of Gary's military benefits. John suggested that we drive to the cemetery that afternoon and look at the new grave spots before deciding where to bury Ann.

When we arrived at Jefferson Barracks National Cemetery, we were impressed by the massive rows of graves. The precision placement of the headstones over the military graves resembled Arlington Cemetery in Washington, D.C. It was a beautifully groomed expanse of hills and wooded areas honoring fallen service members and their families. Following the map to the new grave area, we drove to the top of a hill in the cemetery. Reaching the highest place along the road, we stopped to gaze out over the white rows of grave markers. God gave us confirmation of His presence when we noticed two deer standing by the newest gravesites eating the fresh grave flowers. This would be Ann Marie's resting place, where hind's feet walked on high places. It was a secret moment between God and us. He knew our grief. God had not forgotten us. Ann was with Him now, and we knew that our separation was only temporary. She was saving us a seat in the Sanctuary. We would reunite not only in the same grave, but also in His presence in eternity.

> Ann's heart was that people would come to know Him in a saving faith..

Tuesday morning, Bob Fenn and John Splinter came to my parents' home to talk about the funeral service. We showed them a notebook Ann had made for her seventh grade English class. In it, she had written about her testimony and her family. We also had several of her poems. As we reminisced about her life and all the difficulties she had overcome through prayer and the help of the Lord, we saw her spiritual strength in her physical weakness. We wanted those who attended the funeral service to hear a clear message of the Gospel.

I said to Bob and John, "There is no pressure here, except that NO ONE leaves this funeral service UNSAVED!"

Gary smiled and said, "And we are going to put a ribbon on all of the ones who need to get saved, so you will know who to speak to!"

It was true that we had several family members and friends we were praying God would touch to come to faith in Jesus Christ. Ann was always willing to speak about God. It was a passion of her life. Her heart was that people would come to know Him in a saving faith. Her life had blessed many people, now it was time for her death to call many to repentance and salvation.

Tuesday evening we arrived at Hutchens Funeral home for the visitation time. It would be the first time for us to see Ann Marie's body. She had left in the ambulance on Saturday, and in a twinkling of an eye gone to be in the presence of the Lord. As John Hutchens lead Gary and me into the viewing room, we felt once again the strength of Our Lord helping us to put one foot in front of the other. Ann looked beautifully asleep in her white ruffled blouse and red sweater. In her ear lobes were gold cross earrings, which matched the gold cross necklace around her neck. Her translucent face and blonde hair caught the soft pink light reflecting off the white satin cushion beneath her head. On her left ring finger was her "True Love Waits" ring. I reached up to touch her hand. I was surprised how cold and hard her body felt. It was another confirmation that she was not there. What I was viewing was only a shell she had left behind. Her spirit had entered into the joy of her salvation. She was out of the crucible's refining fire. She had come forth as a reflection of the image of God.

In our few hours of visitation, loved ones and friends wrapped themselves around us. Expressions of sympathy and love surrounded us. Flowers filled the room with the fragrance of Christian prayers lifted to the Throne of God on our behalf. God had spoken through the circumstances of Ann Marie's life. She had been a quiet courageous fighter with an iron will, yet she was full of grace. Her strength of character and loving spirit had touched many lives for the Kingdom of God. Her short fourteen years of life had been significant; now in her tragic death she had eternal worth.

Hundreds of friends and family celebrated the life of Ann Marie Grunick on Wednesday, February 2, 1994, at 11 a.m. Susan's friend had printed beautiful pink bulletins for the funeral service with Ann Marie's picture on the front cover. Phil Roland, Central's music minister, played "Castle on a Cloud" from *Les Miserables* in memory of Ann's favorite piano selection. The congregation stood to praise Our Lord in our opening hymn, "Great Is Thy Faithfulness." Then John Splinter, who had been our first "pastor," rose to deliver the eulogy. He remarked that God is the author and finisher of our faith, and the author and finisher of our lives. He recalled that Ann Marie was a beautiful child who loved the Lord. She blessed the lives she touched with her sweet, gentle and quiet spirit. She had seemed like an angel on loan to us for a short time, then ready to go home and be with the Lord.

Our faith and hope is in the work and person of Jesus Christ..

Randy Mayfield, who had been "Elvis" to Ann Marie's "Cilla," choked back tears as he sang, "When Answers Aren't Enough, There is Jesus."[1] The words of the song spoke of facing a valley, which casts a shadow you cannot overcome. It was true that we were in a deeper valley of the shadow of death than Ann's stroke had been. But, through the years of her recovery, we had grown to trust the Lord Jesus to be there in life and death. We would not ask, *why did it happen?* But, we would ask, *where could this lead us from here?* Many were watching to see if our God was big enough to get us through the sorrow that broke more than our hearts. We had to live by faith, triumphant through the tears as a witness that our hope was in more than a religion. Our faith was more than just knowing the right scripture verse, or prayer to recite. Our faith and hope is in the work and person of Jesus Christ. He is our anchor, which holds us in the storms of life. He is our safe refuge and strength.

After Uncle Tom Werner and my brother Fred read several scripture passages, the congregation stood to sing the hymn, "Because He Lives."

Then Bob Fenn, who had been there from the beginning of Ann's life, gave reflections on her memory. Bob spoke of Ann as an angel sent from God to bring a message. She would want everyone to know that Jesus has prepared a place for them, and He wants them to go to heaven. Bob spoke of her entering the heavenly place greeted by the Lord Jesus, clothed in righteousness, and laying her crown of gold at the feet of Jesus. She is in the heavenly sanctuary singing, *Holy, Holy,*

Holy, is the Lord God Almighty. If Ann Marie could speak from heaven today, she would say, *Beloved, if you do not know Jesus, or do not have the assurance He dwells in your heart, do not leave here without knowing the assurance of your salvation.*

To follow the message about the heavenly place, Randy sang "If You Could See Me Now."[2] Written by Kim G. Noblitt of the traveling Christian music group TRUTH, it spoke of the beauty of heaven and never wanting to come back to earth. This song had prompted Ann Marie's question to me a few months before, "Mom, what if I die before you?" It is an encouragement to know that Ann Marie is standing tall and whole, walking streets paved with gold. She will never limp or stumble again. She sees Jesus face to face. She would never want to leave that place.

Finally, John Splinter gave a meditation on the scripture:

> *Yet those who wait for the Lord*
> *will gain new strength;*
> *they will mount up with wings like eagles,*
> *they will run and not get tired,*
> *they will walk and not become weary.*
> Isaiah 40:31 (NAS)

John spoke the words of truth when he said, "The deepest sadness is the death of a child, but deeper still is the death of a child who did not know the Lord."

As he read some of Ann's poems, it was obvious that Ann had a deep understanding of knowing her Lord. We do not grieve as those who have no hope. We believe that Jesus died and rose again. One day, the clouds will be rolled back as a scroll, and our faith will be sight. God will bring with Jesus those who have died in Him. Our separation is only temporary, and so we will be with the Lord forever. The scripture says to encourage each other with these words. John also encouraged those who are Christians to wrap themselves around us. The tapestry God had woven of grace would surround our souls in ministry and prayers. God would reorder our lives in a direction without Ann Marie. Our Lord would give us a spiritual purpose in ministry through this trial. He would pour out a double blessing to replace the vast emptiness of losing Ann Marie. He would make us strong in the broken places.

<u>Annie's Faith</u>
Waif of Light,
Angel of Might.
Witness to all,
Strong and tall.
With beauty and care,
For the Lord's Fair.
She speaks to us all,
With grace,
For Jesus' face.
Angel of Might,
Waif of Light.

Aunt Cathy Statler
February 2, 1994

CHAPTER TWENTY

Strong in the Broken Places

*Therefore, since we have
so great a cloud of witnesses surrounding us,
let us also lay aside every encumbrance,
and the sin which so easily entangles us,
and let us run with endurance
the race that is set before us,
fixing our eyes on Jesus,
the author and perfecter of faith,
who for the joy set before Him
endured the cross,
despising the shame
and has sat down at the right hand
of the throne of God.*

*Therefore, strengthen the hands that are weak
and the knees that are feeble,
and make straight paths for your feet,
so that the limb which is lame
may not be put out of joint,
but rather be healed.*
Hebrews 12:1-2, 12-13

After the burial at Jefferson Barracks National Cemetery, the women of North Hills United Methodist Church served us a delicious meal in my parents' home. Our immediate family gathered with us in fellowship. Moving through the buffet line in the dining room the reality suddenly struck me that I was not a *mother* anymore. At least, all the responsibilities I had as Ann Marie's mother were over. I had an immediate sense of loss of purpose in life. My life had been being Ann's mother, and helping her with physical and emotional struggles. I was abruptly aware that she did not need me anymore. Now, I did not know why I was left on earth.

Two days after burying Ann Marie, was my forty-fifth birthday. Although my family tried to make it a nice celebration, I felt completely empty of joy. Susan had served a wonderful birthday dinner at her home. It was awkward opening gifts, knowing that Ann Marie had looked forward to my birthday that week. Randy Mayfield was performing a concert that evening at Central Presbyterian, and our whole family was attending. I wanted to move on to normalcy. However, walking back into the Central Presbyterian sanctuary only two days after Ann's casket had rested between the two altar angels was a struggle for us. I just wanted to go home and stay in bed.

When John Splinter met with us on Saturday to do a little grief counseling, I recognized the emotions he explained in the grief cycle. We had gone through shock, disbelief, and denial. The grief cycle had turned to depression. The important thing was not to be stuck in the depression mood. I soon found myself alternating between depression and anger, especially when others were insensitive to our grief. At least I knew what I was experiencing was normal. John cautioned us to take things slower. Our emotions were raw and vulnerable.

During our week in St. Louis, we had remained in contact with Columbia Baptist Church. Jim Perdew had told us of the four-column article printed in the *Washington Post* about Ann Marie. Many were amazed that such an evangelical perspective would be in the national newspaper. My brother's wife Cathy offered to receive a FAX of the news article at her work so we could read it. When we read the *Washington Post* story, we knew that God would use it to bring many people encouragement and conviction regarding their relationship with Jesus Christ. We were grateful the reporter had listened as Gary spoke plainly of Ann's life struggles, healing, and determination in the Lord. Ann's beautiful smiling face must have caught the attention of many of the readers. The last paragraph of the news article quoted Gary.

> *"We knew she would die at any time," Gary Grunick said of his daughter's life and his reaction to her death. "We*

never understood why all this stuff happened to her early on. But we came to the conclusion that she was here to have an impact on other people. We're able to deal with it, with the help of the Lord." [1]

We still had to face a Memorial service in Washington, D.C. Returning to our home would be difficult. Once again, my mother came to help us in a way that only a mother can. The three of us flew back to Dulles on Sunday, February 6, to work through the details of the Memorial service, sort through sympathy cards, delivery of flowers, and receive the love of another body of believers and friends.

Opening the front door to our home, the quiet absence of Ann Marie's life permeated our emotions, while we almost tripped over a pile of Ann Marie's belongings from the retreat center sitting in our front hallway. Someone had dropped them off while we were gone. Obviously, they had not wanted to invade the house but wanted us to know Ann's things had returned.

Unzipping her purple ski bag, I was shocked to find Ann Marie's fanny pack lying on top of her ski boots. She had been wearing the fanny pack at the time of the accident and her blood had soaked into the fabric. Immediately, my mother took the pack upstairs to the bathroom and tried to wash the blood out of it. She stood at the sink crying as she emptied the contents of lip gloss, a small hairbrush, broken sunglasses, and coins from the inside of the pouch. Grieved by what had greeted us at the door, I became angered when I realized that among the things delivered was a pillow that did not belong to Ann Marie. However, her pillow, which matched everything in her bedroom, had not returned. How could someone have taken her pillow and left us with one we did not own?

Lois Cox and a few other women from the church arrived with a meal. We did not feel hungry, but needed to keep our strength up during this emotional time of grief. I certainly did not want to cook. The fried chicken, green beans, mashed potatoes, and gravy were nourishment for our physical bodies. I talked with Lois about Ann Marie's missing pillow. I showed Lois the matching pillow in Ann's bed so she would know what it looked like. Ann had slept on that pillow for the last seven years. It left a missing place in her bed, symbolizing her missing place in our lives. Lois understood my emotions, and said that she would relay the message to the church to help find Ann Marie's pillow. I gave Lois the pillow which did not belong to us to return.

I knew that it probably did not seem important to others that Ann's pillow did not return, but to me it was the last place she had laid her head to sleep. The pillowcase matched the sheets, bedspread, pillow sham, curtains, and canopy. I had made them for her bedroom out of extra sheets to match. A different pillow would not match. Her pillow had not come home. Ann Marie had not come home. Her missing pillow became the focal point of my deeper grief, the loss of our precious daughter.

> Ann had taken none of these things with her except her faith in Jesus Christ.

Gary could not stand to sit at home where every corner of our house felt empty without Ann. He went back to work on Monday morning, leaving Mom and I to sort through things. Ann's place to sit at the kitchen table was vacant. The piano was silent in the family room. At the top of the stairs, the doorway to her bedroom held the memories of fourteen years of laughter and tears. Dolls, games, toys, books, clothes, shoes, jewelry, and hair barrettes were all reminders of past life events. Ann had taken none of these things with her except her faith in Jesus Christ.

Mom and I took a deep breath and entered Ann's bedroom to walk through the memories and share the sorrow of her death. Her poems and stories took on a greater meaning of prophetic truth in her death. We found several profound writings of Ann Marie's thoughts and feelings. Even in her schoolwork, she had expressed a deep faith and trust in Jesus Christ. Two cinquain poems she wrote for English class, a year before her death, described God and herself.

<u>GOD</u>
Powerful, merciful.
Loving, destroying, demanding.
Knows who you are.
LORD.

<u>ANN</u>
Truthful, kind.
Loving, caring, giving.
Will be your friend!
Sweet.
Ann Marie Grunick – February 16, 1993

After reading *Hinds Feet on High Places* by Hannah Hurnard, Ann had written this insight of what she had learned about life.

> *Ann Marie Grunick   September 29, 1993*
>
> *Hinds Feet on High Places*
>
> *I have learned how Resentment and Self Pity can tempt you to not go forward in life. I have also learned how you should trust the shepherd where ever he wants you to go.*

We laughed and cried at an entry in her diary.

> *Another day at school, and I still don't have a boyfriend!*

For some reason, we had the thought of going through Ann Marie's things to "get rid of them." The more we searched through her belongings, the more I knew I was not ready to let go of anything yet. I was having trouble even touching some of her most treasured possessions. When you love someone, everything connected with them becomes dear. Their words written in their own handwriting, pictures captured in familiar moments of time, the sound of their name spoken by others, even the aroma of their perfume on their garments becomes a treasure to those who loved them. Everyone deals differently with the personal effects of a deceased loved one. It takes time. Sometimes it never happens and that should be all right too.

Dr. Doran, principal of Luther Jackson School, and Neil Jones visited our home to talk about the Memorial Service scheduled on that Wednesday night, February 9. Dr. Doran expressed the difficulty many of the students and teachers were having dealing with Ann Marie's death. The teachers had been so encouraged with Ann Marie's progress physically, mentally, and socially. Working out in the weight room with Coach Muniz had made Ann's muscles stronger for coordination and walking. Dave Muniz was taking Ann's death particularly hard. She had shown progress in learning by making the Honor Roll even though everything took her hours longer to accomplish than the other students. The week before her death, she had studied hours for a science test on "light waves." Now she had seen the true "Light." Socially she had touched more lives in friendship than she ever thought. One young man in chorus remembered that Ann Marie always loaned him a pencil when he needed one. Everyone knew she was a Christian girl and in heaven. Her reputation was pure and without blemish.

A terrible ice storm hit the Washington, D.C., area on Wednesday. We had considered canceling the evening Memorial service, but did not know how to let every one know. I received several phone calls that day from people expressing their sympathy and regrets that they would not attend the Memorial service due to the weather. We prepared ourselves for a low attendance and proceeded to the church on extremely slick roads.

Nearly three-hundred people drove through a terrible ice storm on Wednesday night, to attend the Memorial service for Ann Marie at Columbia Baptist Church. The congregation reflected a mixture of the different colored threads our lives had touched. Church members and youth sat next to Ann's schoolteachers, administration, and school friends. Mixed into the crowd were friends in blue military uniforms from several of our air force assignments, now assigned to Washington, D.C. Many of our neighbors and international friends attended the service. Ann's orthodontist Dr. McGrath represented all of the medical care Ann had struggled with during her life.

Gary had cousins from his mother's side of the family living in the D.C. area—George and wife Betty, and Marvin and wife Pauline. We had gotten to know them during the year and a half we had lived in Annandale, Virginia. After sending Christmas cards to each other for twenty-five years, it was good for me to put a face and relationship with a name. Just a few months before Ann's death, we had a small family reunion with the D.C. cousins, and Gary's Uncle Ralph and Aunt Donna. Since Gary's mother and her brother Ralph did not know their parents, Uncle Ralph did extensive genealogical research. Uncle Ralph brought pictures and explained his side of the family to Ann Marie. Seeing photos of her great-grandparents, Ann Marie found a connection with a lost part of her family history. When George and Marvin heard of Ann Marie's death, they got in a car and drove nonstop from Washington, D.C. to her funeral in St. Louis. Now George and Betty sat with my mother and us on the front pew of Columbia Baptist Church, where a remnant of the tapestry gathered representing a larger picture God was weaving.

The Memorial service was another opportunity to scatter the seeds of the Gospel to many who had never been inside a church. Others sought encouragement in their relationship with our Sovereign Lord. Many parents needed to turn their hearts toward their children. Youth saw their mortality and lack of purpose in seeking worldly pleasure. Teachers realized the importance of each student's life they touched. The message would center on faith, family, and friendship as important matters in Ann Marie's life.

Jim Perdew opened the service with a beautiful prayer bringing our questioning hearts before the Throne of God. He spoke of Ann's life not measured in length of years, but in a loving spirit and strength of character. Once again, we sang of God's faithfulness in the old familiar hymn, "Great Is Thy Faithfulness." Calling upon the strong voice of church member Claude Rhea, an attorney with Prison Fellowship, the congregation heard the gospel message in the solo "When Answers Aren't Enough, There Is Jesus." [2]

Principal Dr. Michael Doran took the opportunity to represent the students and teachers of Luther Jackson Middle school, who struggled with the pain and loss of Ann Marie, to express the joy of knowing her. Turning to Coach Muniz for affirmation, Dr. Doran called Ann "a quiet fighter with an iron will." He shared some of the responses from her fellow students about her life.

One student expressed, "Ann Marie was always smiling; she brought everything good into the classroom. She had a glow inside her that made me smile."

Another friend commented, "In chorus, if I was having a bad day, she was the one who encouraged me. She may have been little, but she had a big heart and big voice."

A different classmate stated, "Ann never lost her temper, and never gave a bad impression. She had a twinkle in her eye only certain people have."

Dr. Doran relayed the story in the book Ann had written about "The Loneliest Star." He spoke of her being the young girl who bought the "lonely star," in the way she always saw the potential in others and would reach out to help them. However, she was also like "the star" as she shone brightly in a special home.

Dr. Doran said, "She knew herself!" He said of Ann, quoting Alfred Lloyd Tennyson, "My strength is as the strength of ten because it is pure." He suggested, "Ann Marie inspired us to better understand friendship and faith." Ending his comments, Dr. Doran paraphrased Cornelius Nepos, "She seemed not to relinquish life, but leave home for another."

Following that insightful tribute to our daughter, Gary and I reflected on our life as Ann Marie's parents. It was by the grace of God that we could rise out of our seats and speak to those gathered before us about the strength of His presence in the circumstances of Ann's life and death. Gary and I were honored by the attendance of so many friends considering the treacherous weather. Gary described the ways that God speaks to us as believers. God speaks to us through the Scriptures – His Holy Word. He speaks to us in the circumstances of life. Finally, He speaks to us through other people.

In quoting scripture, Gary explained the kind of godly sorrow that we had which produces repentance without regret, leading to salvation.

I now rejoice not that you were made sorrowful,
but that you were made sorrowful to the point of repentance;
for you were made sorrowful according to the will of God,
in order that you might not suffer loss

> *in anything through us.*
> *For sorrow that is according to the will of God produces*
> *a repentance without regret, leading to salvation;*
> *but the sorrow of the world produces death.*
> II Corinthians 7:9-10 (NAS)

I continued the message of how God spoke through the circumstances of Ann Marie's life. Fourteen years before, we had been walking in darkness. God had given us the little life of Ann to bring us light and show us what God is like. We came to saving faith through the circumstances of Ann Marie's birth and heart defect. We learned to walk in trusting faith through the circumstances of her stroke. Now we were experiencing strengthened faith through the circumstances of her death. Ann had the assurance of her faith throughout her entire life. She had expressed it by writing about her life's testimony ending with the words:

> *Every day He heals me more and more.*

Gary explained the tapestry of grace that God had woven. For the fourteen years of Ann's life, God had brought people into our lives from the seven different communities in which we had lived. Each community had given us a circle of friends, a circle of mentors, and a circle of people we mentored. We were thankful for special friends and special teachers who touched us with God's grace.

I responded that the circle of friends and teachers were present at the Memorial service because Ann did not cross their path by accident. God had woven Ann into the tapestry of their lives, to encourage and strengthen their faith even through her death. We felt the prayers of the Body of Christ, and received great support from a network of Christian friends.

Gary shared how God had prepared us for her death from the time of her birth. Her life had special meaning and significance. Because we came to love her and the Lord through her physical weakness, our faith was made strong. After the accident, we had talked about the fourteen years with Ann. We found no regrets or disappointments with our daughter. At no time did we have an estranged relationship with her to cause any guilt or lack of affection. The notes and comments from her fellow students had reconfirmed what we hoped was the truth. She was a good Christian girl. She was kind and sweet. She was caring and sensitive to others. She was a really hard worker. Although she may have been publicly quiet, at home she had a great sense of humor. She told us jokes and did imitations to make us laugh. She was a neat kid. The kind of person Christ calls each of us to be. She had nothing to be ashamed of in her life.

I closed our reflections by sharing how every morning Ann Marie and I would have a prayer time together before she went to school. We would pray for her safety during the day. We prayed for each teacher by name, and for wisdom for the school administration. Several of her fellow students were prayed for each morning. Finally, I would remember her with the blessing:

> *Yet, I will exult in the LORD,*
> *I will rejoice in the God of my salvation.*
> *The Lord GOD is my strength,*
> *and He has made my feet like hinds' feet,*
> *and makes me walk on my high places.*
> Habakkuk 3:18-19 (NAS)

In Ann Marie's own words, "Everyday He heals me more and more," I responded that she is perfectly healed. She has her hinds' feet, and is in the highest place, waiting to meet us when we arrive.

What I had just spoken flowed into the opening words of the song, "If You Could See Me Now" as Claude Rhea sang:

> *Our prayers have all been answered,*
> *I've finally arrived;*
> *The healing that had been delayed*
> *Has now been realized.* [3]

Neil Jones rose to speak a message to the important people in Ann Marie's life, as heavenly guests surrounded us. He called attention to several special scriptures listed on the right side of the worship bulletin, dealing with worship, identity, family, and youth. He also wanted those present to notice two poems, which Ann Marie had written about her life.

Remember
I seem to remember when I was so strong.
I seem to remember all the days long.
I seem to remember when I was so weak.
I seem to remember that now I am meek.
I seem to remember the angels and heavens above.
And now I remember God's special love.

Healing
Once I was lonely.
I am not lonely any more.
I used to be blind,
But now I see.
And all the while,
I am glad I am Me.
By Ann Marie Grunick - 3/10/93

Regarding the scriptures on worship, Neil stated, "Truth is of eternal significance. Life is either the pursuit of God, or a journey into darkness. Most of what we know of God, we only know in seed form. The God we love tonight is beyond our reach. We cannot plumb the depths of earth, much less the God who made it. Worship is one event on earth, which will be more vastly improved in eternity. We are on our way to see God, she is walking with God."

Then saith Jesus unto him,
"Get thee hence, Satan:
for it is written,
'Thou shalt worship the Lord thy God,
and him only shalt thou serve.'"
Matthew 4:10

Concerning the scriptures on identity, Pastor Jones spoke of the uphill battle Ann Marie faced having an undersized body, which was unable to do everything she wanted to do. However, she was oversized with above average virtue, spark of life and will power.   The rocket booster of her body was jettisoned and burned up, while her real life is now in orbit. She is in the fullness of her life and sees Christ as He is.

Beloved, now are we the sons of God,
and it doth not yet appear what we shall be;
but we know that, when he shall appear,
we shall be like him;
for we shall see him as he is.
And every man that hath this hope in him
purifieth himself, even as he is pure.
I John 3:2-3

Then Neil Jones spoke about Ann and her family. As the pastor of her family, he had watched our lives as we worshipped together. He knew her birth had brought us to the Lord, and our testimony had been recycled back to Ann Marie. He had watched our family role model submission, love, and obedience as we worshipped and prayed together. He had seen the joy of doing missions catch in Ann Marie's life as we packed the *CrossLink* container together as a family.

Neil's next words were directed toward Ann's friends and fellow youth. He warned them, "Don't be childish. Don't seek senseless pleasure, popularity, and power drifting from party to party which will never satisfy, but only disappoint. Don't major on the physical and material." He encouraged them to live for others, as Ann Marie did with her prayer list of friends. He called them to seek ministry to help and minister to others. He spoke directly to the youth saying, "Ann Marie was childlike in her faith. Childlike is beautiful. Childish is terrible."

Let no man despise thy youth;
but be thou an example of the believers,
in word, in conversation, in charity, in spirit, in faith, in purity.
I Timothy 4:12

Finally, quoting what Ann had written about her life, Neil read her words.

Two things have influenced me most in my life.
I thank my parents for having me.
I thank my God for healing me.

Neil ended by asking the question "Where was God?" He answered his own question saying, "When Ann's body struck the pavement and she died, God was in the same place He was when the nails struck the body of His Son on the cross."

Miss Kimberly Welch, Ann's chorus teacher at Luther Jackson Middle School, sang a final solo "Friends" by Michael W. Smith. Ann loved singing in the school chorus. Many of her friends from the chorus class wrote us letters about how much Ann had meant to them in very personal ways. Miss Welch gave us a big envelope with the letters to encourage us that they would miss their friend, Ann.

In the days following Ann Marie's death and for years afterwards, we received many cards and letters from family, friends, and those who just heard about her death. The volume of correspondence would fill another book. We were truly strengthened not only by the outpouring of sympathy, and physical care given us, but also by the prayers lifted to the Throne of God on our behalf for healing our brokenness. The following excerpts from letters we received show the impact one young girl had on the life of others in the short fourteen years she was given to walk among us on earth. We found those parents who had lost children were best able to minister to our emotions of grief.

> *Gary and Libby,*   *Feb 1, 1994*
>
> *There would have been no resurrection without a cross for Ann Marie or Michelle. Christ could bear pain, for the joy of the resurrection and returning to the Father, which was before Him. (Hebrews 12:2) So can you, and so can we bear the pain for the joy of the resurrection and being with our God and our child. Joy comes in the morning!!*
>
> *Love,*
>
> *Fred and Lois Cox*

Peter and Geta Vidu sent condolences all the way from Romania.

> *We are deeply moved by Ann Marie's passing. You are in our hearts and prayers. We pray for you not only as a family, but also as a church. Geta and I know very well what it is to loose a child, so we can share your distress. We pray for you to receive comfort from our Lord and God. One of God's names is God of consolation and He can give you strength and peace.*
>
> *God Bless you,*
>
> *Peter and Geta Vidu*

Later Peter Vidu called us from Romania to talk about Ann Marie's death and encourage us to be strong. One sentence Peter spoke to us has helped us to minister to others who have lost children.

Peter reminded us, "No one leaves the earth too soon."

From one of Gary's former military commanders we received a very insightful letter of sympathy.

> *Dear Gary and Elizabeth,   10 Feb. 1994*
>
> *Somewhere, sometime during the marriage covenant, you know that one of you will probably lose the other, but you are never really prepared to survive a child.*
>
> *As painful as this has to be for you both, how much worse must it be for those without your strong faith and the sure knowledge that your Ann Marie is now forever enveloped in the pure love, happiness and fulfillment that is God.*
>
> *We can only guess at the anguish you must be sharing, but we wanted you to know that you are in our thoughts and prayers.*
>
> *God bless you both,*
>
> *Gloria and Pat O'Brien*

Several of Ann Marie's teachers expressed their sympathy in many ways. Mrs. Sue Grossman, Ann's eighth grade civics teacher, at Luther Jackson Middle School wrote this poem about Ann. Mrs. Grossman had permitted Ann to pursue collecting humanitarian supplies for the *CrossLink* container at school as a Civics project.

Ann Marie
Like a bouquet of yellow roses
She brightened our lives
But like the rose
Her time was short.
She brought joy and sunshine
Into the live of those she touched.
All who knew her will miss her.
But because of who she was,
Her memory will be with us always.

Colonel and Mrs. Grunick:

Thank you for raising such a special child. May God give you the strength to continue sharing your love and generosity with those in need. You have my prayers and admiration.

Sue Grossman

My mother stayed with us during the Memorial service week, but she had a flight scheduled for Saturday morning to return to Dad in St. Louis. On Saturday morning, we woke to a blinding snowstorm blanketing the Delmarva area. Quietly dreading saying "good-bye" and driving her to the airport in a blizzard, we loaded her suitcases into the trunk of the van. Carefully tracking down our driveway, Gary made the sharp turn onto the steep private road out of our small circle of homes. Mounting some speed to ascend the ice-covered road, the tires on our van spun hopelessly stuck in the snow at the bottom of the hill. We were not going to get up the hill to drive to any airport. Even getting back up our driveway was difficult. We unloaded the suitcases and went back into our house to call the airlines. We all were relieved to hear the airline attendant report that Dulles Airport was closing due to the snow and ice storm. Mom was able to stay one more day. She attended worship service with us the next day on a bright sunny Sunday before flying home that afternoon. It was an extra day of healing we needed together.

For the next three months, members of our Sunday school class continued to bring us food, or take us out to dinner. I did not even enter a grocery store for several weeks. One day Lois Cox called and asked what we needed. Laughingly, I replied that we were running out of Kleenex and toilet paper. When Lois came with the needed supplies, I talked with her again about Ann Marie's missing pillow. The church had tried to locate the pillow, including returning to the retreat center to look for it. That pillow was gone and no one knew where it could possibly be. I opened a new box of Kleenex, wiped my eyes, and blew my nose as overwhelming emotions continued to rush over me. Losing Ann was the hardest thing to deal with in our lives.

Lois understood the waves of grief that come and go without any warning. Gary had likened it to "when sorrows like sea billows roll" from the verse in the hymn, "It Is Well with My Soul." You think things are all right and you are standing in a calm ocean, when suddenly you find a wave of sorrow crashing in from behind, taking you under your emotions. Lois hugged me and then spoke her words of wisdom from experience.

Lois said, "Libby, many people are watching you to see if your God is big enough to get you through this. You must give up this pillow, just as you have given up Ann Marie, or it will ruin your testimony. Give the pillow to God. Pray that pillow will bless the head of whoever has it, the same way that it blessed Ann Marie's head." She prayed with me that I would find the courage and strength not to let the missing pillow continue to control my grief and anger.

That afternoon, I stood at the foot of Ann Marie's bed. Through tears, I asked the Lord to bless the head of whoever had the pillow. It was then God reminded me that I had made all of the curtains, pillow shams, and canopy out of an extra set of sheets. Somewhere, deep in a linen closet was an extra matching pillowcase. I rushed to the closet digging through sheets and towels, searching for the unused pillowcase. Finding it still inside the plastic package, I opened it up. I was surprised at how new and clean it looked compared to the one on the bed that was faded after seven years of washing and wear. In the top of the closet was an extra guest pillow. I put the new case on the extra pillow and placed it beside the old pillow on the bed. I realized the two pillows symbolized Ann's life and death. The old pillow represented Ann Marie's earth life, faded and worn out. The new clean pillow signified her new life in heaven. I rejoiced at the lesson God had taught me, once I had given up my selfish bitterness.

> *Remember my affliction and my wandering,*
> *the wormwood and bitterness.*
> *Surely my soul remembers and is bowed down within me.*
> *This I recall to my mind, therefore I have hope.*
> *The LORD's lovingkindnesses indeed never cease,*
> *for His compassions never fail;*
> *they are new every morning;*
> *great is Thy faithfulness.*
> Lamentations 3:19-23 (NAS)

Two weeks after Ann's death, we received a letter encouraging us that Ann Marie still lived with the donation of her eyes.

Medical Eye Bank of Western Pennsylvania

February 14, 1994

Dear Mr. & Mrs. Grunick:

I would like to take this opportunity to express my deepest sympathy to you and your family for the tragic death of your young daughter, Ann Marie. I would like you to know that her gift of eye donation has made a difference.

Both corneas were successfully transplanted to restore sight for two young men, age 14 and 25. Both recipients are recovering nicely and with immeasurable gratitude for this precious gift of sight.

Also, the back part of both eyes was used for research which is studying the disease that affects the lens and the retina. In this way, an additional and valuable contribution has been made to many whose only hope for restored sight is the advancement made in this area.

I realize that this is a difficult time for you, but it is my hope that you are able to find some comfort in your decision to donate your daughter's eyes. Although she is no longer with you, her gift of eye donation will change the lives of those living in a world of darkness.

This ultimate expression of your support of eye donation is deeply appreciated. If I can be of assistance to you in the future, please don't hesitate to contact me.

Ann's death brought the reality home to our family, that death does not always wait for life to grow old. Susan expressed her feelings trying to explain to David and Elizabeth the meaning of death.

Dear Libby and Gary,   March 26, 1994

... I have lived so much of my life unprepared for death and afraid of it. I don't want my kids to live that way. I don't know how Ann felt about death - you know a lot better than I. But I never sensed that she had a fear or a great foreboding of it in spite of her close calls through life. It is comforting to know that she knew the truth. So many people live to be old, and never deal with their feelings about their death, and how they look at it. They just continue to avoid the issue and I think they are really very scared inside. . . .

Love to you both,

Aunt Susan

The eleven friends on Ann Marie's prayer list all attended the *WHY WAIT?* Rally while we were in St. Louis. Josh McDowell and Allen Wilson gave words of tribute to Ann Marie and had a moment of silence for her memory. Although we were not able to attend the event, we received a Josh McDowell *Truth* newsletter in April, which highlighted Ann Marie and the prayer list of friends. We saw Ann's smiling face and name printed on the fifth page under the title "She Carried a List." Thousands of people had received the newsletter with the article. Unfortunately, we were not contacted about the article written in the newsletter. Upon reading the printed article, we barely recognized the story of Ann's life. Most of the details were inaccurate.

I called the editor of the publication and asked her why the Josh McDowell Ministry did not call us for information. She responded that they did not want to bother us during our sensitive time of grief. I explained to her that the true story of Ann Marie's life was so much better than what they had printed; I would send her the background on our family's testimony. The editor was very understanding and gracious on the phone, apologizing for not checking with us before printing the article.

On June 1, 1994, I wrote an eight-page story of Ann Marie's life and impact on those she touched. Before I mailed it to Josh McDowell Ministries, Lois and I went out to lunch and I asked her to read it. The words Lois spoke to me that day spurred me on to continue to look forward with hope, but also honor the past. She said, "Libby, I think you need to write a book. Don't write it yet, but you need to think about writing it in the next five years. Ann's story can minister to so many people."

Another letter from our former pastor in Little Rock, Marlin Howe, encouraged me to think through where God might lead us in the ministry of sharing our testimony with hurting families. Marlin had started a new counseling ministry for hurting families called, "Hope for the Family." His ministry motto was,

Strong Churches Do Not Make Strong Families,
Strong Families Make Strong Churches.

Hello, my dear friends! 7 June 1994

I want you to know that my heart has not stopped hurting since I learned of Ann Marie's death...Ann was a pivotal person and child in your lives. ...

My mind wanders to the question Jesus was asked concerning the person born blind—"was it because of his sin or that of his parents." Jesus responded, "Neither, but that the works of God would be glorified." While we know no human explanation for Ann Marie's death is ever good enough to satisfy the loss and loneliness in your hearts, that God, in some way, will bring glory to himself through it is reason enough. ...

That Ann Marie was your only child makes the loss even worse. ...

God will be glorified through Ann Marie's life, her death, and through you both. You are that kind of people! Patty and I are with you in spirit every day. We love you.

Marlin and Patty Howe

Many marriages do not survive the death of a child. Gary and I had to keep our communication with each other open and frequent. We needed time with each other and to heal where we were broken, then we would rise up stronger than before. We would have an even better marriage and unique platform for ministry. I continued to ask the Lord for several months what direction He intended for my life. The Lord began to show me that I should continue to teach women the Bible through Precept Ministries. My ministry would be especially to young mothers, helping them to train up their children to know the Lord.

As the winter months melted into the promise of springtime, Gary and I began to take long walks together in the evenings. The yellow daffodils, purple and red tulips, and pink and white tree blossoms all promised a resurrected life. We used the time together to talk openly about our day and feelings of grief and joy. We began to look forward to the changes Gary's retirement and our new home in St. Charles would bring. We planned our move to Missouri in June.

Before we left the Washington, D.C. area, Luther Jackson Middle School had planned a special recognition of Ann Marie's life. The last page of the 1994 yearbook was dedicated "In Memory" to Ann Marie. Out of the background of a lovely wooded pathway, Ann Marie's smiling face graced the center of the page, above the words:

We remember with love
Ann Marie Grunick
July 8, 1979 – January 29, 1994

On June 21, 1994, the first day of summer, Coach Dave Muniz asked us to attend a ceremony to dedicate the "Ann Marie Grunick Memorial Weight Room" at Luther Jackson Middle School. Donated weight equipment, formerly used by the Washington Red Skins, and a bronze door plaque engraved with Ann's name were unveiled. Each year one student would have their name placed on a trophy plaque in the room, and receive the "Ann Marie Grunick Award" for overcoming adversity. The administration and students from Ann's Rising Star Team attended the ceremony.

Libby & Gary unveil the bronze door plaque
Coach Muniz and teachers look on.

Coach Muniz wrote a note inside the book of poems he gave us in Ann's memory.

> *We are so proud that Ann Marie's name will go on forever at Luther Jackson. June 21, 1994, the longest day of the year in sunshine, is fitting to Ann Marie. She was full of sunshine and had a "never quit attitude." We hope this book will bring some comfort to the both of you.*
>
> *May God bless you both.*
>
> *Sincerely with Love,*
>
> *The Muniz Family*

Major General Nolan Sklute awarded Gary
The Legion of Merit Medal at
Col. Grunick's Retirement from the U.S. Air Force

On June 29, 1994, exactly five months after Ann Marie's death, Col. Gary A. Grunick, Appellate Judge, Air Force Court of Military Review retired from the United States Air Force. A retirement luncheon and ceremony held at the Bolling Officers' Club on Bolling Air Force Base honored over twenty years of distinguished military service in ten different locations. Gary also served in Incirlik, Turkey, as the Staff Judge Advocate for the Combined Task Force Operation Provide Comfort, supporting security and humanitarian operations in Northern Iraq. Gary was the most productive Appellate Judge in the history of keeping such records. He personally authored over 150 scholarly opinions, which left a profound influence on our military justice system for years to come. His military decorations include the Defense Meritorious Service Medal, the Meritorious Service Medal with four oak leaf clusters, and the Air Force Commendation Medal. The Judge Advocate General, Major General Nolan Sklute, awarded Gary the Legion of Merit Medal upon his retirement. Gary was presented with a flag of the United States, which flew over our Nation's Capitol on Memorial Day 1994.

The pain of grief for the first year without Ann Marie was a hollow ache as we moved through the seasons, holidays, birthdays, and anniversaries. We had to decide how to answer the question, "Do you have any children?" I felt if someone asked the question, it was an opportunity to share Ann's life story and the joy we have in the assurance of her salvation. Many times people would try to avoid saying her name, or talking about her life, thinking that it would make us sad. I loved to hear her name spoken, see a picture of her, or hear stories of her that I had not known. Time heals the wounds of grief. Talking with someone who is willing to listen about your loved one is comforting. Each person heals from the pain differently. They must be allowed to move at their own pace for complete healing.

For the next five years, I continued to remember Lois' words to write a book. However, I could not bring myself to put the words on paper. Finally, after seven years I began to write the story, which I had carried in my heart. I remembered a letter, which our friend Lloyd Ashworth had sent to us. It was a welcomed encouragement to think about writing a book about the tapestry of our lives.

Dear Gary & Libby,   *15 December 1994*

I wanted to write a separate letter to you from our Christmas letter to say just how shocked I was to hear of your tragedy.

Ann Marie was a special girl and I remember well her love of horses and the wonderful way that she seemed so determined to overcome all her disabilities. Many others would not have achieved anywhere near what Ann Marie did in her time here.

I know for you this has been a deep and difficult period, but I wanted you to know that we, and many others I am sure are still praying for you that God will draw near to you in your pain and loss. From the few experiences I have had pastoring people who face sudden loss, it is often months later that they need input into their lives after the initial shock has gone and you try to put your life back into shape. I do not know where you are at concerning this, but please know that we along with many others are standing with you to support you through this time.

We want answers for hard questions. I still have none for the loss of both my parents, my mother when I was just 14 years old. Many try to explain "why" but in the end, there is just that sense that God somehow knows best beyond our limited understanding. This somehow, most of the time, fails to supply an adequate answer, but you can be assured that one day you will know the full story and why, and perhaps only then will you receive the full release of your grief and sense of loss.

I am sure that you carry many special and happy memories of Ann Marie and will treasure these all your life. I know that she now would want you to get on with your lives and take on new challenges, and not become bogged down with thinking about the past. Just as she would have done. I know this that she could not have wished for better parents in you both, you have had the joy of parenting Ann Marie for those years, and she has been and will continue to be for you one of the most powerful shaping ingredients in your life.

I think of the tapestry, which rich colors and hours of concentrated effort produce a masterpiece. But turn it over, and the cottons are a mess on the back. Sometimes life is like that; from our side it looks all disfigured and unplanned and even tangled, but somehow allow the Lord to lift you both up to see His side of tapestry. It looks just fine, and one day from eternity, you too will enjoy with Him the picture that He is weaving of your lives and Ann Marie's....

The other matter I wanted to share with you, and this may be premature, but still... have you thought what God might be opening up for you in the future now as a couple? For whatever reason you are now freer to travel and move into a new phase of your lives and ministry. It may be that this is too soon, and this will take time to work through, but there will be purpose in this tragedy not just for Ann Marie's life but also for yours together. Can I encourage you to seek the Lord and ask Him to make this plain and clear to you both. I know you were sensing that your retirement from the Air Force was going to mean some new possibilities. Gary and Libby, both of you have much to give and share with others. Especially now through this "valley" that you have and are walking. Allow the Lord to use you both....

Please know my heart, that all I want to do is in whatever way I can, encourage you both and try to lift you up to the Lord who is the source of all comfort.

Sincerely in Christ,

Lloyd Ashworth, Executive Director

International Needs New Zealand

Elizabeth Grunick

Realizing that many believers and unbelievers are watching to see if our God is strong enough to get us through the worst nightmare any parent might have to face, we continue to share our testimony of His faithfulness. The LORD has surely given us the oil of joy for mourning, and the garment of praise for the spirit of heaviness. We look forward to the day when we wake up, holding God's hand and taking our first breath of celestial air. We will never have to say "Good-bye" again. The marriage feast will have begun. We will be seated in the Heavenly Sanctuary, rejoicing together for our work on this side of eternity.

CHAPTER TWENTY-ONE

Worthy of Our Calling

I, therefore, the prisoner of the Lord,
entreat you to walk in a manner worthy of the calling
with which you have been called,
with all humility and gentleness,
with patience,
showing forbearance to one another in love,
being diligent to preserve the unity of the Spirit
in the bond of peace.
Ephesians 4:1-3 (NAS)

With Ann Marie's passing, God closed a special chapter in our lives that we will treasure forever. The next chapter has taken many twists and turns causing us to grow deeper in our faith, teaching us to walk worthy of our calling. We have had to learn not to run ahead of the Lord, but wait for renewed strength. As our hearts continue to heal, He opens greater doors of ministry to us. Always connecting the tapestry threads, He weaves grace into our growing faith.

Losing an only child means the end of a family legacy on earth. There will be no wedding or grandchildren to continue our heritage. It leaves a particular emptiness to earth life and a desire and hope of our calling focused on a future eternal life. Our inheritance has gone ahead of us to a heavenly home, and we are moving toward that home. We have

> Always connecting the tapestry threads, He weaves grace into our growing faith.

an appreciation of how short life and time can be on earth. Such a perspective on life can lead to disappointment with those who take family, time, health, wealth, and life for granted. However, it gives us a desire to help them realize the importance of eternal relationships and ministry opportunities. God has given us everything we have on earth, and God can take it away. It is not how the present seems to be, but how things end that matters.

For where your treasure is,
there will your heart be also.
Luke 12:34 (NAS)

The first year after Ann's death was a painful walk through waves of emotions, pushing and pulling us along the healing processes. We were off the stress chart as we made a major move halfway across the country, changed careers, churches, friends, and built a new home after the death of our daughter. The end of June, upon arriving in St. Louis after the retirement ceremony, we discovered our new home was being built wrong. Thankfully, it was not even near completion and all of the framing on the bedroom side of the house was torn out and corrected. The faith growing processes continued when we had to place everything into storage and live with my parents while the new construction progressed painfully slow. It would be four more months before we moved into our completed home in October.

In July, Susan sang at the Family Life Conference in Montreat, North Carolina. The guest speaker was Dr. Leighton Ford. Susan shared with him about Ann Marie's death, since his son Sandy had died as a young adult. A few weeks later, Dr. Leighton Ford called us to talk about our daughter's death and pray with us. As we talked on the phone, I spoke to Dr. Ford concerning the book he had written about Sandy. I particularly loved the words he had written on the last page of the final chapter, "Finishing the Race." He wrote about chatting with Sandy, who had been dead for two months. His concern was that as time passed, they would lose any sense of nearness.

The reply from Sandy was, "But why, Dad? You're moving closer to eternity every day. You're no longer moving from, but to me! And besides, the 'Wall' between is so thin—you would laugh if you could see it."[1]

Leighton Ford then told us that he believes there is an awesome group of youth in heaven, and when we talk to each other about our loved ones who have gone ahead, God allows them to meet in heaven. Ann Marie and Sandy have met each other. The thought of moving closer to eternity every day has given us the assurance we will be together again.

Gary and I celebrated our twenty-fifth wedding anniversary in August 1994 at a quaint bed and breakfast hotel in Hannibal, Missouri. It was in Hannibal that we had renewed our marriage vows on our first lay renewal almost fifteen years before. That renewed vow caused us to grow stronger in our marriage each day as we faced the testing of our faith through difficult trials, which could have ended our marriage. Bonded together in our covenant love and faith, we knew our marriage could stand the test for better or worse, for richer or poorer, in sickness and in health, till death do us part.

We hand-carried Ann Marie's small pumpkin back to St. Louis in the spring. She selected it at the Single's Retreat in Virginia the previous fall, and it was still firm and whole. During the summer, we planted a garden on the farm property which my parents owned. Mom took the seeds from Ann Marie's pumpkin and sowed them at one end of the garden. By October, we had an "Ann Marie Pumpkin Patch" full of sugar pie pumpkins! Ann Marie's cousin Olivia Rose helped us save some of the seeds. Each year, we take the seeds from the pumpkins and continue a tradition of spreading seeds and growing pumpkins in Ann's memory. One small pumpkin has produced hundreds of pumpkins over the years.

Our new home helped us to start fresh, and develop new relationships while restoring old friendships. Boxes and boxes of Ann Marie's clothing, toys, and games were closed off into the unfinished part of the basement. Eventually, I was able to give most of her clothing away. However, other treasures were far too personal. Sometimes, I would wear one of her sweaters, or just hold it and smell her perfume scent. I still love the smell of her favorite perfume.

We were humbled that Dr. Barry Byer and several team members had continued *CrossLink*. In May before we left Washington, D.C., a second forty-foot container was filled and sent to Central Baptist Church in Moscow, Russia; with $241,000 worth of food, clothing, and medical supplies. The work of faith continued when a few months later a smaller container was shipped with $85,000 worth of humanitarian supplies. Roy Winston had become a regular volunteer with the ministry. He told us that sometimes the volunteer force coming to help sort the supplies was so large that they actually had to turn volunteers away. Barry Byer sent us reports of the *CrossLink* effort as 1994 ended with a fourth shipment to the Russian congregation.

> *Dear Gary and Libby,*
>
> *Thank you for your letter. I hope all is going well with your new home and job…. CrossLink is really expanding. We are all so grateful to you for your vision and hard work in getting it started. Our fourth container left before Thanksgiving packed with over 15,000 pounds of winter clothes and some medical supplies. The members of Moscow Baptist Church will be the best dressed congregation in all of Moscow…*
>
> *I'm sure God will use you two in many wonderful ways in your new church home. Sharyn and I send our warmest regards. You are two of the most inspiring Christians we know. Keep me informed about how you are doing. Your friendship has been one of God's richest gifts to us!*
>
> *Your friends,*
> *Barry and Sharyn Byer*

Gary's Air Force retirement pay allowed us time before making future employment and ministry decisions. After several interviews, Gary accepted a position with a private St. Charles law firm. It was an adjustment from practicing military law to a civilian practice. Coming from a twenty-one-year military career and retirement as an Appellate Judge did not bring any clients with it, so a partnership in the firm was not given consideration. After his many years of experience in a courtroom, he started as a new associate with the same pay as a younger attorney just out of law school. He discovered the world of billable hours, where he had to keep track of every six minutes of his time in order to bill clients. He worked long hours, six days a week, driving all over St. Charles and St. Louis.

Maintaining a Christian witness in the civilian practice of law is challenging. The shine of being in a law firm quickly wore off. After ten months of sweating in new suits, white shirts, and ties; Gary and the firm came to a mutual departure.

We found our new church to be welcoming and ready to involve us in ministry. Even before we moved to St. Charles, I started teaching Precept with two other Precept teachers in September. The study was a timely one, *God Where Are You When Bad Things Happen?* It was the study of Habakkuk, and included the scripture of "hinds feet in high places." I continued to teach Precept for the next two years, as the group of women grew to almost forty when I taught the book of *Daniel.*

I was on the women's council, and Gary was elected a deacon. The church, known for its pageants at Christmas and Easter, asked us to give our testimony at the 1994 Christmas concert of "God with Us." Several hundred people heard our story of faith over the three nights of production. Gary's sister Donna and her children began attending church and participating in the musical performances.

Gary and I taught a family values Sunday school where the children and parents attended together.

In the spring, our friends The Flying Wallendas came to St. Louis. Tino Wallenda set up his high wire inside the church worship center and walked across it while giving his testimony from a wireless microphone. The church sat breathlessly as they watched Tino stand on his head and skip rope on the slim cable above us. After church, we invited our Sunday school class to our new home for lunch with The Wallendas. It was great fellowship as parents and children enjoyed a sandwich and dessert, while Tino and his family shared their faith walk in a personal touch.

Another opportunity came our way for mission ministry in the summer of 1996. Gary was asked to be the chairman of a choir mission trip to Jamaica. The church wanted to take their Easter drama to the island; much like our Romanian choir had done in 1992. Gary thought we would not take more than thirty to forty people on the trip; it quickly mushroomed to one-hundred and seventy people wanting to go. Expenses and logistics for travel, housing, and meals for that number of people were astronomical. Gary questioned the wisdom of taking such a large group and spending so much money for one mission trip. Soon planning meetings were being held without the chairman invited to attend.

A chartered private airplane for the group locked the church into a commitment, which cost thousands of dollars. Lack of proper paperwork with customs officials left humanitarian supplies and stage equipment tied up at the Jamaican port. The trip was an extravaganza of building a stage in the Caribbean heat on the Montego Bay beach, feeding one-hundred and seventy choir members for a week in three different hotels, and thousands of Jamaicans attending the free outdoor performance. Two men on the team were threatened by attempted robberies; one in his hotel room, the other at knifepoint in the food market. The church found itself $40,000 in debt when the choir returned home from Jamaica. Gary's wisdom and concerns had been ignored. The results were damaging to the church financially and spiritually.

Jealousy, arrogance, immorality, abuse, and financial misappropriation have no place in the Lord's work. Churches do not win the evangelism game by leaving "bloody bodies" all over the playing field. People leave churches over such things. When people leave churches, families leave churches. Many times, they never find another church. Soon you have a whole nation that has left the church.

The Jamaica trip was just a symptom of a bigger problem in a church that continued to unravel God's tapestry of grace. Within a few years, only a remnant was left of what once was a growing vital church. Five years later, a staff member came to our home and apologized for how we were treated. It had bothered him for all those years, and he needed to ask our forgiveness. We had found another church by then. Unfortunately, Gary's sister and children had left church altogether.

Almost two years after Ann's death, we received the following card from Race and Linda Lariscy. For years thinking they would never have a child, the Lord had miraculously blessed them with a baby daughter named Hope. The Holy Spirit used this note to encourage us at a time of seeking God's will in a new ministry direction.

Dear Gary and Libby,   October 17, 1995

Greetings in the name of Jesus our Lord. While praying and ministering to the Lord this morning, the Lord impressed you two upon my heart and so I'm writing. Race and I still weep when we think about Ann Marie, but the Lord always tells us there is no need as she is constantly rejoicing in His care. I wanted to share my heart with you about some things and mainly express thanks to you. When Race and I first came to RVBC you were the first people we met in the Church. Do you know how much that encouraged us? You were with us and knew and understood what we desired to do at RVBC. You were instrumental in bringing a great Lay Renewal and we remember it as being a true blessing to the Body. That was at the very beginning. We've now been here 7 years and at this point we're starting over again due to the draw down of troops. We've seen so many come and go and there have been many who have touched our lives in a special way and you are one of them. We love you and want to encourage you wherever God has you at this point in your lives. There is so much rich deep joy in His presence. I pray that you remain in His presence and in that joy all the days of your life and that you are constantly filled and refilled with His Spirit and Grace.

I'd like to introduce you to Hope. She is now a curly-haired three-year old. Just know we are often moved to pray for you and thank God for you every time we remember you. In love over flowing,

Linda, Race, and Hope

While we were in Germany, Dr. Andy Jumper, pastor of Central Presbyterian Church died from a long battle with cancer. Dr. Jumper had led the church into the Evangelical Presbyterian Church (EPC), a newly formed denomination. Compromises on the authority of scripture and other denominational positions had caused many large churches to split from the mainline Presbyterian denomination.

Central Presbyterian Church called a new pastor, Tim Brewer, while we were in Washington, D.C.

Shortly after moving back to St. Charles, Lay Renewal Ministries approached Gary about being the visiting lay team coordinator for a renewal at Central Presbyterian. We had come full circle in the fifteen years since we first walked to the front of that church and gave our lives to Jesus Christ. Now we would be bringing a team of lay people to share their testimonies with the congregation that had prayed for us so many times. The Central Presbyterian members who would coordinate the church logistics of the renewal were Alan and Sue Schaffer. We remembered when Alan had prayed in the Mainz Cathedral for God to shake Germany, and then taken credit for the Berlin Wall falling the next day.

The renewal plans started almost a year before the scheduled event, so that prayer would guide all of the decisions. Gary met with Central pastor, Tim Brewer, several times about the renewal scheduled for November 11-15, 1995. However, in March all of St. Louis was shocked when a train struck the young dynamic pastor while vacationing in Colorado. Tim had his leg amputated, but seemed to be recovering from the accident.

Then on July 20, 1995, Dr. Timothy D. Brewer ended his thirty-six years of life in a tragic suicide, leaving his family, friends, and congregation devastated by the loss.

Central Presbyterian considered canceling the renewal, but it became obvious that the congregation needed a formal opportunity to come together and share the pain of their grief. The visiting team was a weaving of new and old threads of friendship for us. Tino Wallenda shared his testimony. Our dear friends, Steve and Billie Tomberlin, drove all the way from Montgomery, Alabama, to be part of the team. They had a powerful testimony of Christian growth since the first days we met them and began a mentoring relationship. We had become friends with former St. Louis Cardinal Football player, Roger Wehrli and his wife Gayle. Roger gave his testimony at one of the men's luncheons, drawing a large crowd. During the evening afterglows, many church members poured out their hearts about the pain and doubts that Tim's suicide had created in their personal faith. As the renewal team ministered to them, healing began to take root, watered by the tears of sharing.

A new friend from the Central Renewal, Rev. Chris Pierce, who was a pastor in the adjoining county, contacted us about helping host the Belarus National Choir in February 1996. Ted Hope from Chattanooga was bringing the thirty-six-member choir on tour to St. Louis and needed American host homes. Chris had scheduled the churches for concerts, but placing the choir members with local church members would save the expense of hotel rooms. We worked with the list of strange Russian names; sometimes trying to figure out if they were male or female, married or single. I called several families in our church giving them the opportunity to host one or two of the choir members. After a few weeks, we had the choir scheduled to stay in several homes. Gary and I kept the Belarusian pastor, the choir director, and one choir member in our home.

Just one day before the choir was to arrive; a host family called and canceled keeping two of the single women in the choir. It was Super Bowl weekend and they were having a Super Bowl party instead of hosting the foreigners. Desperate at such a late notice of cancellation, I started calling more church families. Several turned me down. Finally, I called Carl and Virginia Hall. Carl was a little unsure that they wanted to keep two young women from this strange country called Belarus.

I begged and pleaded with him, until he said, "Well, okay, I guess we can keep them for a few days."

The next day when the choir arrived, all of the host families were anxiously waiting to take their new friends home. When Carl saw Kate and Mila, he and Virginia instantly bonded with them. Out of the thirty-six choir members, only two were fluent in English. Mila, a pastor's daughter, was one of them. These two special young women touched the lives of their host family for only four short days, but it seemed like they had known each other all of their lives. On the morning of the choir's departure, Carl had tears streaming down his face as he said good-bye to his new adopted Belarusian daughters.

The experience expanded Carl's thinking beyond the walls of the local church. In September 1998, Carl made a trip to Belarus with another church member, Dave Sutton. From that trip, Carl and Dave started sponsoring a Belarusian missionary. Gary told them about *CrossLink* and they started collecting used medical equipment and supplies; which they sent to Belarus through the assistance of Ted Hope and Slavic Gospel Association. Within a few years, Carl was hooked on sharing the gospel in mission ministry after his first trip to Venezuela in 2000, when he led a woman to receive Christ. Carl and Virginia continue to remain in contact with Mila and her family.

Another renewal team member, Lynn Williamson, soon became a new close friend. Lynn was involved with a ministry called International Students, Inc. (ISI). She encouraged us to attend one of the Friday night dinners where 100-200 international college students from all over the St. Louis area gathered for fellowship with American families. The first night at ISI, we met Jennifer Wang from Taiwan. Jennifer was beautiful, slender, with long dark hair and a newlywed. Her husband William attended St. Louis University as an Asian business student. Within the month, Jennifer and William shared dessert with us as their new American friends.

The first time William and Jennifer came to our house, they walked up to our Christmas tree and gazed in awe at the twinkling lights and ornaments.

Then William, being a business major, said, "I never realized what an economic opportunity Christmas is!"

I turned their attention to our Advent wreath, and began to explain the true meaning of Christmas. We certainly had some work cut out for us to help them understand the Christian side of Christmas. Eventually, they both became Christians and started attending a Chinese-American church in St. Louis.

Each month we would get together with our new Taiwanese friends and go somewhere or visit each other's homes for a meal. When The Flying Wallendas came to St. Louis to perform in Circus Flora, we took William and Jennifer to see the show. Several times, we took them to the farm to fish and eat barbeque with my family. The first time William caught a catfish out of the farm pond, Gary helped him clean it.

When Gary cut the head off the catfish and threw it to the farm cats, William said, "You cut the head off of the fish! Thirty percent of the nutrients are in the head!"

Gary replied, "Well, we give it to the cats!"

Then Jennifer appeared with a plastic bucket to put the fish parts in and said, "You cut the head off of the fish! Thirty percent of the nutrients are in the head!"

It was then Gary learned that in Taiwan it is an honor to receive the head of the catfish to eat. Usually it is a gift to the oldest family member.

Understanding English was sometimes complicated. When Jennifer became pregnant, she and William wanted to attended Lamaze classes.

One night William told Gary, "You won't believe what we have to bring to the Lamaze class. We need to bring a blanket, pillow, and the coach! I don't know how I am going to get the coach out of the living room and into the back of our car!"

Gary realized that William was thinking about the living room couch, not the coach. Gary said, "No! No! The coach—you are the coach!"

We laughed for a half hour thinking of William struggling to get the couch into his car. Over the next five years, they became parents to a son Edward, and then a daughter Emily. We felt like the American grandparents to their precious children with dark hair and Asian eyes. Eventually, they moved back to Taiwan where William became a successful executive, and Jennifer a good mother.

What may have seemed like a devastating set of circumstances when Gary left the law firm, God used to move us in a new career direction. International Needs gave us a phone call in May 1995. International Needs – USA was looking for a part-time Developmental Officer to help raise funds for the ministry. Lloyd Ashworth was still with International Needs in New Zealand, and Peter Vidu was on the International Needs Board of Directors in Romania. Gary accepted the part-time position with International Needs (IN), while he started his own private practice of law from our home. We were delighted with the concept of helping nationals do ministry in their own countries. I joined the board of Women's International Needs Network (WINN), helping women to encourage and minister to each other throughout the world.

Besides raising funds for the IN ministry, we were also required to raise our own support. It was a lesson in faith to seek personal financial support from friends and relatives, and raise funds for the much-needed ministry projects around the world. Many times, we directed personal support offers towards the ministry projects because we felt the projects were in much more urgent need of the funds. We also realized that there is no "part-time" Christian ministry. Fund-raising is a difficult job in a non-profit organization, especially when it involves raising your own funds at the same time you are raising ministry funds. One of the greatest gifts was working with the Christian nationals from countries all around the world. We hosted in our home nationals from India, Ghana, Romania, and New Zealand.

Gary traveled several weeks on deputation with nationals from other countries raising funds for their work. At our own expense, we used our home office equipment, administrative skills, and hospitality to serve the Lord through the nationals who we grew to love.

We had received mixed messages about whether we needed to continue to raise our own funds, or if a salaried structure would replace our personal support efforts. After a year, our personal support had more than doubled what the ministry required. Sometimes, other ministries with which we were involved, and Gary's private law practice, seemed to conflict with expectations of the part-time position with International Needs. This happened when we scheduled a lay renewal at Signal Mountain, Tennessee, months before we knew Cynthia Davidason would be coming to Atlanta from Sri Lanka for a deputation tour the same week.

Cynthia Davidason was the head mistress for a Christian children's school in Columbo, Sri Lanka. Gary and I had a grand time taking Cynthia and two schoolchildren, Rebecca and Timothy from Sri Lanka, on a 5,000-mile deputation in Atlanta, to Texas and Kansas for several weeks in the fall of 1996. Rebecca and Timothy would sing for church congregations, while Cynthia would tell about the children's school she ran in Columbo, Sri Lanka. Gary and Timothy had the most fun in Wal-Mart buying cowboy hats in Texas. They would pretend to have a gunfight dressed in their hats and sunglasses.

On our trip to Atlanta with the Sri Lanka deputation, we visited with our friends, Dr. Phil Roberts, and his wife Anya. The Roberts' two children, Naomi and Mark, had grown into preteens since we had visited them in Oradea, Romania during the choir trip. Dr. Roberts was the Vice-President of Evangelism at the North American Mission Board in Alpharetta, Georgia. Re-establishing our relationship with Phil Roberts would lead us on other paths of ministry in our future.

Putting the Sri Lanka team on an airplane from Atlanta, Georgia, to Seattle, Washington; Gary and I drove to the lay renewal on Signal Mountain. We were excited to be part of the lay renewal team to Signal Mountain Presbyterian Church in Chattanooga, Tennessee, from September 28 to October 1, 1996. Bill Dudley had moved from Memorial Presbyterian Church to pastor Signal Mountain Presbyterian several years before. My sister Susan was also on the team as the music leader. It was an opportunity for us to minister together by giving our testimony, and Susan singing at the worship service. We felt a special bonding with the Dudleys, who had lost their adopted son, David. The threads of tapestry continued to flow through God's grace in our relationships with fellow believers.

We longed to return to Romania and work with Peter and Geta Vidu, and the Romanian Executive Director of International Needs-Titi Bulzan. We first met Titi and Ligia Bulzan at the February 1996 International Needs board meeting in Phoenix, Arizona. Ligia asked me to come to Romania and teach a women's Precept class. Then in June, we met the Bulzan family in Washington, D.C., for a vacation tour of our nation's capitol. Titi was working on his doctorate at Southeastern Baptist Theological Seminary and preparing to go back to Romania. We began to plan a trip for the summer of 1997 to coincide with a July Precept Women's Conference in Romania.

Gary and I made an appointment with the Eurasian Precept trainers, Mia and Costel Oglice from Romania, who would be at Precept Ministries in Chattanooga at the same time as the lay renewal at Signal Mountain. We sat in a conference room with Mia talking about the trip. Suddenly my mentor and role model Kay Arthur walked into the room. I was so excited to see her again in person. Gary said I had not been that excited since our honeymoon. Of course, I had never seen him jump up to stand at attention in the presence of a woman since military retirement. Kay was so gracious to spend time talking with us about our plans and encourage us.

I told Kay Arthur that I was starting a Precept class in January at our new church. She suggested the Lord Series study of the Gospel of

John, *God Are You There?*, as a good beginning class. For the next four years, I taught Precept to hundreds of women in a weekly Bible study. Eventually, I coordinated and recruited teachers for several women's Bible studies as our women's ministry began to grow.

By March 1997, plans were firming up for our pastor, his wife, and two young sons to make the Romanian trip with us. Our hope was a partnership would develop between our new church and the work of International Needs in Romania. I purchased Precept books written in Romanian for teaching a group of women, *Lord, I Want to Know You!*

In April, we had to change our trip plans, because of the school situation of one of the pastor's sons. August would work out better for them to travel as a family to Europe. Reluctantly, I called Precept and told them I would not be able to speak at the Romanian Women's Conference in July. It was a great disappointment to me, after over a year of planning to attend the conference.

In May of 1997, Gary traveled with Titi Bulzan for twenty days through five states, driving 2,800 miles, to thirty-seven church meetings on a deputation tour for International Needs. While staying at our home, Titi Bulzan met our pastor, and we made new plans for the Romanian trip. Our first stop would be at a Youth Discipleship Camp (sleeping in tents) in the Carpathian Mountains of Transylvania, Romania. New dates were August 3-14. I would teach the Precept *Lord, I Want to Know You!* to the women at the camp. Gary would work with Titi to get sponsors for IN Romanian church planters, do advanced coordination for short-term mission work, and medical teams at the Arad Ministry Center. Our pastor would do a teaching series on leadership for the Romanian young adults. After the youth camp, we would travel to Oradea, to stay with Peter and Geta Vidu. The new Emmanuel Baptist Church was now complete, and the first seminary building was almost finished on the seventeen-acre campus hillside. Our pastor would preach in several village churches and the large Emmanuel Baptist Church.

Peter, Geta, and Adonis Vidu came to the U.S. to visit us in July. When they stayed at our home for several days, we firmed up the plans for our August visit. Peter was concerned about our rendezvous point with Titi to go to the youth camp. We were to meet Titi at a PECO gas station as we drove into the city of Oravita at 6 p.m. on Wednesday,

August 6. From our meeting point, Titi would take us to the youth camp in the forest. Peter said that it was not a good part of Romania, and that there might be viper snakes at the campsite. We decided to take anti-snake venom serum just in case.

Titi had requested us to bring some important supplies to the camping area. We packed two tents, which we would leave in Romania, along with sleeping bags and air mattresses. The summer season had been exceptionally rainy and mosquitoes invaded the countryside of Romania. We packed mosquito repellant, citronella candles, instant hot chocolate for eighty people, marshmallows, toilet paper, and a blue tarp (to cover the cooking area). Other requested necessities from the U.S. included instant coffee, amaretto coffee creamer, Thai meat marinade, lemon-pepper, peanut butter, strawberry jelly, powdered Ranch dressing, and toothpaste.

Arriving in Vienna, we picked up our two rental cars and went to bed at the NOVOTEL hotel next to the airport. The next morning, after a late breakfast, we were off to Hungary. Knowing that we still would need another day to recover from the flight, we drove only a few hours to a beautiful resort hotel just outside of Budapest. Stopping for lunch in Budapest, our pastor's wife remarked that she had expected things to look worse. I told her, "It goes down hill from here!"

Things did go "down hill" from there! The plan was to leave the Hungarian hotel by 9 a.m. the next morning. Delays caused us to leave almost two hours later than planned the next morning. We were scheduled to meet at a new McDonald's for lunch with evangelist Dinu Bulzesc, professor of chemical engineering at the University of Timisoara. Driving in our two cars, rough road construction and bad weather slowed our travel even more. We arrived in Timisoara, Romania, around 3 p.m. long after lunchtime, and needing a gas and potty stop. We had first met Dinu and his wife, Lydia, when they came with Peter and Geta to our church in Germany in 1990. Dinu now owned one of the few gas stations in Timisoara, and supported five Romanian pastors with the profits. Dinu filled our cars with gas, gave us some refreshments, and then led us out of town headed toward Oravita to meet Titi Bulzan.

The roads grew worse as we headed south toward the border with Serbia. Horse carts and hay wagons blocked traffic on the rural narrow roads. At one point, an oncoming car honked at a horse walking on the side of the road. The horse jumped and darted between our car and our pastor's car following us. It was a narrow escape, but our pastor missed hitting the horse. The sun was setting as we arrived at the PECO station in Oravita around 8:15 p.m., over two hours late.

There was no one waiting for us at the PECO station, which was still under construction. We had no cell phone, since very few people even owned a phone in Romania. Peter and Dinu had warned us not to drive the roads at night because of highway robbers. We could not imagine where Titi was, but it was obvious that we were in a very strange isolated place and unable to speak Romanian. (Titi had waited for two hours for us and decided we were not coming. We had missed him by fifteen minutes.)

From an outdoor bar across the street, God sent a man who could speak German to help us. We decided that he was really an angel named Sebastian. Sebastian helped us to get a room in the only "hotel" in town. He took us to a restaurant to eat where there was a phone. At midnight, Gary called Peter Vidu in Oradea from the restaurant phone and explained our situation. Peter warned us not to drive on the roads at night. He suggested that we stay in the hotel that night, and go back to Dinu in Timisoara the next day.

We spent one night in the dirtiest pre-revolutionary hotel in Romania. When we were shown our room, the hotel clerk screwed the single light bulb into the light socket. There was no running water in the room or the bathroom. In the corner was a pitcher of drinking water and two glasses. The pitcher of drinking water had evaporated four inches and had a scum of dead flies and bugs on its surface. When we sat down on our hard single beds, dust flew up from the stinky bedspread. Through the night, Sebastian and his friends guarded our cars on the parking lot from thieves. Looking back at it, we were convinced God was making us realize what Romania was like for many of its people.

Dinu was able to schedule us into a church in Arad the next evening when we arrived back in Timisoara. Pastor Doru Popa hosted us at Maranatha Baptist Church for a worship service where our pastor preached. Then Pastor Popa gave us the privilege of sleeping in one of the Christian orphanages that night on clean sheets. After a Romanian breakfast at the orphanage, we knew that the opportunity to minister at the youth camp was gone. We unloaded all of our tents, sleeping bags, blue tarp, hot chocolate, and children's gifts from our two cars and gave them to the orphanage. The orphanage had been praying for some camping equipment to help with a children's camp. Unknowingly, we had taken the detour to answer their prayers. We had to remain flexible for God to use us in ministry.

The next day, Friday, we arrived in Oradea and into the welcoming arms of Peter and Geta Vidu. Gary and I cried tears of joy when we toured the new Emmanuel Baptist Church and saw the worship center which could seat twenty-five-hundred. It had been under construction when our German choir sang in the communist sports hall five years before. The beautiful building reminded us of a wedding cake with white columns, pale pink wall paint, and marble floors. Peter explained that the price of flooring for the church had been so expensive in Romania, that when they heard a marble factory in Italy was going out of business, they purchased the entire factory for a good price. All the floors in the church, education building, and seminary were a beautiful pink and white marble.

On Sunday morning, our pastor preached before the largest congregation in all of Europe at Emmanuel Baptist Church. When he and Gary walked to the platform with the other Romanian pastors, the twenty-seven hundred-member congregation stood to its feet out of respect for the pastors. It was an emotional moment after a difficult and tiring week.

Many times when we face the storms of life that come as failure or disappointments, God will lift us up to soar as an eagle on the wind above the storm. We can use the storm to lift us higher instead of letting it overcome us. As the Romanian countryside was in full harvest, so was the spiritual harvest of new believers. We were encouraged by the perseverance of the believers in economic hardship and runaway inflation rates. Signs of change were peaking through the dark polluted cloud of former communist oppression. New gasoline stations and McDonald's golden arches were springing up in larger cities. A new Coca-Cola plant produced the best cola using Romanian mineral water. A new dormitory at the seminary would open at the start of the school year.

Ministry worthy of our calling will come under spiritual warfare if it is striking a blow for the Kingdom of God. Facing great stress and conflict teaches us to trust in God's grace to get us through the valley. As He walks beside us, His Holy Spirit gives us wisdom, discernment, and protection. We can see many dangers, toils, and snares along the path of righteousness. His plans are not always our plans. Totally stripped of our plans, we could only trust in Him to lead us on the right path. He had closed one door and opened another to run the race with endurance, worthy of our calling.

CHAPTER TWENTY-TWO

A Future and a Hope

"For I know the plans that I have for you,"
declares the LORD,
"Plans for welfare and not for calamity
to give you a future and a hope."
Jeremiah 29:11 (NAS)

After we returned from Romania, Randy Mayfield and John Splinter invited Gary to go on a trip to the Ukraine for a men's conference in November of 1997. Gary gave his testimony to several hundred Ukrainian men in a former communist hall. He also spoke in a radio interview, which caused the women to want to come to the conference, too.

While Gary was in the Ukraine, he met a men's singing group called *Kovcheg,* or The Ark Singers in English. They had sung for the Billy Graham Crusade in Moscow, Russia, in 1992. The Ark Singers came in 1999 for a Midwest tour of the United States. Gary made all of the concert arrangements and traveled with them from Wisconsin to Mississippi for a month. When they were not on the road tour, they stayed at our home. The five singers consumed seventy pounds of bananas, sixty pounds of apples, and fifty pounds of grapes. They raised enough funds to buy the small house next to a Ukrainian church for Sunday school meetings. They returned to our home in March 2005 for another Midwest tour raising funds for two orphanages and children's summer camps.

Over the years, we have done several more lay renewals in St. Louis, Missouri and one in Detroit, Michigan. At one renewal in Cape Girardeau, Missouri, the church coordinator was David Limbaugh, brother to Rush Limbaugh. When Gary was the team coordinator, I was usually the women's luncheon speaker.

One of our greatest joys has been watching God multiply the *CrossLink* ministry started in 1993 with a few cans of green beans and asparagus. Ann Marie has probably witnessed from heaven the blessing poured forth on the poorest of the poor all over the world. When a local church comes together in a mission ministry with lay people able to express their Christian faith in a hands-on way, the love of Christ impacts the world.

> *CrossLink is a God ordained work with a spiritual impact*
> *that we will never fully know this side of eternity.*
> *What a future celebration that will be.*
> *Col. Gary A. Grunick*

The U.S. State Department discontinued the container shipment program of the "Fund for Democracy and Development" under the Clinton Administration. *CrossLink* ministry at Columbia Baptist Church had grown so large that it was time for a major step toward independence. In November 1996, *CrossLink* International was incorporated as a nonprofit, nondenominational, humanitarian aid organization.[2] *CrossLink* International started sending medical supplies outside of the Russian Baptist Church to other countries. Belarus received over $1 million worth of supplies, when Gary connected the Belarusian choir and the Missouri Baptist Convention together with *CrossLink.* Shortly after those shipments, Prison Fellowship entered into a partnership with *CrossLink,* and sent supplies to prisoners in Moldova. With Brazil, Estonia/Latvia, and Sierra Leone added to the list of shipments, more than $4 million worth of supplies, medicines, and clothing were sent in containers during the year.[3]

The step to become a nonprofit organization took off in 1997 when over twenty-four countries spanning the globe received aid totaling more than two-million dollars. The NOVA Mobile Clinic and the Arlington Free Clinic in Arlington, Virginia, received free medicines. Supplies were sent with medical mission teams to Haiti, Venezuela, Ecuador, and the Caribbean. Medical hospitals and dental clinics in Korea, Tanzania, Belize, Liberia, Guatemala, Ukraine, Kenya, Madagascar, Togo, Zambia, Benin, Bulgaria, and Romania received supplies of medicine and equipment.[4] The Virginia Board of Pharmacy licensed *CrossLink* in 1998 as the only nonprofit distributor/warehouse of proprietary medicines in the Commonwealth of Virginia.[5] *CrossLink* extended their partnership with Lions International to distribute refurbished eyeglasses free of charge to people in other countries.[6]

In June 2000, Gary and I received a special invitation to an "Affirmation Dinner" for *CrossLink* International celebrating the past years of ministry, and looking to where God would continue to lead it. On June 3, we gathered in the fellowship hall of Columbia Baptist Church with over one-hundred and eighty friends and volunteers linked together to form one body in Christ, making a powerful difference in the world. Special guests who had received aid from *CrossLink* gave testimonials. The history of *CrossLink* recorded in a printed report listed our first container in 1993 along with all of the other shipments until May 2000. The total value of *CrossLink* projects as of May 2000 was $15,451,035 sent to seventy countries around the world.[7]

Many of those present at the dinner never knew the story of the start of *CrossLink*. For them it started sometime after the first container was shipped, or when *CrossLink* became a nonprofit organization. However, on the inside of the last page of the report, Jim Perdew wrote about how the ministry was started as God wove the tapestry of grace.

The history of CrossLink has been one of God placing key individuals in key positions at key times. Gary Grunick, an Air Force attorney who had been involved in getting humanitarian supplies from Germany to Romania, was the organizing and implementing force behind our first container to Moscow called 'CrossLink I.' The mission and the name caught on, people got excited, God opened doors and hearts, and a ministry named CrossLink was born. God multiplied the meager financial resources available and hurting people were served in the name of Christ.

What a joy it is to continue to promote CrossLink, pray for its future and thank God that I was a part of its beginning.

Rev. Jim Perdew, Gray Summit, MO. [8]

The day after the *CrossLink* dinner, we went on a tour of the two warehouses that *CrossLink* used for storage of medicines, equipment, and eyeglasses. Both facilities were stacked full of boxes that had been inventoried and labeled, using the original label format Gary had designed for the first container.

Because Pastor Neil Jones and Jim Perdew were secure in their ministry as church staff, they allowed church members to take the *CrossLink* ministry and run with it, watching as God blessed it. Since *CrossLink* International incorporated in November 1996, it has sent over twenty-five-million dollars to one-hundred and eighteen countries including the United States. [9]

Before leaving Washington, D.C., we stopped by Luther Jackson Middle School to see Coach Muniz. He showed us the plaque in the "Ann Marie Weight Room" with all of the student names of those who had received the yearly award. More weight equipment had been added to the room. Dave Muniz told us that he would come to the weight room to workout and often thought of Ann Marie. However, Coach Muniz had one more surprise for us. In front of the school, he had supervised a group of male students as they created a memory garden. In the circle garden of flowering shrubs were plaques in memory of Ann Marie and another student who had died after her.

Gary's private law practice enabled us to take a month to travel in Europe and attend the wedding of Adonis and Adriana Vidu in Romania during June to July 2000. It had only been three years since our last visit to Oradea, but significant improvements in the economy were reflected in the wedding. The glorious wedding followed by a five-course meal reception lasted eight hours, and was well worth the trip. We arrived the day before the wedding and watched as the young girls of the church decorated the reception hall with balloons, flowers, and bows. In the kitchen, the older women and Hungarian chef prepared several dishes to serve two-hundred guests. They carefully stuffed grape leaves and pounded chicken breasts. Ice cream served with wedding cake was kept cold in a refrigerator truck behind the church building. Dr. Paul Negrut, president of the seminary, performed the two-hour wedding ceremony.

Cornel Iova took us around Oradea to see several possible ministry opportunities. His wife Michela was a dentist who had received two dental chairs from *CrossLink*. We videotaped a seminary student in one of the dental chairs. Another ministry had taken an old communist meeting hall and made it into a kindergarten and Down's syndrome school. A young man, Elijah, and his father had made a miraculous change in the facility. A third *CrossLink* dental chair was in use at the kindergarten.

To our delight, we saw the new Emmanuel University and Seminary full of students studying from several countries. The seminary had broken ground for a new chapel and cafeteria. They also were growing their food supply in greenhouses. The vision of educating pastors was coming to fruition.

We returned to Ramstein for the week of July 4 to stay with Steve and Teresa Kahne. Their nice home in Miesenbach was a few blocks from our former German home. Their daughter, Rachael Kahne, was the president of the Ramstein High School senior class. When she heard the story of the Romanian kindergarten and Down's syndrome school, she decided to make it the senior class project. We gave her the contact information for Elijah in Romania. Her class collected almost $7,000 to help the Romanian school during the next year.

While we were in Ramstein, we called our old German landlord Karl. Gerda answered the phone. In her broken English, she told us that Karl had died the year before from cancer. We visited her and son Gernot during that week. They took us to Karl's gravesite. Their grief was still raw as they placed fresh flowers on his grave and wept.

We visited Faith Baptist Church and met the pastor. Jimmy Martin was called to be the pastor after we had moved to Washington, D.C. He had been at the church for seven years when we visited. We encouraged him to understand the importance of the Romanian ministry that continued with Oradea. Gary and I also reminded him of the many lives Faith Baptist Church touches as men and women rotate in and out of Germany. One of the military members of our early Romanian mission team had felt called to the pastorate. He was serving in another European Baptist Church.

The next week we drove to Interlaken, Switzerland, for the European Baptist Convention. Our friend Phil Roberts and his family were attending the convention. His pastor, Dr. Johnny Hunt, was the platform speaker. Dr. Roberts was traveling with Dr. Bob

Reccord, president of the North American Mission Board (NAMB), of the Southern Baptist Convention. Dr. Reccord's wife Cheryl was with him. We were amazed two days into the conference, when Phil Roberts turned to us at lunch and requested that we escort Dr. and Mrs. Reccord for the next four days in Switzerland. Phil needed to catch a flight back to the States. We knew the countryside, since it was a few miles from the Eiger Mountain, where we had skied many times. We were delighted to escort Bob and Cheryl Reccord. Walking up an Alpine mountain trail to a small restaurant in Wengen, Bob Reccord asked us about our children. As we told the story of Ann Marie's life, Bob suddenly stopped on the trail. He was visibly moved with compassion by her testimony of life and death. He encouraged me to write about it. Every time Bob and Cheryl Reccord see us, they hug us and say, "Let's go to Europe together again!"

From Switzerland, we drove to Prague, Czech Republic to see our friends, Bob and Lynn Williamson, who had done international student ministry with us. Bob had taken a consultant job in Prague, Czech Republic with Boeing Aircraft. The year before, in January 1999, the Williamsons had invited us to ski at Crested Butte, Colorado and stay with them in their time-share apartment. It was the first time for Gary and me to ski after Ann Marie's death. Pulling out our ski equipment five years after we had last used it brought back a flood of memories. Bob and Lynn had been so gracious to consider our emotions during the anniversary week, but encouraged us to experience the exhilaration of downhill skiing once again. It was a wonderful week of healing as we felt the freedom of flying down the mountains and enjoying their friendship.

The Williamson had been in Prague almost a year when we visited them. Lynn knew all the famous places and history of Prague. She took us on shopping/walking tours for two days. The people of Prague were still recovering from the former communist rule. They did not trust anyone, and had suffered through the revolution with a split between the Czech and Slovak people.

So many people had encouraged me to write a book about Ann Marie's story and our lives of adventure and travel. I began to work on the book in September 2000. It was difficult, but therapeutic to begin to put on paper the amazing tapestry God has woven into our lives. It all began with the heart defect of one tiny baby. I struggled for months praying to find a focused direction. Then the Lord gave me the answer in a shocking phone call.

On March 21, 2001, I received the phone call from Mrs. Kyle, who had been Ann Marie's guidance counselor at Luther Jackson Middle School. Dave Muniz was working out in the weight room when he suffered a massive heart attack and died. Maybe Dave had been thinking of Ann Marie, and suddenly went home to see her and the Lord. As their two lives touched each other here on earth, surely they have touched in heaven. I understood the focus of our earthly relationships to our spiritual relationships.

However, the Lord had another twist in the tapestry thread for our lives. In February 2001, our friend Dr. Phil Roberts became the president of Midwestern Baptist Theological Seminary (MBTS) in Kansas City, Missouri. When we called him in March to welcome him to Missouri, he suggested that we come for a visit. Scheduling the visit for April, we asked our dear friend Cindy Province to make the trip to Kansas City with us. We wanted Phil and Cindy to meet each other. Phil was so gracious to give us a grand tour of the seminary campus. He and Cindy had a mutual friend in the president of Southeastern Baptist Theological Seminary (SEBTS), Dr. Paige Patterson. They immediately developed a friendship that came to serve MBTS well. Sitting in Dr. Roberts' large executive office, he spoke to us about the vision he had for the future of the campus and the beautiful one-hundred and eighty acres of property. Knowing that Gary was a trusted friend with degrees in Business Administration and Law, Phil approached the subject of needing a business manager. He wanted Gary to come and work for him at the seminary. Phil needed a trusted friend in the business side of the seminary.

Then he asked me how my Bible study was going. When I told him that I was not currently teaching, but writing a book, he said, "Would you like to see the president's mansion on campus? They call it the Vivion Farm Home."

Excited to go inside the great white three-story historical home, we agreed to take a tour. MBTS had been without a president to live in the grand home for over two years. Mrs. Roberts was still in Atlanta until Mark was finished with his school year. She had seen the Vivion

Farm Home, and she was not excited about the run-down condition. When Anya Roberts saw the property, one of the eight massive columns supporting the walkout balcony was lying on the ground in the backyard. The basement leaked and a moldy smell permeated the entire home. Mark Roberts had severe asthma and could not possibly live in such a dirty moldy environment. Estimates were it would cost $250,000 to repair and renovate the home. The Roberts had decided not to live in the Vivion Farm Home, but Dr. Roberts wanted to use it as a hospitality center to host special guests.

Approaching the hand carved arched front doorway, we noticed that a squirrel had eaten a corner of the storm door. As Phil unlocked the entry door to the massive front hallway, we stepped over a swarm of ants busily feasting on some leftover dessert spilled on the oak floor. The moldy, wet, wooly smell reminded me of many of the parsonage homes my grandparents had lived in. The once light-green carpet looked worn and soiled after thirty-five years. At the two French doors in the dining room leading to a large green and gray slate stone patio, two black paths of dirt tracked across the carpet into the butler's pantry. The dreary rooms were bare of furniture and dark without lamps or overhead lights. A large dingy crystal chandelier hung from the ceiling of the second floor over the curving handcrafted staircase to the upstairs bedrooms. I felt sadness in the winding, turning hallways leading to massive bedrooms and closets. The finished attic had several cedar closets surrounding a staircase to the rooftop widow's walk. In the damp, spidery basement, antiques piled into unlocked storage rooms. Gorgeous gold gilded mirrors rested on marble-topped tables coated with a layer of sooty dust. My attention was drawn to one ancient European desk, intricately hand carved with angels and flowers. Carefully, I ran my hand across the wood, wondering how glorious the home must have been. The condition of the house was a parable of the seminary.

Phil could see that my heart was drawn to the possibility of the mansion being a grand place once more. Knowing my experience with entertaining large groups as a military wife, Phil revealed the other half of the plan.

He said, "Libby, you could come to the seminary with Gary and be a hostess for the Vivion Farm Home. It needs restoration, and I want to use it for chapel luncheons. Eventually, we can raise funds for furnishing the five bedrooms and have special overnight guests."

Gary and I did not want to move from our beautiful home in St. Charles to Kansas City, so Phil Roberts finished the vision for us. He offered for us to live in the master bedroom of the Vivion Farm Home (VFH) during the week and drive home to St. Charles on the weekends. Cindy was ecstatic with the prospects of fixing up the home. She lived in a historical home in Defiance, Missouri, and could see the possibilities of using the grand mansion for campus hospitality. At Southeastern Baptist Theological Seminary (SEBTS), President and Mrs. Patterson had taken a smaller home and made it into a campus showplace for entertaining called "Magnolia Hill." Cindy wanted to help make this home into the treasure it once had been.

Gary and I thought that the idea was workable, and just possibly a new direction the Lord was opening to us. After a few weeks of prayer, we knew that we needed to talk with our pastor about the opportunity and ask for his blessing of the ministry. Our pastor wanted to see MBTS prosper under the direction of Phil Roberts. He encouraged us to take the challenge. He also warned us of some potential conflicts at the seminary.

The Vivion Farm Home was about to become the Executive Mansion for campus hospitality. It needed extensive renovation and repair. It was a grand historical landmark given to the seminary by Mrs. Sheffa Vivion Foster at the time of her death in 1966, along with much of the early 1900s estate furnishings. The home had five bedrooms, seven bathrooms, and three fireplaces. Several stairways and an elevator could access the basement, main floor, and upstairs.

Before I cooked our first meal, I had to run across the street to K-Mart and buy pots, pans, knives, and cooking utensils. Every night that first month at dinnertime, I would look out the back kitchen window towards the campus and see Gary's car winding down the long driveway followed by the president's car. Phil was living alone in a two-bedroom mission apartment until Anya and Mark arrived in August. He had been through some tough months before we arrived. After the first week, he sat with us for dessert on the slate patio watching the deer at dusk.

Phil said, "This has been my best week here. It is good to have you as my friends."

I scrubbed, polished, and vacuumed the old mansion. Like the Vivion Farm Home, the seminary had drifted for two years with no president to give it care and vision. As the business manager, Gary began restoration of the campus facilities. He had the dead leaves cleaned out of the beautiful fountain and painted. When the sparkling water sprayed out once again welcoming visitors, it was a sign of new life and hope. The spirit of the campus began to improve as broken sidewalks were repaired, grass cut, new paint applied to worn buildings, and landscaping projects enhanced the physical property.

There were those who did not want to see improvements. They had an agenda to close the seminary, and the new president and his friends were changing the plans. The challenges of an academic atmosphere are different from any other environment. Degreed egos and titles of importance struggle for recognition. Within two weeks of coming to the seminary, the honeymoon was over. We were in a spiritual warfare far beyond any we could comprehend.

As Gary would later say, "The Gulf War was easier than this! At least I knew who the enemy was!"

The first week on campus, we had a heavy rainstorm. I went to the basement of the house to get some supplies and stepped into two inches of water flooding the basement floor. Valuable antique furniture sat soaking in the water. Gary and campus operations surveyed the situation. After sucking the stinky water out of the basement with a wet-vacuum, we moved several of the antique pieces upstairs into appropriate rooms. Gary noticed that the gutter on the west side of the roof was blown off its mounting and lying on top of the widow's walk. No one knew how long it had been that way, but it was fixed immediately. The next week, two men from Carpenters' for Christ spent about seventy dollars for black plastic drain pipes and installed them on every downspout, channeling the water away from the basement walls. The old mansion never leaked again while we lived there. Previous estimates for eliminating the damp basement situation had run in the thousands of dollars to hire professionals to dig a French drain around the home. Volunteers had fixed it for much less money and in a few hours time.

My first official function was an executive trustee reception three weeks after moving into the mansion. When one of the female trustees entered the front hallway for the dinner, she smiled brightly and said, "Someone has been cleaning this place!"

Later that week, the tapestry weaving came full circle with our special dinner guest from Russia. Dr. Srgei Nikolaev, who had spoken about the medical needs of the Russian hospital when we attended the 1989 European Baptist Convention in Wiesbaden, Germany, sat at our mansion dinner table. He had the privilege of seeing a rare glimpse of the campus red fox that evening from the patio. He was surprised that Gary could remember him from the Wiesbaden conference. Then we told him how he had inspired us to send medical supplies to Moscow in the *CrossLink* container. He had benefited from some of those much-needed medical supplies, and appreciated knowing how the connection was made.

Dr. Roberts needed an executive assistant when his secretary resigned shortly after our arrival. He decided I should be the interim until he could hire someone permanently. Then the dean approached me about directing the student wives WISDOM program and teaching Precept during the first semester until his wife could arrive on campus. Reluctantly, I took on the extra temporary responsibilities. The president's inauguration was scheduled for October 22, and much of the responsibility suddenly became mine. Often, I had to remind Phil Roberts that I was not "superwoman!"

Anya Roberts' nephew, Peter from Poland, came to live with us in the house. It was Peter's first time to the United States, and he would be a student in the master's program. Speaking very little English, Peter helped me with the entertaining, while Gary and I shared the kitchen and living quarters with him. Peter was thirty-six years old. What might have been a disastrous relationship grew into one of us mentoring Peter. We understood the cultural shock of living in a foreign country. Every evening when Peter walked home from working on campus and seminary classes, he would eat dinner with us in the kitchen.

Clearing the dinner dishes, he would say, "I have the gift of dishwashing."

From July to December 2001, I hosted fifty-two events and seven-hundred guests. I served meals, gave tours, and hosted several overnight guests in the VFH. During those months, we lived and worked around major renovations including seven-thousand square feet of new mauve carpet donated by friends of the seminary and installed by volunteers. Contractors and volunteers replaced two old furnaces, and grounded inside electrical wiring for the entire house. Old dangerously frayed outside power lines were removed, and were replaced with new electric lines running underground. We had several bedrooms and the living room painted. New den furniture was purchased so we could sit on something other than antique dining room chairs.

Chapel luncheons were served once or twice a week along with other special events. I planned the menu, purchased the food, cooked, and served all of these events. I did all of the vacuuming, cleaning, and laundry. Often, Cindy Province would drive across Missouri from St. Charles to Kansas City to help me with special receptions and trustee meetings. She would spend the night in the "Cindy Province bedroom."

For the first time in several years, the Vivion Farm Home glowed with electric candles in every window and Christmas decorations in all of the downstairs rooms and staircase. One very important Christmas tea included our neighbor, Mrs. Anita Gorhman, who lived in the mansion across Vivion Road. The adjoining Anita Gorhman Park and fountain were named for her. Also attending was Jonathan Kemper from the Kemper Arena family. Mrs. Gorhman told stories of the Vivion family she had known growing-up. Looking around the mansion, she gave me a stunning compliment.

She said, "Libby, Sheffa Vivion would be so proud to see what you have done with the home."

Gary signed the check and title paperwork a few months later, to add twenty-four acres of property and a 34,000 square foot building to the campus for the purchase price of $1.4 million. The building was a former retreat center for Farmland Corp., overlooking a three-acre lake. It brought meeting space for students, and facilities for the faculty, staff, and expanded library. The building had more than fifty rooms which did not need major renovation. It was obvious that MBTS had no intention of closing down. God was working out His plan and purpose. The seminary was moving forward with a future and a hope.

In January, I coordinated Precept training for thirty-six pastors and wives on campus. I welcomed Precept trainer Jan Priddy to stay in the mansion during that week. One evening, I could hear Jan walking around upstairs – counting. She reported that there were fifty-three doors in the mansion. She did not know how I could take care of such a large mansion, and not receive any help or compensation for the work. I told her that I saw it as a ministry, but I was wearing out; especially traveling back to St. Louis every weekend and trying to keep my own home there. The dark circles under my eyes testified to the fact that I really needed some help. My back was also in constant pain.

I enjoyed serving many of the honored guests for chapel luncheons, all of whom had graciously thanked me for a wonderful lunch. However, Dr. James Merritt was an extremely impressive guest. He was genuinely interested in the students who attended the lunch, by asking them all sorts of questions about themselves. He asked Gary and me about our children. We responded with Ann Marie's story. He sincerely looked at us as if God had predestined our luncheon; and told us that he was returning to Georgia to perform a funeral for a teenager who had been killed in his church. He asked our advice on what to say to the parents of the young man who had died. When we responded with the encouragement that we would see Ann Marie again, he seemed saddened that in the case of the parents in his church that might not be their assurance. I explained to him the book I was writing. He encouraged me that pastors need to know what I was writing to help understand how to handle the death of children in their congregations.

Dr. Phil Roberts was a trustee for Emmanuel University and Seminary in Oradea, Romania. Phil's connections had brought Dr. Radu Gheorghita as a professor of New Testament to MBTS. We had met Radu's father, Nicolae "Dr. Nic" Gheorghita, in Romania ten years before. Dr. Nic had founded the Christian Romanian Clinic where we had sent medicine and a dental chair from *CrossLink*. Now the second generation of Romanians was carrying on the faith not only in Romania, but also in the United States.

One afternoon, Dr. Roberts pulled up in the driveway and Dr. Paul Negrut, the president of Emmanuel Seminary in Oradea, Romania, got out of the car. I had just cleaned one of the extra guestrooms.

Paul stood at the backdoor of the VFH with his suitcases and asked, "Where should I sleep this week!"

What a wonderful week we had of bonding again with Romania, as Gary and I took Dr. Negrut to several churches in Kansas to speak.

Gary and I were the campus sponsors for the chaplain's fellowship. We started with two students who were interested in becoming military chaplains. After a few monthly meetings in the Vivion Farm Home, with me serving soup and sandwiches, the group grew to around twelve. Several of the young seminary students were encouraged to become military chaplains from this fellowship. I believe it was Gary and I sharing with them our military experience, and the need for strong men of God to minister on our military installations in the chapel.

In March, at the spring trustee meeting, I hosted a tea and tour of the Vivion Farm Home for the trustee wives. Many of the wives had never been inside the mansion, and they loved the history and antiques. They were honored to be served tea and pastries on the estate Limoges china from Sheffa Vivion's engraved silver tea service.

Getting ready for the graduation reception began weeks in advance. The siding on the home and windows were power washed. I planted new plants and flowers around the garden areas, which Gary and Peter had dug. They had worked hard making a decorative border out of Windsor stones and filling it with dirt and mulch. Gary, Peter, and I painted white columns, doors, patio furniture, and black wrought iron railings. Crawling out of the upstairs window, I painted the white front balcony one day. The next day, I painted the white wrought iron loveseats that always sat on the front lawn. On May 17, the lawn and gardens were ready for the reception of one-hundred and fifty guests outside at circular tables decorated with vases of fresh peonies from the estate gardens. I could relate when Dr. Rick Ferguson gave the commencement speech the next day on "servant hood."

He said, "You will never know what it is like to be a servant until you are treated like one!"

To which I replied, "Amen."

Within a few days, I was at home in St. Charles. I had severely strained my back and could not get out of bed. During my recovery time my dad had minor surgery. However, he did not come out of the anesthetic properly and suffered a serious stroke. He was unable to talk. Through the prayers of family and friends, the Lord began to heal his speech. During the next week, he suffered several other medical issues, which led him to come to total brokenness over his relationship with the Lord Jesus. In tears, he lay in the hospital bed and cried out for Jesus to come and save him. He confessed his past antagonistic attitude toward Jesus; and true repentance of his sin. Since that time, his life has continued to display a redeeming grace of genuine faith. We rejoice that he will be in the circle of our family in eternity.

Dr. Roberts hired a wonderful administrative assistant named Susan Reed. Susan was a single mother with a sixteen-year-old daughter named Elizabeth. Elizabeth had a rare neurological disease called Neurofibromatosis 2 (NF2). On June 8, 2002, Elizabeth went home to be with the Lord. Of all the reasons for us to be at the seminary, probably one of the most important was to minister to Susan during the loss of her only child. Susan was all alone without a husband to support her during the darkest days of grief. Within the next two years, Susan was called as a missionary to Poland with her dog Gracie. She taught English to several Polish college students while leading a Bible study. In 2008, Susan re-married and became our neighbor.

The summer months included me teaching a ten-week Precept Bible study at the VFH to seventeen women. They loved sitting in the large living room and learning about the names of God. One young girl came faithfully in her wheelchair. Gary and Peter would put the ramp up to the back door so she could enter the house and enjoy the Bible study. I made many wonderful friendships with those future pastors' wives. I am sure they began Precept classes in the churches they were called to serve.

Our first honored luncheon guests for the fall 2002 school year were former MBTS president and wife, Dr. Milton and Betty Ferguson. It was a special treat to welcome the Fergusons back to the grand home, which they had lived in previously for twenty-three years. I knew that during their time in the Vivion Farm Home, one of their teenage daughters had been killed in a car accident. We immediately bonded. They spent most of the afternoon visiting and touring the house. Both of them expressed deep sympathy for Ann Marie's death; encouraging me, and sharing much wisdom from their experience. They also understood the difficult and strenuous ministry of living in the campus "fishbowl" and constant entertaining. They suggested that I get some help with the hosting, or it would take a tremendous physical toll on my body. I knew my back often caused me pain, and the constant stress was becoming unbearable.

By October 2002, Gary and I felt that we had accomplished the major part of our work at MBTS to the glory of God. The seminary passed a difficult accreditation visit in October. Gary achieved many goals in the business office and campus facilities. We hosted more than one-hundred and fifty events and served over fifteen-hundred guests in the year and a half of renovation of the Vivion Farm Home. Driving Interstate HWY 70 between St. Charles and Kansas City every week was dangerous and exhausting. Our home in St. Charles had suffered considerable neglect during our absence. It was time to bring a fresh team onto the playing field.

We loved most of those we worked with. Others who refused to move forward or give their best to the Lord's work were a distraction to the progress. The decision came to leave our work at the end of the semester in December.

It was the right decision in God's timing. Gary's father became deathly ill in Arizona during the last few weeks of our time at the seminary. He went to a rehab center after several weeks of hospitalization. His condition continued to deteriorate. Placed in a hospice bed in January, he slipped into a coma. Don died a few days later on January 30, 2003, in Phoenix, Arizona. It was the day after Ann Marie's death date and a difficult time of the year for us. We flew to Phoenix to be with Gary's mother. We had not seen her for almost thirteen years. It was a precious time of grieving and restoring a relationship that been kept apart for years because of Don's illness. Laura was free from the constant care she had selflessly given to Don. She missed him, but knew there was nothing left in Arizona for her. We planned a memorial service in March for her to come back to St. Louis. Eventually, she sold her home and furniture. Gary and I found a nice senior apartment in

St. Charles for her. Within the next year, she moved back to where her children and grandchildren live.

Gary and I inherited nine acres of farmland, which once belonged to my grandfather. In 2006, we built a new home on top of the hillside; and enjoy walking the fields, raising chickens, planting our garden and pumpkin patch. My family lives across the creek.

Adjoining the land is the cemetery where many of my ancestors are buried. I often visit the graves of my great-great-grandparents, Elizabeth Eleanor Irvin Logan and Robert Reynolds Logan. My favorite gravestone is that of Elizabeth's mother, Jane Doak Irvin. The top of the stone is etched with an anchor and the word *HOPE*. What a legacy of faith is spoken from that gravestone to future generations to place the anchor of their hope in Jesus Christ. He is able to hold our faith in any storm of life.

This hope we have as an anchor of the soul,
A hope both sure and steadfast
and one which enters within the veil,
Where Jesus has entered as a forerunner for us,…
Hebrews 6:19-20 (NAS)

EPILOGUE

We believe that leadership sets the tone in ministry. We have seen the damage that ripples out like shock waves from a tsunami when "brothers and sisters in Christ" do not preserve the unity of the Spirit in the Body of Christ. Often, ministries and churches drifting in a sea of division move toward a shipwreck while the leadership is busy straightening the deck chairs. Oppressive, insecure leadership stifles lay people from blossoming in their spiritual gifts, leaving them grasping at pieces of a shipwreck trying to stay afloat. Leadership that refuses accountability usually blows apart with exposed sin. Their eyes are on earthly kingdoms instead of a heavenly home. It is difficult for new leadership to turn a drifting ship away from dangerous waters and back to the chartered course of safe waters. Sometimes many waves of turnover are needed for an organization to cleanse itself of past neglect and mistakes. Often times there are casualties of good people in the cleansing process.

The Lord has spoken to our hearts many times to move on as He closes the door behind us and opens new doors. The Lord continues to call us to new ministries and friendships as we learn the lessons of our faith walk.

In June 2004, Gary was elected a trustee of LifeWay Christian Resources with the Southern Baptist Convention. He was re-elected for a second term in 2008. In many ways, God had taught us important lessons about trustee responsibility through our experience at Midwestern Baptist Seminary. Gary also learned about board dynamics as a member of the Board of Directors for Lay Renewal Ministry from 2000-2002.

During the years since Ann's death, several threads in the tapestry have gone on to be with the Lord. Thelma Mease, who taught Ann, passed away shortly after Ann Marie in 1994. Margaret Kautt, who taught me so much about air force life during our first military assignment, suffered a stroke and died in 1997. My grandmother Mimmy died October 8, 1997 at the age of ninety-three. Marlin Howe, our pastor in Little Rock, was killed in a private airplane crash in 1998. Our fifteen-year old dog, Winchester, suffering from kidney disease and heart failure, died in 2000. Before Gray Wilson died, in May 2003, she called her teaching associate, Diane Gibson, and talked about going to see Ann Marie in heaven. Now, they have seen their part of the tapestry from the top side of God's plan and purpose.

For months after Ann Marie's death, I longed to see and hear her. I missed combing her hair, and hearing her voice. One night, the Lord gave me a special dream. I was sitting in a theater waiting for the dark-red velvet curtain to rise on the stage. I could hear Ann Marie laughing and twirling around backstage in the folds of the curtain. I grasped at the curtain trying to break through and touch her.

Her laughing words came from behind the heavy fabric, "No Mom. It is not time yet for you to see me. But when you do, you will be so surprised!"

Since there will come a day when we will all give an account to God for our work on this side of eternity, we must keep our eyes on Jesus; walking with all humility, in gentleness, with patience. We must show forbearance to one another in love, diligent to preserve the unity of the Spirit in the bond of peace. We are to finish the race, worthy of our calling. Then we will hear the words, "Well done, my good and faithful servant."

For I am not ashamed of the gospel,
because it is God's power for salvation
to everyone who believes,
first to the Jew, and also to the Greek.
For in it God's righteousness is revealed
<u>from faith to faith,</u>
just as it is written:
The righteous will live by faith.
Romans 1:16-17(NAS)

FOOTNOTES

Chapter One
The Lost Generation

[1] Morris, Margaret Logan, IRVINS, DOAKS, LOGANS, AND McCAMPBELLS OF VIRGINIA AND KENTUCKY. Compiled and Edited by Mrs. Margaret Logan Morris, Corydon, Indiana. There is no date confirming the time Irvins, Doaks, Logans and McCampbells of Virginia and Kentucky was published. It is believed that the book was written approximately 1915.

[2] Ibid. pages 1 & 2 Appendix

[3] Ibid. pages 7 & 8.

[4] Ibid. page 38.

[5] Ibid. page 70.

[6] A History of Southeast Missouri, published 1888, Goodspeed Publishing Company, Chicago, Illinois. Historical research by Goldie Marie (Cole) Statler, edited by Fred J. Statler, Jr.

[7] Barry McGuire, Eve of Destruction, 1965.

Chapter Two
On a Wing and a Prayer

[1] History's Greatest Speeches, *Hale Boggs, US Representative of Louisiana: Discloses Soviet invasion of Czechoslovakia*, electronically retrieved: < www. historychannel. com/ speeches/ archive/ speech - 23.html>

[2] Mike Miller, Sept. 14 'Wins' Draft Lottery, Washington, news article appeared in newspapers December 2, 1969. *15th Field Artillery Regiment 1917-2003 - "Fighting 15th" - Vietnam War-Draft Lottery: The Military Draft and 1969 Draft Lottery for the*

Vietnam War, electronically retrieved: <www.landscaper.net/ timelin.htm>

3   15th Webmaster note. *15th Field Artillery Regiment 1917-2003 - "Fighting 15th" - Vietnam War - Draft Lottery: The Military Draft and 1969 Draft Lottery for the Vietnam War,* electronically retrieved: <www.landscaper.net/timelin.htm>

4   Vietnam War, electronically retrieved: <www.Historychannel. com>.

Chapter Eight
Tribes of Every Nation

1   Stephen Foster, Oh Susanna!, 1848

2   History of Memorial Presbyterian Church, Member Directory 1982, Memorial Presbyterian Church, Montgomery, AL.

3   Ibid.

4   John Kuykendall, The Faith Story in Glass, text by The Reverend Dr. John W. Kuykendall, President, Davidson College, Davidson, N.C., Memorial Presbyterian Church, Montgomery, AL.

5   Gail Pichon, The Key Partner, *AFP 30-34, Air Force Family Matters, Department of the Air Force,* Dennis P. Tewell, Col, USAF, Chief, Air Force Family Matters Office (AFFAM), 14June1985

6   The Gathering of Eagles, United States Air Force Museum, Oct.9 through 10, 1998, electronically retrieved: www.wpafb.af.mil/ museum/ eagles/ eagle 1.htm

   Major Lennard (Larry) W. Lee, Jr., *Gathering of Eagles-First in Flight Home Page,* ACSC/DEOT, June2003, electronically retrieved:<www.au.af.mil/au/goe/admin/Goehome.htm>

Chapter Ten
Peace Be With You

1   Tino Wallenda of The Flying Wallendas, Walking the Straight and Narrow: Lessons in Faith From the High Wire, Bridge-Logos, Gainesville, FL 32614, Copyright 2005. The Flying Wallendas, electronically retrieved <www.wallenda.com/history.html>

Chapter Eleven
The Valley of the Shadow of Death

[1] Thomas L. Spray M.D. (D), <u>Medical Records of Ann Marie Grunick, St. Louis Children's Hospital, Operative Report, 04-26-84, Record # 2754901/79-11523.</u>

Chapter Twelve
Do You Want To Be Made Well?

[1] <u>1996 -- Annual Report to Congress -- 18th Annual Report on the Implementation of Individuals with Disabilities Education Act (IDEA) P. L. 94-142.</u> Since 1975 provides free appropriate public education for all children with disabilities. Before IDEA, one million children were excluded from school, and many others housed in institutions that did not address their educational needs. Special Educational Services were developed to integrate disabled children into public school.

[2] <u>New Age Dawning—The Five Year Plan for Evangelism in the Presbyterian Church (USA)</u>, Presbyterian Church (USA)

[3] Marj Carpenter, <u>Ogilvie Asks Worshippers To "Receive Spirit of Living God In Fresh Way,"</u> *Congress Courier--Presbyterian Congress on Renewal*, Wednesday morning, January 9, 1985. Bruce Larson, editor. *The Power to Make Things New*, <u>Message: "Perfect Makes Practice,"</u> Dr. Lloyd John Ogilvie, Word, Inc., Copyright 1986.

[4] Leighton Frederick Sandys Ford, Jr**.,** <u>Sandy—A Heart for God</u>, InterVarsity Press, Downers Grove, Illinois, Copyright 1985.

Chapter Fourteen
A Light Shines In the Darkness

[1] <u>Kristallnacht</u>, *The Expanded Columbia Electronic Encyclopedia*, Copyright 2003, Columbia University Press, electronically retrieved: <www.historychannel.com>

[2] Ibid. <u>World War II</u>.

3   <u>Gail S. Halvorsen, Great Moments in Aviation History.</u> This collection of biographical sketches accompanies the lithograph entitled, *Great Moments in Aviation History.* The lithograph was made from an oil painting by William J. Reynolds, which was commissioned by the Air Command and Staff College Class of 1982.

4   <u>Berlin Blockade</u>, <u>Berlin Airlift</u>, <u>Berlin Wall</u>, *The Expanded Columbia Electronic Encyclopedia*, Copyright2003, Columbia University Press, electronically retrieved: <www.historychannel.com>

5   Ibid. <u>Cold War</u>.

6   Ibid. <u>Disarmament, nuclear</u>, <u>Reagan</u>, <u>Gorbachev</u>.

7   Electronically retrieved: <www.annefrank.nl/eng/af.html>
    Martijn Luns, <u>The Anne Frank House Amsterdam,</u> tour brochure, composition: Martijn Luns/ Amsterdam, Illustration: Lex van de Oudeweetering/ Amsterdam, The Anne Frank Foundation, Prinsengracht 263, 1016 GV Amsterdam.
    Otto H. Frank, <u>Anne Frank: The Diary of a Young Girl,</u> copyright 1952. Preface copyright 1958 by Simon & Schuster Inc, 1230 Avenue of the Americas, New York, N.Y. 10020.

8   Electronically retrieved: <http://timelines.ws/countries/LEBANON.html>

Chapter Fifteen
Fall of the Wall

1   Craig and Sandy Koontz, <u>Driving to Berlin</u>, driving information compiled by Craig and Sandy Koontz for a successful trip through Eastern Germany and Berlin.

2   Electronically retrieved: <http:// www.bkohg.com/ multi/ English/ Brandenburger_ Tor_ Info_ 3_E.html>

3   <u>Welcome to Germany 1988-89</u>, *Off Duty Magazine*, Off Duty Enterprises, 3303 Harbor Blvd., Suite C-2, Costa Mesa, California, 92626, a private firm in no way connected with the Department of Defense. Publishers: Walter B. Rios, Dagmar M. Rios.

4   Berlin Airlift Memorial Ceremony Brochure, 26 September 1989. Produced under the auspices of the Berlin Airlift Memorial by Capital Markets Group. Concept and text: W. I. Norton, Design: Ben Daniele. Printing: Dhyana Druck, Copyright 1988, Luftbrucke Chapter, Airlift Association.

5   Frankfurter Night brochure for the Berlin Airlift Veteran's Reunion, 26 September 1989.

6   General T. R. Milton, biography, electronically retrieved: <www. af.mil/bios/bio>

7   David C. Turnley, Peter Turnley, and Mort Rosenblum, Moments of Revolution—Eastern Europe, Copyright 1990, Publishers: Stewart, Tabori & Chang, Inc., 575 Broadway, New York, New York 10012

Chapter Sixteen
Romanian Rhapsody

1   Welcome to Germany 1989-90, *Off Duty Magazine,* Off Duty Enterprises, 3303 Harbor Blvd., Suite C-2, Costa Mesa, California, 92626, a private firm in no way connected with the Department of Defense. Publishers: Walter B. Rios, Dagmar M. Rios

2   A Tour through Trier, published by the Verkehrsamt der Stadt Trier, printed by Lintz & Co. GmbH, 1988, printed in Germany, Fourth Edition.

3   Published by the Parish Council of the Emperor Wilhelm Memorial Church, Text: The Rev. Erwin Gerlach; English: The Rev. Dr. Roger Aus

4   David A. Deese, Persian Gulf War of 1991, *World Book Online Reference Center*, 2004, World Book, Inc., 1 Sept 2004, electronically retrieved: <http://www. aolsvc. worldbook. aol. com/wb/Article?id+ar424190>

5   Ibid.

6   Operation Provide Comfort, electronically retrieved: http: www. globalsecurity. org/ military/ ops/ provide_comfort.htm, accessed 8/30/2004, USAFE Humanitarian Operations: 1945-1997, elect

ronicallyretrieved:<http:www.globalsecurity.org/military/library/report/1997/humanops.htm>, accessed 8/30/2004

Chapter Seventeen
Crosslink

[1] U. S. Department of State, Benjamin Franklin State Dining Room, electronically retrieved: <http:// www. state. gov/ www/ about_state/ diprooms/ franklinobjects. html>, accessed 11/26/2004

[2] U. S. Department of State, Architect's Table, electronically retrieved: <http://www. state. gov/ www/about_state/diprooms/ d67.90.html>, accessed 11/26/2004

[3] Excerpts from Columbia Baptist Church: A Short History and Interpretation, October 1991 – Church Membership Directory.

[4] Charles W. Colson with Ellen Santilli Vaughn, The Body: Being Light in Darkness, copyright 1992, WORD Publishing, Dallas-London-Vancouver-Melbourne.

Chapter Nineteen
Out of the Crucible

[1] Scott Wesley Brown, When Answers Aren't Enough, ©Greg Nelson/Scott Wesley Brown, 1985 BMG Songs, Inc.\Careers-BMG Music Publishing, Inc.\Pamela Kay Music\Greg Nelson Music (Admin. By BMG Music Publishing)

[2] Kim Noblitt, If You Could See Me Now, ©1992 Integrity's Praise! Music and Dad & Dann Music, % Integrity Music, Inc., P.O. Box 16813, Mobile, AL 36616.

Chapter Twenty
Strong in the Broken Places

1 Carlos Sanchez, Washington Post Staff Writer, *The Washington Post, Metro Section, Monday, January 31, 1994*, <u>Va. Girl, 14, Killed After Van Overturns, Falls Church Teen Was on Church Ski Trip in Pa.</u>, and <u>Falls Church Girl Dies After Ski-Trip Van Flips</u>, *Church*, From B1.

2 Scott Wesley Brown, <u>When Answers Aren't Enough</u> ©Greg Nelson/Scott Wesley Brown, 1985 BMG Songs, Inc.\Careers-BMG Music Publishing, Inc.\Pamela Kay Music\Greg Nelson Music (Admin. By BMG Music Publishing)

3 Kim Noblitt, <u>If You Could See Me Now</u>, ©1992 Integrity's Praise! Music and Dad & Dann Music, % Integrity Music, Inc., P.O. Box 16813, Mobile, AL 36616.

Chapter Twenty-One
Worthy of Our Calling

1 Leighton Ford, <u>Sandy, A Heart for God</u>, page 171, copyright 1985, InterVarsity Press, Downers Grove, Illinois 60515.

2 <u>CrossLink International, Making A World Of Difference, Linking Resources With A World In Need</u>, June 1999, page 1, Newsletter.

3 <u>CrossLink International, Making a world of difference, Linking Surplus Medical Resource to Missons Around the World</u>, page 4, project report from the *Affirmation Dinner June 2000*.

4 Ibid, page 4, 5, 6.

5 <u>CrossLink International, Making A World Of Difference, Linking Resources With A World In Need</u>, June 1999, page 1, Newsletter.

6 <u>CrossLink International, Making a world of difference, Linking Surplus Medical Resource to Missons Around the World</u>, page 2, project report from the *Affirmation Dinner June 2000*.

7 Ibid, page 17.

8 Ibid, page 18.

9   <u>CrossLink International</u>, http://www.crosslinkinternational.net, Executive Director, Linda Cook, accessed 2/17/2005.

ABOUT THE AUTHOR

Elizabeth (Libby) Grunick has been a Precept Bible Study teacher for over twenty-three years. For the past thirty years, she has served with women's ministry boards, Bible studies, and mission ministries. She has traveled and lived in Europe for several years during her husband's military career and retirement. Libby and her attorney husband, Gary, live in Missouri. Their daughter Ann Marie is with the Lord.

LaVergne, TN USA
15 December 2009
167125LV00001B/128/P